THE ZADDIK

THE ZADDIK

THE DOCTRINE OF THE ZADDIK
ACCORDING TO THE WRITINGS
OF RABBI YAAKOV YOSEF OF POLNOY

BY SAMUEL H. DRESNER

SCHOCKEN BOOKS · NEW YORK

To

Abraham Joshua Heschel

רבי ומורי

צדיק הדור

Preface

The Holy of Holies in the Temple at Jerusalem was a place which only the High Priest was allowed to enter once a year, on the Day of Atonement. Now even the Holy of Holies was occasionally in need of repair. To provide for such an occasion, there were openings in the Upper Chamber leading through the ceiling of the Holy of Holies and close to its walls. Through these openings they used to lower the workmen in boxes (*Tevot*), which were open only to the walls, "so that they should not feast their eyes on the Holy of Holies."

It is said that the Upper Chamber of the Holy of Holies was even less accessible than the Holy of Holies, for the High Priest entered the Holy of Holies once a year, whereas the Upper Chamber was entered only once in fifty years to see whether any repairs were required.

The great Hasidim were the repair men of the Holy of Holies. In Hebrew *tevot* means both boxes and *words*. It was through the word that they entered the Holy of Holies. In the Hasidic movement the spirit was alive in the word. It was a voice, not a mere idea. It emanated in words that had the power to repair, to revive, to create.

Judaism today is in need of repair. The spirit is stifled, the word is emaciated; we do not know how to find access to the "Upper Chamber."

Hasidism withers when placed on exhibition. Its substance is not perceptible to the eye. It is not enough to read its written word; one must hear it, one must learn to be perceptive to the voice. Fortunately there are words in many of its records which still ring with the passion and enthusiasm of those who spoke them. The problem is how to hear the voice through the words.

Neither the Baal Shem nor most of his disciples have written down their utterances. One of the very few who did write was Rabbi Yaakov Yosef. The surprise, the joy, the refreshment which the publication of his books brought to the Jewish world are quite understandable to those who are acquainted with the spiritual atmosphere of the eighteenth century. It was like questioning the Ptolemaic theory in the time of Copernicus. These books offered a transvaluation of accepted values, a fresh vision of what is at stake in Jewish faith and existence, and a singular sensitivity for the divine. These are words that originated in Paradise, said one of the contemporaries. In other books one must read many pages until the presence of God is sensed; in the writings of Rabbi Yaakov Yosef, God's presence is felt on each page.

Hasidism was not a homogeneous movement. After the departure of the Founder it developed in different directions. For an understanding of the teachings and attitudes of the Baal Shem one must turn to the writings of Rabbi Yaakov Yosef. Unfortunately, very little research was done on the writings of Rabbi Yaakov Yosef. The study by Rabbi Dresner is a successful attempt to analyze and to evaluate one of the major themes in Hasidic thinking. His conscientious study is a very valuable contribution to the study of Hasidism.

ABRAHAM J. HESCHEL

Contents

II. THE SOLUTION

Criticism of rabbi and maggid for failure to preach Musar; the appeal for Musar; the way to speak Musar; Musar to be given out of love; the zaddik must hearken to his own Musar; God's responsibility.

Introduction

The crisis of our time is a crisis in leadership. The spiritual decay and the peril of world-wide disaster cry out for exalted men to draw us out of the pit of the twentieth century. Present day thinkers are frantically searching the past for guidance. The zaddik is a supreme example of what they seek. Rarely in history has there existed such an amazing manner of leadership as that which Hasidism brought about in the role of the zaddik. Martin Buber, whose influence today is enormous upon thinkers and writers, ranging all the way from Biblical scholars and philosophers to social scientists and novelists, writes that "the zaddikim offer us a number of religious personalities of a vitality, a spiritual strength, a manifold originality such as never, to my knowledge, appeared together in so short a time-span in the history of religion."[1]

These men were saint-mystics of a most practical order. They did not forsake this world for another world. Their goal was to join the two, to build that rarest of phenomena in history—the religious community. They represented a paradox of solitude and communion. He who attained the highest degree of spiritual solitude, who was capable of being alone with God, was at the same time the true center of the community. To live among ordinary men and yet to be alone with God, to speak common words and yet to draw strength to live from the source of all existence—this was the supreme achievement of the zaddik.

Perhaps that is why Buber can proclaim with such certainty to modern man: "I consider hasidic truth vitally important for Jews, Christians and others; and at this particular hour more important than ever before. For now is the hour when we are in danger of forgetting for what purpose we are on earth, and I know of no other teaching that reminds us of this so forcibly."[2]

The subject of this book is Hasidism, and in particular the hasidic leader, the zaddik.

The hasidic movement in Judaism, which sprang up in Eastern Europe during the eighteenth century and within the span of several decades gathered to its banner and won as loyal devotees to its teachings nearly half of the Jewish population in that area, has now disappeared. It was the last great flowering of the Jewish spirit and succeeded in working a veritable revolution of the soul in the life of the people. It brought a renewed sense of God's presence and God's concern, and it was this which produced a remarkable expression of prayer, humility, and compassion; plus a feeling of holy joy and devotion in performing the mitzvot. It created a new kind of leader, called the zaddik, and a new kind of community, composed of the zaddik and his loyal disciples, called hasidim. It is only natural that such a movement, like all the great movements in Judaism before it, should have left an indelible mark both on the thought and the life of the people. It has, to be sure, but there is a strangeness in the modern Jewish attitude to Hasidism which requires comment.

One would think that such a treasury of the spirit as Hasidism—witness the words of Martin Buber—would have been carefully cultivated by Jewish scholars in the religious wasteland of the twentieth century as one of the most fruitful areas of study. Such, however, has not been the case. It is to this very day ignored in the curricula of most academies of higher Jewish learning. Hardly any serious studies of its doctrines or even of its history have been published. A few works have appeared from time to time, but they are in no way comprehensive or adequate. Hasidism has been shunted aside as a subject of serious research for so long that, owing to the recent catastrophe, we may soon find ourselves too distant from the living tradition to know it at all.

One is compelled to ask why in an age as sterile in religious values as ours, the wealth of hasidic literature has not been plumbed, examined and made available; why, for example, critical editions have not been printed. There are more than three thousand hasidic books. How many are known and being studied today? And how much hasidic literature has to offer! One of the reasons for ignorance of this literature is, undoubtedly, the difficulties it presents the reader. It is unsystematic, epigrammatic and moves in a universe of discourse—both rabbinic and kabbalistic—which is strange to the modern student. But there is another reason for the prevailing ignorance of hasidic literature on the part of modern scholars—prejudice, the prejudice of the Western rationalistic approach which, in the last century and part of the present one, viewed with suspicion and reduced to magic anything that might be labelled "mysticism." It was this prejudice unfortunately which has dominated Jewish scholarship and, more than anything else, hampered any serious study of Hasidism. Upon examination, it is amazing how little the learned scholars of *die Wissenschaft des Judentums* knew of hasidic literature. Ignorance, however, did not prevent them from issuing against it pronouncements whose authority has only recently been challenged.

Steinschneider, probably the greatest scholar that modern Jewry has produced, the master bibliographer, who considered Hasidism a "malady of Judaism," admitted on more than one occasion that he was unfamiliar with its literature, an admission doubly significant in the case of this born bibliographer endowed with insatiable curiosity for the smallest leaflet written in Hebrew on any subject.[3]

Heinrich Graetz is another case in point. Considered by many the leading Jewish historian in modern times, his *History of the Jews* is still today, almost a century after it first appeared, the most popular work on the subject. Period after period of Jewish history is treated in such a brilliant and unforgettable manner, with such insight and understanding, that even though our knowledge of historical fact and theory has increased considerably since he wrote, it remains in many ways unexcelled. But when he treats the forbidden subject of Hasidism, *mirabile dictu*, all scholarship and all insight are cast away. To read the ninth chapter of his fifth volume, which deals with this subject, one would more easily believe he was reading a bigot or a pamphleteer than a distinguished historian. Hasidism, he says, "the new sect, a daughter of darkness, was born in gloom, and even today proceeds stealthily on its mysterious way.... As ugly as the name *Besht* was the form of the founder and the order he called into existence." To Graetz the Baal Shem was simply a "wonder-worker" who would "see into the future" and "perform miracles." He cannot decide whether this was deliberate "trickery" or only "self-delusion." He accuses the Maggid of Mezritch, the Baal Shem's successor, of "indulging in vulgar jokes" and of deceit. "It was an accepted fact," he writes, "that the zaddik had to be enthusiastic in prayer, had to have ecstatic dreams and visions. How can a clever plotter appear inspired? Alcohol...now had to take the place of the inspiring demon.... To predict the future was a more difficult task, yet it had to be accomplished; his reputation depended upon it.... Among his intimates were expert spies, worthy of serving on the secret police. They discovered many secrets and told them to their leader; thus he was enabled to assume an appearance of omniscience. Or his emissaries committed robberies; if the victims came to the 'Saint' in his hermitage to find them out, he was able to indicate the exact spot where the missing articles were lying." Graetz speaks of the "Chasidean witches' Sabbath" and describes the "hermitage" of the zaddik as "his dirty little retired chamber" where he conducted himself as "the papal vicar of God upon earth." The relationship of the hasid to the zaddik "seems like a return to the days of the priests of Baal, so vulgar and disgusting do these perversities appear. The saddest part of all is that this teaching, worthy of a fetish-worshiping people, met with approbation in Poland.... All these absurd fancies owed their origin to the superstitious doctrines of the Kabbala which...still clouded the minds of the Polish Jews."

Yet after this landslide of condemnation, Graetz calmly admits that "only a few circumstances which contributed to its [hasidism's] rise and propagation are known."[4] There is no evidence that Graetz had anything but the meagerest familiarity with hasidic literature. In spite of all this, his conscience was clear and he felt quite justified in publishing his opinions. So powerful was the prejudice of the time.

As a result of this negative attitude on the part of Western Jewish scholars, we possess today only a few really reliable books on hasidism. There are, of course, numerous works available. But they are either, on the one hand, brief enthusiastic pictures of the movement, collections of stories and popular essays; or, on the other hand, bitter, almost slanderous attacks and misrepresentations. Hasidism thus has been either maligned or glamorized. But there is a glaring lack of adequate scientific studies of the teaching and history of Hasidism, such as one would normally expect—certainly in English.

I have dealt with this literary problem at some length because it is important to indicate the strange paradox which is involved; the paradox of generations experiencing the shaking of the foundations of their faith and desperately in need of religious insight, at the very same time ignoring—even despising—what might well have been and still may be the single most important contribution to that insight—hasidic teaching. To resolve this paradox and correct this error is more than a literary matter, more than adding footnotes to Steinschneider, Graetz, *et al.* It is a matter of revealing a living fountain of the spirit for a thirsting age. Hasidic teaching in its authentic form must be made available now in order to bring about the renaissance of modern Judaism for which our time and our people wait.

This volume is a modest attempt in that direction. I have selected only one hasidic writer—albeit the greatest of them— and only one aspect of his thought—albeit one of the most important aspects—to present to the reader. It represents little more than an entry and an introduction to the vast areas which still lay untapped and the rich material which waits to be uncovered for the modern reader.

Perhaps the most amazing fact about Hasidism, according to the great authority on Jewish mysticism, Gershom Scholem, is that "within a geographically small area and also within a surprisingly short period, the ghetto gave birth to a whole galaxy of saint-mystics, each of them a startling individuality. The incredible intensity of creative religious feeling, which manifested itself in Hasidism between 1750 and 1800, produced a wealth of truly original religious types which, as far as one can judge, surpassed even the harvest of the classical period of Safed. Something like a rebellion of religious energy against petrified religious values must have taken place."[5]

It is the zaddik—the "saint-mystic" as Scholem calls him— with whom I am concerned in this book, and it is to the writings of Rabbi Yaakov Yosef of Polnoy that I have gone for the classic portrayal in hasidic literature.

Rabbi Yaakov Yosef of Polnoy was the first and is still to this day the most important hasidic writer. It was he who set down and expounded in so masterly a fashion the teachings of the Baal Shem Tov, his revered master and the founder of Hasidism, that his work was never superseded in all the hasidic literature that followed. There is to be found in his writings such a scathing denunciation of the leadership of the time as has rarely appeared in the history of Jewish literature. The reaction was violent, and his writings were publicly burned on several occasions—also a rare occurrence in the history of Jewish literature. But together with the denunciation came an exalted blueprint of the new leader, the zaddik, who was to revolutionize the spiritual life of East-European Jewry and introduce a remarkable era into Jewish history, the hasidic era, which in some ways has not yet ended even today.

Rabbi Yaakov Yosef's teachings on the nature of the zaddik represent a clear insight into his *Weltanschauung*. I have attempted to present a systematic account of his thinking on this subject, quoting at length from his writings in order to give the English reader for the first time a taste of the profound and brilliant manner of the classic hasidic literature, and to permit Rabbi Yaakov Yosef, as much as possible, to speak for himself. I have concerned myself with an analysis and description of the doctrine of the zaddik in Rabbi Yaakov Yosef's writings and have not attempted to write a genealogy of the various motifs nor an accounting of their development in later generations. Nor have I set down anything previously unknown about his times and life. I felt that the brief historical chapter presented here was necessary for the reader unfamiliar with the subject in order to better acquaint him with the background out of which the doctrine of the zaddik emerged. Likewise, the chapter on the life of Rabbi Yaakov Yosef is not meant to be a scientific account, for the historical biography is yet to be written. However, by way of introduction to his teachings I have sketched a rough picture of the man, relying to some extent on legendary sources.

The text of this book has been written so that it might stand by itself. The Hebrew notes at the rear may thus be ignored by the lay reader. They are meant for the scholar in whose eyes the value of this volume will, I hope, thereby be enhanced.

This work is based upon a dissertation presented to the Jewish Theological Seminary of America in 1954 for the degree of Doctor of Hebrew Letters.

I express my appreciation to Mrs. Elliot Potter, who has read the manuscript with care, to Dr. Menahem Glenn who has corrected the notes, to Rabbi Levy Krakovsky for his help in my understanding the kabbalistic references, and to Rabbis Felix Levy, Fritz Rothschild and Jules Harlow who have read the manuscript and offered numerous suggestions. To Mr. Lew Schwartz and Miss Joyce Engelson I am deeply indebted for their patient understanding and constant guidance. I first learned of hasidism from my revered teacher, Dr. Abraham J. Heschel, who is today the outstanding authority on that subject. He guided my studies for many years and introduced me to the texts themselves. But more than that, he symbolized to me in his very person the teachings of Hasidism itself. I gratefully acknowledge my indebtedness to my teacher and master. May the Almighty grant him many more years of life and may his merit be a shield for us.

I

THE PROBLEM

CHAPTER I

The Conditions of the Time

EXTERNAL DECLINE

The sixteenth and seventeenth centuries in Poland saw Jewry at the zenith of its powers.

Encouraged to immigrate earlier by tolerant monarchs who understood that a land consisting only of nobles and peasants could well benefit from the merchant and trading talents of the Jews, and driven forth from central Europe first by the fires of the crusades and later by the flames of the persecutions which followed the Black Plague, the Jews of Poland numbered about half a million by the beginning of the seventeenth century. They were economically prosperous, protected by the crown, and lived an almost autonomous life, a nation within a nation, with their own courts and synods fully recognized by the government. The Council of Four Lands (Great Poland, Little Poland [Cracow], Ruthenia and Volhynia) was the overarching organization that united Polish Jewry into a single, powerful body, with authority to legislate not only for taxes, for which purpose it had originally been constituted, but also for cultural and religious matters.

Study of the Torah had rarely reached greater heights in the history of Israel. Men such as Shalom Shakhna (1500-1588), rabbi of Lublin, Moses Isserles (1530-1572), codifier of East-European practices for Caro's Shulhan Arukh, and Solomon Luria (1510-1573) were the products of this age. European Jewry began to look to Poland for its rabbis and leaders.

This position of eminence, however, was not to remain long

undisturbed. In 1648 the Greek-Catholic peasants of the Ukraine, led by Chmelnitzki, rose up in revolt against their tyrannical Roman-Catholic lords and slaughtered Pole and Jew alike. The terrible massacres by Chmelnitzki's Cossacks laid waste much of Ukrainian Jewry, and sweeping invasions by the Russians and Swedes, as well as the animosity of the Poles, brought terrible suffering to large sections of East-European Jewry.

The losses inflicted upon the Jews of Poland during the fatal decade of 1648-1658 were appalling. In the reports of the chroniclers, the number of Jewish victims varies between one hundred thousand and five hundred thousand. But even if we accept the lower figure, the number of victims still remains colossal, even exceeding the catastrophes of the Crusades and the Black Death in Western Europe. Some seven hundred Jewish communities in Poland had suffered massacre and pillage. In the Ukrainian cities situated on the left banks of the Dnieper, the region populated by the Cossacks, the Jewish communities had almost completely disappeared. In the localities on the right shore of the Dnieper or in the Polish part of the Ukraine as well as those of Volhynia and Podolia, wherever the Cossacks had made their appearance, only about one-tenth of the Jewish population survived. The others had either perished or had been carried off by the Tatars into Turkey, or had emigrated to Lithuania, the central provinces of Poland, or the countries of Western Europe. All over Europe and Asia, Jewish refugees or prisoners of war could be met who had fled from Poland, or had been carried off by the Tatars, and ransomed by their brethren. Everywhere the wanderers told a terrible tale of the woes of their compatriots and of the martydom of hundreds of Jewish communities.[1]

From this time on the situation of the Jews in Poland declined. Though they attempted to rebuild their previous life, they could not easily restore its former glory. The central government of Poland had been considerably weakened so that the nobles gained more power, and the old protector of the Jews, the royal court, could no longer help. Matters reached such a state that in 1740 the nobles even proposed a bill which would have made the Jews their slaves. Though the bill itself was defeated, in reality the Jews were little more than slaves, completely exposed to the malice and caprice of the nobles. In the memoirs of one Polish lord, we find the following:

Fifth of January. Since Hershke, the tenant-farmer, has not yet paid the ninety-one taler which he owes me and the time for payment has passed, I am forced to resort to indirect means. According to the wording of the contract between us, if he fails to pay his debt, I have the right to forcibly conscript into my service both him and his family until such time as the debt is paid. Yesterday, I ordered that he be bound in chains and shut up in the pigsty, but his wife and sons I allowed to stay at the inn. His youngest son, Layzya [Eliezer], I brought to my house, and ordered that he be taught the principles of our religion, and our prayers. The boy is unusually talented. I intend to have him baptized, and have already written concerning this matter to the bishop, who has promised to come in order to prepare the soul of the boy. At first, Layzya did not want to accept Christianity, or to learn our prayers; but Strilitzki [the teacher] has beaten him, and today he has already eaten the flesh of pigs. The excellent priest of our church, Bonifati... has been laboring hard in order to overcome the stubbornness of the boy, and to bring him into our faith.[2]

Three weeks later, after noting that he intends to slaughter the young pigs of his American sow in honor of his birthday, the Polish noble recorded the following: "Jews from Berditchev have arrived and have payed Hershke's debt of ninety-one taler; in addition, they brought a gift of sugar and coffee. I ordered the release of Hershke, but I wanted to keep his son with me, for he is now about to enter the Catholic faith. However, the Jews pleaded so much that I was compelled to free him also. Nevertheless, I am confident that the Jew will not be able to pay the next time his obligation is due, and, in the end, Layzya will become a Christian. I must wait until the twenty-fourth of March."[3]

The Catholic priests looked upon the Jews as "infidels" and tried to reinstate many of the anti-Jewish medieval laws, which would have outlawed the building of new synagogues, prohibited Jews from having Christian servants, forced them to bury their dead only at night, and forbade their appearing on the street during Christian festivals. It was not uncommon for priests to close the synagogues of a town, and then demand huge ransoms for reopening. One rabbi described how the people stood weeping on the steps of the synagogue while listening to his sermon, in which he "raised his voice with a great cry that the day of the Lord is near, the 'Days of Awe' are approaching, and we have no place to pray!"[4]

Stirred up by fanatical priests, Poles made frequent accusations that Jews used the blood of Christian children to bake their Passover matzot, and terrible were the sufferings which followed. The Council of the Four Lands sent a special delegate to Rome to beseech the Pope. As in the past, after a thorough investigation, he declared the charges false; but, also as in the past, the local priests—this time the Polish priests—ignored the report and similar accusations were soon heard again.

By the eighteenth century the burden of taxation had become unbearable. First there was the great sum given yearly to the government, then the vast amounts demanded by the nobles, and finally the payments made to the priests. Nothing could be done without bribery; even religious appointments and observance were proscribed. Speaking of the condition of the Jews, a contemporary Christian wrote: "The very conduct of your life and your freedom to carry out the laws of your religion you buy from Christian nobles. You cannot even appoint a rabbi unless he purchases his position for life or for a limited time from a Christian noble. The position of *parnas* [communal leader], too, must be purchased for a small sum.

Only after you have filled the treasuries of the government, the princes and their ministers, the officials and the different nobles, can you build a synagogue, and are you permitted to live according to the religion of Moses and Israel."[5]

We see, then, that in eighteenth-century Poland where confusion reigned [the state was in dissolution, its kings had little power, its legislature was indecisive, its princes disloyal, its peasants oppressed] the Jew dwelt alone amidst a Christian society with no protection. The nobles forced him into menial duties, allowed him only just enough to eat and held him in scorn; the priest could only speak of him with contempt on his lips; while the Russian peasant despised both noble, Polish priest and Jew, and waited for the day when he might hang all three of them to a tree along with the head of a dog (which actually happened). The city dweller and artisan hated the Jew because of commercial competition and sought to make his life difficult by ever restricting his trade. The officials readily took bribes, though often even this did not help. And beyond these difficulties was the royal government which ignored the plight of the Jew (just as it ignored the misery of the Polish peasant) and was concerned with only one thing—to collect its full measure of taxes.[6]

INTERNAL DECAY

Conditions had reached a critical stage; poverty was widespread and persecution continued unabated.

But internally, too, a radical change had taken place. Out of the bitterness and woe of a downtrodden people there arose a hope which was to raise them from the depths of despair to the heights of exaltation—promising relief from suffering, redemption from agony and the coming of the kingdom of heaven for those who had faith—only to cast them back once again, still deeper than before, into the misery of despair and disillusion: the false messiah, Sabbatai Zevi. He, together with the movement and the myths that grew up around him, worked untold damage among both the people and their leaders, leaving them in a state of spiritual exhaustion. Further evidence of internal decay was the disastrous decline of the high level of Torah study which had previously characterized Polish Jewry and been its glory, especially in those areas where the destruction of life and property had been worst during the seventeenth-century wars and pogroms. The nature of the religious literature now changed; it abounded in fruitless controversies. Cases of petty hairsplitting occupied the time and pens of the rabbis, to the exclusion of the legitimate needs and problems of the people. But perhaps the clearest sign of degeneration from within and one of the most disastrous from the point of view of the community as a whole, its unity, power and character, was the dissolution of the great autonomous body, the *Vaad Arba Aratzot* [Council of Four Lands]. The main source of organizational strength for Polish Jewry and the symbol to the Jewish world of a great and unified community dedicated to noble goals, the Council of Four Lands issued a last ineffective decree just before it was abolished by the government, to put an end to the ever-increasing bickering which had broken out among factions of the people in various cities, and to gain a breath of peace in the face of never-ending local quarrels that threatened to disrupt the communal life of the Jews and shame them in the eyes of gentiles.

The readiness with which the people were drawn after the will-o'-the-wisp vagaries and promises of a false messiah, the decline in Torah study as well as its perversion, and the collapse of the Council of Four Lands all testified to the radical change which had taken place in the spiritual life of the people.

Rabbi Yaakov Yosef—who died in 1782—was well aware of the physical suffering of his people. Each day he walked amidst hatred from noble, king and priest, as well as from peasant and tradesman, a hatred which crushed and tormented the innocent. He saw how lack of work and empty larders caused aching

hearts and empty stomachs. He suffered for the physical suffering of the people, knew their hunger, poverty and pain—
not only through the sympathy of his soul, but also because of
the wretched life he himself endured. But he suffered infinitely
more for their spiritual privation: felt ever so much more
keenly the prevalent lack of inwardness in observance of the
mitzvot, the use of Torah study for the sake of show, the
bickering among the people, the lack of unity between people
and leader and among the leaders themselves, the corruption
on the part of appointed officials who "purchased" their appointments, the aloofness of the rabbis and the contempt in
which they held the people. He understood the problem of his
time as essentially an inner one, a spiritual one, and when he
wrote of the pressing need for *takannah* (reform),[7] he referred
primarily neither to social nor economic breakdown, but to the
fact that "after a number of generations reverence has diminished"[8] among the people. What distressed him most was a crisis
of the spirit—the spiritual condition of the people. His writings
serve as a classic source and record of this spiritual climate.

According to the Talmud, "neglect of Torah study" was
responsible for the destruction of the first Temple while
"needless hatred" caused the destruction of the second
Temple.[9] In the eyes of Rabbi Yaakov Yosef, it was as if that
destruction had taken place again in his own time, as if the
great sanctuary of Polish Jewry, once a mighty source of
learning and piety, had been overturned, because these sins,
once again rampant, had destroyed its foundations.

Regarding the first cause of destruction, the sin of "neglect
of Torah study," Yaakov Yosef did not complain that the
Torah was not "studied," that it was ignored, put aside for
other and less worthy pursuits; rather that Torah study was not
motivated by "love and fear that it might rise heavenwards,"[10]
but by pride and vainglory. And this desire "to be elevated
and aggrandized through it, is the cause of its downfall."[11]

Striking testimony to the depths to which Torah study and those who were its masters had sunk was given by one who was not himself a hasid, Rabbi Yosef Hakohen, author of the book *Berit Avraham*:

Now, gentle reader, observe with a clear eye how dreadful a stumbling block has been erected because of *pilpul* [legal dialectics], the method of study which is the fashion in our time. We shall walk together, gentle reader, hand in hand, in love, and I shall tell you what my own eyes have seen.

There was a rabbi of great learning, a master of *pilpul*, who used to study the halakhah [law] and tosaphot [talmudic commentaries] in a hairsplitting fashion for two or three weeks at the beginning of the spring and fall of each year. He did this in order to prepare the discourse he would deliver on the Great Sabbath before Passover, and on the Sabbath of Repentance between Rosh Hashanah and Yom Kippur, as is the custom.

Now, it once happened that, while he was busy studying the problem of "wool and flax" for such a discourse, a poorly dressed woman from the lowest class came to him and placed before him her troubles concerning her livelihood. The rabbi rebuked her scornfully for having disturbed him, and the woman went away with a heavy heart.

The poor creature told an important member of the community what had happened to her. He went to the rabbi, greeted him pleasantly, and in the midst of their conversation, hinted politely that he had been derelict in not helping one in such dire need. The rabbi answered him in a loud, angry voice: "Is it not written, 'the study of Torah takes precedence over all'? I was busily engaged in the problem of 'wool and flax'—a most intricate and complicated law—with only two days remaining before my discourse must be delivered. At such a time this woman came to me. Is it proper for me to put aside my study in order to judge between one person and another—especially in such an insignificant matter?"[12]

The second cause of destruction, "needless hatred," Rabbi Yaakov Yosef also found to be widespread, "for the cause of our misery in this bitter exile is that there is no brotherliness or unity."[13] "This exile continues because of the needless hatred which exists."[14] "No one inquires into the welfare of his neighbor, but one hates the other."[15] "Hatred brings about division between men 'below,' causing division 'above'.... Therefore the commandment which encompasses the whole Torah is, 'Thou shalt love thy neighbor as thyself. I am the Lord'; that is, one should take pity on the glory of the Lord, encouraging brotherliness and love between a man and his neighbors, so that hatred and division on earth should not cause, God forbid, separation between the letters of His name in heaven."[16] But so deep had this evil buried itself within the hearts of the people that at times there seemed to be no possible solution, and the man who dared to seek one was filled with bitterness and despair. Thus the verse, "I have set your seed as the sand upon the sea" (Gen. 32:13), was interpreted to mean: "Just as it is not possible by any natural means to form threads out of sand, so by any natural means is it not possible to form a bond between one Jew and another."[17] "It is impossible to repair this breakdown [needless hatred] by means of a preacher or rabbi...."[18]

It is only in the passage of the Talmud which depicts the spiritual decay of the people of that period that Rabbi Yaakov Yosef found words adequate to describe the conditions of his own time:

"Since the destruction of the Temple, learned men and those of good families have become ashamed, and have lowered their heads. Men of deeds have diminished, and men of power and tongue begin to rule. There is no one who seeks, or pleads, or asks for the people. Upon whom shall we rely? Only upon our Father in heaven."[19]

He explains these sentences from a different age as if they were contemporaneous: "Since the destruction of the Temple, piety and words of learning have ceased, so that those who would engage in words of learning as of old are ashamed before this generation.... The learned are ashamed to publicly admonish the people to return to the good way. Since everyone observes that 'men of deeds are few, and men of power and tongue begin to rule,' it is not at all possible to admonish, while those who cleave to the Lord are beaten. It is as the prophet laments, '...yet will I lay my case before Thee: Why does the way of the wicked prosper? Why do all the faithless live in comfort?' 'There is no one who seeks, or pleads, or asks for the people. Upon whom shall we rely? Only upon our Father in heaven.' "[20]

The fact that "reverence had diminished" expressed itself in the daily religious life of the people. The ritual cleanliness of meat could, in some cases, no longer be relied upon.[21] There were those "small in spirit who contract the way of the Lord, whether in prayer or in the mitzvot which they perform in an off-handed manner, as if learned by rote."[22] They were in the habit of giving only "a little charity, and have never in their lives bought an *etrog* or a *megillah*. To them it is sufficient on the eve of Yom Kippur merely to contribute money for candles."[23]

According to Rabbi Yaakov Yosef, the Sabbath, which is to the rest of the weekdays what the soul is to the body, needed to be given to the Jews all over again.

This is why the passage in the Torah which warns about the observance of the Sabbath is followed by the passage concerning the building of the sanctuary.... It is written in the Zohar: "Moses assembled all the congregation of the children of Israel" (Ex. 22:1). The object... of this assembling was to give them anew the law of the Sabbath, for the previous promulgation of the Sabbath before the Israelites was not observed by the mixed multitude.... The profanation of the Sabbath is later explained in the Zohar: "Once the holy people enter into the precincts of the synagogue on

Sabbath, it is forbidden for them to concern themselves with anything save words of thanksgiving and prayer and the study of the Torah. Whoever directs his mind to worldly matters profanes the Sabbath, and thus has no portion among the people of Israel. For such a one two angels are appointed on the day of the Sabbath, who proclaim: 'Woe to So-and-So who has no portion in the Holy One, blessed be He'. "[24]

From this passage you can understand the profanation of the Sabbath in our own generation.... It is not enough that they speak of worldly matters in the synagogue, but they also burden the congregation with delaying the *borechu* prayer of the Sabbath service for the important members to arrive—until those who cleave to the Lord are separated....[25]

Perhaps no aspect of religious life suffered so much as prayer, which, because of its exalted naure, is easily profaned. According to ritual law, a Jew may not have *hametz* [anything which is leavened] in his possession during Passover. Before the holiday every dwelling and shop was carefully examined and all traces of *hametz* removed. Explaining why we are required before Passover to inspect even the synagogues for *hametz*, Rabbi Yaakov Yosef said: "It is well that we are taught to 'examine' the synagogues too, for the houses of study and the houses of prayer need to be searched for the *hametz* [leavening] of the *yetzer hara*, the evil impulse. Thus we must search out the custom of honoring and 'raising' a man when he attends services on the Sabbath or on a holiday... because very often he comes only for that honoring. Likewise, it is well to search out the idle gossip, arguments, jealousy and hatred there."[26] Many of the people "are satisfied with a minimum of worship, going to the synagogue only in the morning, and even these prayers are recited by rote, and in a hurried fashion."[27] They are "humble regarding spiritual matters, being satisfied with a minimum, but this is not the case with material matters, the pleasures of this world, for they feel that no one is entitled to wealth and honor except themselves."[28] The prayers of such persons jeopardize all communal prayer, for "it is impossible to pray with a congregation which observes the commands by rote."[29]

That a breakdown in the spiritual life of the people had occurred, a breakdown which affected the community itself in its relation to the outside world, seems beyond question. Yaakov Yosef even confesses the occurrence of the worst crime one Jew could commit against another: "In our time there has been informing before the government."[30] This breakdown, however, did not express itself in a radical outer change. On the surface everything seemed to continue as before: the Sabbath was kept, the holy days were marked, the Torah was studied, *talit* and *tefillin* were donned, few persons ate nonkosher food. The institutions of Jewish life apparently maintained their traditional functions, and yet, according to Yaakov Yosef, something had gone wrong, something was lacking— that inner devotion for which all else existed. The mitzvot were ordained that man might come closer to his Creator, that a bit of spirit might enter his life. They were to be the means to a higher end, but, in the course of time, they had become ends in themselves and thus, as an inevitable consequence, the very means were corrupted. The body of the tradition remained, but the soul was lacking. What was left was often hard, rigid, unbending, easily giving rise to anger and strife, engendering hatred and rivalry, opening the door to the chief of all transgressions—pride.

A parable which Rabbi Yaakov Yosef was fond of telling and retelling perhaps best portrays the condition of his age:

"I heard a tale of an apprentice who learned his trade from a smith. After he had mastered it, he made a list, point after point, of how he must go about his craft. He did not mark down, however, that he should first ignite a spark for the fire, because this was obvious and hardly needed to be mentioned.

Now he went to work at the king's palace, but, alas, found to his dismay that he was unable to perform his duties. He was soon dismissed. Finally he returned to his master, who reminded him of the first principle, which he had forgotten."[31]

The young blacksmith may have learned how to wield the hammer, how to shape the metal, how to blow the bellows; he may have mastered all the skills of his craft, but one thing he had forgotten, without which all his knowledge, all his talent, all his experience were of no avail—how to kindle the spark.

So it was with the Jewry of that time. They produced mighty scholars whose heads were crammed with quotations, whose lips spoke long and involved discourses, whose hands were busy putting ink to paper so that books poured forth in a mighty stream from the presses. They maintained the outward observance of the Law: synagogues were attended daily for prayer, stores were closed on Sabbath and Festival, unleavened bread was not eaten on the Passover, huts were built for Sukkot, fasting was universal on Yom Kippur and Tisha b'Av. But one thing was missing, without which all the knowledge, all the study, all the books, all the apparent meticulous observance of the Law was of no benefit—the spark which gave life to all else.

The duties of "Torah study and prayer" have to be fulfilled, "but above all else is the yearning, the spark of flame which sets fire to *hitlahavut*—the craving, the longing for His love."[32] Forgotten was the obvious and self-evident, that all the commandments of the Torah—study and prayer, Sabbath and Festival—were only for the sake of drawing closer to the Lord. A relearning of "the first principle" was necessary. A return to the Master to learn that first principle once again was the spiritual need of the time.

Before proceeding further with our analysis, let us consider who was this man, Rabbi Yaakov Yosef, whose bitter and passionate words concerning the conditions of the time we have quoted, and whose writings serve as the source for the remainder of this book as well.

CHAPTER 2

The Life of Rabbi Yaakov Yosef

HIS CONVERSION BY THE BAAL SHEM TOV

" 'Israel loved Joseph' (Gen. 37:3) and gave him of his glory, his offering to the priest...."[2] Israel, son of Eliezer, popularly known as the Baal Shem Tov (Master of the Good Name), the founder of Hasidism, that great spiritual movement which swept the Jews of eastern Europe in the eighteenth and nineteenth centuries and whose influence is still felt in modern Jewry, once remarked: "The Blessed One will thank me that I have found for Him a Yosele such as this!"[3] The "Yosele" to whom he referred was Yaakov Yosef Hakohen, rabbi and head of the *bet din* of Sharogrod, Rashkov, Nemirov and finally Polnoy [Polonne].[4] A profound scholar, born of a family of scholars, steeped in both rabbinic and kabbalistic learning[5] and destined to become the foremost literary disciple of the Baal Shem Tov, he was the creator of those books which formed the very groundwork of the hasidic movement and gave classic expression to the doctrines of the Besht (Baal Shem Tov). In his own lifetime and afterward he was the teacher par excellence of Beshtian Hasidism.

At first, while he was rabbi in Sharogrod [c. 174?-1748], Yaakov Yosef was not sympathetic to the way of his future master. This attitude was typical of the rabbinic leadership of the time. As a talmudist, he engaged in the customary hairsplitting dialectics; as a kabbalist, he was a devoted pupil of the dominant school of Luria which breathed an unhealthy asceticism. Since these two trends of thinking were contrary to the way of the Besht, how did it happen that Rabbi Yaakov Yosef became one of his most loyal and distinguished followers?

The Baal Shem did not act in solitude. It is true that he spent years of his life in a mountain retreat, secluded from society, seldom coming into contact with other men. He lived apart during these years in order to better prepare himself for the task which lay ahead: of healing what had become sick, of recalling what had been forgotten, of bringing new life into the decadent Jewry of his time. But when he left those lonely hills, he needed helpers to join him in his work. The circle which subsequently gathered around the Besht included some of the greatest personalities of the time, strong and devoted men, ready to fight for what they believed and suffer for what they held dear. It did not matter to the Besht that at first his views often differed from the men he wanted about him. The very strength of their opposition was often an asset, for when he made them his disciples they became strong in the new way he marked out for them. The conversion of Rabbi Yaakov Yosef is a case in point. Regarding its biographical particulars, hasidic literature contains both fact and fancy inextricably intertwined.

The Besht, it seems, knew of the young rabbi of Sharogrod. Despite their differing views, he felt he possessed latent powers and was eager to win him as a disciple.

One summer morning at the hour when the cattle were taken to the pasture the Besht came to Sharogrod where the *Toldot* [the title of Yaakov Yosef's chief work, after which he was often called] was the rabbi. He stopped in the market place with his wagon, called to the first man who came along leading his cow and began to tell him a story. Another passer-by stopped to hear what the stranger was saying. A third did the same. At last the Besht had caused all the passers-by—among whom was the sexton of the synagogue—to stop and listen to his tales. Now, it was the custom of the *Toldot* to commence his morning prayers at eight o'clock in the summer, and the sexton had been on his way to open the doors of the synagogue at six-thirty as usual. When the *Toldot* arrived at the synagogue that day, he found it still locked, and because of his short temper (which is well known), he grew angry over the delay.

The sexton finally left the circle of listeners and went to open the doors of the synagogue. When the *Toldot* saw him, he was vexed and asked why the men who usually came each day for prayer were not there. At being told that a certain stranger was standing in the market place telling stories and that everyone was gathered around him, listening, the rabbi bristled with anger. Powerless to do anything about it, however, he was forced to pray alone.

Rabbi Yaakov Yosef had heard of the Besht, but had never met him. Certainly he did not believe in him. Nevertheless the Besht wanted to draw him to himself. After the morning prayers the *Toldot* ordered the sexton to bring the visiting "storyteller" to him, that he might be flogged for interrupting communal prayer. In the meantime the Baal Shem Tov had at last finished his stories and retired to the inn. After the sexton found him and told him that the rabbi of the city ordered that he appear before him, the Besht immediately presented himself.

When he arrived, the *Toldot* asked indignantly (using familiar address): "Are *you* the one who interrupted the communal prayer?" He answered: "Rabbi, I am the one." (The Besht called him "rabbi"—"my teacher"!) The Baal Shem continued, "I request his eminence not to be angry with me. Let me tell him a story." Rabbi Yaakov Yosef listened to the story and was deeply moved by it. He regained peace of mind and was no longer angry. He began to speak to the Besht in a respectful manner, calling him "his eminence," while the Besht no longer called him "rabbi," but "his eminence."

The Besht continued: "If his eminence would like, I shall tell him another tale." "Tell it to me," he replied. When the Besht had finished still a third story, the *Toldot* entered into conversation with him and immediately "was joined" to him.

Then the Besht said, "I have not prayed yet; I wish to go and pray." While he prayed, the *Toldot* prepared a meal for him, and after the meal the two of them walked and talked together. All the city followed after and saw what had happened, that the Besht had drawn their *rav* to him. From this time forth the *Toldot* was a devoted disciple of the Besht.[6]

But the struggle for the soul of Rabbi Yaakov Yosef was too great an event in the history of Hasidism to be dismissed with so brief and esoteric an account. Many are the reports of what transpired during that first meeting in Sharogrod, each generation handing down the tradition and perhaps adding a few words of its own.

According to one description, we are told that when the Baal Shem was ordered to come before the rabbi of Sharogrod for having disturbed his daily routine and caused him to pray alone, he responded at once to the summons, since he had been awaiting just this opportunity for many months. He entered the house of the rabbi at a time when the latter was reproving one of his congregation who had come to pour out his heart because of the miserable poverty in which he found himself. Out of bitter pain and infinite heartache, the man moaned:

"My teacher and master, I am in desperate need, and my situation worsens each day. Yet I well know that it is the multitude of my sins which are the cause of all my trouble, as it is written in the Mishnah: 'I have done evil, and I have lost my livelihood.'"[7]

Rabbi Yaakov Yosef interrupted him and interjected mockingly:

"There is a vast difference between the words of the Mishnah and your complaint. The Mishnah stresses the first part of the passage, 'I have done evil,' while you seem to be concerned only with the last part of the passage, 'I have lost my livelihood.'"

A groan emerged from the heart of this miserable creature. And the heart of the Baal Shem, who was standing nearby and had overheard the conversation, contracted within him. His sense of compassion was stirred for the unfortunate penitent and, turning to Rabbi Yaakov Yosef, he remarked:

"Even our father Jacob understood the importance of earning a living when he said, 'If God will be with me... and will give me bread to eat and clothes to wear... *then* shall the Lord be my God' (Gen. 28:20-21). First we must ask the Lord to provide every one of the children of Israel with bread to eat and clothes to wear; only afterward may we ask the children of Israel to mend their ways, that the Lord should be their God."

Rabbi Yaakov Yosef raised the great brows over his deep black eyes, twisted his lips in mild scorn, turned to the Baal Shem and said:

"They say that you are an expert at storytelling. Perhaps you will favor me with one of your tales."

"I am prepared," replied the Besht, "to fulfill your wish and shall relate to you an incident that truly happened. In a certain house there dwelt two Jews and their families. One was a learned scholar, the other a poor laborer. Each day the scholar would rise from his sleep at the break of dawn and go to the synagogue where first he would study a page of Talmud and then, as the pious men of old were wont to do, wait a short time, direct his heart to heaven, and say the morning prayers quietly and slowly, drawing out his worship until almost midday. His neighbor, the poor laborer, also rose early and went to work, back-breaking work that strained the body and soul at once, until midday—there being no time to go to the synagogue to pray with the congregation at the proper hour. When noon arrived, the scholar left the synagogue to return home filled with a sense of self-satisfaction: he had busied himself with Torah and prayer and had scrupulously performed the will of his Creator. On his way from the synagogue he would meet his neighbor, the poor laborer, hurrying to the house of worship where he would recite the morning prayers in great haste, with anguish and regret for his tardiness. When the poor laborer passed his neighbor on the street, he would utter a mournful groan, that the other had already finished his study and prayer in leisure and he himself had not yet begun; while the lips of the scholar would curl mockingly, and in his heart he would think: Master of the world, see the difference between this creature and me. We both rise early in the morning. I rise for Torah and prayer—but he...?

"So the days, weeks, months and years passed. Each of the two men's lives was spent in a different fashion: one in the freedom of Torah and prayer, the other in the slavery of earning a livelihood. And when, from time to time, their paths would cross, the scholar would smirk and the laborer would groan.

"As it must to all men, death came, at last, to the scholar and, shortly afterward, to his neighbor, the laborer. The scholar was called before the heavenly tribunal to give an accounting of his deeds. 'What have you done with the days of your years?' a voice from on high called out. 'I am thankful,' replied the scholar with a firm voice in which could be detected more than a little pride, 'that all my days I served my Creator, studying much Torah and praying with a pure heart.' 'But,' commented the heavenly Accuser, 'he always mocked his neighbor, the poor worker, when they would meet near the synagogue.' The voice from on high was heard: 'Bring the scales!' On one side they put all the Torah that he had learned and all the prayers that he had prayed, while on the other side they put that faint smirk which hovered over his lips each day when he met his neighbor, and, behold, the weight of the smirk turned the scale to—Guilty!

"After the case of the scholar had been completed, they brought before the heavenly tribunal the poor laborer. 'What have you done with your life?' asked the voice from on high. 'All my life I have had to work hard in order to provide for my wife and children. I did not have the time to pray with the congregation at the proper time. Nor did I have the leisure to study much Torah for there were hungry mouths at home to feed,' answered the laborer in shame and grief. 'But,' commented the heavenly Advocate, 'each day when he met his neighbor, the scholar, there issued from the depth of his soul a groan. He felt that he had not fulfilled his duties to the Lord.' Again the scales were brought and the weight of the groan of the poor worker turned the scale to—Innocent."[8]

According to another tradition, the Besht had arrived in Sharogrod to win over Rabbi Yaakov Yosef. He preached both Friday night and on the Sabbath day, but the rabbi did not come to listen. Only at the "third meal" toward sunset, impressed by reports of the Besht's sermons, did he reluctantly join the others to hear him speak, hoping that in the fading light of the Sabbath he would not be noticed. He stood in the darkened corner of the room, but the Besht knew that he was there, and began to tell a story.

It concerned a certain rabbi, deeply learned in Torah, who at the beginning of the month of Nisan had begun to prepare his halachic discourse for *Shabbat Hagadol*. Some days before that Sabbath, when he was still busy preparing this traditionally intricate and involved address, and annoyed by the many people who came to his house with questions regarding the Passover laws, he went to the *bet hamidrash* to review his discourse. Through the window he saw a water-carrier and called to him to bring some water, but not hearing him or not wanting to hear him, the water-carrier did not come. The rabbi was enraged. When the water-carrier passed the *bet hamidrash* a short time later, he called out louder than at first. When again he did not come, the rabbi leaped through the window, ran after the man and struck him many times. After his anger left him, he regretted his action and sought to repent for his sin, but to this day he has not discovered how he should make atonement.

"If that rabbi would come to me," concluded the Baal Shem, "I would heal him with good advice and show him the path of repentance which is fitting for him, and he would be forgiven for his sin."

When Rabbi Yaakov Yosef heard this story, he could not believe his ears. For it had all happened to him. He had beaten the water-carrier in an uncontrollable fit of anger, but thought no one knew of it except himself and the victim.[9]

The first appearance of the Besht in Sharogrod was not sufficient to transform the way of the young rabbi, but the Besht's initial encounter with Rabbi Yaakov Yosef, the words or stories which he spoke, had succeeded in planting seeds of concern in Yaakov Yosef's mind. The reports which reached him from that time on about the doings of the Besht and his followers, while in all probability told him in derision—for the people of his city were fierce opponents of the new way—he now listened to with a new interest, struggling to subdue the stirrings of concern that had begun to move within him. The Besht, however, was not satisfied to leave matters as they stood. The struggle into which he had entered for the soul of Rabbi Yaakov Yosef was too momentous to be terminated. In his desire to further the work he had begun, he sent one of his most trusted and gifted disciples, the *Mochiah* or Preacher,[10] as he was called, to Sharogrod. It is recorded in the name of Rabbi Yaakov Yosef himself that "the *Mochiah*... came to the holy community of Sharogrod for the Sabbath and requested that he might lodge with him. This was allowed, and he was also given permission to arrange a *minyan* for himself in the rabbi's house. But Rabbi Yaakov Yosef went to the synagogue. On the Sabbath, when the *Mochiah* went to preach, he asked the rabbi to come and listen. When he arrived, the *Mochiah* proceeded to envelop him with sermon from the soles of his feet to the top of his head. The rabbi said to himself, "This is none other than a prophet, for how does he know my thoughts?' He 'joined himself' to him."[11]

The accounts of the conversion of Rabbi Yaakov Yosef which hasidic tradition has handed down to us are not all of one piece. They are only the scattered fragments of a precious mosaic which must be put together with great care and in the knowledge it will always remain incomplete. Nevertheless it contains the record of one of the most significant encounters in all of Jewish history. There is no doubt that at first, the young and brilliant rabbi of Sharogrod had heard much about the Baal Shem, had even met and spoken with some of his disciples, but he remained certain that his own way was the right way, that there could in fact be no other way in the service of God. Then came the first meeting with the Besht himself, and, while he may have rejected what he heard and been angered by the strange manner and the simple parables of the other—the one about the scholar and the poor laborer, perhaps, or the one about the arrogant rabbi—after the Besht left, doubt gnawed at him. Perhaps he began to question the correctness of his own way, shaking the rigid wall of certainty that had formerly encased him, that had assured him of the rightness of his attitude and protected him from any self-criticism; while the tale which the simple villager told him about his preference for the Besht's counsel, and the disturbing sermon of the *Mochiah* who stood before him as a living representative of the master, made Rabbi Yaakov Yosef even more eager to travel to the Baal Shem himself, and to confront him face to face.

That he did go to the Besht we know from the Rabbi of Sharogrod's own testimony. It was this trip which sealed the bond between these two men.

"I heard from the distinguished, pious and wise rabbi of the holy community of Polnoy that, when he was the chief judge of the holy community of Sharogrod, he heard that the Besht was coming to the holy community of Mohilev. He said to himself, 'I too shall travel there.' He arrived before the morning prayers on Friday, and saw the Besht smoking a pipe. This surprised him.

"'*Later*,' said Rabbi Yaakov Yosef, '*while praying, I wept a great weeping, the like of which I had never wept in all my life. I understood that this weeping was not from myself.* Afterwards, the Besht set out for the land of Israel, and I remained desolate until his return. Then I began to travel to him, and stayed with him for a time. The Besht used to say that it was necessary to "elevate" me, so I dwelt with him for a period of weeks, and inquired when his honor would elevate me.'"[12]

The final conversion of Rabbi Yaakov Yosef took place during the first and subsequent visits to the Besht; there the great task the Besht had undertaken, to win over to the new movement the turbulent spirit of Yaakov Yosef, was completed. It was providential that these two souls, so apparently different from each other, so distant in their way of serving God, should have been united. The conversion of Rabbi Yaakov Yosef to Hasidism prepared the way for its eventual victory and added immeasurably to the strength of its future influence.

Rabbi Yaakov Yosef came, at last, to the Besht—that much we know—but precisely what transpired there, exactly how the Besht "elevated" his soul (to use the peculiar but wonderfully pregnant expression of this oldest report we possess), despite the multipilicity of legends, remains a secret of God. And perhaps it can only be so. What took place between those two men must be the story of mind meeting mind, heart meeting heart, soul meeting soul, the joining of two flaming brands into one.

And yet we can be sure that those nights and days of debate, discussion and, then, learning, covered the entire range of the teachings of the young movement of Hasidism, for they are all expounded with consummate mastery in the books which the new disciple spent the rest of his days composing.

The Besht must have revealed to Rabbi Yaakov Yosef his unbounded love for God and Israel—for *all* of Israel, the learned, the unlearned, even the sinners; his conviction that "the whole world is filled with His glory," that there is no place where God is not to be found and no hour when God is not to be found, if only one knows how to search for Him; that His remoteness is only a mirage, a wall of the imagination, which, impregnable as it appears, can be breached at any moment man desires, and opens into the very throne of the King; that, in truth, God is not remote at all, but as close to every human creature as the mouth is to the ear, yearning only to enter his heart and life and soul; that arrogance is hateful to God, driving Him away and erecting a barrier of pride which He cannot penetrate, while humility is an invitation for Him to enter, man's welcome to the presence of the Divine; that one should serve God every hour of the day and every day of one's life, not only through the prescribed rituals, but by every action, whether it be in the house of study, in the privacy of the home or in the market place; that one should "know Him in *all* thy ways" (Prov. 3:6); that somberness is akin to sinfulness and a sign that man is not grateful for the simple joy of living; that God wants man to serve him in happiness and song, not through fasting and mortification of the flesh; that prayer is in its most profound sense a portion of the living God, the most precious possession of man, in which he is asked to invest his very life; that the Torah is filled with mysteries within mysteries and that, in spite of all the study which the generations of the past had given to it and all the books that the wisest of sages had written to explain it, still it remains as when first it was given, complete and almost unknown, for "The Torah of the Lord is *perfect*" (Ps. 19:8); that the soul of man has been separated from its source, wandering in exile in a strange land—"I am a stranger on earth" (Ps. 119:19)—ever yearning to return to that from which it first sprang and cleave to the Soul of all souls; that as the soul is in exile so Israel is in exile, and as Israel is in exile so the *Shechinah*, a part of the Lord Himself, is in exile; that, above all, in this period of inner decay and outer crisis Israel needs dedicated, selfless leaders who neither stand aloof from the people nor hold them in contempt, but go out to them in love and concern and compassion to heal and raise them; and, finally, that nothing which he, the Baal Shem, taught was new, an invention of his own mind, but all a part of the ancient tradition of Israel, that he, the Baal Shem, was only recalling once again to the people what had almost been forgotten.[13]

These visits with the Besht worked a revolution in the soul of Rabbi Yaakov Yosef, a revolution that meant suffering and sacrifice for the rest of his days. He became a loyal advocate of the new way, attempted to introduce this way into his own community—and reaped disaster.

Thereafter, he [Rabbi Yaakov Yosef] began to urge the men of the community to come to the "third meal" on the Sabbath, according to hasidic custom. This surprised them, for they knew that he had been at odds with the hasidim in the past. When the rabbi continued to maintain the justice of his cause, the men of the city began to dispute with him, and came to hate him. The dissension increased in intensity until at last they drove him from the city on the eve of the Sabbath and he was forced to spend the Sabbath in a village.

The Besht was not far away, and when he "saw" the situation, he said to his followers, "Let us travel to such and such a village, for I know that Rabbi Yaakov Yosef is desolate. We shall spend the Sabbath there with the rabbi of Sharogrod, that we might ease his suffering."

Rabbi Yaakov Yosef later traveled to Rashkov, where he was appointed rabbi. There he performed many acts of repentance. He possessed a thousand pieces of coin and gave them all away, returning all the fines which he had formerly received and the money of any business dealing about which there could be the slightest question. He proclaimed that anyone from whom he had received money improperly should present himself, and he would return it. Until he was reduced to poverty.[14]

HIS REPENTANCE

From these stories concerning Yaakov Yosef before his conversion and in spite of the contradictions inherent in them, we can piece together the picture of a harsh, officious man, rigorous in his personal observance, devoted to study, aloof from the people and their problems, given to outbursts of anger and assertions of authority—all of which, most probably, made him more feared than loved. The change which the Besht wrought in his soul was the turning point of his life. It reached down to the core of his being, opened his eyes to what he had really been and revealed what he must become. The old values were put aside and in their place new ones arose. The prayer of tears which the Besht had wrung from him, the laying bare of his tendency to anger, his proneness to judge severely, the exposure of his hard, narrow ways before his very eyes through tale and parable, worked a revolution in his soul, though traces of the old ways still remained. He was filled with regret for his past life and a fierce yearning for repentance and change. These, he felt, must take place in the people at large as well, for the wrong he saw was not in himself, but in those about him too—a common malady. First, however, his own soul had to undergo this repentance and change; it had to be an action of his own.

We have already remarked that he gave all his money away. We hear again of this in a specific case which is recounted in the name of a personal witness.

I heard the following from Rabbi Joel of the holy community of Nemirov, whose place of burial is in the land of Israel, in Jerusalem (may his soul be bound up in the bond of life). Once while he was traveling to the holy community of Meziboz with the *rav* of Rashkov (R. Yaakov Yosef), they came to the town of Bar. After they had prayed there with a *minyan* at an inn, Rabbi Yaakov Yosef departed, and they went to seek him. Learning that he had just left the house of a goldsmith, they inquired after him: "What did the rabbi do in your house?" The smith did not want to tell, because Yaakov Yosef had forbidden him to do so. But when the leading citizens of the community who had accompanied the rabbi grew angry and demanded that he tell them the truth, the goldsmith spoke: "I see in this [my] punishment. When I lived in Rashkov, he took a fine of two ducats from me. Now, in place of this money which he wants to return but cannot, he has given me his Sabbath *talit* until he returns from the trip and is able to redeem it from me."

The men ordered: "You must release him from his debt at once and return the *talit* to him." Rabbi Yaakov Yosef did not want to take it until the smith had given him his hand in assurance that he had forgiven him with a whole heart. Only then did he accept the *talit*.[15]

The poverty in which he lived was well known. "When the rabbi of the holy community of Polnoy was the chief judge of Rashkov, the angels complained to the Baal Shem Tov: 'Why are you silent while the rabbi of the holy community of Rashkov has no livelihood?' " How could it be otherwise, "for he did not have enough to provide for his family."[16] Despite this, "he redeemed captives and gave much charity."[17] "Once when his son complained to him of their privation and want, he replied: 'It is written, *Let the poor be the children of thy house.*' "[18]

OVERCOMING HIS ASCETICISM

Rabbi Yaakov Yosef had been a fervent adherent to the school of Lurianic Kabbalah.[19] It is not difficult to understand, therefore, that the Lurianic contempt for the body and its consequent asceticism retained a strong grip on him, in spite of his new adherence to the Besht.[20] Indeed, the Besht was compelled to exert special influence to weaken this grip.

We are told of his custom of fasting in Nemirov, a center of Hasidism, where he was appointed rabbi after leaving Rashkov.

He used to fast each day until nightfall and once every month he would fast from Sabbath to Sabbath [each day until midnight]. No one of his household knew of this fasting, with the exception of one girl, his niece, who alone was permitted to bring him his food and remove [the food or empty dishes as the occasion required]. Thus his conduct was hidden from the members of his own family. So it was for five years. In the sixth year, during a fast from Sabbath to Sabbath, the Besht happened to be traveling nearby and heard a heavenly voice; "Go with all haste to him, otherwise he will die." He went to him with such haste that his horse of twenty ducats' value died on the way. On arriving, he said to the rabbi, "My horse of twenty ducats' value died on the road for your sake. Let it, therefore, be an 'atonement' in your stead." Immediately he ate and obeyed him afterward.[21]

That more than a kernel of truth is contained in this story, and that the Besht took issue with Rabbi Yaakov Yosef over the question of fasting, is clearly revealed in the letter which the Besht sent to him. It is one of the very few extant letters of the Besht.

From the community of Meziboz to the community of Nemirov... to my beloved, beloved of my soul, the *rav*, the great luminary, righthand pillar, strong hammer, renowned in piety, perfect scholar, he who is full of wonder and works wonders, who is bound up in the chambers of my heart, more close to me than a brother— our teacher Yosef Hakohen:

Behold, I have received the letter composed by your unsullied hand and saw from its first two lines that his eminence believes fasting necessary. This shocked me to my innermost soul. By the counsel of God and His *Shechinah* I order you not to bring yourself into this danger, for this way is dark and bitter and leads to depression and melancholy. The glory of God does not dwell where there is depression but where the joy in performing His mitzvah prevails, as is known to his eminence—words which I have taught many times. Let them be upon your heart.

Regarding the branches of your thought which bring you to this fasting, let me advise you, that God may be with you as a Mighty One of strength: each morning at the time of your study, cleave completely to the letters of the words in worship of the Creator, may He be blessed and His name blessed. Then the judgments will be sweetened at their roots and will be light upon you. "Hide not thyself from thine own flesh" (Isa. 58:7), God forbid, fasting more than one is obliged to or than is necessary. If you hearken to my words, God will be with you. And with this I shall conclude my brief lines and say *shalom*, from him who ever seeks your welfare.

Signed: ISRAEL BAAL SHEM TOV [22]

It seems obvious from this letter that Rabbi Yaakov Yosef had inquired from the Besht concerning his fasting, expressing the compulsion he felt. But the answer of the Besht was direct and demanding. " 'Hide not thyself from thine own flesh'... the glory of God does not dwell where there is depression but where the joy in performing His mitzvah prevails... *words which I have taught many times.*" For Rabbi Yaakov Yosef, this letter remained the definitive word on the subject and is an important document in the struggle for his soul. Its influence is to be found in his later writings: "The body must be strong for the worship of the Lord; therefore one must not weaken the body."[23] The Besht was eager that his precious disciple be brought completely to his way of thinking. Not only did he fight for his soul, but for his body as well.

SOME OF HIS SPIRITUAL TRAITS

A grandson of the Besht, Rabbi Baruch of Meziboz, although the arch-critic of the zaddikim, greatly admired Rabbi Yaakov Yosef and wrote the following about him:

Once I traveled with the holy Rabbi Pinhas (may the memory of a zaddik live on in the future world) to spend a Sabbath with Rabbi Yaakov Yosef of Polnoy. The holy rabbi of Polnoy loved me dearly. Out of respect—for I was young in years and he an old man—I would not sit down in his presence. But neither would he seat himself in my presence. Thus I was compelled to be seated in order that he, too, should do so. I took out my pipe to smoke. He said to me, "Baruchel, I heard from your grandfather, the Besht, that you would fill his place. Are you then able to smoke tobacco like the Besht? For when the Besht wanted to ascend to the higher worlds, he would smoke tobacco and each time he puffed he went from one world to another."

After the Sabbath a messenger came to Rabbi Pinhas telling him that he must return home at once, because pressing affairs awaited him. Now it so happened that at that hour the holy rabbi of Polnoy was in "seclusion" [*hitboddut*] in his private room. Rabbi Pinhas was troubled and did not know what to do. To delay returning home until after the "seclusion" of the rabbi of Polnoy was not possible, since such periods of concealment usually lasted twenty-four hours or more. To depart without the knowledge of the rabbi was likewise not possible. Thus the holy Rabbi Pinhas asked me to go to the *rav*, to the room of his "seclusion," and request him to give Rabbi Pinhas permission to return home on urgent business. When Rabbi Pinhas asked this of me, I found myself in a dilemma: if I went to the room of the *rav*, I was afraid I might disturb him; if I did not go, I would disobey Rabbi Pinhas.... Therefore I suggested to him that both of us go to his room together.

And so it was that the two of us came to his door. It was old and warped. When my hand touched the knob, it fell to the floor and the door opened of itself. We entered the room—and behold, a heavenly *maggid* was studying with him! Such fear fell upon Rabbi Pinhas, that he was afraid to stay there. But I remained standing in the room. *And it is because of this that I know what an angel is!*"

"I had known," Rabbi Baruch adds later by way of further comment, "that the Rabbi of Polnoy had a *maggid* [a heavenly mentor] with whom he studied. But my grandfather, the Besht, saw that this *maggid* was not one of the true *maggidim*, and so he took that *maggid* away from him and gave him one of the true *maggidim*."[24]

The Besht was not only concerned that Rabbi Yaakov Yosef have the proper earthly teacher, but also that he have the proper heavenly teacher.

What records we possess of his spiritual life are all too few; nevertheless, those which have been preserved tell us much about the man.

"Each day he used to study in *talit* and *tefillin*. Before eating he would master seven pages of Talmud, and even while he ate, between each piece of food, his mouth did not cease to recite the holy words. After breakfast he would take a short nap, rise from his sleep, put on his *tefillin* and study until time for the afternoon prayers. In the evenings, too, he would spend many hours with his books. Not one night passed, whether

winter or summer, weekday, Sabbath or holiday, that he did
not rise at midnight to study. His study of Torah, his prayer
and all his holy acts he performed with such vigor that his
very flesh trembled for him."[25] In the letter to his brother-in-
law, Rabbi Gershon Kitover, the Besht wrote of Rabbi Yaakov
Yosef as "one whose deeds find favor before God, for all his
deeds are for the sake of heaven."[26] The Maggid of Mezritch
said that he "received revelations from Elijah and attained
other exalted rungs of the spirit."[27] Rabbi Pinhas of Koretz,
who considered himself more of an equal than a disciple of the
Besht, "was especially emphatic in glorifying the rabbi of
Polnoy and said, 'even in the days of the *tannaim* there was no
one who had a mind such as his.' "[28]

Great as he was in Torah, the *Toldot* was likewise great in
prayer. It was the Besht who had taught him the true meaning
of worship that day he went to Meziboz to visit him, where,
while praying, he "wept a great weeping the like of which he
had never wept in all his life."[29] As for his habits of prayer, the
author of *Shivhe Habesht* wrote: "I have seen that the rabbi of
the holy community of Polnoy would examine the *tefillin* before
and after the *shemoneh esreh* prayer. When he finished the
blessing, 'He who blesses his people with peace,' he would
again examine his *tefillin* immediately. (I have written all this
to learn from it zeal in the worship of the Creator.) He would
always pray the *shemoneh esreh* in a loud voice, while looking
into the prayer book, and would listen to the one who chanted
the service."[30] But later, it seems, "he was accustomed always
to pray before the ark himself." This custom was to him as a
vow from which he rarely released himself and then only
"before three men."[31]

His power of prayer was known even to people of distant
communities, and he was often asked to pray for them in time
of trouble.

"I heard from a certain man, whose name is Rabbi David,

and at that time lived in Sharogrod, that one day the rabbi of this holy community, Rabbi Mordecai, ordered that they send a special messenger to the rabbi of the holy community of Nemirov [Yaakov Yosef] to request him to pray... for them. They sent a messenger... but he said there was no need for the messenger, since the rabbi of Nemirov already 'knew.' May the Lord save his people from all suffering and privation. Amen."[32]

It was believed that his prayer had effect on individuals as well as communities. "I heard the following from Rabbi Susya of Hanipol regarding the time he traveled from his brother Rabbi Elimelech by way of Zolkva. 'I stood in a certain place in the *bet hamidrash* to pray. The prayer which I prayed was pure and clear like the prayer of the Besht, and I did not know the cause. Then they told me that this place was the place of the author of the book *Toldot Yaakov Yosef*!'"[33] And yet, despite the power of his prayer, which was already famous among his contempories, even compared to that of the Baal Shem Tov, within Rabbi Yaakov Yosef himself a different opinion prevailed. What seemed wonderful and easy to others was the most difficult of achievements to him, an unending struggle. "The zaddik, Yaakov Yosef, used to say that it was easier for him to learn ten talmudic discourses than to pray a single *shemoneh esreh*!"[34]

It is significant to note that at this point, however, the world of music and melody seems to have been a foreign one to him. He rarely refers to it in his writings, and, unlike many of the other great zaddikim, there is no *nigun* which is sung in his name. Indeed, according to the testimony of his grandson, he was not able to sing. In a movement where music played such a vital role, this failing must be considered with some care in any attempt to understand his personality.[34a]

When Rabbi Yaakov Yosef became a follower of the Besht and began "to travel to him" so that he might be "elevated," he was no longer satisfied with his own spiritual life, nor was he content with the spiritual life of his community. He had been "elevated" and he wanted to "elevate" others. His eyes were opened to the spiritual shortcomings of those about him as well as to his own failings. And so, in a long passage filled with bitterness and heartache, after describing the poor state of affairs which existed in the community at large, in the lives of the appointed leaders, both lay and religious, and in the very synagogue itself, and after recounting several shameful incidents,[35] he concludes by declaring that "all the above events, from beginning to end, happened to me, the writer, and demonstrate why I ordered the establishment of a separate *bet hamidrash* in Sharogrod."[36]

But the changes which Yaakov Yosef called for and which he tried to institute were not accepted readily by the people, some of whom perhaps reminded him with no little cynicism of his own earlier views. The tension between the rabbi and his community mounted and broke into the open. It ended, as we have mentioned, with his being driven from the city on the eve of the Sabbath. Nor was this to be the last of his privations. For his devotion to the new way of the Besht, he had to pay dearly throughout his life. Often when he describes in his books the suffering which the zaddik endures, and perhaps must endure by virtue of the nature of his mission—how he is given "no rest" by the people,[37] is the "cornerstone which the builders rejected,"[38] is exiled not only by the nations but also by his own people,[39] "mocked,"[40] "slandered,"[41] "hated,"[42] "trampled upon,"[43] even "beaten,"[44] "driven from his city,"[45] his place of study and prayer abolished[46]—one feels that it is from the well of bitterness of his own life that he draws.

In several of Rabbi Yaakov Yosef's *responsa*, which he presumably wrote in Rashkov[47] (where he took up residence after having been banished from Sharogrod), he reveals the suffering which he had undergone in those years after the expulsion and how he had been forced to leave in such haste that he could take with him nothing but his most necessary belongings. In answering a question regarding the dietary laws, he writes, "I shall be brief, like a dog licking water from the sea, and even if I err, do not hold me guilty, for I have neither *Tur* nor *Bet Yosef* nor any Code [books of religious law], but only that little knowledge which I myself possess...."[48] In another *responsum* he writes, "... this is not the time for me to speak cleverly or to compose a handsome phrase, for I have been burdened with hardship from the time of my being cast out from my dwelling place until now. 'I have not been at ease, nor at peace and now distress comes' (Job 3:26) to Joseph,[49] for I have been punished by the death of my dear brother...."[50]

"It is by no means a pleasant task to teach others. Rather is it more pleasant to seclude oneself and receive the outpouring from above."[51] These are the words which came from his innermost heart in an hour of anguish and despair which he could not conceal. He reveals the heavy burden of his mission and his desire for respite. True, it would have been more "pleasant" to be secluded in study and prayer away from the stormy controversy into which he had thrown himself, but he knew that it was his duty to enter that conflict in spite of the suffering, privation and persecution he might encounter. The force of his new convictions carried him beyond himself, out and down to the people. The struggle was not only with himself but with them as well. As a loyal captain he had joined the great battle which the Besht proclaimed. Nevertheless, in moments of pain and suffering, when the present was discouraging and the future seemed hopeless, he was often tempted to flee from the raging conflict which daily tore at his heart and gave him no peace. Time and again he was turned back.

Rabbi Pinhas of Koretz testified that the rabbi of Polnoy received a "letter from heaven...."

Once the rabbi (may his memory be for a blessing) wanted to emigrate to the land of Israel and requested permission from the Besht (may his memory be for a blessing). But he prevented him, saying, "You must be a rabbi in Poland!" Afterward, in his old age, he felt that, since he could no longer accomplish as much in the rabbinate as in his younger years, it would be better to go up to the land of Israel—without the knowledge of the Besht. But, through the holy spirit, the Besht became aware of his intentions and wrote him a letter instructing him not to go. Indeed, the letter of his teacher was so precious in his eyes that he put it in a box in a place where no one could touch it.

Many years later, when the Besht was long dead, he again wanted, at last, to leave for the land of Israel and thought that since he was now very old and weak, even his master, were he still alive, would give his approval. So he prepared the wagons, and arranged for a festive meal on the day of his intended departure. After the meal he went to a room in the rear of the house for something and, on the way, came upon the very letter which the Besht had sent him many years before. He picked it up and placed it underneath the tablecloth, intending to show it to his guests, for he believed that it was God's providence that this letter, telling him not to leave, should turn up at that moment. Now when he opened the box where he had originally put it, he found the Besht's letter lying in its hiding place as always.... The letter he had come across must have been a "letter from heaven."[52]

The urge to escape the battlefield of Europe for the quiet land of his dreams was strong in the heart of Rabbi Yaakov Yosef. Even the most selfless and dedicated of men seek to find shelter from persecution and an opportunity to put aside weapons of war for more peaceful pursuits. He was no exception. "Many times the rabbi wanted to travel to the Holy Land, but the Besht said he should not go."[53] The Besht knew only too well that he was one of his most valiant captains, whose presence and active participation in the great struggle was necessary for victory. "*You must be a rabbi in Poland,*" the Besht said to him when he expressed his desire to leave. What would have happened to the hasidic movement in that crucial hour of its birth if this brilliant, impetuous and fearless leader had gone to Israel, perhaps never to return?

The Besht exerted all of his energies to keep him. Even heaven played a role.

According to legend, there was great controversy in the heavenly chambers when the pure soul of the Baal Shem Tov was born. It refused at first to descend to the earth for fear that the evil serpents which exist in every generation might seek it out and destroy it. Thus, in order to guarantee his safety the Baal Shem was promised a special guard of sixty mighty men—like the sixty mighty men who guarded the bed of Solomon the king—to guard him against the evil ones. These sixty mighty men were the sixty disciples of the Besht, the zaddikim. Among the mightiest of these disciples was Rabbi Yaakov Yosef of Polnoy, who cleared a path for the master and his teachings among the scholars and the people, who fought the battle of Hasidism which the Baal Shem had proclaimed fearlessly and ceaselessly, with the conviction of his heart, the force of his mind and the brilliance of his pen. It was his very life that he offered up upon the altar of the new movement.

THE SUCCESSION TO THE BESHT

When the Baal Shem Tov died, it was not Rabbi Yaakov Yosef who succeeded him. In spite of the *Toldot's* closeness to his master[54] and his unrivaled understanding of his teachings, the successor was another, Rabbi Ber, the Maggid of Mezritch. The Maggid was not a disciple of the Besht of long standing.

It is reported that "he was with the Besht only twice. But the second time he stayed with him for half a year and the Besht transmitted everything to him. Each evening Rabbi Ber came to him, for he studied with him by night in order that the other hasidim should not be jealous."[55] "When the Maggid (may his memory be for a blessing) took leave of the Besht, the Besht blessed him. Then the Besht bent his head to receive a blessing in return, but the Maggid drew back. So the Baal Shem took the Maggid's hand and laid it on his own head. Thus he blessed him."[56]

It seems, however, that the Besht's disciples were either unaware that the master himself had chosen the Maggid or, aware of the decision, were opposed to him, for only a handful of them accepted him as their leader.[57] Both his teachings and his customs were, in a number of significant respects, different from those of the Besht.[58] There were no doubt some who believed that Rabbi Yaakov Yosef was the truer disciple and the one who rightfully should have sat upon their master's throne. This was apparently the feeling of Rabbi Pinhas of Koretz who, according to hasidic tradition, once said to Rabbi Yaakov Yosef: "I am astonished that such is the course of events, that when the king himself does not place his crown, it is put on a peg. Is the crown not sufficiently important that the king himself should place it on the other's head? Why did not one of the king's princes take it, that there might not be this desecration of honor? But the answer is thus: the man upon whose head the crown is put—if the king himself does not place it—may grow arrogant and say in his heart: 'I too am like the king.' But the peg is dumb and is incapable of arrogance."[59]

Rabbi Yaakov Yosef himself did not hesitate, at first, to express his opposition to the Maggid. The story is told that "once Rabbi Yaakov Yosef travelled to Mezritch, where Rabbi Ber [the Maggid] had established the new center of Hasidism, and wanted to enter Rabbi Ber's room. But the Maggid was already conducting his affairs with such formality that a servant had been stationed before his door. The servant, not recognizing Rabbi Yaakov Yosef, put his hand out to stop him, but the rabbi, who was by nature temperamental, struck him on the cheek, pushed through into Rabbi Ber's room, removed his hat and asked him in Polish, 'Are you a nobleman that a guard must stand by your door?' The Maggid excused himself; he explained that he was ill and had many visitors, and because of that someone had to stand at his door. The Maggid asked him to be seated. But he did not stay long."[60]

Within a short time the fame of the Maggid spread far and wide, attracting many distinguished disciples. There could no longer be any doubt that the succession was complete, a fact which Rabbi Yaakov Yosef himself cryptically admitted. "What can be done," he wrote, "for since the day when the Besht ascended to heaven, the *Shechinah* and her belongings have gone from Meziboz [the home of the Besht] to Mezritch [the home of the Maggid], and we are forced to bend our head in submission!"[61] Later, "however... in the year 1765 in a sermon preached on *Shabbat Hagadol* he quotes words of Torah which he heard in the Maggid's name, referring to him as 'our teacher, the hasid, Dov Ber Tortziner.' "[62]

Why Rabbi Yaakov Yosef was not chosen to succeed the Baal Shem is not clear. The master never made known his reason. It may be that, since he was a man of passionate nature and given to outbursts of anger, the Rabbi of Sharogrod was not considered fit for the all-important task of providing practical leadership to the new movement in its crucial period of expansion, when daily decisions based on calm and objective judgment were required. Furthermore, it may have been the wish of the Baal Shem to grant another the active leadership so that Yaakov Yosef himself could be spared to sit within the quiet walls of his study and create the lasting works which his pen produced.

It is in this latter sense that he must, indeed, be considered as sharing the leadership of the movement, for, while outer guidance was in the hands of the Maggid, the inner instruction, the truest teachings of the master himself, remained with Rabbi Yaakov Yosef. To him was given the momentous task of creating those fortresses of the spirit which, for thousands of persons, his books became. It is to these books that we now turn.

CHAPTER 3

The Writings of Rabbi Yaakov Yosef[1]

THE MAN AND HIS BOOKS

There is more to be found in hasidic literature about Rabbi Yaakov Yosef's writings than about his life. The story of the book is, in some ways, even more interesting than the story of the man.

When, in 1772, the first *herem* was issued from Vilna (and later Brody) against the hasidic movement—a ban which bore the signature, among others, of no less an authority than the Gaon Elijah of Vilna himself—many thought that with the enactment of this strong measure the death knell of the young movement had been sounded and that Hasidism would die aborning.[2] But a few years later, in 1780, there occurred an event which was destined to strengthen Hasidism immeasurably and at the same time strike a deadly blow at its opponents. This event was the appearance of the *Toldot Yaakov Yosef*, the first hasidic book, which to this day has remained the single most important work in the entire hasidic literature. It made a great impression upon the people as a declaration of revolution of the spirit: a profound and moving document which was written by one who, between the lines, betrays a life of suffering and struggle for the ideas in which he believed, and which revealed, along with an indisputable mastery of the older literature, a freshness of insight that again and again surprised the reader by its boldness, its ingenuity and its inescapable truth. Even the two dots (earmarks) printed above words the author wanted to emphasize, were believed by some to harbor hidden meanings, and so the book was at times called the "*Toldot* with the dots."[3] So famous did it become that, as we have noted, Rabbi Yaakov Yosef himself was often referred to as "the author of the *Toldot*" or simply as the "*Toldot*." The Baal Shem is mentioned by name only on the title page and in the preface. The *Toldot*'s usual manner of introducing quotations from the Baal Shem was to write, "I heard from my teacher." These "I-heard-from-my-teacher's" [for so the quotations were commonly called] were held in awe and reverence by the people. Indeed, Rabbi Pinhas of Koretz used to say that with an "I-heard-from-my-teacher" it is even possible to revive the dead.[4]

THE MAIN SOURCE OF THE BESHT'S TEACHINGS

The book, *Toldot Yaakov Yosef*, is most significant as the main source for the teachings of the Baal Shem Tov, the founder of Hasidism. Apart from a few letters and a will which, in all probability, he did not write himself, we have nothing from the Besht's own pen. What Rabbi Yaakov Yosef did was to devotedly and scrupulously record the teachings of his master, and to elucidate and develop them through his own thinking in a manner so rich and fruitful that what had been the treasured property of a select few was made available to all. The author of *Seder Hadorot Hehadash*, an early description of the Besht and his followers, writes this:

> Our teacher, Rabbi Yaakov Yosef Hakohen—gaon, hasid of the priesthood, holy and pure, one of the most high, divine kabbalist, head of the court of Polnoy—was among the greatest of the disciples of our teacher, the Besht (may his memory be for a blessing). By virtue of his mouth and pen do we possess all the teachings of the Besht, both secrets of Torah and mysteries of Hasidism. In no book of the holy disciples is there found such an abundance of words of

their holy master as in his holy books. He built all his wo
words of his master, and the words of his master are like the
which smites the rock and scatters many sparks.... In
is in truth "Joseph the provider," for all the holy ones wno quote
the words of the Besht (peace be to him) heard them from the very
mouth of the holy one of God, our teacher Rabbi Yaakov Yosef, or
from his holy books.... [5]

It is reported in the name of "the author of the book of *Rav
Yevi*,[6] a disciple of the holy Maggid of Mezritch (may his
memory be for a blessing), that in his old age the author of the
Toldot once visited him [the author of *Rav Yevi*, who was rabbi
of Ostro] in Ostro. Rabbi Yaakov Yosef was very old and weak
and his legs were sickly, so that he had to lay himself down
upon the bed to rest. The rabbi of Ostro came to his bed and
asked him the meaning of a statement which he had quoted in
his book, the *Toldot Yaakov Yosef*, in the name of the Besht
(may his memory be for a blessing). Then the face of Rabbi
Yaakov Yosef shone like a torch of fire, flames spread all about
him, he was lifted upward from his bed several feet, and the
words he spoke were as if given from Sinai, in awe and fear,
with thunder and lightning. May his merit shield us."[7]

Rabbi Yaakov Yosef devoted his life to disseminating his
master's words, for he knew and believed what was written in
the celebrated letter which the Besht sent to his brother-
in-law, Gershon Kitover. Once, in an "ascension of soul... I
entered the sanctuary of the messiah where he studied Torah
with all the *tannaim*, the zaddikim and the seven shepherds....
I asked the messiah when he would come. He answered me,
'By this you shall know: When your teaching—which I have
taught you—has been revealed and spread in the world and
the waters from your well have been scattered about.' "[8] To
spread the Besht's teaching and to scatter to all the world the
waters from the well of his master was the avowed goal of
Yaakov Yosef.

The publication of Yaakov Yosef's books, particularly the *Toldot*, fed the fires of controversy which raged for many years and eventually included the majority of East-European Jewry.

According to hasidic records, he did not find it easy to distribute copies of the *Toldot*, and so traveled from town to town, peddling them. When "Rabbi Yaakov Yosef came to Berditchev to sell his book, he set a price of one golden ducat per volume, and sat himself down in the inn to await buyers. But no one came, either to buy or to inquire. He grew angry, and because of his anger, the city was 'accused from above,' and its destruction virtually decreed. When Rabbi Zev of Zitomer,[9] a disciple of the Maggid, learned what had happened, he traveled at once to Berditchev and asked Rabbi Yaakov Yosef what it was that had aroused his wrath. The author of the *Toldot* answered excitedly that he had come to sell his book which contained the teachings of his master, but that no one wanted to buy it. Rabbi Zev replied: 'Why should this upset you so? Are you greater than the Holy One, blessed be He, who wandered about with His Torah among all the nations while none would take it?'

"Rabbi Yaakov Yosef grew calm, and the heavenly decree was annulled."[10]

Though copies of the book may not have reached as many people as its author might have desired, nonetheless its message quickly swept across the land, giving strength and a weapon to the followers of the Besht, and raising a frenzied storm of protest from his opponents. The masterful presentation of the teachings of the Baal Shem within the covers of a book for the first time, the admirable elucidation of the basic ideas of the young movement and their application to the immediate situation, won for Hasidism many determined followers. On the other hand, the author's sharp criticism of the evils of the day stirred up fierce opposition. His scathing denunciation of the aloofness and arrogance of some of the rabbis and scholars who were more concerned in perfecting their own wisdom than in helping the people, was misinterpreted as an irresponsible attack upon the institutions of Torah and rabbinic leadership in general, and called forth a ban from Vilna.

In *Zemir Aritzim*,[11] an early pamphlet attacking the hasidic movement, the *Toldot* is denounced in the harshest terms:

"I write you regarding the book which has reached your land in the month of *Menahem Av*, 1718, which the *rav* of the community of Polnoy, Yaakov Yosef, has written. It contains moral teachings and novel expositions which the hasidim expound from the weekly portion of the Torah at the third meal of the Sabbath, according to their custom. It represents a new way which they have learned from their teacher, called Israel Baal Shem (who claims that his teacher was Ahiyah Hashiloni), regarding whom he writes, 'I-heard-from-my-teacher.' His [Yaakov Yosef's] purpose is to entice all Israel to walk in their [the followers of the Baal Shem] path; but they do not walk in the path of our holy Torah, the path of our ancient ones (may their memories be for a blessing). Their main goal is to destroy the study of Torah, whether it be Talmud or Kabbalah, which they aver are not at all necessary.... He calls this book *Bet Yaakov Yosef* (*sic!*) [which is printed] without any 'approval.' I shall quote for you some passages—you may read them without end—which are fit to be burned...."[12]

The author of *Zemir Aritzim* then proceeds to quote Rabbi Yaakov Yosef's bitterest attacks against some of the rabbis and scholars of the period (not hesitating, at times, to alter the text to suit his fancy),[13] without admitting that it is not the study of Torah per se which Yaakov Yosef opposes—his entire life and every page of his works testify to the contrary—but its perversion at the hands of the arrogant.

Such attacks, oral and written, upon the writings of Rabbi Yaakov Yosef were not infrequent, nor did they fall upon deaf ears. Conflict and controversy were stirred up in many Jewish communities, some of which were nearly torn asunder by dissension. "When he [Rabbi Pinhas of Koretz] was visiting the holy community of Vishnivitz to perform the wedding of his son, there was a dispute over the books of the Rabbi of Polnoy. He rebuked the people and put them to shame. 'How could you display such irreverence by disputing over a man who, as is known to all of you, received a letter from heaven[14] regarding his intended trip to the Holy Land.... All the evil decrees which have been decreed against you were only because of your discord. Your remedy may be found by going to his grave, becoming reconciled with him, and accepting his books as holy books.' "[15]

So it was that the man was adored by the hasidim and despised by their opponents, welcomed as the leading disciple of the master and driven out of his own community; while his book, cherished with reverence by the followers of the Besht, was publicly burned by his adversaries. The ban from Vilna in 1781, which sharply condemned the book, also forbade social and commercial intercourse with the members of the new movement, even to the extent of prohibiting "marriage with them or helping to bury them."[16]

To the best of our knowledge the book was burned in Vilna,[17] Cracow,[18] and Brody.[19] The latter city seems to have been a place of particularly fierce oppostion. It is reported that *Keter Shem Tov*, a volume which comprises all the quotations from the Besht found in Yaakov Yosef's works, was cut into pieces, dipped in sulphur and made into matches![20] In the city of Brody, by the decision of the *bet din*, the *Toldot* was publicly set afire in front of the house of the Maggid, Rabbi Michal of Zlotchov, a friend of the author.[21] The son of the Maggid of Koznitz bears witness: "Mine eyes have seen how, when my father and teacher, my master, the holy Maggid of Koznitz, was visiting Brody, he passed down a street in the course of his business and suddenly stopped before a certain house. He was asked, 'How is this house different from others, that his honor [stops and] stares at it? He answered that he was not able to bear the impurity of the house. After thorough inquiry, it was learned that it was in this very place that the copies of *Toldot Yaakov Yosef* had been burned (may the Merciful One save us). It was the stench of this impurity that the Maggid of Koznitz still felt."[22] The house in question was that of Rabbi Michal.

Hasidic lore weaves a rich tapestry of legend over this infamous event of bookburning which, we are told, moved even the upper worlds to consternation.

The youngest son of the holy *rav*, Rabbi Michal of Zlotchov, Joseph by name, was once taken seriously ill. At that time the rabbi learned that in a certain land they intended to burn the holy books of Rabbi Yaakov Yosef of Polnoy. Rabbi Michal departed from his house, giving orders to his household that if, God forbid, his son should die, the burial was to be delayed until his return. After his departure, the sick boy fainted, fell into a deep sleep... and seemed dead. Three days later perspiration appeared, and his soul returned to his body. When he had recovered somewhat, he recounted all that had happened.

"As soon as my soul departed [he said], an angel took it and brought it to a chamber which he himself could not enter, but into which I was permitted. I stood near the door watching the heavenly court in session. I also saw two messengers bearing a book which weighed heavily upon them and in which were inscribed my transgressions. Another angel soon appeared with the book of my good deeds. The good deeds were not equal to the transgressions, so a third book was brought in which were the sufferings I had undergone, and many of my transgressions then disappeared. Nevertheless, because the remaining transgressions still outweighed my good deeds, they wanted to condemn me to death and to write out the decree.

"At that moment my father, Rabbi Michal, entered the heavenly chamber with the cry that, upon earth, they intended to burn the books of the Rabbi Yaakov Yosef, and pleaded: '*Is it not revealed and known before Him Who spoke and the world came to be, that he did not write for his own honor, but for the honor of the Lord and His Torah?*' Now when he saw me standing near the door, he asked, 'My son, what are you doing here?' I replied, 'I have been standing here a long time, and I know not why nor for what reason.'

"I asked him to intercede in my behalf. My father answered, 'If I do not forget, I shall intercede for you.' Then he again began to cry out because of the books, as at first. The *bet din* declared: 'This matter is not proper for our court, but for a higher one!'

"Meanwhile the holy *rav*, Rabbi Yaakov Yosef himself, the author of the *Toldot*, ascended to that chamber and, in tears, bitterly complained about the intended burning of his books. He too saw me standing near the door and inquired, 'What are you doing here?' I answered him as I had answered my father, and asked him to intercede in my behalf. The author of the *Toldot* replied, 'If I do not forget, I shall indeed intercede in your behalf.' The court answered the rabbi's complaint as they had answered Rabbi Michal. He departed, also, and I remained there in despair, for there was no help.

"Then the sound of a great roaring was heard, as the roaring of all the worlds, proclaiming, 'Make way, the Besht is approaching!' The Besht entered, saw me standing near the door, and asked, 'Joseph, what business have you here?' I answered him as I had answered both my father and the author of the *Toldot*, and added, 'I begged my father and the rabbi of the holy community of Polnoy to intercede in my behalf, but they forgot about me. So I ask your most holy honor to do so.' The Besht requested the court to let me go in peace, and they ordered me to return home."[23]

The striking fact which emerges from this dramatic fantasy is that in his anxiety over the books of Yaakov Yosef, Rabbi Michal could forget to plead for his own son's life! The life of these books, it would seem, was more precious to him than that of his child; his concern for the printed word was greater than his concern for his own flesh and blood. Instead of turning to help him, as one would expect a father to do, he first had to declare to the court that Rabbi Yaakov Yosef was innocent, that his books were pure, that "he did not write for his own honor but for the honor of the Lord and His Torah."

A second tale dealing with the heavenly debate which raged over the burning of the *Toldot* is told in the name of Uri of Titivo.

The author of the *Toldot* entered the chamber of the heavenly court, crying out in anger against those who were destroying his book, and against the Polish government, which had issued a decree for the burning of the book. "I demand that you examine my book carefully, page by page, and tell me if you find in it anything which is not proper." The upper chamber could not stand against his rage, and the book was handed over for examination. They searched and searched, but found nothing objectionable. "Examine it a second time," he shouted angrily, lowering his great eyebrows, "perhaps you will find something!" But this time too they found nothing. "Examine the earmarks [dots placed over words to be emphasized] which are in my book; perhaps you will find an earmark written out of pride." The heavenly court then decreed, "Whoever agitates against the *Toldot* will end in apostasy to the God of Israel, and the government which decreed its burning will be abolished!"[24]

The most important story about the burning of the *Toldot*, like the others, ends with a vindication of the book; but this time the scene of action takes place primarily on earth. The story is contained in a small pamphlet, *Divre Noam*, which was published several times and widely circulated. It reports a discussion between Rabbi Yaakov Shimshon of Shpetivkah, one of the outstanding scholars among the hasidic leaders,[25] a disciple of the *Mochiah*, Rabbi Leib of Polnoy, and Ezekiel Landau, the famous rabbi of Prague, a forthright opponent of the hasidim.[26]

"At the time the holy book, *Toldot Yaakov Yosef*, by the Rabbi and Zaddik of Polnoy appeared upon the face of the

earth, the Gaon, Rabbi Ezekial Landau, was head of the
rabbinical court of the holy community of Prague, and one of
the leading opponents of the Besht's followers. When the book
reached the hand of the Rabbi of Prague, he ordered it burned,
and he himself trampled it beneath his feet! In heaven, this
act brought anguish to the deceased rabbi, the Zaddik of
Polnoy. Thus it was that he came in a dream to his holy disciple
of Shpetivkah, Yaakov Shimshon, and bade him travel to the
Rabbi of Prague."

Yaakov Shimshon went to Prague, dressed in the rags of a
pauper. When he came to the door of Rabbi Landau and requested help, the latter told him that he was occupied in the
study of Torah which "precedes all things," and could not be
of any help to him. Through ingenious interpretations of the
Bible, Rabbi Yaakov proved to him that if his learning did
not teach him to aid one in need, it had not fulfilled its purpose.
Rabbi Yaakov revealed a mastery of Talmud which astounded
Rabbi Landau and his pupils by the brilliance of the expositions of rabbinic texts, unlike anything they had ever heard.
Rabbi Landau, realizing that this was no ordinary beggar,
asked who he was and why he had come. He answered that he
was a hasid. When requested to define the title, he replied, "*A
hasid is one who repairs what has previously been broken down.*" After
defending this definition with another array of talmudic dialectics which left Rabbi Landau in deep admiration, and, also,
delivering an astonishing extemporaneous halakhic discourse
before the scholars of the city, Rabbi Landau again asked the
disguised pauper "what his purpose was, why he had come to
him and who he really was?"

"The pauper answered: 'Let it be known before his honor
that I am the least of the least of the disciples of the holy
Zaddik of Polnoy. Thus you can appreciate the brilliance and
learning of his average disciple, and from both of us you can
appreciate the great, indeed, the surpassing brilliance and

learning of the holy rabbi himself, the gaon, author of the book *Toldot Yaakov Yosef*. We have heard that the Rabbi of Prague wants to have it burned. Therefore I have come to make known to him who his adversaries are, for 'there is no punishment without warning.'[27]

"When the Rabbi of Prague heard these words, he at once took the book from beneath his feet where he had placed it, raised it up and kissed it."[28]

Whether these stories are based upon historical fact or are the product of fancy is not our problem, for in either case they demonstrate the attempt of the hasidim to defend Rabbi Yaakov Yosef and his books from the fierce and unremitting attacks which were leveled against them. In the story quoted above, the Rabbi of Shpetivkah succeeded in coming to the very heart of the matter with his brief definition of the new movement's objective. "A hasid," he declared, "is one who repairs what has previously been broken down." The sharp criticism which Yaakov Yosef brought against the scholars and the study of Torah was motivated neither by ignorance (he was a man of great learning) nor by the desire to oppose the study of Torah (he encouraged Torah study in every way possible), but by his uncompromising desire to "repair" the study of Torah, which had "broken down," to make of it once again a means of coming close to God and a guide for one's daily life, rather than a means to display one's knowledge.

RABBI YAAKOV YOSEF'S WRITINGS AND THE RISE OF HASIDISM

We can understand now why hasidic lore contains so much about the books of Rabbi Yaakov Yosef. There are no books in all hasidic literature which are treated with such deep interest, whose history, both in defeat and victory, is told with such concern and such passion. And the reason is clear, for the life of these books mirrors that of the movement itself. They were born as creations of hope and promise in a time of spiritual despair; they knew the pains of persecution in their early years; they overcame, at last, all obstacles and conquered vast areas of Jewry. Thus the victory of these books symbolized the victory of Hasidism. It is true that the future of Hasidism after the death of the Besht depended largely on the practical efforts of the Maggid to reorganize it and to provide it with leaders. But ultimately it depended just as much upon the writings of Rabbi Yaakov Yosef, which gave to the leaders and the people the teachings by which they might live and engage in their holy work.

Though the early editions of these books were printed about a hundred and seventy years ago, these editions have been exceedingly rare for some time, because their contents were devoured by eager spirits with such appetite that they were literally worn to pieces.[29] There was something in these books which was not to be found in the other works of the age, something for which there had been a great hungering but no food, a deep thirst but nothing to quench it. How else can we explain the statement of Pinhas of Koretz, a man whose words were few and cautious: "Of the books that have been written in the past seventy years, none are altogether truthful, except the works of the Rabbi of Polnoy. There is no book in all the world which can compare to them...."[30] Nor did Rabbi Pinhas speak only for himself when he later remarked: "Books such as these have never existed, for they are Torah from Paradise!"[31]

CHAPTER 4

A Critique of Leadership

The life and the writings of Rabbi Yaakov Yosef were devoted to a rehabilitation of the spiritual condition of the time. Internal decay had slowly made its way into many areas of the religious life of the people and the situation had become so critical as to require nothing less than a radical solution. The "spark," without which all else was insufficient, had almost been extinguished. Externals had taken the place of inwardness: instead of feeling there was formality, instead of conviction habit, instead of devotion hypocrisy.

Who was to blame for this situation?

This is the question which is posed, a question that all religious reformers who condemn the way of life of their time must pose before they can point out the new way. It was a simple matter of placing responsibility, but one which Rabbi Yaakov Yosef took with the utmost seriousness, for his conclusions were to be revolutionary.

THE PEOPLE'S RESPONSIBILITY: THE MASSES AND THE RICH

In the past, the blame for such conditions was usually laid upon the people. They were urged to repent, to mend their evil ways, and to return to the Lord. "Return, O ye backsliders!" had been the cry of old. And there is no doubt that the people, both the masses and the rich, were partly responsible for the situation at hand. The finite and fallible nature of man tends to corruption unless constant vigilance is exercised.

It is not surprising, then, that many were concerned only with material desires, and that along with the denial of spiritual needs came the repudiation of their spiritual leaders.

"The common people despise the Torah and the learned. '[The people] cast truth [the learned] to the earth (Dan. 8:12), so that 'truth' is banished... and Israel bows down before an idolatrous 'truth.'"[1] "Indeed, our own eyes have seen the endless humiliation of the wise before the common people."[2] "The zaddikim seek the love of the common people, to humble them in holiness, through Torah and Musar, yet the attitude of the people is not love, but the opposite."[3] "The unlearned bring heaven, that is, the learned ones, down from their rung."[4] "They are called slaves whose service to the Lord is servitude, serving only for the sake of the reward and not because there is joy in the service itself.... Therefore their worship is without devotion, merely habit, simply a custom inherited from their fathers. And not only do they worship without devotion, but they take offense at those who do the mitzvot of the Lord with joy...."[5]

Maimonides has written that, "just as there are illnesses of the body, as when a sweet matter tastes bitter, so there are illnesses of the soul. And just as the cure for the former is to be found by going to the physicians of the body, so the cure for the latter is to be found by going to physicians of the soul.... Of those who do not go to them, it is said: 'Wisdom and correction they despise'" (Prov. 1:7).... One must understand why it is that, in truth, such people do not go to the scholars, the physicians of the soul. If, for a bodily illness, one goes to a physician of the body, then why should one not seek a cure for the soul, which is of higher account than the body?... Further, why are the physicians of the body deemed important, while the physicians of the spirit, who are indeed sages, are held up to mockery and not deemed important?[6]

The learned are rejected and avoided by the people. The verse, "How does the city sit in solitude" (Lam. 1:1), refers to the *hakham*, the wise head of the city, who remains in solitude... for the wisdom of the scholars is like an unpleasant odor to them. The verse continues, "she has become like a widow"; that is, the people have a husband—the rabbi—but only so they can brag to others that they have an important husband. In reality, however, they are widows, for they desire not his leadership.... [7] [They do not know the proper duty of honoring the learned and following their guidance.] Everyone says, "In the stubbornness of my heart I shall walk, for I am as good as the leader."[8]

Lack of respect for scholars was especially rampant among the rich ruling class,[9] whose sense of its own importance prevented its following the leadership of the learned.

I heard a story in the name of the late Rabbi Ephraim, the preacher of the holy community of Brod. A man from Cracow, having grown rich, was made a representative to the city council. Once the council sat in deliberation until the darkness of evening had fallen, and when he set out to return home, his servant walked before him, lantern in hand, to light up the way. Now this proud man was so offended to have his servant walk before him that he shouted angrily, "Who are you, that you should walk in front of me?" and struck him. Truly, there was no sense in his words.... He was a great fool to become angry at the poor servant who only walked before him to show him the way.

This is, alas, the situation between the leaders of each generation and the wealthy of every city.... In every generation, the rabbis and the other learned men want to strengthen our faith, teaching the people the path upon which they should walk and the deed which they should perform, by the light of the Torah. They want to give the people light and to walk before them. (The *Sanhedrin* was called "the eyes of the community.")[10] But there are those coarse persons, swollen in pride, who despise the learned who seek to walk before them to illumine the way. Thus it is written in the Talmud: "Jerusalem was destroyed only because the people despised the learned; as it is written, *'they mocked the messengers of God.'*"[11]

To learn, one must feel in need of learning; to repent, one must feel in need of repentance: but he whose heart is shut with self-righteousness wants neither learning nor repentance. "The Torah is called light, for the learned, in whose hand is the light of the Torah, will light up the darkness of the night, so that you can search out the *hametz*, which is the *yetzer hara*, to destroy it.... He who is humble in his own eyes, knowing the bitterness of his soul and that he walks in darkness, will honor those who fear the Lord that they may go before him to shed light with the light of the Torah. But this is not so of him who does not know he walks in the darkness of the night. He thinks he has no need for the light of the flame."[12]

For the hypocrite all things are possible. He can pretend to believe and yet not believe, pretend to accept God, who is apparently remote, and yet reject his messengers, the learned and the pious, whose demands are disturbingly near. The rich say that at Sinai no pledge was given to accept the yoke of the learned and their authority. " 'We are obliged [they claim] to obey the Lord [only,] as we promised [at Sinai]. But it is not honorable for them to bear [the yoke] of the learned, that they go before them.' "[13] Israel's submission to the nations is likened to the scholars' submission to the rich, "for we find, that just as among the nations, Israel, who is called the head, is bowed down, while the idolaters, who are called the tail, rule; so it is within the people of Israel itself, that the learned and those who fear sin, who are the head, are bowed down. 'The wisdom of the scholars is as a stench; those who fear sin are despised; the young shame the elders.'[14] The common people, who are the tail, rule."[15]

The attitude of the rich expressed itself not only in their refusal to respect the teachings of the learned, but also in their failure to provide adequately for the scholars, who found themselves in a serious economic plight. Time and again we are told the following paradoxical story. "A wise man, when asked whether wisdom or wealth is of higher value, replied, 'Wisdom is greater....' 'If so,' they further questioned, 'why do the wise hasten to the doors of the rich, while the rich do not hasten to the doors of the wise?'"[16] The plea which was made to King David, "Thy people, Israel, are in need of a livelihood,"[17] refers to the learned who labor in the Torah and are called Israel, "since there is no support or stay for them that they might have a livelihood."[18] "The learned ones are destitute and paupers."[19] It is the rich who should provide, but "the majority of the rich are miserly."[20] The scholars should not be forced to travel from city to city in search of help; "each city should support its own poor and learned,"[21] for "the students of the Torah are poor and need support."[22] Instead of ignoring the scholar, forcing him to search for assistance, driving him from their door, "the rich should pursue after him."[23] It is only "proper that you men of wealth should hasten to the homes of the wise to learn Torah and Musar so that it will not be necessary for them to descend to the level of degradation because of you,"[24] for "the understanding of the wealthy" is like that of "the animal or the fool who walks in darkness, not comprehending the value of wisdom."[25]

THE LEADER'S RESPONSIBILITY

Rabbi Yaakov Yosef was aware of the faults of the masses and the sins of the rich—their failure to respect the students and teachers of the Torah or to provide adequately for them, their pride and drive for power, their material desires—and therefore he laid some responsibility for the conditions of the age at the door of the people, as had been the practice since ancient times. But he believed that there was a more basic reason, embedded at the very root of the evil and sending its poison up through the branches to rot all it touched. One cannot blame the people alone—even the rich among them—for the main responsibility must be charged against the spiritual leaders of the generation, the rabbis, the scholars, the teachers, in short, the men of supposed learning and piety. It is upon their shoulders that the mantle of leadership over the people had been placed and, therefore, those very shoulders should bear the major burden of shame.

This was a revolutionary conclusion and was soon to stir up great wrath among those very leaders, shaking their fortresses of security, threatening their accustomed ways and exposing their crimes against the people and against God Himself; a conclusion which was to help bring about the new leader which Hasidism produced—the zaddik.

"I once heard from the deceased Rabbi Leib Pistener[26] an explanation of the verse, 'Save, O Lord, because the pious one is gone, because the faithful have disappeared from among the children of men' (Ps. 12:2). 'The faithful from among the children of men have disappeared,' he explained in the accepted fashion, '*therefore* the pious one [the true leader] is gone, for by means of their common unity, the one influences the other.' *But it was revealed to him in a dream that perhaps the explanation of the verse was the opposite: the pious one is gone; therefore the faithful from among the children of men have disappeared.*"[27]

This statement should be examined with some care, for it is basic to Yaakov Yosef's thought and admirably illustrates what must have happened at the very beginning of the hasidic movement. The usual explanation of the above verse from the book of Psalms, that the people are to blame, (the "pious one" or the leader is gone, *because* the "faithful" among the people have disappeared) was also the usual explanation of every spiritual crisis—the people have sinned, they are the cause of our misery, of our lack of leadership; let them repent. Rabbi Leib Pistener at first interpreted the verse in orthodox fashion, but he was not happy with it; he felt a sense of disquietude, that uneasiness which comes from a decision too lightly rendered. Then, something so novel and so striking occurred to him that only heaven itself could have been the author. In a dream, a new explanation of the verse awoke within him and, with it, a new explanation of his time and his people's situation. Perhaps the "pious one," the learned one, the rabbi, is to blame; because of him, his shortcomings, his selfishness, his pride, his bigotry, his contempt, his jealousy, because of *him* the people are in such a state. The true leader is no more to be found; *"therefore* the faithful from among the children of men have disappeared." The people are the flock: they are always at hand; it is the shepherd who cannot be found. The leader stands responsible for his generation.[28]

A revolution indeed.

The dream of Rabbi Pistener was seized upon by Rabbi Yaakov Yosef, repeated again and again throughout the pages of his books, told and retold, hinted at and alluded to, so that one is left with little doubt but that the "perhaps" of the dream had become a "certainty"[29] to him, and that nothing less than a thoroughgoing rehabilitation of Jewish leadership, a cleansing of its soul, a washing of its mouth and a breaking of its proud heart would suffice to save the people. In moving toward his analysis of the rabbi and the learned, let us begin with Rabbi Yaakov Yosef's treatment of the lesser officials.

"I heard from a wise man that the *yetzer hara* [evil desire] has of late grown shrewd, perceiving that it is not necessary to entice into its net every single individual, but only those through whom the others stumble."[30] Thus, if the butcher "offers unfit meat to the people, they are caught in the net because of him. So it is with the *sheliah tzibbur*, the cantor, who is the intermediary between Israel and our Father in Heaven. The rabbis have warned us... that the *sheliah tzibbur* should be the most select of the people which, alas, as is well known, is not the case now, for he is the least select. One cannot speak more of this."[31] The verse, "they bless with their mouth, but inwardly they curse" (Ps. 62:5), refers to those cantors who with their mouths recite *borechu* with only a melody, "in order that men and women might find pleasure in their voices; but inwardly they curse [God]."[32]

Our souls are sick with listening to *hazzanim*, for in every fine and pious community the plague has spread. They sin and bring others to sin. When they prolong their melodies without end, the people gossip in the synagogue, interrupting the silence of prayer at times when it is forbidden to interrupt. Therefore the *hazzan* brings evil upon himself and upon others. From whence did this custom spread? Originally, I heard, he sang devoutly and without payment, for the *hazzan* was the most important person in the city, as is stated in the *Shulhan Aruch*, Chapter 55. It is further recorded in the writings of the *Ari* that the three letters of the word *hazzan* (*h z n*) represent: embrace (Hibbuk), union (Zivug) and kiss (Nishuk); for through the *hazzan*, the divine embrace, union and kiss were achieved.... In the past the *hazzan* used to express the proper *kavannah* for each word of the service through the melody he sang. Therefore it is our tradition not to change the melodies even for the Days of Awe, for they fit to the words of the prayers. But, in the course of time, when the generation was no longer pure, *only the melody remained, while the hazzan ceased to pray at all.* He sinned and brought others to sin. Woe for the disgrace! How has he the shamelessness to stand up as the advocate, the messenger of the congregation, the intermediary between Israel and our Father in heaven, before the great and awful King, the root and source of all worlds...?

So it is with the teachers. Originally, they would study and teach the children devoutly and without payment, for the *Shulhan Aruch* states in Chapter 246,[33] "It is forbidden to receive a salary for teaching the oral law, as it is written, 'behold, I [Moses] have taught you statutes and laws as the Lord my God commanded me' (Deut. 4:5).... Just as I [Moses] learned without payment, so have you learned from me without payment. And thus you shall teach without payment in the generations to come...." In later times the teachers were paid [but not for the teaching of Torah, only] for the loss of time [which could have otherwise been used to earn a livelihood]. Nevertheless, they performed their task sincerely; as it is written in *Sefer Hasidim*, "one should not stand and talk with the teacher of children lest with your words you keep him from his task." But in recent times they have grown crafty, as we hear in the story of the wise man who met a teacher who had absented himself from his duties.[34] "Why are you not teaching the children?" he asked. "Even if you have no shame before the Creator, surely you should have shame before those who pay your salary!" The teacher answered, "In the past, I used to busy myself with the children during the entire year. *But I have found that it is better to busy myself for a few weeks with their fathers to ingratiate myself with them. After that, I need not bother with the children at all!*"[35]

THE RABBI AND THE SCHOLAR

Yet it is not with these lesser dignitaries, the *hazzan*, the *shochet* and the teacher, that Yaakov Yosef was most concerned. He passes over them rather quickly, though in a manner so bitter and incisive, so impassioned and outraged, that one cannot easily forget his words. His main objective was something, or rather someone, else. Behind the people, both poor and rich, and behind the minor officials, stood the rabbis and the scholars of the time. It is as if our author were pushing aside one veil after another, treating one aspect after another of the spiritual decline of the day—the masses, the rich, the butcher, the cantor, the teacher—until at last he could concentrate his attention upon those who were principally responsible, "for *the Shechinah is in exile, because we have no leader, no one to give us strength.*"[36]

It is especially to the rabbi that Leib Pistener's dream, so profound and so characteristic of the hasidic movement and of Yaakov Yosef's thinking, applied. "The pious one"—the true leader—"is gone; *therefore*, the faithful from among the children of men have disappeared." The rabbis and scholars were the spiritual leaders of the community. The blame, though borne by others too, lay principally with them. Theirs was the central task and responsibility. Therefore, it is upon them that Rabbi Yaakov Yosef casts the piercing rays of his criticism, exposing the malpractices in which they participated, the sins which they committed, and the deeds which they had left undone. He disclosed their self-interest, their pride and vainglory, their concern for themselves and contempt for the people. It was not easy for him to speak in this way; he did not do so from desire—because he really wished to—but out of the uttermost necessity, because he was compelled to. He was like "the faithful physician who, loving the man to whom he gives a remedy, must first uncover his wounds and sores. Only then is he able to heal him."[37] For "it is imposible for the physician to heal if he does not open up the wound and lay bare its evil."[38] So thoroughly did he uncover the ugly sores and lay bare the festering evil that the state of affairs which existed could not remain the same for long. Whoever read his books knew that the day of reckoning had come.

One of the central themes of Rabbi Yaakov Yosef's works is a criticism of the rabbi of the time and a picture of the ideal rabbi of the future. Unlike the Baal Shem Tov and some of his circle, Yaakov Yosef had himself served as a rabbi in several communities and was, therefore, even more keenly aware than they of the problems of rabbinic leadership. He spoke out of his own inner struggle, his own bitter experience, and his own deep concern with the kind of leadership the people received. Unsparing in his denunciation of the abuses of the rabbis, he was at the same time transported by his picture of the ideal leader; but throughout it all there runs a core of realism which kept him from adopting the grandiose views of the zaddik which were held by some of the later hasidic leaders.

CONSEQUENCES OF THE PRIDE OF THE LEARNED

The task of the Jewish leader, whether he be judge, prophet or rabbi, is to bring his people closer to the Lord, so that they walk in His ways and bend their will to His. He stands midway between God and the people, both of whom he serves. It may sometimes happen, however, that the power he wields, the knowledge he possesses and the place of distinction which he occupies go to his head, filling him to overflowing with pride. Then all his glory and power, even all his knowledge, become perverted, for they are now no longer bent toward the service of God and the people, but toward the service of his own ego. The canker of egotism reaches everywhere. It destroys him and, ultimately, the people as well. "For the foundation is the basis of a structure. If the foundation totters, the whole building will fall. So it is with the man whose very foundation totters, the man of pride. All his good deeds are built on an unstable base."[39] So it was with that generation of eighteenth-century Poland. The greatness of its Torah and houses of study, of its learning and *yeshivot* was built upon an unstable foundation. How different were the leaders of old.

" 'Herewith shall Aaron come into the holy place.... He shall put on the holy linen tunic, and he shall have the linen breeches upon his flesh, and shall be girded with the linen girdle, and with the linen mitre shall he be attired. They are the holy garments.... And he did as the Lord commanded Moses' (Lev. 16:3, 34). This passage brings praise to Aaron, because he did not don the priestly robes for his own aggrandizement, but only to fulfill the command of the King.[40] It is the reverse with the rabbis who clothe themselves with the raiment of their calling because of their pride."[41]

So far had they traveled along the road of pride that humility was no longer a simple possibility; only the naked fear of God in their hearts might bring it about. Therefore the Torah did not begin, as it might have, with the first mitzvah mentioned in it, that of declaring the new moon (which only occurs many chapters later); for the moon is the symbol of humility, since it constantly humbles itself before the sun. But the Torah began with *bereshit*, for it is the symbol of *yir'ah*, fear of God. In other words, humility should be the first command to the leaders, but their hearts are too filled with pride for them to become humble without prior preparation. Therefore, first the dread and awe of the Almighty must shake them from the arrogance of their self-satisfaction.[42]

According to Rabbi Yaakov Yosef three principal consequences followed from the pride of the learned:

1. *The breakdown of the place of Torah*, which became, for the scholar, a means of achieving glory and fame.

2. *The drive for personal security*, which resulted in corruption, and in subservience to the rich.

3. *The concern for spiritual security*, the salvation of the leader's own soul, which led to the neglect of the people's salvation.

THE BREAKDOWN OF THE PLACE OF TORAH

"There are those who become proud when they study much Torah."[43] "There are learned men whose every action is for show, who are the first to enter the synagogue and who study there only in order to display their prowess."[44] Pride is "most common amongst the learned."[45] For many of the rabbis of the time the Torah had become "a means of display, so that the people might remark, 'he is a wise man,' "[46] "for there is a natural tendency to pride through much study."[47] The only antidote for this is humility. "If the scholars would learn the traits of humility and modesty, then all would be well; but this is not at all the case, since it is well known to everyone that *the more learned they are the more vain they are*."[48]

The purpose of the entire Torah and all the mitzvot is that one might cleave to Him Who is blessed, as it is written, "that thou mayest cleave to Him" (Deut. 10:20), and as the commentary to the second chapter of Maimonides' *Hilchot Yesode Hatorah* explains, "When you study the words of the Torah... your soul will yearn to cleave to Him... for all the mitzvot were only given in order that we might reach that rung, as it says, 'choose life that you might live' " (Deut. 30:19).... But in the course of years the hearts of our leaders have shrunk so that they no longer understand these words. They only make of the Torah a crown with which to be exalted and glorified. Even repentance is for the sake of show. When a man learns one halachah, he is only a little proud; when he learns more, he becomes prouder still; and when he learns the codes or kabbalah he is even more filled with pride and is cut off from the Lord. As it says in the Talmud, "regarding the man of arrogance, I and he cannot dwell in the same world."[49] *The more the scholars travel from city to city to study, the farther they seem to travel away from the Lord.*[50]

I heard from my teacher an explanation of the following talmudic passage: "Then shall ye again discern between the righteous and the wicked, between one that serves the Lord and one that serves Him not" (Mal. 3:18). In regard to a question on this verse, Hillel remarked, "He that serves Him and he that serves Him not both refer to the completely righteous, but he that repeated his lesson a hundred times is not to be compared with him who repeated it a hundred and one times."[51]

One must endeavor to understand this, for is it true that because a man lacks one repetition of the lesson, he should be called "wicked," one that "serves Him not"? My teacher explained... that if the basis of his Torah and service is pride, even if he serves

God it is nothing, because he is lacking the "One," that is, the Lord. Therefore, we should know that *even if he serves God [with Torah], it is as if he did not serve Him... for he lacks the One.*[52]

A plague has spread among the rabbis regarding the sermons they preach on the Sabbath before Passover and on the Sabbath of Repentance, for the principal purpose of the sermon should be to show the people the path upon which they should tread, as the great codifiers have written and as we learn from the Talmud and the tosafot and from Moses our teacher (may he rest in peace) who showed the impure among the Israelites how they might be sanctified for the service of the Lord.... So it is proper for all generations that they be shown the way to be sanctified for the service of the Lord. But at the present time it is otherwise, for the rabbis use most of their sermons to display their brilliance and their knowledge, while toward the end they just mention a few laws regarding Passover, and none at all on the Sabbath of Repentance.[53]

How easy it is for one to lose himself in his own words, especially if they are clever words and reflect his own cleverness. How easy it is not only to forget the people whom you serve but the God whom you serve as well.[54] "When one scholar discusses Torah with others, precisely at that moment should he love the Lord and not himself (God forbid), making a display of his knowledge and brilliance that he might gain renown among other scholars."[55]

It was only natural that once the Torah became merely a spade to dig with, a means of achieving fame and glory—not studied or taught for the sake of heaven, but for the sake of the ego—that the spirit of brotherhood which often characterized Jewish scholars would give way to the fierce clash of personalities. Jealousy is ever the bitter fruit of pride.

Many of the rabbis regarded one another, not as brothers joined together for a holy task, but with rivalry and bitterness. There was often bitter "dispute between the learned. They should not mock one another, but their dispute should be for the sake of heaven."[56] "When a certain scholar settled in a city... he began to pass judgment on the judge of the city, to dispute and contend with him."[57] It was not the truth they were interested in but only in asserting their own point of view. "There are rabbis who do not respect the Torah of another scholar but only their own, and when they hear the Torah of others, they pass it off as something of no interest...."[58] "One who does not study the Torah for its own sake turns his ear from hearing the Torah and Musar of another, since he does not consider it fitting that he learn from another but only that he himself speak and the others listen."[59]

I heard a parable in the name of my teacher (may his memory live on in the future world). A very tall man was exposed to the heat of the sun all day, until he had become blackened by its rays. A wise man observed his plight: that he had no water for his parched tongue. What did he do? He approached him, sat down, took out his container of water and drank from it, so that the other might observe him. Even with the water bottle, he was too short to reach the tall man who would have had to bend over to drink the water. Now, it was because of his pride that he would not bend down, for this would indicate that he was in need of another's help. The wise man understood this, and could find no other way of getting some water to him other than by throwing it upward into his face. But, concerned only with his pride and what others might think of him, the thirsty man tightened his lips one against the other so that not even the slightest bit of the other's water should reach his mouth... and so he died.[60]

The pride of the learned so encased them—so the parable implies—that when they could benefit from others in learning and wisdom, when they were parched and the living water of Torah was available, they did not seek it out. Even when it was brought to them and they had but to open their mouths to taste its sweetness, their lips were tightly closed, their backs straight, their heads high, lest it seem they were not self-sufficient, that there was any wisdom other than their own which could benefit them. They were stubborn even until their souls had become dry and emptied of all life.

In many cases the rivalry among the rabbis gave rise to petty quarrels and a diversion of attention from the plight of the people. The plague of locusts in Egypt is compared to "the multiplication of leaders, for there is not one leader to the generation but all of them would be leaders-in-chief."[61] "Each one puffs himself up, saying, 'I shall rule, I am the greater scholar.'"[62] Just as the locusts covered the land so that one could not see it, so "the multiplication of leaders has covered the face of the earth so that none is able to see the earth, that is, the people, to care for them."[63] This too was a result of jealousy. Rabbi Yaakov Yosef issues a warning to the Jewish communities against the drive for power which motivated some of the rabbis—when a new community is founded and "you say: 'I shall set a king over me,' that is, you want to have a rabbi; be careful that *you* set a king over you, before one sets himself up."[64]

Along with the scholars' jealousy of each other was their feeling of bitterness toward the truly pious, whose piety they mocked and whose influence over the people they sometimes opposed. This mockery of the pious was bitter in intent and expression and was the cause of no little anguish. "Rabbi Akiba remarked: 'When I was an *am ha'aretz* [one of the unlettered], I said to myself that if I were near a learned man, I would bite him as does a *hamor* [donkey].'[65] For the bite of the unlettered man is not like the bite of the *hamor* [the Zohar explains the letters of the word *hamor* as referring to *h*acham *m*ufla *v*'rav *r*abbanim, thus equating donkey and scholar]. For the bite of the scholar is terrible in its wickedness."[66]

The pious ones, the zaddikim, tried to draw the people to themselves, to influence them. This is one of the great goals of

Hasidism, for once the people have joined themselves to the true man of piety, then they have in a measure joined themselves to the Lord also; as the Mechilta comments on the verse, "They believed in the Lord and in Moses His servant" (Ex. 14:31): "If one believes in the shepherd of Israel, it is as if he believes in Him who spoke and the world was created."[67] To cleave to the pious means to cleave to the Lord. Such a union "below" causes a union "above" in the upper spheres as well, so that the separated letters of God's name may once again be brought together. It is an endless disaster, therefore, which some of the learned help to bring about, contributing to the diabolical forces of separation which threaten the world. The eternal "mixed multitude are the learned, *those who are wise to do evil*, for they separate the letters of God's name; they divide the mass of the people from the zaddikim of the generation."[68]

Scorn for the righteous caused Jerusalem to be destroyed and it is the scorn for the righteous which constantly brings Jerusalem to ruins. "'Jerusalem was destroyed only because the scholars were mocked'[69]...as it is written, 'And the Lord, the God of their fathers, sent to them by His messengers, sending betimes and often; because he had compassion on His people and His dwelling place; but they mocked the messengers of God, and despised His words and scoffed at His prophets, until the wrath of the Lord arose against His people, and there was no remedy' (II Chr. 36:15-16). This was because of the scholars of the time... and I heard that they put to death the prophet Zechariah."[70]

The learned mock the pious because of the proud man's hatred for him whose life and words are joined, thus serving the Lord in truth. In a sense he is jealous of the inner life of the pious man, which moves in a world unknown to him. But since it is unknown to him, how foolish of him to mock the man of piety. This is the meaning of the following parable.

Once a king wanted to have the walls of the palace illustrated with pictures. Artists from all the lands of the king gathered to see who could produce the finest piece of work. One drew a corn stalk upon which was perched a small bird, and the people were very much impressed. Then there came a gentile of the lowest rank and heaped scorn upon it: "A cornstalk in a field always sways in the wind, while this one stands quite still." The same artist arose, drew a plough with the workmen following after it, and again it gained favor in the eyes of the king and nobles. But the same gentile again was critical: "A plough usually goes to the right, but he has painted it going to the left." The painter was embarrassed. So it continued in this fashion many times until, finally, he painted a maiden serving and adorning the queen in the innermost chamber. When again the critic found fault, he was given a flogging. "How can you criticize a painting of the queen's handmaidens in the innermost chambers which you, in all your days, have never seen?" So he who criticizes the saintly ones of Israel who adorn the heavenly queen, of which he knows nothing, deserves rebuke.[71]

When the *Toldot* remarks, "Our eyes see that most of the simple people love the rabbis,"[72] he testifies to what has ever been the case in Israel. But such a condition was bound to decay under the pressure of the dissension among the leaders themselves, for, "the learned ones and the rabbis mock one another, as is well known."[73] "The leaders are divided one from the other; what one permits the other forbids."[74] It was only natural then for the people to become less and less respectful toward their leaders. The reason "why *the people hold the leaders in contempt is that they contemn one another.*"[75] Indeed, even the failure of the wealthy to provide adequately for them was partly their own fault. "Because the learned mock one another, they are mocked by the unlearned, the rich, who do not support them."[76] Thus the spiritual illness which the rankling among the learned produced not only affected the truly pious, who became objects of mockery, but reached down to the people as well.

The study of the Torah should be *lishmah*, for its own sake, and not for the sake of one's pride, that is, for ulterior motives. This principle does not strictly apply to the common people, who must at all costs be encouraged to study, even if it be for ulterior motives. But those of the learned class whose motives are false must be taken to task. Such men have been excoriated in Jewish history, from the false prophets of the Bible to the false scholars of Rabbi Yaakov Yosef's time. The Talmud is harsh in its estimate of such persons,[77] and proclaims: "Woe unto those who occupy themselves with the Torah but have no fear of heaven."[78] In the Zohar the proud scholars who make a show of their learning are called "Jewish demons," while the *Sefer Hakaneh* states that "a man is called wise [*hacham*] only if his learning is for the sake of his Maker... if not, he is 'wise *to do evil*.'[79] Even though he has learned the Sifra, Sifre and all of the Talmud, he is not to be considered one of the wise [*hacham*], but merely one of the learned [*lamdan*]."[80] The verse "It is not in heaven" (Deut. 30:12) refers to the Torah and means that "the Torah is not in heaven, that is, it is not with the arrogant and lofty of spirit,"[81] with those who, though they may be learned enough, look down haughtily upon others as if they themselves were in heaven, those whose main purpose in being learned was only that they might be able to look down upon others. The real Torah is not with them.

Knowledge alone, when unbounded by humility, can easily lead to pride. Perhaps Jewish scholars, because of Judaism's great emphasis on learning and study, are particularly prone to the sin of pride, and so it is that time and again in Jewish literature we read stern admonitions against the learned proud whose dead weight threatened to crush the inner spirit of the people. Many of the rabbis and the scholars of Rabbi Yaakov Yosef's time seem to fall into this category. His cry is that, in spite of the fact that they study Torah, their pride shuts out the true light, that even their Torah is false, for they never reach the inner Torah, the deeper Torah, that which lies beneath the letters, the spirit which pervades them and for the sake of which they are to be studied. They only know the outer husks of Torah, that which appears superficially on the surface, which is not the true Torah. Thus even the scholar's claim to learning is false. For the man who hears only his own voice, and never the voice of others, shuts himself off not only from his fellow man but from the Lord as well. The word of God is lost in the din of his own words. It is difficult to feel the Lord's love when filled with self-love.

THE DRIVE FOR PERSONAL SECURITY

If the pride of the learned turned their interests inward and led to a *breakdown of the place of Torah* in the life of the scholar, so that study became a means of achieving glory and fame, and aroused the jealousy of their fellow scholars and mockery of the pious, it led, as well, to *a desire for personal security* and, therefore, obsequiousness, flattery of and submission to the ruling classes.

Rabbi Yaakov Yosef complains about "the scholars who turn their hearts to wastefulness and the gathering of money,"[82] and, commenting on the custom of giving the rabbis money during the Hanukah season, he speaks of the degeneration of the rabbinate from selflessness to selfishness.

From a wise man I heard a reason why the rabbis travel from village to village during Hanukah. In previous generations, when the rabbis served devoutly and without payment, they traveled from village to village in the same spirit. All year long they were in the city, engrossed in the study and teaching of Torah or engaged in other noble pursuits. Only during the Hanukah period, which was a holiday, could they travel from village to village to improve the spiritual conditions of the people, whether it be regarding desecration of the Sabbath or examination of the butchers or other similar matters. For all this they refused to take the smallest amount of pay from the villagers.... After a number of generations, however, reverence for God diminished and these rabbis who traveled from village to village found an excuse to accepts gifts, namely, as payment for the income they could have otherwise earned during the time they spent traveling. Still later, in a generation weak of spirit, they no longer bothered with the problems of the community and made the trip only to collect the gifts. And so, in the course of time, it became an official decree that this payment was to be taken, *even against the will of the people, and it no longer became necessary for the rabbis even to make the trip, for the Hanukah-money was sent to their very houses.*"[83]

The rabbi and the people are to be compared to a shepherd and his flock. But one should take care that "by a shepherd is meant one who truly shepherds and watches over the flock so that they are well fed and *not one who feeds himself and rules over them....*"[84] The strife between the scholars which pride engendered naturally led to competition for material advantages, "for the jealousy and hatred which is rampant between one man and another, particularly among the learned, is due to their struggle for a livelihood, each one thinking, 'The higher position I have among the people, the higher salary I shall receive.' "[85]

Our author explains Isaiah's outcry in the first chapter of his prophecies as referring to the rabbis who, concerned for their salary, flatter the rich and compete among themselves.

> Hear, O heavens, and give ear, O earth,
> For the Lord hath spoken:
> Children I have reared, and brought up,
> And they have rebelled against Me.
> The ox knoweth his owner,
> And the ass his master's crib
> But Israel doth not know (Is. 1:2, 3)....

" 'The ox knoweth his owner,' which is not true of the ass who does not discern the Master Himself," but confuses the crib with the Owner, the apparent provider with the Real Provider, the wealthy rulers with the True Ruler. " 'Israel doth not know, my people do not understand,' for if Israel (the learned ones) would know this, then there would be no occasion for one scholar to hate the other because he believes that he deprives him of a livelihood. Thus no artisan would hate his fellow artisan—nor would the innkeeper or the shopkeeper— since he would realize that his craft is but a crib, the vessel into which his livelihood flows from his Master, who is the Lord. For if this crib is broken, is his Master not able to make another crib? The crib is not the essential thing, but the Master, who is able to make any number of cribs for every one of His creatures to secure a livelihood for them. And if Israel (the rabbis) would take this to their hearts, they would neither hate one another nor would they need to curry favor with those who pay them, making of their Torah and their prayer a display to impress the people, but they would instead devote themselves to their Creator, who is their Master. But, alas, they do not act in this manner; they think that the crib is the essential thing and are suspicious lest their livelihood be jeopardized by their associates. So they are greater fools than the ass. And this is the meaning of the verse, 'Israel doth not know.' "[86]

Slavishly to coddle the rich and compete with other rabbis and scholars for positions is the result of a reversal of centers. "Trust not in princes," for the real provider is not the rich man but God;[87] therefore service must be rendered to God, not to men, not even to the rich among them. "It is proper to praise and seek favor only with the Creator, may He be blessed."[88]

The desire for personal security and material well-being led directly to an attitude of submissiveness to the rich, who controlled the rabbinical positions. "The rabbis... whose livelihood comes to them from the people of the community and its leaders, tend to flatter them and to make a display of their achievements and the splendor of their wisdom... in order to be able to benefit from them."[89] To gain favor with the wealthy, the rabbi would often "eat and drink and carouse with them like the fox who cautiously looks behind while acting as if he were the leader; but it would be better if he were a tail to the lions and not a head to the foxes."[90] In bitterness and heartache Rabbi Yaakov Yosef echoes the words of the Psalmist, "May the Lord cut off all flattering lips!"[91]

It was a custom in certain localities for the government to sell rabbinical positions to the highest bidder,[92] a malpractice which the heads of the communities and sometimes even the rabbis themselves, often fostered. "The verse 'Do not make a god of gold' (Ex. 20:23) refers to gods [rabbis] who come for the sake of gold.[93] The *Maharsha* further explains: 'They committed two evils. They were appointed for gold which they gave to the government and, furthermore, they themselves wanted to gather gold and silver.'[94] In the Palestinian Talmud it is written, 'Rabbi Mana said: Scorn those who are appointed for money. Rabbi Ammi calls them gods of gold and states that one should not call such a person rabbi, nor stand up before him. The *talit* which he wears is like the saddle of a donkey!' "[95]

Such rabbis, of course, could not be expected to denounce the sins of the ruling class nor even to fulfill their own duties to the people. They did not build their communities; they destroyed them. " 'The little foxes who destroy the vineyard' (Song 2:15) are the rabbis who purchase their positions for silver. They are nothing but weak little children, for when those who are the leaders of the generation enter into the battle of the Lord, they must be strong and courageous, so that their curse is a curse and their blessing is a blessing. But this is not the case."[96]

"The golden calf refers to the gods of gold [the rabbis] who are appointed by the government for gold. And if the rabbi does not have the means to pay, he arranges a proper marriage for himself in the city." Those who built the golden calf wanted a god who would go before them and always be available. "Nowadays the cities are full of rabbis 'who go before us' and lust after power—both the rabbis and their relatives—until, because of this, quarrels and strife break out in the city. This is the meaning of the passage: 'And Moses turned, and went down from the mount, with the two tables of testimony in his hand.... And when Joshua heard the noise of the people as they shouted, he said unto Moses: "There is a noise of war in the camp."... And it came to pass, as soon as he came nigh unto the camp, that he saw the calf and the dancing; and Moses' anger waxed hot, and he cast the tables out of his hands, and broke them beneath the mount' (Ex. 32:15-19). Finally, the Lord, in his mercy, again sent Moses, and he ground up the golden calf into dust in order to show that it possessed no value, even though it had gone before them. And they again accepted him [Moses] as their rabbi."[97]

The rabbis who bought their offices are like the golden calf. They are false idols of gold who cause dissension and strife in the city through their struggle for power and wealth. But Moses, who is the symbol of the true leader, the zaddik, will show the people how vain and empty this little god is. Even though he seems to do their bidding, acceding to their wishes, walking before them (yet in reality following after them) he seeks only self-glory. Therefore he must be utterly destroyed, and the true leader, the zaddik, must be accepted as rabbi.

The moral corruption which existed was due partly to the lack of courage to withstand the widespread malpractices. Though the stench of corruption was everywhere, the rabbis, weak in spirit and afraid to protest, often ignored the problems and accepted the standard of the time. They said in effect: "It is not within our power to establish the laws of our religion, so we have taken on the character of the foxes who act as if they smell no stench."[98] They saw that the "scholars were considered unimportant... and so became unimportant in their own eyes as well. Since apparently the ways of the wicked prospered, they chose their ways too... eating and drinking and carousing with them. They acted like the little foxes who walk in front but whose habit it is to constantly look to those behind them; thus they try to give the appearance of being leaders and men of importance...."[99]

Having lost the sense of their true task and become devoted to the furtherance of their own welfare, they permitted the ruling class to act as it pleased, as long as their own positions were secure. They were blind to all that went on about them. " 'The eyes of Israel were heavy with age, and he was no longer able to see' (Gen. 48:10). This verse means that the leaders of the generation, who are called 'the eyes of Israel,' upon whom rests the duty of carefully watching over the communal activities, are asleep. Everyone does what is right in his own eyes, for they do not concern themselves with the rulers of the city, to lead them on the straight path."[100] They did not see, "because of their desire for the pleasures of this world, which is called the land of Egypt. Darkness covers this land so that no man sees his brother, and everyone does what is right in his own eyes. In this manner we are to understand the words from Scripture: 'And there was a thick darkness in all the land of Egypt three days; they did not see one another.' "[101]

The rabbis should have reproached these men with strong words, preaching confession and repentance, but they failed to do so. "It is necessary for the scholar to bribe the authorities in order to be appointed head of the court. Therefore he does not preach against them, lest they take a dislike to him and withhold his salary."[102] To win the favor of the rich, to flatter them and be submissive to them was the task which some of the rabbis set for themselves. "Because the learned chase after the rich, the rich find a reason to despise learning.... Because the learned run after the rich, they profane the name of heaven."[103] "The Talmud remarks regarding... those rabbis upon whom the city elders look favorably, that it is not because of their good qualities that this is so, but rather because they do not reprove them with words of Torah. This is why Noah was able to live at ease [*nah*] with those in heaven and at ease with those on earth... for he should have reproved his generation, but instead Scripture says that 'Noah walked with God,' that is, he did not reprove the people of his generation but fled from them and secluded himself with God."[104]

Governed by their own self-interest and desire for material security, many of the rabbis were hesitant to take any action which might threaten the benefits they possessed. They submitted to the wishes of the wealthy. At times conditions came to such a pass as to defy recording lest this stand as an everlasting shame in the annals of Israel. So Rabbi Yaakov Yosef testifies from personal experience: "With my own eyes I have observed the ways of rabbis and leaders in communal affairs *which one cannot permit to be written down!*"[105]

For the common people to worry about material needs over and above spiritual ones does not occasion surprise. They were busy from early morning to late evening with the endless task of earning a living and had time for little else. But for those whose task it was to spiritualize the material, to raise the people to a higher level of living, and whose days were given over to the study of Torah so that they could draw strength from this well of salvation to withstand temptation and to lead others from it, for these men to don the garment of the scholar, to pore over thick books and wear a long *talit*, and then lead a life of acquisition and greed—this was foul indeed. Rabbi Yaakov Yosef's rage mounts higher and higher in his denunciation of the objects of his wrath.

"A scholar who engages in such spiritual matters as Torah and prayer, but whose mind is occupied with material concerns, deserves not the title of *hacham* [a wise man] but *am ha'aretz* [a man of the earth, an ignoramus], since his mind is on earthly matters."[106] But to remove his title and call him an ignoramus is not a sufficiently strong disapprobation. There is everything false in the character of the man who does one thing and means another. Using the parable of Jacob's ladder, he is contrasted to the true leader, Moses. " 'He dreamed and beheld a ladder fixed in the earth whose head reached the heavens, and angels of the Lord were going up and down it' (Gen. 28:12). There are those who, like our teacher Moses (peace be to him), go up the ladder, for even though he was fixed in the earth so far as his work in the world was concerned, his head, that is, his thoughts, reached into the heavens to cleave to the Lord.... And there are those who go down the ladder, for even though they are engaged in Torah and prayer—heavenly matters— nevertheless, at that very moment, they are 'fixed in the earth,' that is, their thoughts are bound up with earthly things... that their Torah and prayer should be a source of wealth and honor to them.... *They are liars even in their Torah and prayer.*"[107]

Even worse, subservience to the rich amounts to a kind of *idolatry*. The command "Thou shalt not bow down before a foreign god" (Ps. 81:10) becomes a "warning to the scholars, that they should not bend before the rich for the sake of their livelihood...."[108] Conditions of the time justified this warning because "for the sake of food and drink and salary they bow down and prostrate themselves before the wealthy of the generation that they might be the means of their welfare (as if God Himself is not able to care for the livelihood of each one). Such a one is called an idolater."[109] The harshest accusation, however, is yet to be made. Rabbi Yaakov Yosef denounces this type of rabbi and scholar not only as an ignoramus, a liar and an idolater, but says he is meaner still; for to pray to God and study Torah and, at the same time, to think of money is, in reality, a form of *adultery*. "Just as the unfaithful wife who, in the very moment when she lies with her husband, thinks of the lewdness of her adulteries, so it is with the learned who, *while they study the Torah, commit adultery with the wealthy members of the community*."[110]

THE CONCERN FOR SPIRITUAL SECURITY

Pride led to a *breakdown of the place of Torah* in the life of the scholar, and therefore to jealousy of his fellow scholars; and to the desire for *personal security* and therefore submissiveness to the rich. It likewise led to the desire for *spiritual security* and therefore seclusion from and contempt for the masses of the people.

Spiritual security is a noble goal to pursue when it encompasses more than one's own soul and leads to compassion for other men as well But when it is the result of excessive self-concern, with the seeking of self-perfection without regard for others, it can easily become a path of selfishness. To put it another way, the yearning for personal salvation is good so far as it goes; the trouble is, it often does not go far enough: it does not include others. This exclusion of others, furthermore, can impair the prior motive in seeking self-perfection itself, so that it may turn out to be not so noble an undertaking after all, but simply the stirrings of pride.

This was the deplorable situation, according to Rabbi Yaakov Yosef, with many of his learned contemporaries. They were concerned for their own spiritual security, with adding to their own knowledge, with taking meticulous care in their own personal ritual observance, with spending hours over their books in study to make them even more learned, and with the scrupulous observance of the commandments to guarantee the propriety of their own life in this world and the world to come. Yet all this had little to do with the people. They had neither learning nor piety. There could be no common meeting point for folk and rabbi.[111] The latter's respect was limited to those like himself who were learned. As the aristocracy of a nation often looks down upon the masses, he looked down upon those whose leisure for study may have been consumed by the bitter struggle to earn their daily bread,[112] who, plagued with a thousand worries, could find little time for study and were ignorant of the details of the ritual code. The rabbi and the people were at opposite "extremities." "There is no brotherhood between them, for they [the rabbis, the learned] hate them [the people] and lead them astray."[113] They felt little obligation to the people and often did not have the desire to teach them. "No one explains to the people the laws regarding what is forbidden and what is permitted."[114] It was a sort of emergency religion. If a Jew had a ritual question to ask or a legal matter to inquire into—to whom a certain piece of property belonged or whether an animal was *kasher* or not—he would go to the rabbi for a decision. But to suppose that the rabbi would seek to look after the needs of the people was another matter. He was like the shepherd who "does not notice if one of the flock dies or is injured, because he does not look after them."[115] This attitude towards the people may be described as one of *contempt*.

CONTEMPT FOR AND SECLUSION FROM THE PEOPLE

Contempt for the people made it easy to despise them and to look down upon them. It led to the people's fear of the learned and to their need to appease the latter. They suffered under the rule of the learned and yearned for deliverance from them. So the prayer of Jacob that he be delivered from Esau becomes

the prayer of the people to be delivered from the learned:
" 'Save me from the hand of my brother,' for the learned one
is Esau—he who is learned to do evil...."[116] "Save me from
my brother who is always filled with hatred like Esau, for
between friends and lovers there is anger, and this wrath, like
Esau's, is a constant one. 'For I fear him lest he come and
smite me, the mother [the learned] against the children [the
common people].' "[117] "It is a scandal that the communal
leaders indulge in one of the injustices which must stand in the
way of Redemption, namely, acting arrogantly toward the
community... for all their greatness and wisdom derives not
from themselves, but from the people...."[118]

Contempt for the people gave many of the scholars all the
justification they needed for the custom of seclusion. Since they
considered the people to be beneath their spiritual dignity,
and, in addition, that contact with them might lead them into
sin and temptation, they remained within the four walls of
their own studies, immersed in Torah, safe in lofty seclusion.

THE SYMBOL OF NOAH

The symbol of the contemptuous and secluded leader, who is
held up as an object of scorn by Yaakov Yosef, is Noah.
Scripture tells us that "in his generation Noah was a righteous
man," that "he walked with God" (Gen. 6:9), and that
he was spared when all others were destroyed by the flood.
Wherein then does his sin lie, how can he be criticized? When
compared to Abraham, however, Noah is found wanting.[119]
While it is true that he was a righteous man in his generation,
he would have accounted for little in the generation of
Abraham, and his walking "*with* God" is really the sign of his
egotism, of his concern for his own salvation, of his contempt
for and seclusion from the people. " 'Noah walked *with* God,'

that is, he was always in the house of prayer or the house of study, though he should have gone out to the people and brought them to repentance." Abraham's way was different. Scripture tells us that he walked "*before* God" (Gen. 17:1), that is, he went out to the people, trying to save them as well as himself. "For there is a difference between the righteous man who secludes himself before the Lord and is not able to save his generation, only himself, and the righteous man who goes into the midst of the city, returns them to the good way and saves his generation as well.... Why did the first righteous man [Noah] not save his generation? Because he secluded himself with the Lord and was not in the midst of the city."[120]

Noah was like some of the rabbis of the time who observed the letter of the Law, studied, prayed and fasted regularly, fastidiously carrying out all the ritual details. He fulfilled the commandments, it is true, but it was an outward fulfillment, a selfish fulfillment. He "walked *with* God," in seclusion. He kept to his study and synagogue, concerned with his own spiritual welfare, but did not possess the courage or the concern to venture out to help others. "He did not reprove the people but drew far from them....[121]" He did not feel the inner yearning to rescue his fellow man less fortunate than he, to leave the seclusion of his study and step into the darkness of the world, bringing a light that might illumine another's way; did not understand that he was but a vessel which was to carry the word of the Lord to the people; and that God had given him all his learning only for their sake.[122]

A man such as Noah, who was supremely confident that he walked side by side with the Lord, and who in his arrogance and lack of concern held the people in contempt and took refuge in his own spiritual seclusion in order to guarantee his own salvation, could not long go unpunished. God would not long tolerate this kind of leader for His people.

It is a mistake, therefore, to think, as is commonly the case, that Noah saved the world at the time of the flood. Noah is not to be praised for surviving the flood. His stature is less than that of Abraham. Not only did he neglect the people of his time, but he was actually the one most to blame for the catastrophe and in a sense the worst offender of his day. " 'There were ten generations from Adam to Noah to indicate to you how forgiving God was,'[123] for all the ten generations caused Him anger but they were not punished until the generation of Noah. God would still have forgiven them, but Noah stirred up wrath. *He brought the flood upon them.*"[124]

The ark, furthermore, was not a haven of safety for a righteous man, but a prison house of punishment for a guilty one. God made Noah suffer in the ark to atone for his great sins, each in its own measure. God said to him: "You did not go out to save your people, to purify them and teach them how to serve their Creator but only locked yourself in your house (which Abraham did not do); therefore, you shall be locked up in the ark, where you will suffer. You were not a shepherd to your people, sometimes going without sleep in an effort to reach them, to help them and raise them; therefore you shall now be a shepherd to the animals, and, in the work of caring for them, sleep shall vanish from your eyes...."[125]

The pride of many of the rabbis prevented them from seeing the plight of the others; it spun a web of self-concern which turned their eyes inward so that they saw only their own needs, their own desires, their own hurt, their own situation, and were blinded to the need, desire and hurt of the people. The self-centered rabbi was aloof, removed from day-to-day concerns; he "was unaware of the people to care for them."[126] Pride not only blinded him to all but himself, but filled him with contempt for the people and, therefore, justified, in his own mind, his seclusion from them. For this situation there should be weeping and wailing, fasting and contrition, a new *Tisha b'Av* for a new destruction. So is the first verse of the

Book of Lamentations to be understood. " 'How does the city dwell alone' (Lam. 1:1); that is, the people of the city who remain alone, apart from the leaders who are there."[127]

Can a leader achieve salvation for himself when he gives no thought to the salvation of the people? One who is concerned for his own spiritual security and not that of the people he serves, secures neither the spiritual welfare of the people nor his own, for they are bound together into one bond. Contempt for others renders his own life impure. " 'The eyes of Israel were dim from age so that he could not see' (Gen. 48:10). This verse refers to the leaders, who are the eyes of the community, and are obliged to see and be concerned with the community. Not only are they unconcerned with others, but they do not even take care with themselves, to see that they themselves should walk uprightly. That is why it is written, 'The eyes of Israel were dim from age [habit]'; therefore, as a result, 'he could not see' even himself... for he had fallen into the habit of forbearance."[128]

Leaders who hold the people in contempt and stand in lofty seclusion from them, oblivious of their sufferings and needs, are the embodiment of the *yetzer hara*, the evil desire. At the time of creation, when the *yetzer hara* saw God breathe the soul, which is the zaddik (the righteous leader) into the body, which is the people of Israel, he raised a hue and cry that pierced the heavenly chambers: "Why have you created me in vain?" He complained that, since the true leader, the zaddik, had been created, "he would surely lead the people to goodness, just as the soul gives life to the body, and therefore, he, the *yetzer hara*, would no longer have a task to perform. *Therefore, in opposition to the zaddik, there were created the destructive leaders, 'the Jewish demons,' who try and tempt the people.*"[129]

Perud

From the contempt—even hatred—which the learned felt for

the people and their consequent seclusion from them, there followed a rending asunder of what the generations had striven for—unity of leader and people. As form is to matter or soul to body, so the leader stands in relation to the people, comprising a *komah shelemah*, a perfect whole. The rupturing of this unity is called *perud*, and it is this condition of *perud* which carries within it the portents of disaster.

The power of man is great and what is wrought in heaven is wrought first on earth. If man depends on God, God also depends on man; if earth needs heaven, heaven needs earth as well. It is the destiny of Israel to unify the great and holy name of God. But it is by first unifying that which is split in the earthly realm that heaven itself is unified. This holy work of unification, however, is halted through *perud*. *Perud* interrupts and restrains the forces striving to join the divisive elements within man, to join man and his fellowman, man and God, and even God Himself. In the beginning a divine harmony reigned within the universe, but this harmony has been disrupted and the original unity broken, the very vessels of creation have been shattered so that disharmony and separation now run rampant through the worlds, human and divine. Thus God's oneness will be a true oneness only in the future: "On that day the Lord *will* be one and His name one" (Zech. 14:9). Likewise, the people are not yet one, but stand broken, split. The true exile is, thus, the exile of the soul from the body, the leader from the people, God from the world. To infuse spirit into the body, to bring leader and people together, so that they are indeed one, is redemption. For then the Lord will be One, reunited with His *Shechinah*. Israel's task, therefore, is to bring together what had been broken, to unite what had been separated, to join together what had been rendered asunder—to restore the original harmony. The fate of God thus hangs upon the fate of man.

The goal was sublime, but the vision was wanting. Many of

the leaders had become "Jewish demons," conquered by a pride which acted in three major areas. First, it *perverted their Torah* into a device for acquiring fame and fanned the flames of jealousy for other scholars; second, it caused them to look after their own needs and seek *personal security*, thus submitting to current malpractices and to the ruling element whom they flattered and dared not reprove; and, third, it led them to seek *spiritual security*, which meant concern for their own salvation, but not the salvation of the people, whom they scorned, held in contempt and ignored. All this brought about the condition of *perud*, radical separation between the learned class and the people and, therefore, *perud* within God Himself. Rabbi Yaakov Yosef understood this to be the greatest tragedy of his age.

A note of despair is sometimes sounded in Rabbi Yaakov Yosef's analysis which leaves little hope for an improvement in conditions. The gap between leaders and followers seemed so wide as to promise a bleak future for which only some outside force could bring help. "In the Midrash to Kohelet[131] there is a story about a man who once told a shoemaker: 'Sew up this broken mortar.' The shoemaker mockingly showed him a handful of sand and said: 'Make a thread out of this sand for me, and I shall sew up the mortar for you.' It was to anger the shoemaker that the man showed him the broken mortar, for surely there was no hope of its repair. Through this he hinted to him that *the children of Israel had been shattered as a potter's bowl is shattered*. And by the shoemaker's reply, regarding the sand, he hinted that if Israel were united like the threads of a cord, then God would bind up their fracture." There is doubt whether the shoemaker's hope of a united Israel could in reality ever be achieved. "Indeed, just as it is not possible in the order of nature to unite grains of sand into a thread, so is it not possible, in the order of nature, to unite one Jew and another because of the abyss which exists between them—

unless the Lord sends Elijah the prophet. Then 'he will return the heart of the fathers to the sons and the heart of the sons to the fathers.' "[132]

Matters had gone too far to expect any of the "natural" remedies to heal the breach. Patchwork formulas would no longer suffice. It was a radical solution that was called for.

II

THE SOLUTION

CHAPTER 5

The Zaddik

The primary cause of the inner decline and the religious formalism that accompanied it, which ignored the kernel while leaving the shell intact and brought greed and corruption in its wake, was corrupted spiritual leadership. The solution to the problem, the way to kindle the spark that would infuse a new spirit into the body of the people, likewise lay in the hands of the spiritual leaders.

RENEWAL OF THE INDIVIDUAL AND THE COMMUNITY

In asserting the above, Rabbi Yaakov Yosef does not mean to imply that once a bad leader is replaced by a good one, all problems and difficulties will immediately and automatically disappear. He expresses great concern for the task which each individual Jew has: to conquer the evil desire within, to rid himself of hatred, and allow the love and fear of God to rule over him. He appeals to those of the learned class to liberate themselves from the curse of pride and become reconciled in love to the people.[1] He implores the lower religious functionaries, the teacher, the cantor and the butcher, not to defile their callings by sacrificing principles for the sake of salary, but to become rededicated to the true goals of their callings:[2] the teacher to impart the beginnings of Torah to the children, the cantor to be the true messenger of the community in prayer, and the butcher to provide holy food for a holy people. Even more insistent is he that the wealthy class be charitable, and support those men whose lives are devoted to Torah and those institutions which despense Torah to the people.[3] In this sense, the rich man too can be a kind of zaddik, not by giving of his spirit, but by giving of his possessions. "If one man gives to another he is called a zaddik. There are two kinds of zaddikim, one in regard to Torah, one in regard to charity."[4]

Rabbi Yaakov Yosef also expressed concern for problems of the community as a whole. Because of the "breakdown" of communal religious life, he fostered a policy of segregation by which, it was believed, renewal and rehabilitation could be achieved. It was this policy of segregation which contributed greatly toward the formation of what soon developed into the separate hasidic community.[5]

One "breakdown" was that of *kashrut*. "In the matter of food our generation is not pure, for everyone and anyone has adopted the title of *shochet*, even those who are noted neither for their knowledge of the laws of *shechitah* nor for their fear of heaven. This is contrary to our holy rabbis, who have warned us in the early and later codes that the *shochet* should be a fearer of heaven, particularly regarding the examination of knives, which depends upon the reverence of his heart." Ignorance of the dietary laws was common among the people themselves. "Many are not expert in the laws of salting and soaking meat, from which numerous regulations are derived.... There used to be many preachers who would go about explaining to each woman the laws of salting, but that is not now the case. Surely he who wishes to be holy should not sit at the table of such people [who are ignorant of the laws of *kashrut*]. He who separates himself from the food of the 'world' shall be called holy."[6]

Another "repair" which our author saw as necessary and which demanded separation, concerned a "breakdown" even more serious and all-pervading. This corruption expressed itself in the bad habits which were current in the synagogue: the hurried, mechanical way in which prayers were said, the lack of *kavannah*, the pride of the *hazzan*, the desire for honor on the part of the rich, the ambition of the rabbis and the lack of respect on the part of the people. Only the action of a small group of faithful ones, creating their own circle of worshipers, could avail. "Moses gathered together all the people of Israel... saying: 'Take from among you an offering for the Lord.' " The newly created hasidic community was to be such an "offering" as a group of spiritually elite, for this verse "implies for the future that a *bet hamidrash* should be created for the select of Israel who are to be set apart from the common people, for it is impossible that there should be a united community."[7] *"He who wants to be holy should set himself apart to pray in a* minyan *of his own, since it is not possible to pray with a congregation which performs the mitzvot by rote."*[8] And this is "just as it was in the Sanctuary: a chamber for the priests and a chamber for the people."

With a boldness that knew no fear, Yaakov Yosef concludes his analysis of the community, in which he depicts the corruption which was rampant and the low state to which Torah and prayer had fallen, with one of the few purely personal utterances to be found in his works. *"The above events, from beginning to end, occurred to me, the writer, and indicate why I ordered the establishment of a* bet hamidrash *in Sharogrod!"*[9] This act, which may well have been the establishment of the first hasidic house of prayer and study, was of the highest importance in the history of Judaism, paving the way for the founding of separate synagogues for hasidim, a fundamental step in the creation of the hasidic movement.[10]

The commonly accepted view, therefore, that the message of Hasidism was directed to the masses must be severely qualified. In its origins at least, it was, in some respects, the opposite: a movement of the few, not the many; of the learned, not the ignorant; of the pious, not the common people. Nevertheless, such a policy of separation was not construed as an ideal for the community, but rather as an emergency measure. "It is a repair for that which first broke down."[11]

THE ZADDIK AS THE ANSWER TO THE CRISIS OF THE TIME

Above and beyond or, rather, within and beneath the individual and the community, as the inspiration for the one, the initiator for the other and the guarantor of both, was the spiritual leader, the rabbi. The disease which infected the religious life of the people had reached all levels of society. No area remained immune. The people had fallen away from Torah and respect for the rabbis, the rich ruled with an iron fist, the cantors sang but did not pray, the teachers were not sincere, the butchers unreliable, the rabbis arrogant and full of contempt for the masses. How to attack such a widespread illness was the problem. It was impossible to begin with every area of life at once. There was neither the time nor the strength; what little energy was available would have been frittered away. Rabbi Yaakov Yosef believed he knew how to find the answer to the problem. He believed that if one reaches to the cornerstone and begins to rebuild there, then, eventually, all else may fall into place.

The cornerstone was the rabbi.

The realization was needed that Israel, which was to be a kingdom of priests and a holy nation, had retained only the garments of its former glory. Out of a power derived from such a conviction and from fearlessness, the false leader of the time could be exposed for what he was and a new leader fashioned, one whose humility would permit the word of God to penetrate his mind and heart, giving him unshakable faith and the willingness to sacrifice, one who was strong in belief and compassion at once and could perform the double miracle of going out to the people while at the same time remaining bound up with God. Through such a man all else would be effected. Around the zaddik a new community of souls could gather; both synagogue and school could be transformed; teacher and cantor rededicated; rich and poor brought to repentance. "The zaddik is called the cornerstone upon which the world is built."[12] He is the "foundation of the world,"[13] and it is on this foundation that all else either stands or falls. Therefore, all energy, infinite care and devotion should be concentrated on fashioning the new "cornerstone," the new "foundation," the zaddik, upon and around whom the world of late eighteenth-century East-European Jewry was to be rebuilt into a mighty tower of the faithful.

THE CALL FOR THE ZADDIK

Great was the need for the new leader—"The zaddik is the foundation of the world." Great was the pain at his absence— "We have no one on whom to rely now."[14] Great was the cry, therefore, for his appearance:

One who loves Him Who is blessed above all else will not be afraid to offer up his life, for he feels anguish over the anguish and exile of the *Shechinah* which wanders homeless because of our sins. *We have no one to lead us, no one of strength. And yet, the fate of the Shechinah depends upon us*—for we can bring out those who are locked in the dungeons of the spirit and bring forth from the prison house those who are imprisoned. Therefore, in the place where there are no men, be thou a man, turning many from sin and doing what is pleasing to the wandering feet of the dove, until the spirit from above is aroused for us.[15]

Let all of us who are here today go out into this battle: to awaken ourselves from the heavy sleep, to rouse our pure hearts over our fate, *over the absence of zaddikim* and the exile of the *Shechinah*, to join in the anguish of the weakened and confused ones, to cry out bitterly and in distress as one who gives birth. The sound of our shout rises with the sound of the *shofar* to awaken the Upper Man from his sleep so that he may draw down mercy and compassion from the watchful Eye which never sleeps."[16]

Two things the man of spirit must realize: the crisis which prevails, and the power which is his. One who is aware of the power of man "is considered wise, for it is wonderful wisdom regarding the service of the Creator that he be not despised in his own eyes, but should rather say, 'When will my deeds reach the deeds of the first fathers?' Especially is this true in our time, when the *Shechinah* is in exile, for the 'dove finds no resting place for the sole of her foot.' For as soon as a man performs his deeds for the sake of heaven, he becomes the throne for the *Shechinah*, which will rest upon him. And he will be considered greater than the earlier generations when there were many zaddikim in the world, which is not the case in our times, for *the pious man and his Creator have disappeared.* Surely, then, one must gird up his loins like a man to deal mercifully with the *Shechinah*, and thereby become a throne for the quality of mercy. Just as in the generation of Abraham there was no helpmate for the *Shechinah* except through Abraham, so now no one sets his heart upon being a helpmate and stay for the *Shechinah*, who dwells in this bitter exile, save for a scant number who offer up their souls and truly become a throne for the *Shechinah*.... May the Name Who is blessed help us to serve Him in truth and innocence, that this message proceed out of our deeds, well spoken and well fulfilled."[17]

Such was the fervent cry for the zaddik.[18]

The zaddik was not a completely new institution in Judaism, a creation out of nothing, so to speak. The search for the right kind of leader had gone on throughout Jewish history, bringing about at different periods radical changes in the type of leadership which existed and, at times, creating new types of leaders. So it had always been from the priests, judges, kings, prophets and scribes of the Bible to the rabbis of the Talmud. There were wicked kings, corrupt priests, false prophets and arrogant rabbis, while the good, uncorrupted, true, humble leaders were always needed and sought. The needs of the times did not remain static, nor did the level of leadership remain stationary. Changes took place which had to be dealt with by changes within the leadership. But never since the days of the Talmud, or perhaps since the time of the prophets, was such a serious, deliberate effort made to analyze the defects of the contemporary leadership, to enunciate what type of leader was desired, and to attempt to produce such leaders. Hasidism achieved a revolution in Jewish life, because it succeeded in creating an exalted blueprint of the kind of leadership it wanted. It placed great emphasis on the development of the devoted, selfless leader, certain that once this was achieved all else would go easier. By beginning at the head, the whole body of Israel was to be affected. The verse, *"Ki tissa' et rosh benei Yisrael"* (Ex. 30:12), is interpreted to mean that one must raise up from the dust the head, the leader of the people of Israel. Only then will the body be raised.[19] "Everything depends on the head of the people."[20] "There is no hope for the people without the learned ones."[21]

It is as if the people of Israel were once more standing at Sinai in the most decisive moment of their history, unable to decide whether to receive the Torah or not, until the Lord lifted the mountain over their heads and forced them to accept. Only now it is not the Torah but the zaddik whom He wants them to take, and their decision is to be just as decisive as when they were offered the Torah itself. Again they are a wandering nation, harassed and distraught; again they find themselves in a wilderness where temptation and danger lurk on every side;

again there seems to be no guide, no way for them. The Torah has become a deadletter, the mitzvot are performed perfunctorily, while the ravages of arrogance and hatred threaten to destroy the community. Again they are in need of a Torah. But this time the written Torah will not suffice; it must be a Torah come alive, the living Torah, the zaddik. They must make a committment as grave and as binding as the one their ancestors made generations ago at Mount Sinai and which guaranteed the destiny of Israel throughout the centuries. The mountain is once more lifted over their heads, and God says, "If you accept my Torah, that is, my learned ones [the zaddikim], it will be well for you; but if not, then this will be your burial ground."[22] Whether the people were to live or die depended on the zaddik.

The creation of the new leader—the perfected man who serves God in the midst of the world—as the main solution to the crisis of the time was undertaken with such a solemn as well as a passionate earnestness that momentous results were inevitable.

What is particularly remarkable about Hasidism, writes Gershom Scholem, is "that within a geographically small area and also within a surprisingly short period, the ghetto gave birth to a whole galaxy of saint-mystics, each of them a startling individuality. The incredible intensity of creative religious feeling which manifested itself in Hasidism between 1750 and 1800 produced a wealth of truly original religious types which, as far as one can judge, surpassed even the harvest of the classical period of Safed. Something like a rebellion of religious energy against petrified religious values must have taken place."

Buber goes beyond even Scholem in his estimate. It is well to quote him at length.

The appearance of Hasidism within the history of faith of Judaism and its importance for the general history of religion cannot be understood on the basis of its teaching as such.... The decisive factor for the nature and greatness of Hasidism is not found in a teaching, but in a mode of life; and, indeed, in a mode of life which shapes a community, and regulates a community in accordance with its own character.... The Baal Shem himself belongs to those central figures in the history of religion who have done their work by living in a certain way, that is to say, not starting out from a teaching but aiming toward a teaching, who lived in such a way that their life acted as a teaching, as a teaching not translated into words. The life of such people stands in need of a theological commentary.... Two different things must be added to this.

Firstly, the nature of this life is given by a wholly personal mode of faith, and nevertheless this faith acts in such a way as to form a community. Let it be noted: it does not form a fraternity, it does not form a separate order which guards an esoteric teaching apart from public life; it forms a community, a community of people. These people continue living their life within their family rank, and public activity, some of them being bound more closely, others more loosely, to the master. But all these people imprint on their own, free, public life the system of life which they have received by association with the master. The determining factor is that the master does not live alone by himself, or lead a secluded life with a group of disciples, but that he lives in the world and with the world. It is just this living in the world and with the world which belongs to the innermost core of his mode of faith.

Secondly, there arises a circle of people within the community, who lead the same kind of life independently of the master, but who, through him, have received the decisive stimulation, the decisive molding, people in different stages, of very different natures, but all endowed with just the one, common, basic trend to carry the the teachings on by their lives, until everything they say is but a marginal gloss on it. Each life is a life in itself, for its part forming the community; and it is a life in the world and with the world, and a life which again gives birth to people of the same kind.

The flowering period of the hasidic movement... lasted five generations from the Baal Shem.... The zaddikim of these five generations offer us a number of religious personalities of a vitality, a spiritual strength, a manifold originality as have *never, to my know-*

ledge, appeared together in so short a time-span in the history of religion. But the most important thing about these zaddikim is that each of them was surrounded by a community that lived a brotherly life, and who could live in this way because there was a leading person in their midst who brought each one nearer to the other by bringing them all nearer to that in which they believed. In a century which was, apart from this, not very productive religiously, obscure Polish and Ukrainian Jewry produced the greatest phenomenom we know in the history of the spirit... a society which lives by its faith.

MAN AS A SOURCE OF HOLINESS

Belief in the holiness of man, or in man as the source of holiness, is, perhaps, the underlying assumption which made the doctrine of the zaddik possible.[23] God created the heavens and the earth, the stars, the mountains and the animals, but He breathed His spirit into man alone. The righteous man was the object of all creation and he occupies a superior place in the world of creation—superior even to the Temple or the Torah. Indeed, the Temple was destroyed and the tablets were shattered because of what man did. Man stands above both and is the object of both. The tabernacle was a holy place which the people built lovingly for God to dwell in, but "this is the purpose of the tabernacle: that 'I shall dwell amidst *them*,' that is amidst the leaders, who are the temple of the Lord, and not amidst the wood and the stones of the Tabernacle.... Do not think that building the tabernacle or the synagogue is [God's] purpose, but God's purpose is to create the scholar.... One must not confuse the means with the ends... for the common custom is to build a synagogue and to make light of the scholar's honor, while, in truth, it should be the reverse, for 'I shall dwell amidst *them*' (Ex. 25:8), amidst the scholars who are worthy...."[24] It is in the soul of the great man that God dwells; he is the true tabernacle of the Lord.

As it is with the House of God, so it is with the Book of God. The Torah is something more than a collection of words and sentences. Its existence depends upon those who read it and make its words a part of their lives, so that, in a sense, those for whose sake the Torah was given *become* Torah, a living Torah. The very word "Torah" means "teaching," which implies there are those who are being taught. Torah, then, is an intermediary, incomplete in itself, finding its completion in the man who, studying, learning, and loving it, becomes himself a kind of living Torah. "Why do people stand up before the Torah but not before him who is filled with the Torah?" the Talmud asks. The book is composed of words on a page. He who teaches the words and lives the words, who teaches the words by the way he lives the words, makes the book come alive. It is easy to ask, as a later writer does, "Why should I travel to the zaddik and seek Torah from his lips; are there not many holy books of ethics and sermons on every aspect of Torah and piety?"[25] But spiritual illness requires more than the reading of a book. It requires the application of the principles of the book through human means, through the living reality. Man, therefore, is not only the goal of Torah but man himself can also become its very source.[26]

The spirit of God is contained more in the spirit of the great man than in any building or any book. What is holy is the word of compassion at the right moment, the act of kindness when needed. What is holy is the life of the righteous man. The well of holiness exists in man; it has but to be uncovered for its waters to overflow the ground and give nourishment to all who come near. The great Jews of all ages were such a well.

So was the zaddik in his age.

THE ZADDIK STANDS BETWEEN HEAVEN AND EARTH

In kabbalistic thought, the holy man has a task to perform in relation to the upper spheres and apart from the people. He is the leader of the people, but his destiny is not primarily with them. His primary concern is heaven. He is cast in a cosmological role, moving among the forces of creation, endeavoring to influence the upper spheres, to hasten the coming of the messiah.

The zaddik, in contradistinction, must always be understood in relation to the people. He has no completely independent part to play. He stands between heaven and earth, "between God and the people,"[27] "just as Moses was the intermediary between Israel and the Holy One, blessed be He."[28] Indeed, through the zaddik, the austere loftiness of heaven and the abject lowliness of earth, the transcendence of God and the humanity of man meet. What seems set apart and unalterably opposed find in him a mediating principle which brings them together. "It is only possible to join together two opposites through a third force."[29] "The zaddik is the foundation of the universe, which is peace, for he joins together two opposites as when one makes peace between a man and his neighbor."[30] Flesh and spirit within man, man and his neighbor between men, and man and God beyond man—with all these the zaddik struggles, striving to join them together; between all these the zaddik makes peace.

The zaddik stands between heaven and earth. His relationship is twofold. On the one hand, he is the means by which heaven reaches the people. On the other hand, he is the means by which the people reach heaven. He brings heaven to earth and raises earth to heaven.

What is the manner in which the zaddik achieves this double aim?

God did not forsake the world after having created it. His love
for His creation manifests itself in His constant effort to reach
down to it. At Sinai His voice broke through the curtain which
man had painstakingly erected. Never again was it heard so
clearly and so decisively, but the effort on His part to speak to
His creatures never ceases. Saintly souls of all ages have caught
echoes of the beyond: "A voice goes out from Mount Horeb
every day...."[31] This outpouring from heaven to man is called,
in kabbalistic terminology, *shefa*, and may be likened to the rays
which emanate from the sun, ceaselessly reaching out to
brighten the darkness of the world. To receive the spiritual
outpouring which endlessly and lovingly flows from heaven
and to transmit it to his people is the task of the zaddik. In this
sense the zaddik is spoken of as a "channel."

"I heard from my teacher (may his memory live on in the
future world) an explanation of the following passage. 'A
heavenly voice declared: "All the world is sustained for the
sake of (*bishveel*) Hanina, my son, and Hanina, my son, is
sustained by the fruit of the carob tree from the eve of one
Sabbath to the eve of the next Sabbath." '[32] The word *bishveel*
implies that he made a channel (*sheveel*)* to bring to all the
world the heavenly outpouring, and therefore it says, all the
world is sustained through the channel of Hanina, my son."[33]
These are the words of his teacher, the Baal Shem Tov. Rabbi
Yaakov Yosef, however, adds a striking remark of his own
which lends deeper meaning to the idea. "But it seems to me
that, not only did Hanina *make* a channel, but that *he himself
became the channel* through which the outpouring passes."[34] The
zaddik makes the channel by means of his fitness for the task,

*The Hebrew word *bishveel*, "for the sake of," can mean "through the
sheveel," "through the channel of."

and that channel which he makes is his own self. "The zaddik is called the heart of the body, for he is a channel which draws the bounty of life from the Life of all Life to all the other limbs, which are the people of his generation."[35]

"A vessel is placed under the Sabbath light to receive the sparks."[36] This law of the Mishnah refers to the "zaddik, who is called the vessel of the *Shechinah*, which is light, for the Torah is called light; that is, the study of Torah and performance of the mitzvot is light. The zaddikim are the throne for the *Shechinah*, as it says of Abraham, 'And the Lord *went up* from Abraham' (Gen. 22:17). The zaddikim are the channels through which the sparks of the *Shechinah* pass that they might scatter to all the world."[37]

The Torah commands, "Thou shalt be holy." But how is it possible that all of Israel should reach the category of holiness, which is an exalted rung? It is as the Talmud remarks, " 'Everything is in the hands of heaven except the fear of heaven, as it is written, "Now, O Israel, what does the Lord your God require of you but to fear the Lord your God?" (Deut. 12:10) But is the fear of heaven such a small matter?... Yes, for one like Moses it was indeed a small matter.'[38] [At this point] the *Maharsha* [a seventeenth-century talmudic commentator] raises a difficulty: 'This statement refers, not to Moses but to the people of Israel, and, as far as they were concerned, the fear of God was no small matter.' " Rabbi Yaakov Yosef resolves the difficulty. "Moses our teacher opened the channel of fear of God into the world.... The statement, 'Yes, it was a small matter to Moses,' means that to that generation which was in the time of Moses when the channel of fear was opened into the world, the fear of God was a small matter too.... It is similar with the question of holiness, which I have already raised. How could all the people be holy? But when the whole community of Israel was close to Moses, then it was easy for them to be in the category of holiness, which was drawn to them from the holiness of Moses."[39]

Sometimes the way from heaven to earth is obstructed. Then it is for the zaddik to open that channel so that once again the outpouring from heaven continues, for "he draws the Holy Spirit down over mankind."[40] The zaddik opens the channel for what was always there, waiting to descend; and it is in his own being that the heavenly outpouring reaches the people. The whole generation is affected by the zaddik. "The leaders of the generation are the channel by which the generation is influenced, in the likeness of Moses our teacher of whom it is written, 'And I will take from the spirit which was upon thee and place it upon them'" (Num. 17:11).[41] Because Moses was great, his generation was great and is called "the generation of knowledge" of God. "Through the mediation of Moses, the spirit of wisdom and prophecy rested upon them. *So it is with every generation and its leaders, the spirit of the Lord goes from him [the leader] to the people.*"[42] "Just as Moses was the head of all of his generation... so it is with every generation. The leaders have sparks [within the flame of their souls] from our teacher Moses (peace be to him)."[43]

To understand how to open up the heavens is the particular genius of the zaddik. As a channel between earth and heaven, he reaches upward, touches the heavens, is transformed and turns to transform others. He becomes a source of spirit for the people. From the symbol of the zaddik as a channel, several inferences can be drawn.

As a channel is merely the means to join two ends, the zaddik is the humble link between God and the people. As a channel or tube can only receive at one end what it dispenses at the other, the zaddik is obliged to give in order to receive, to teach in order to learn. The zaddik can only take from heaven if he gives to man. "If he who receives *shefa* does not hand it over to others, it will be cut off from him as well.... If he wants to receive, he must give to others, as if he were a bridge for the outpourings of heaven."[44] To a large extent, it is the desire and willingness to bestow upon others the treasures of his spirit which permits the zaddik to draw strength from above.

THE ZADDIK AND DEVEKUT OR THE MEANS OF EARTH REACHING HEAVEN

The zaddik not only brings heaven down to the people; he also acts as a means by which the people rise upward toward heaven.[45] This is accomplished by *devekut*. *Devekut* is one of the key words in hasidic literature,[46] and means the clinging or cleaving of man to God. It is the object of all the commandments and the goal of all spiritual living. "There is one mitzvah in the Torah which includes everything, and that is 'Thou shalt cleave unto Him'" (Deut. 10:20).[47] It is "the heart of all the mitzvot,"[48] for it is their source, giving them life. If it be fulfilled, it is as if all the Torah were fulfilled.[49] "*Even if one acquires the world-to-come through Torah and mitzvot, this is not the main goal. The main goal is to acquire the rung of drawing close to Me,*"[50] which is *devekut*. It can be achieved through the inner yearning of man for the nearness of God, through prayer and study. But there is yet another way, especially for those who are not learned and have little time for study or meditation—by means of the power of the zaddik.

To the simple man heaven is something so remote that he easily despairs of coming close to it. His mind is not occupied with Torah, but filled with the selling of potatoes; his tongue is not busy with prayer, but heavy with the matters of the market place. How, then, can he taste something of the sweetness of heaven? It is through the zaddik that he is able to achieve this. "The purpose of all the mitzvot is that one may merit the rung of 'and thou shalt cleave unto Him' (Deut. 10:20)... but this is not possible for all men.... Therefore the sages say, 'Cleave to the learned man who cleaves to the Name

Who is blessed,' and, then, through him, he too will be able to cleave to the Name Who is blessed."[51]

"There are two kinds of *devekut*. One is that of the learned who cleaves to God directly, and the other is that of common people who do not know how to cleave to the Lord directly. Therefore the Torah commands them, 'Thou shalt cleave unto Him,' meaning, to cleave to the learned, which is like cleaving to God."[52] " 'When Moses raised his hand, the people were victorious' (Ex. 17:11). But could the hands of Moses do battle? The verse teaches you that all the while that Israel gazed upward and subjugated their hearts to their Father in heaven, they were victorious."[53] " 'All the while that Israel gazed upward,' that is, toward the learned; for Israel clings to the learned face to face like the cherubs whose faces were toward each other, gazing upward toward the faces of the wise. In this manner they subjugated their hearts to their Father in heaven, for the wise are also called their father, as Elisha said of Elijah, 'My father, my father, chariot of Israel' (II Kings 12:2). For, by means of their gazing upward, the cleaving of the common people with the learned, strength and elevation was given to their heart to subjugate it to their Father in heaven."[54]

"To join the *tzurah*, which is the spiritual world, with the *homer*, which is the material world, is a thing of wonder, as the *Rama* writes in the *Orah Hayim:* 'It is wonderful how God watches over the soul of man which is within the body, binding together spirit and matter.'[55]... But how is it possible for man, who is flesh and blood, to cleave to God, who is the spirit of all spirits and the life of all life? Still more difficult is the verse which explicitly declares, 'Thou shalt cleave unto Him' (Deut. 10:20), which means a binding and cleaving of spirit and matter to the Creator. How is this possible? There is, however, a means through which the man of flesh and blood can cleave to Him whose Name is blessed. Moses our teacher was the

mediator between Israel and the Holy One, blessed be He."[56]
"When one joins himself to the scholar on whom the *Shechinah*
rests, he actually joins himself to the Lord, as it is written, 'and
they believed in the Lord' (Ex. 31:14), which is faith in and
cleaving to God himself. How was that possible...? The very
same verse explains: 'and in Moses His servant.' For 'one who
believes in a shepherd of Israel, it is as if he believed in God,'
as the sages have explained the verse."[57]

The Torah commands, "'And thou shalt cleave unto Him'
(Deut. 10:20). The rabbis (may their memories be for a
blessing) explain it as follows: 'Is He not a devouring fire? The
verse, therefore, means to cleave to the learned.'[58] Yet, one
might object that it is written, 'Thou shalt cleave unto Him'
(Deut. 10:20) and truly means *Him*. How then can one distort
the verse to mean cleaving to the learned, which is not the
same as cleaving to God? It is necessary to explain, therefore,
that if one cleaves to the learned, he cleaves *with him* to the
Lord as well. (And this is the meaning of the tale of the two
merrymakers who by turning sorrow to joy, joined others to
themselves and thus to God.)[59] See and understand that this
is the highest rung, for the purpose of all the commandments
is to enable one to cleave to God. And if one does not know the
order of cleaving to God, the Torah has wisely commanded
him to cleave to the learned, by means of whom he will be
raised."[60]

In cleaving to the zaddik, the people not only join themselves
to him, but also they are raised *with him*. This is an action of the
zaddik himself.

One who leads the community for the sake of heaven must direct
the people both in worldly and in spiritual matters, not with words
and deeds alone, but also in thought, joining himself to the Lord
with the people of his generation and raising them so that they
might cleave to the Lord, under the condition that they too will
join themselves to the leaders of the generation. Then the leaders

of the generation can seize their hands and raise them.... This is the meaning of the passage, "When one believes in a shepherd of Israel, it is as if he believes in the Lord Himself,'[61] for the one is the means to the other.... By a shepherd is meant one who shepherds and watches over the flock so that they are well fed... acting for the sake of heaven, for the welfare of Israel. It is good to believe in such a man."[62]

Rabbi Akiba taught that reverence for the scholar was like reverence for God. We are told that Rabbi Shimon explained every time the word *et* occurs in the Torah but could not explain the *et* in the verse, "Fear the Lord your God" *(et adonai elohecha tirah,* Deut. 10:20), "until Rabbi Akiba came and explained the word *et* here to include the scholars."[63] Thus the verse would mean that one must revere the scholar just as one reveres God. And the reason why no one other than Rabbi Akiba could explain this verse was that in his youth he himself was unlearned, hated the scholars and did not have reverence for the Lord. It was the repentance which he had experienced in his own life, during which he had been transformed into the greatest sage of his time, that brought him to this understanding. *"Reverence for the scholar brought him reverence for God."*[64]

In cleaving to the zaddik, there is hope even for the wicked, the disbelievers. "Even though they are wicked in regard to heaven, nevertheless, if they are good in regard to the zaddikim, cleaving to them, so that there is peace between them, their judgment too is cleft together with the zaddikim. But this is not true if they hate the zaddikim who are among them, for then they are wicked toward heaven *and* earth.... Thus we find regarding Korah, that, though he denied the prophecy of Moses our teacher (peace be to him), declaring that the Torah was not from heaven,[65] punishment did not strike him until he separated himself from the community, as it is written, 'and Korah took' (Num. 16:1), which the Talmud explains

as: 'He took *himself* to one side to be separated from the community...." [66] A man may be filled with doubt; he may be
wicked toward heaven; he may even deny the Torah itself.
But if he remains close to the zaddik, who is his earthly hope,
there is always the possibility that he will be delivered.

THE ZADDIK AS AN INSTITUTION

The inconsistent manner in which the term "zaddik" is
employed in the writings of Rabbi Yaakov Yosef indicates
that during his lifetime the new leader had not yet become an
institution. Nevertheless, the dependency of a man upon the
zaddik who alone can save that man is expressed several times.
This is the meaning given to the following talmudic passage:
"He who is slothful to lament a sage deserves to be buried
alive." [67] "Every zaddik is the soul of his generation. If a
zaddik dies and you neither take it to heart nor feel the lack,
you are like a body without a soul and deserve to be buried
alive." [68] For though you are maintained in life so far as all
outward manifestations are concerned, it is as if you were
dead, "a body without a soul, an orphan without a father, a
castle without a leader, a ship without a captain." [69]

While later writers emphasized the teaching that each man
has a particular zaddik and none other, [70] the beginnings of
this doctrine are to be found in the writings of Yaakov Yosef.
"When a zaddik leaves the world, one must cry out bitterly
at the loss." One should not say: "Are there not other zaddikim...? For perhaps this zaddik was the portion of life of
this particular man? It is well known that the body possesses
two hundred and forty-eight bones and three hundred and
sixty-five sinews. Now, the soul too possesses a like number of
bones and sinews, which are spiritual. Just as it is with the
human body so is it with the body of Israel which forms one

corpus, the people being the physical limbs and sinews while the zaddikim of the generation are the spiritual limbs and sinews which give life... to them. Every zaddik, who is a limb of the limbs of the soul, gives life... to one physical limb, which is a single man of the common people."[71]

The message of this passage is that each human personality is unique. Though one man may seem very much like his neighbor, he is an entity complete in himself, unduplicated anywhere in exactly the same fashion. "For man stamps many coins with the one seal and they are all like one another; but the King of Kings, the Holy One, blessed be He, has stamped every man with the seal of the first man, yet not one of them is like his fellow."[72] If the rise of the new leader, the zaddik, means that a new interest is to be taken in the spiritual life of the people, then not only is the community to be transformed but a new understanding for the individual members of that community was also to make itself felt. And since no two men are alike, it may be that every man does not have the same zaddik, but that each one must find the zaddik who can best help him. Cleaving to a zaddik is not a casual act, to be placed on the same level as ordinary events. It is an action of ultimate significance, a joining and meeting of the spirit. There may be a zaddik somewhere who has the key that will unlock the hidden caverns of pain and doubt which destroy a man. That zaddik is the spirit to his body.

Despite the intimate relationship between the zaddik and his followers, Yaakov Yosef, like the Baal Shem before him, did not teach complete dependence upon the zaddik. This is important to emphasize, because it highlights a difference in attitude toward the zaddik between the earlier and later generations of Hasidism. For example, it became the custom for hasidim to visit the zaddik to consult and learn from him. Great stress was placed upon these journeys and they were looked upon as holy pilgrimages. But such visits are nowhere urged by Rabbi Yaakov Yosef. Indeed, the reverse is the case. It is not the people who are told to go to the zaddik, but the zaddik who is told to go out to the people. The over-emphasis which later writers sometimes placed on the power and glory of the zaddik, as well as complete dependency upon him, is rarely found in Rabbi Yaakov Yosef's works. He is fond of quoting the following story in his teacher's name.

In a certain country there was a mighty warrior in whom all the people of the land put their trust. They did not bother to learn the arts of war, for they relied upon this mighty warrior who was among them. War broke out later and the mighty warrior wanted to make ready his weapons, but one of the enemy, a clever man, had stolen his weapons one by one, until he was left with nothing to fight with. The people who had relied on him were taken captive with him. (The words of the wise are full of grace!) Thus we can understand the verse, "Happy is the *people* who know the joyful shout" (Ps. 16:89). That is to say, when the people do not rely on a mighty warrior, but *they themselves* know the joyful shout of war, then "they walk, O Lord, in the light of Thy countenance." They do not rely on the great ones alone.[73]

Martin Buber, in his delineation of the role of the zaddik, is quick to stress the independence of his followers.

How was man, in particular the "simple man," with whom the hasidic movement is primarily concerned, to arrive at living his life in fervent joy? How, in the fires of temptation, was he to recast the Evil Urge into an urge for what is good? How, in the wonted fulfilling of the commandments was he to develop the rapturous bond with the upper worlds? How, in his meeting with creatures and things, grow aware of the divine sparks hidden within them? How, through holy *kavannah* illumine everyday life? We do, indeed, know that all that is necessary, is to have a soul united within itself and indivisibly directed to its divine goal. But how, in the chaos of life on our earth, are we to keep the holy goal in sight? How retain unity in the midst of peril and pressure, in the midst of thousands of disappointments and delusions? And once unity is lost, how recover it? Man needs counsel and aid, he must be lifted and redeemed. And he does not need all this only in regard to his soul, for in some way or other, the domains of the soul are intertwined with big and little cares, the griefs and despairs of life itself, and if these are not dealt with, how shall those loftier concerns be approached? A helper is needed, a helper for both body and soul, for both earthly and heavenly matters. This helper is called the zaddik. He can heal both the ailing body and the ailing soul, for he knows how one is bound up with the other, and his knowledge gives him the power to influence both. It is he who can teach you to conduct your affairs so that your soul remains free, and he can teach you to strengthen your soul, to keep you steadfast beneath the blows of destiny. And over and over he takes you by the hand and guides you until you are able to venture on alone. He does not relieve you of doing what you have grown strong enough to do for yourself. He does not lighten your soul of the struggle it must wage in order to accomplish its particular task in the world.

And all this holds for communication of the soul with God. The zaddik must make communication with God easier for his hasidim, but he cannot take their place. This is the teaching of the Baal Shem and all the great hasidim followed it; everything else is distortion and the signs of it appear relatively early. The zaddik strengthens his hasid in the hours of doubting, but he does not infiltrate him with truth. He only helps him conquer and reconquer it for himself. He develops the hasid's own power for right prayer, he teaches him how to give the words of prayer the right direction, and he joins his own prayer to that of his disciple and therewith lends him courage, an increase of power—wings. In hours of need, he prays for his disciple and gives all of himself, but he never permits the soul of the hasid to rely so wholly on his own that it relinquishes independent concentration and tension, in other words, that striving-to-God of the soul without which life on this earth is bound to be unfulfilled. Not only in the realm of human passions does the zaddik point over and over to the limits of counsel and help. He does this also in the realm of association with God; again and again he emphasizes the limits of mediation. One man can take the place of another only as far as the threshold of the inner sanctum.[74]

HOMER AND TZURAH

Basic to the understanding of the relationship between the zaddik and the people is the doctrine of matter (*homer*) and form (*tzurah*).[75] This dualistic concept runs through the thought of Yaakov Yosef regarding both the nature of man himself and that of the people-zaddik relationship. The doctrine predicates a world composed of matter and form, coexistent and conflictive, yet necessary to one another. Two processes are constant and simultaneous, one good, the other bad, one constructive, the other destructive: matter is being changed into form and form is being changed into matter. These two entities compose a relationship which may be described as both dynamic and integral. It is dynamic in that there is no lull; one element is constantly struggling and conquering the other. It is integral in that the two compose a single unit which is greater than either of its component parts.

Man is created out of form and matter, which are two opposites, matter tending toward material domination [*kelipot*] and form yearning for spiritual things. The purpose of man's creation is that he should convert matter into form, creating a unity. As this is the purpose of the creation of the individual man, so is it with the nation as a whole. The masses are called "people of the earth," because their concern is with earthly, material things, and so they are "matter." The zaddikim, who engage in Torah and prayer, are "form." The purpose of all this is that matter should be transformed into form, as it is said, "The lips of the priest do keep knowledge, and they should seek Torah from his mouth; for he is the messenger of the Lord of Hosts. The law of truth was in his mouth, and unrighteousness was not found on his lips; he walked with Me

in peace and uprightness, and did turn many away from iniquity' "
(Mal. 2:7,6).[76]

The principal purpose of the creation of man, who was made out
of form and matter, is that he should strive all his days to turn
matter into form. After he has achieved this in himself, he should
endeavor to transform others, for the zaddik is the form or soul of
the whole world, while the wicked are the matter or body of the
whole world. The zaddik must strive all his days to change matter
into form, to bring the wicked under the wings of the *Shechinah*,
which is the goal and purpose of everything."[77]

The purpose of creation was a disharmony which can and
should be made harmonious, through the efforts of man with the
help of God. The zaddik must spiritualize the people, converting
matter into form, leading them, raising them, ennobling
them. However, the people stand as a constant challenge
and threat to the zaddik. They need him, but even so, they
may defeat him, by changing him from "form" into the
"matter" which they are, or simply by separating from him.
Separation, or *perud*, means the defeat of the zaddik. It is this
continuous struggle between zaddik and people which lends
to their relationship its dynamic character.

AHDUT—UNITY

In Oriental mysticism, and some aspects of Greek philosophy,
matter is considered the source of all evil, and form (or soul)
the source of all good. The separation of the two, whether in
death, freeing the soul from the prison of the body, or within
the community, freeing the holy man from the contamination
of the people, is the ideal goal. Opposed to this is the character-
ization of the people and the zaddik as matter and form or
body and soul, implying that each is incomplete without the
other, since each is a part of a larger whole. The zaddik does

not seek to escape from the people, for separation, *perud*, is, far from being desirable, the worst possible evil, signifying the sundering of the underlying unity.[78]

Within a single man, the soul should not act arrogantly toward the body, boasting that she is a holy soul, hewn from a holy place beneath the Throne of Glory, while the body comes from the dust and is created from a fetid drop... for the soul descends into this world in order to perform the commandments in a perfect manner *by means of the bodily limbs....* Thus, all the more so, the body should not act arrogantly toward the soul, boasting that she nourishes the soul, for when the soul is divided from the body, the body putrefies. *They are each in need of the other* as a man and his wife, each one being only half a person. So it is, in general, that the scholars and zaddikim should not say that they do not need the common people, for they are the bearers of the Torah, and many commandments are fulfilled through the people. All the more so, the people should not say that they do not need the scholars, nor act arrogantly toward them because they support them, since the reverse is really true, as the sages say: "The world is sustained because of Hanina, my son." So it is that *each is only a half*. If both form and matter, individually and collectively, unite, then they become one complete man.[79]

The zaddik alone is incomplete, as the soul alone is incomplete, as man alone is incomplete. Each is in need of a mate—a people, a body, a wife.

"One of the great principles of hasidism," Buber tells us, "is that the zaddik and the people are dependent on one another. Again and again, their relationship is compared to that between substance and form in the life of the individual, between body and soul. The soul must not boast that it is more holy than the body, for only in that it has climbed down into the body and works through its limbs can the soul attain to its own perfection. The body, on the other hand, may not brag of supporting the soul, for when the soul leaves, the flesh falls into decay. Thus the zaddikim need the multitude, and the multitude need the zaddikim. The realities of hasidic teaching depend on this inter-relationship."[80] Rabbi Israel of Rizhyn taught that the zaddikim and their hasidim are to be compared to the letters and the vowels of the Hebrew alphabet. Just as the letters without the vowels are voiceless and the vowels without the letters are meaningless, so the zaddikim and the hasidim have need of one another and are bound up with one another. The zaddikim are the letters and the hasidim are the vowels. The hasidim need the zaddik, but he has need of them as well. When joined together, they possess voice and meaning; apart they are mute and sterile.

There is a unity running throughout all levels of creation which joins the blade of grass to the star, man to heaven. This unity is only a pattern now, the drive which urges all creatures to return to their source. It is only a pattern, because its original reality has been shattered. Our world is a world torn asunder in which each act of man helps either to widen the breach or to cast a bridge across. For there is a division which now spreads through all levels of creation, just as in the beginning unity prevailed. So deep is this division that it divides man from man, man from God and God from Himself. Even He is not truly one. Thus our cry, "Hear, O Israel, the Lord our God, the Lord is one," is but a memory and a prayer, not a reality. It is a memory because in the beginning such a unity did reign; it is a prayer because we dare ask that such a unity may reign again. It is not a reality because we live our lives in a broken universe. And this is the deepest meaning of exile, not only an exile of the body, a physical exile, but an exile of the soul, a spiritual exile. Exile means separation, division, *perud*. Thus the individual, the people and the *Shechinah* are all in exile: the individual from the soul, the people from the zaddik, the *Shechinah* from the Lord. Each yearns to return: "The *Shechinah* is love-sick to unite with her beloved."[81] But for this heavenly union, we must wait until all human *perud* will have disappeared, when the hatred and the pride which set a man apart from his neighbor and against his neighbor will have fled, and love will have united each man with his fellow man and all men with God. "On that day the Lord shall be one and His Name one" (Zech. 9:14).[82]

But the Name of the Lord is not truly one now.

"The zaddikim are... the first two letters of the Divine Name. The common people are the last two letters."[83] Behind this brief passage stands a daring theory which includes not only all of creation but the Creator Himself, and points to the zaddik as the one who can help to redeem the entire universe.

The Divine Name consists of four letters in Hebrew, YHWH. Furthermore, to speak of the Divine Name is only another way of speaking of God. Thus, if the zaddikim are the first two letters of the Divine Name and the people are the last two letters, then whether the letters are united, that is, if God is truly one, or whether the letters are divided, that is, if the unity of God is impaired, depends on the relationship between leader and people. Hatred and division between leader and people not only destroys the human community, but affects God Himself. By joining leader and people in a bond out of which emerges a holy community that obeys the Torah and performs the mitzvot with the love and fear of heaven, the letters of the Divine Name are joined and the divine wound is healed. God Himself is made whole. Redemption is at hand.

God did not create man and then abandon him. So great is His concern for His creatures that He involves Himself in their lives. Not only are they dependent upon Him, but He too is dependent upon them. Not only do they need Him, but He needs them as well. The Torah is a divine gift without which man becomes an animal and the world turns back to chaos and void. But the implementation and the realization of the Torah is a human venture. Thus while the fate of man hangs upon God, the fate of God hangs upon man. It was with fearful dismay, therefore, that Rabbi Yaakov Yosef viewed the prevailing division between leader and people and wrote of the terrible need for an intimate and enduring bond that would bind them together. He believed that this is not a human affair alone which ends with man, but one in which the Lord takes part. For to heal the rift between leader and people means to heal the rift within God himself. And who is it that must begin this fearful mission? It is the man who is himself united. The zaddik. He plays the leading role in this drama.

The unity of God's Name, which means the unity of God, depends on the unity of the leader and people. The *perud* which separates him from the people must be overcome. The abyss which divides the leader from the people, thus dividing God Himself, must be joined. It is the momentous task of the zaddik to cast a bridge over the chasm and then to draw the mountains together, so that in time, the perilous bridge which began the venture becomes superfluous and the two walls merge into one. Then the mountain reaches up and draws the very heavens together. This unity, this *ahdut*, which is redemption, is the solemn goal that the zaddik strives to achieve above all else. For unity is not only a memory of the past and a prayer for the future, but a constant possibility in the present. Even though the day of final unity is in the distant future, at the end of days, the possibility of achieving an aspect of unity in the present is always at hand. Each word, each act of man, depending on the manner in which it is spoken and the way it is performed, serves either to widen the breach or to help restore the unity that once prevailed. The eschatological drive for the final unity, which characterized Lurianic Kabbalah and which had little to do with the affairs of men, was replaced in Hasidism by the countless opportunities for *yihud* which each day offered, though the final task is never forgotten. Emphasis was put on that inner harmony within man and that social harmony between men which would alone produce the holy community. God would be one only when mankind would be one.

CHAPTER 6

Humility

A PRIMARY QUALITY OF THE ZADDIK

Pride was one of the principal failings of many of the rabbis of the time, and was the underlying cause of much of the evil which abounded. Humility was one of the central virtues of the zaddik, and is a key to the understanding of his personality and his place in the newly fashioned community.

The zaddik does not possess that fullness of arrogance which leaves little room for God or man. The self is not the center of his life: God and people are the center, or, better, they are the poles between which he moves. He is a channel which draws from above to below. He is a vessel which brings water to irrigate a field, that it may be fruitful and feed the hungry. The field is important and the water is important, but the vessel is mere clay. It only serves to join the water with the dry earth. So the zaddik is a vessel through which God might reach His people Israel for the sake of all mankind. The zaddik exists only for this reason: that heaven and earth might meet.

Because Moses could declare, "Blot me out of Thy book" (Ex. 32:32), he was chosen to lead the people. Because Joseph did not consider himself worthy before Pharaoh, he was selected to rule over Egypt. Because of Hanina's humility, "for he was content with a little, a piece of carob fruit from one Sabbath eve to another, he was set apart to be the channel of the Lord."[1] "The truest sign that a man cleaves to the Lord, Who is the life of all life, is humility."[2] "It is the truest sign," according to Rabbi Jacob Emden, "that a man fulfills the verse, 'I shall set the Lord before me at all times' " (Ps. 8:16).³ "It is the zaddikim, before whom the Lord is at all times, who humble themselves unto the dust; for when they behold the majesty of the Lord, his angels and pious ones, they are as nothing in their own eyes."⁴ Humility is the "qualification for the *Shechinah*'s resting upon a man, as with Moses our teacher who humbled himself. He knew that the *Shechinah* did not rest upon him because of his own virtues, but because of the virtues of another, of Israel. Thus he said, 'Because of *you*, the word was united with me,' as it is written, 'I shall dwell with the broken in heart' " (Isa. 15:57).

THE ZADDIK'S SENSE OF SELF-CRITICISM AND SERVICE

Characteristic of the zaddik is his self-criticism; characteristic of the wicked person is his self-satisfaction. One never achieves enough; the other thinks he has achieved everything. This thought is expressed in an explanation of the verse, "He who goes weeping, bears his measure of seed. He who comes in joy, bears his sheaves" (Ps. 126:6): "All the day long the zaddik is immersed in the service of the Lord, and ever finds himself inadequate."⁶ "He weeps and is in distress over his 'going away' from the service of the Lord," but, "in the end, 'he bears his measure of seed.' This is not so with the one who feels that he has arrived"⁷ in Torah and the service of God, who feels that he is close to the Lord. He is filled with the false joy of self-satisfaction, "for in the end he bears his sheaves *without the seed*."⁸

"His impurity and his sin are before the eyes of the zaddik at all times, which is not so of the wicked who consider themselves pure.... The man who thinks himself pure reveals a sign of impurity.... In this manner is the verse 'Thou shalt be holy' to be understood. The goal of knowledge is for one to know that he does not know. Even one who is in a lofty state should feel that he is in a lowly state and should *look forward* to salvation, asking, 'When will I merit the category of "Thou *shalt be* holy?" '—which implies the future, not the present—'for I the Lord *am* holy'; that is, only God *is* in the highest degree of holiness. But this is impossible for man. Therefore he should always consider himself lacking the category of holiness."[9] Since the verse "Thou *shalt be* holy" (Lev. 2:19) is in the future tense, the zaddik constantly strives to be holy, feeling that it is a rung he never reaches. It is always a future hope to him, never a present possibility. God alone *is* holy.

The zaddik's humility is one of the signs of his greatness. "Man is a 'ladder fixed in the earth, whose head reaches the heavens, and the angels of the Lord ascend and descend it' (Gen. 28:12). That is to say, when he thinks he is far from the Lord—'fixed in the earth,' and one of those who 'descend'—he is in reality close to the Lord and 'his head reaches the heavens.' But when he thinks he is close to the Lord—that 'His head reaches the heavens,' and of those who 'ascend'—he is in reality far from the Lord, 'fixed in the earth.' "[10] "Through humility and meekness, one is worthy of coming closer to God."[11]

"Truly the pillar of Torah is the central support for the world,"[12] but he who dispenses it "must humble himself with each and every person." "For the pillar of Torah which is the support of the world requires *the quality of humility*. Without it, it is not [the support of the world]." The proud scholar is not interested in the Torah of others; the humble scholar is willing to learn from any man. " 'Who is the wise man? He who learns from all men,'[13] for he knows that it is necessary to learn also from another."[14] "The wise man learns from all men. That is, even though he is wise, nevertheless, he learns from all men, because of the humility which is his,"[15] "turning to listen to the teachings of Torah... from even the lowliest of men."[16]

The rabbinate is not a source of power but of service, and one should not so much desire it as be compelled to accept its duties. "There are two kinds of rabbis: one is of evil desire, wishing to acquire wealth and fame through the rabbinate; the other is filled with the Lord and His service. It is not of his wish, but he is compelled [to become a rabbi], as it is written in the Talmud that he [R. Gamliel] wanted to appoint them [R. Jochanan B. Gudgada and R. Eleazar B. Chasma] as rabbis. They did not want to accept until he said to them: 'You thought that I was going to offer you "authority" and so, in humility, you wanted to evade the honor. But it is "servitude" that I offer you, as it is said, "If thou wilt be a servant unto the people this day"' (I Kings 12:7).[17] ... The one who is compelled out of inner constraint to become a rabbi, not for authority, but for servitude, is sanctified."[18] He is sanctified because his role of leadership does not come from any ulterior motive, but from an inner constraint which he cannot halt and which turns his life, whether he wants it thus or not, into a path of hardship and suffering and endless responsibility. The zaddik understands the words of Amos which he spoke when he tried to explain to others why he became a prophet. "I was no prophet, neither was I a prophet's son; but I was a herdman, and a dresser of sycamore trees; and the Lord took me from following the flock, and the Lord said unto me: 'Go, prophesy unto my people Israel.' Now therefore hear thou the word of the Lord" (Amos 7:14-16). The zaddik knows that "it is not easy to bestow the outpouring of heaven on another. It is easier to go into seclusion, to receive for oneself the heavenly outpouring from above."[19] It is not a personal ambition,[20] but the pressing urge of the time which fills him with the spirit of the Lord and "His service" that "compels him" to enter the battle. To be a rabbi is not a matter of delight or pleasure, not like any other profession, but the task requiring most devotion and sacrifice. It does not offer power but servitude, does not come as an easy choice, but as an implacable compulsion, for "by means of the rabbinate one can watch

over the needs of the community."[21] And all this is true, not
when "the rabbi... is appointed by the government," but
when "*he is appointed by the Lord*."[22]

THE ZADDIK'S RELATION TO GOD AND ISRAEL

The abilities and position of the zaddik are not a source of
pride, because he feels himself moved by a higher power. If
the zaddik "performs a great mitzvah or studies much Torah
or prays with *kavannah*, no self-glory enters his heart that *he* has
achieved this."[23] It is the divine within him, "the *Shechinah*,...
which has done all this, and not he himself."[24] "Therefore
Moses our teacher... knew that all his accomplishments and
good deeds were not from himself but from the *Shechinah*."[25]
For the life of God can be a part of the life of the zaddik—and
of every man—since man is not a self-contained unit, but is
embedded in another dimension of reality. There is a power
other than himself at work within him.[26] Indeed, the "I" of
man is something more than man.[27]

While the ability and knowledge of the zaddik have their
origin in the *Shechinah*, they belong to the people. "The Mishnah,
'Give to him what is his'[28] is to be understood by the talmudic
passage 'I have given you greatness, only for the sake of
Israel.'[29]... The zaddik possesses knowledge and understanding
that he might be able to lead the people and teach them the
laws of truth and righteousness. As Solomon said, 'And now,
O Lord my God, Thou hast made thy servant king instead of
David my father; and I am but a little child; I know not how
to go out or come in. And Thy servant is in the midst of Thy
people, that cannot be numbered nor counted for multitude.
Give Thy servant therefore an understanding heart to judge
this people, that I may discern between good and evil; for who
is able to judge this Thy great people?' (I Kings 3:7-9) There-

fore, 'Give to him [Israel] what is his [Israel's], for you [the zaddik] and all you have [your learning and authority] are his';[30] and so it is from 'what is his' that you teach him and make straight his path."[31]

Thus we see again the twofold relationship of the zaddik, standing between God and the people, and the emphasis therefore upon humility and service. The zaddik cannot be proud of his learning and his talents, because they are not his. They belong to God and to the people. They belong to God since they have their origin in the *Shechinah*, for it is the divine aspect of his nature from which his abilities derive. They belong to the people since they exist only for their sake, for whatever he possesses, he possesses on their account. He gives to them only what is already theirs, since he and all he has are theirs.

Pride blinds a man's eyes to what is around him, turning his sight inward so that he sees only his own problems. The center of such a man's life is himself. Humility removes the blinders so that he sees the problems of others. The center of his life is not himself, but God, and thus he turns to concerns beyond himself. The humility of the zaddik, lifting the barrier of conceit, opens his soul to the cares of the people, allowing him to give himself to them with all his heart and soul. "The [zaddik] should acquire the trait of humility [until he is] like the dust of the earth... descending from his rung to lift up those who dwell in the dust."[32]

When the mother of Rabbi Yitzhak Meir of Ger died, he followed after the coffin, crying bitterly and asking for forgiveness. Just before they were about to fill up the grave with earth, he said to her: "I have achieved much fame and honor here on earth, and I am even called Rabbi. But now you will enter into heaven, which is the world of truth, and there you will discover that all these people are mistaken. Grant me forgiveness, therefore, and bear me no grudge. What can I do, if the people are mistaken in me!"

CHAPTER 7

The Descent of the Zaddik

The "descent of the zaddik" is the name given to the most crucial aspect of the doctrine of the zaddik. It represented the manner in which the zaddik was to meet the crisis of the time. According to Rabbi Yaakov Yosef, a chasm existed between the people and the leaders. This chasm began in the heart of man, reached the very heavens, and was encouraged by the contemptuous attitude of the scholars, who secluded themselves from the people and were concerned principally with their own wants. The zaddik was void of the pride which characterized many of his contemporaries. Because of the humility which resulted from his awareness of God's presence and his own task, he was filled with "the fullness of God and His service," and was ready to act for the people. One of the principal characteristics of the zaddik, therefore, is his going out to the people, to save them.

He takes the initiative to heal the breach, not waiting for the people to act. A world of chaos and void, of division between matter and spirit, of chasm unending, stands before him. The zaddik must "arouse himself, as in the beginning of creation."[1] It is he who must begin the labor of binding together what has been broken in order that the former harmony be restored. The people cannot be expected to come to him; he must take the first step toward them. The zaddikim "are warned: 'Do not depart from the people!' Even though the people do not go to the wise men, healers of the souls, nevertheless the wise men should go after them, as the Zohar teaches, 'Happy is he who pursues after the guilty.'[2] God commanded Moses: 'Go to the people and sanctify them today' (Ex. 10:19). Regarding this verse the *Alshech* remarks, 'It teaches us that Moses was not to wait for the people to come to him to seek the way of the Lord, but that he should go with them, to teach them.'"[3]

Aaron, too, is an example for the zaddik to imitate. "Aaron the priest, the man of compassion, opened the channel of love. This is the meaning of the passage 'Be of the disciples of Aaron, loving peace, pursuing peace and bringing them to Torah.'[4] Even when your friend does not seek peace with you, nevertheless, you should be 'pursuing peace.'[5] Even though he flees, you should pursue and be the first to open the channel of love, loving men, bringing them to Torah. Then, 'as in water face answereth to face, so the heart of man' (Prov. 27:19), and they will love you also."[6] "Love thy neighbor as thyself" (Lev. 19:18) means: "'Love thy neighbor,' then he will be 'as thyself,'"[7] and love you. The zaddik, as a disciple of Aaron, must act first, not waiting for the people to love. He must pursue them in love, even when they do not want his love. Only in this way will they, too, come to love. For there is merely a "curtain separating"[8] them which needs but to be pierced by the rays of love. This was the way of Aaron, and this alone is the way for the zaddik. The prophet first "will turn the heart of the fathers to the children"; only then "the heart of the children to the fathers."[9] The fathers are the zaddikim: first they must turn their hearts to the children, who are the people; only then will the heart of the people, who are in truth their children, be turned to them.[10]

The action which the zaddik initiates not only carries him *out* after the people, but also, and primarily, *down* to them. To be able to find them at all, so that he might love them and bind and heal them, he must descend to their level, seeking them out wherever they may be, in order to raise them. Otherwise all his good intentions will be in vain. If a man wants to take one out of a pit, he himself must go down into that pit. It is the peculiar task and the peculiar genius of the zaddik to be able to move between the higher and lower realms in order to deliver the wicked man. "The wicked must be turned to good until they become one with the righteous. And this is as it is written, 'Thus saith the Lord: Surely my covenant is with day and night; surely I have appointed the laws of heaven and earth' (Jer. 22:25); that is, to unite, through the *zaddik, who is called the 'covenant of day and night,'* the two classes of men mentioned above. For the purpose of the creation of heaven and earth (which are the two classes of men) is to unite them that they become *one....* 'It was evening and it was morning, one day'" (Gen 1:5).[11] The zaddik is a righteous man. But he is more. His mission is to move *between* the righteous and the unrighteous, "to turn many from sin, to change night into day."[12] He is the "covenant between night and day," "the law between heaven and earth." His duty is to join the two so that earth is transformed into heaven and night fades into day. For this to be a possibility at all, however, he knows that he must leave the radiant heights of Torah study and prayer where he finds a heavenly shelter and go down into the dark night of the soul, into the dreary earthly life of his people. This is what is meant by the "descent of the zaddik."

Commenting on a passage in the Song of Songs, Yaakov Yosef contrasts the high and mighty manner of some of the contemporary rabbis with the new manner of the zaddik. The former had no success, but the latter, breathing love and concern, is destined to reach the people. "The watchmen who go about the city found me: 'Have you seen him whom I love?' Scarcely did I leave them when I found him whom I love. I held him and would not let him go until I brought him to my mother's house, to the chamber of her who bore me" (Song 3:3, 4). The zaddik strives to save the people whom he loves and goes seeking them. He asks the "watchmen" of the city, who are "the leaders of the generation," the rabbis of the time, if they know how to reach the people, "to be close to them," to save them. "But [the watchmen] give no answer, for they have failed." They had not "come close" to the people But "scarcely did I leave them, that is, their ways," when I was able to find a way to the people "whom my soul loves." Then "I held him and would not let him go until I brought him to my mother's house." For the Lord "has given [the leader] the congregation of Israel to tend as a shepherd, not to rule over them, but to watch over them...."[13] "Not only must the great men, the heads of the generation, set themselves right, but [it is necessary] to caution them regarding the little men, the wicked, who are little in faith; it is necessary to warn the great men to return the little men also to right conduct."[14]

THE SYMBOL OF ABRAHAM

As we have seen, Noah is the symbol of the false leader, the secluded scholar. He was a righteous man in his own way, doing his duty to God as he envisioned his duty to be, "conducting himself in the highest manner in his own house"[15] and performing all the commandments of the Lord. He was sure his own soul was secure. Noah "walked with God." Proof of this was the fact that when the flood came, he was saved. What better evidence could there be that he was without sin? He spent his time in his ark, in his synagogue, in seclusion. There were others who sought such seclusion and joined Noah. With them he passed his hours. But were they the ones that most needed his help? "Whoever wanted to seclude himself in holiness, came *of himself* to the ark (the synagogue) to lock himself in. This is not true, however, of the sinner, who is drawn after worldly pleasures; he surely would not come willingly to lock himself in the ark for the worship of God...

which to the wicked is not a delight but a punishment.... Indeed, they would rather be destroyed in the flood (the world) than be enclosed in the ark (the synagogue) to worship God."[16]

Noah saw his duty fulfilled by being personally scrupulous and associating with the select few who came to the ark. But how can the people be saved in this manner? Only those who are *already* saved come to the ark in the first place. The real task is just with those who remain distant, who hate the ark, who are lost in the midst of wordly living and prefer death to the life of the spirit. Noah did not understand this.

Abraham, on the other hand, is the symbol of the true leader, the zaddik. "He not only purified himself, but others as well... as it is written, 'He called on the name of the Lord' (Gen. 12:8), which the sages explain to mean: 'He caused the Name of Heaven to be familiar in the mouth of men.' "[17] His entire life was a constant wandering. He left the seclusion of his home and the security of his country to go from land to land, seeking to bring to others the vision which exploded in his own soul. He could not contain it, for it was not meant for him alone. The Bible speaks of "The souls he *made* in Haran" (Gen. 12:5), which means, according to the sages, that he converted people to believe in God.[18] He fought for the wicked; even the people of Sodom found a defender in him. He did not live in seclusion, but was a "zaddik *in the midst of the city*,"[19] in order that he might turn others from sin. To achieve all this, Abraham had to descend to the people.[20]

"Abraham wanted to make known to the world the fact that the Lord was God, to turn people to God. But they did not listen to him, for he had nothing in common with them, since he was on a high rung and they on a low one. So, out of concern for the glory of God, he descended from his rung that he might have something in common with them and be able to raise them. 'Walk before me and be perfect' (Gen. 17:1) was the command God gave to Abraham, to teach the leader that by lowering himself—walking *before* me into the world, not *with* me in seclusion from it—he will be able to join himself with the common people and raise them. Then he will be *tamim*, complete or perfect. Only after he has purified himself *and* others, can he be called complete and whole. But if he does not [purify the others], he is called half [a man]."21 "A man is complete only in union with his fellow man."22

Noah and Abraham are more than two Biblical characters; they represent two different types of leaders. "For there is a difference between the zaddik who secludes himself with God, who cannot save his generation but only himself, and the zaddik who goes 'into the city,' admonishes the people and saves the generation also."23 Noah walked with God; Abraham walked before God. Noah remained aloof; Abraham went to the people. Noah sought personal security to save himself; Abraham exposed himself to wickedness and sin to save others. Noah held the people in contempt; Abraham had compassion for them. Noah caused God's anger; Abraham caused His mercy.24 Noah brought *perud*, separation; Abraham brought *ahdut*, unity. Noah destroyed the world; Abraham saved the world.25

The Maggid of Mezritch explained the verse "The zaddik shall flourish like the palm tree; he shall grow like a cedar in Lebanon" (Ps. 92:13) to mean that there are two kinds of zaddikim. One kind devote themselves to the people, teaching them and seeking to help them. Another kind devote themselves to study and the performance of the commandments. The first are like the date palm which bears fruit; the second are like the cedar: lofty and without fruit.

The rabbi of Kotzk once described a noted rabbi to his hasidim as a zaddik in a fur coat. In answer to their questions as to what was meant by this description, he replied that there are two ways to keep warm in a cold room. One can put on a fur coat or one can light a fire. What is the difference? The first man only wants to keep himself warm. The second wants to bring warmth to others as well.

THE DESCENT OF THE ZADDIK AS A DOCTRINE OF CONCERN

The lofty attitude of the false leader, the scholars who stood apart from the people, has been characterized as one of contempt—which stemmed from pride, justified seclusion and contributed to the prevailing condition of *perud*. The attitude of the true leader, the zaddik, can also be characterized by a term—*concern*.

Humility makes concern possible, because it implies the awareness of the other's existence. But concern is more than awareness of another's existence. It means to care: to go out of oneself toward one's fellow man, to help him, to heal him, to raise him. It means the drawing together of what has been shattered. It means that a man alone is incomplete, only half a man, and that he must feel for another in order to be whole himself.[26] Only by helping to heal others is he himself healed. "The essence of returning to God is to turn others also."[27] It means that the outpouring of God's concern for man overflows the zaddik's heart, reaching out to touch other men. God's concern for man becomes the zaddik's concern for God's concern and, therefore, concern for man himself. "The zaddik thinks that each Israelite is a limb of the *Shechinah*,"[28] and thus, concern for the anguish of the *Shechinah* becomes concern for the anguish of the people. *Concern* means love and compassion. The zaddik loves the people and finds even among the plainest of them signs of holiness. "I heard that a woman from the holy community of Meziboz said in the Russian language, 'It is well for us that we have chosen our God, but it is likewise well for Him that He has chosen Israel, for see how simple Feibush sanctifies the Name Who is blessed.'"[29] Even for the least of men the zaddik has compassion. The zaddik "loves the lowly creatures in whom there is no perfection other than their being His creatures—nonetheless it is proper to love them, to draw them to the Torah... to descend to the rung of the people in order to make them holy."[30] "Noah only knew the fear of God... but Abraham reached the rung of the love of God."[31] Fear is restrictive, harsh, bringing punishment; love is expansive, embracing others, bringing forgiveness. The zaddik "follows after the wicked, putting out his hand to him; perhaps he will repent."[32] The entire life of Moses was one of constant concern for the people. "Whom do we have greater than Moses, the master of all Israel? Surely all his deeds, all his prayers, and all his learning was only for this—that he stretched out his hand to Israel that they might seize it, in order to raise them."[33] The very word "zaddik" implies concern, for it means "to declare the people innocent."[34] Just as *contempt* is the key word in understanding the scholar's aloof attitude to the people, so *concern* is the key word in understanding the zaddik's compassionate attitude toward the people.

Before proceeding to a detailed analysis of the "descent of the zaddik," which is the primary expression of his concern for the people, it is advisable to examine how this concern manifests itself in several other related respects: the zaddik's constant thought of the people, his willingness to suffer for them, his understanding of their poverty, and his belief in the principle of "rung." They will be dealt with in this order.

THE ZADDIK'S CONSTANT THOUGHT OF THE PEOPLE

Nothing which the zaddik does is done solely for himself. He is the leader of the people and must be worthy of such a trust. "First, one should set himself right; afterward, he should set others right."[35] This passage from the Talmud is quoted again and again in Yaakov Yosef's treatment of the zaddik,[36] for the influence of his words "depends upon his deeds."[37] The zaddik must be worthy of leading the people and healing their hurt. Therefore, before he can presume to lead them, he must heal his own hurt, prepare his own soul, strengthen his own spirit. But this was true of the aloof leader of the time as well, of Noah as well as Abraham, for both of them tried to perfect themselves through prayer and Torah. The difference between them was that while "setting oneself right" was the end of the matter for the one—a fully justifiable goal in and of itself—it was merely the beginning of the matter for the other, only the means to the end. He set himself right first, so that afterward he might be worthy of setting others right. One was concerned principally with his own perfection; the other was concerned with his own perfection for the sake of the perfection of others. "If one wants to mend the community, first he must mend himself."

Even this, however, is not sufficient. The concern of the zaddik for the people causes him to think of the people at all times, creating a union of leader and people which permits no exception. To emphasize this point Rabbi Yaakov Yosef adds a further explanation to the above quoted passage: "'First, one should set himself right; afterward, he should set others right.' One must not think that there is an interval between setting oneself right and setting others right, as if the others are apart from him, and therefore that he should set himself right first *alone*, not having the intention in mind of including others with him. Through such action they would, in truth, remain separate by themselves. *It is necessary that at the very time he sets himself right, to also include his generation with him*, and then it will be easier to mend them and return them to right conduct."[38]

The zaddik must correct himself and afterwards correct others. This is necessary, and is a higher goal than that of the

self-centered leader. But it is not sufficient. He must understand further that these are not two distinct acts—correcting
himself and correcting others—that there is no "interval"
between them. For if he understands his task correctly, he will
know that even in the very moment of self-perfection, when
his own soul is being cleansed, he must include the people in
himself. Never for a moment must he forget that he is not an
autonomous unit, but joined in an unbreakable bond with his
generation. Therefore, no act, not even the very act of preparation, can be an act in which he thinks only of himself, for
there too he "must include his generation with him." It is the
concern of the zaddik for the people which unites him with the
people so that all his thoughts and all his deeds are for them.

THE ZADDIK'S WILLINGNESS TO SUFFER FOR THE PEOPLE

His willingness to undergo persecution for their sake is palpable
evidence of the zaddik's concern for the people. His life is often
one of peril and suffering. Indeed, "the healers of the soul must
go down to Gehinom to raise the wicked."[39] In descending to
the wicked he lowers himself into the pit and puts his very life
at stake, "for he who descends from his rung is called dead. In
this manner we understand both the dictum of Resh Lakish,
'The words of the Torah are only fulfilled by one who is willing
to give his life for it,'"[40] and the dictum of Yaakov Yosef: "He
who wishes to live, finds death; he who is willing to die, finds
life."[41]

"The zaddik dies two kinds of death: actual death and
apparent death."[42] "Weep ye not for the dead, neither bemoan
him; but weep sore for him that goeth away" (Jer. 22:10). The
prophet's words are to be understood in the following way:
"Weep ye not for the dead,' that is, for the zaddik who actually
dies.... For to the contrary, the actual death of the zaddik is

called a *hilulla*, a time of joyous festivity, because he goes from
this vale of sorrows to the tranquillity of the next world. 'But
weep for him that goeth away'... that is, for the zaddik who
does not actually die, but who descends from his rung, going
down to join himself to the common people in order to raise
them.... For if they do not wish to be joined to him and raised,
it was all for nothing that he went away from the security
of his rung."[43] It is for this latter death that the zaddik should
be mourned and bemoaned, that he died again and again
for the people, descending into the pit for their sake, to no
avail. Yet, despite failure, anxiety, and even, at times, despair—"all this is for the suffering of Israel and not for his own
suffering."[44]

To deliver the wicked the zaddik goes to them and learns
the wickedness of their ways. "He has no joy in this world
because of worry over the danger of the *yetzer hara*, that it might
seize him in its grasp."[45] "The zaddik, the servant of the Lord,
knows the battle with the *yetzer hara* and with the enemies who
wait along the way of one who serves the Lord. This way is a
way of danger, for he must ever live a life of anguish—how to
escape from their net and how to warn others of the dangers
from these enemies. 'The more knowledge, the more pain
(Eccl. 1:18).' "[46]

The zaddik is in peril from enemies of the spirit who threaten
the life of his soul. He is in peril also from enemies of the flesh
who oppose and hamper him every step of the way.[47] "The
earthly ones cause the heavenly ones to fall from their rung."[48]
"Woe to the wicked who turn the soul [the zaddik] into a body,
for they give the zaddikim no rest, even though they are in the
service of the Lord...! Woe unto them, for they bring evil to
their own souls!"[49] "Moses too was of the persecuted and not
of the persecutors."[50] Though the zaddik may be able to save
the people, he is not accepted by all of them. He is the " 'stone
which the builders rejected' (Ps. 118:22). The zaddik is called

the cornerstone, the foundation of the world, for upon him the entire world is situated. But the builders, who are the scholars, have rejected him."[51] The zaddik suffers exile. "One is filled with anguish over the exile of the learned who serve the Lord, from the learned who are the prophets of Baal and because of whom the Temple was destroyed."[52] Indeed, the exile of the zaddik is the bitterest of all exiles. "There are three kinds of exile: first, the exile of Israel from the nations; second, the exile of the learned from the unlearned; third, the exile of the faithful ones of Israel, the servants of the Lord, from the scholars who are motivated by fame and show. This latter exile is the most severe... for the people suffer one exile, the scholar two, and the pious all three!"[53] But this exile, bitter and harsh as it is, must be expected and borne by the zaddik. In the Song of Songs reference is found to the exile of the zaddik. The soul speaks: "'I adjure you, O daughters of Jerusalem, if you find my beloved, what will you tell him? That I am lovesick' (Song 5:8). 'Daughters of Jerusalem,' you are the zaddikim. 'I adjure you' to bear the exile of the wicked as I, the soul, bear the sickness of the ugly body because of the love of my beloved.... You must do the same. 'If you find my beloved' in the exile of the wicked, through your prayers, tell him that the soul, which is a portion of the *Shechinah*, is lovesick."[54]

The zaddik must be ready to receive criticism for striking out on a new path, for "because he joins himself to the common people, he is mocked."[55] The *hitlahavut* or fervor which characterized his worship, his study and his observance of the mitzvot was also an object of scorn. "The people hate the zaddikim who fear the Lord and guard His way, because they are two opposites. The people are small of spirit and shorten the way of the Lord, whether in prayer or mitzvah, which they perform in a sluggish manner, by rote. This is not the case with the zaddikim, who take pains with the way of the Lord. The Torah is fulfilled only by one who offers his life for it."[56] "Not only do they observe the mitzvot sluggishly, but they are angry with the zaddik who observes the mitzvot of the Lord with joy and fervor."[57] "Not only do they forsake the Lord, but they despise the holy ones of Israel, the faithful ones of Israel who act for His Name Who is blessed, who sanctify themselves in many ways of holiness. *They despise them, because they do not act as they do.*"[58]

Envy lies beneath this hatred and, because of it "they slander the holy ones on high."[59] The truth is that those who mock the zaddik "are jealous of him,"[60] for in their heart of hearts they know what he is. "Everyone recognizes the rung of the zaddik and renders him honor. Even the wicked know his rung, only they do not speak his praise with their mouth."[61]

"And Joseph brought evil report of them [his brothers] unto their father" (Gen. 37:2). Now one must ask himself, "How could Joseph transgress?" It is likewise difficult to understand how this shameful act could be written in the Torah in the first place. Furthermore, the verses which follow the above one also present a problem. "Now Israel loved Joseph more than all his children.... And when his brethren saw that their father loved him more than all his brethren, they hated him and could not speak peaceably to him" (Gen. 37:3, 4). Are we not shocked that the founders of the tribes of the Lord transgressed the negative commandment, "Thou shalt not hate thy brother" (Lev. 19:17), and the positive commandment, "Thou shalt love thy neighbor as thyself" (Lev. 19:18)?

But according to our explanation, it is all quite understandable. "And Joseph brought evil report of them to their father," that is, to their Father in heaven. For all the evil which he saw in them he took upon himself in part and made confession before their Father in heaven, because he joined himself with them. This is the mystery of the zaddik. And that is why it is written, "And Israel loved Joseph." For to take upon oneself[62] all the reproach of mankind, fulfilling the verse, "And thou shalt love thy neighbor," is to stand upon a lofty rung. Therefore, Israel (his Father in heaven) loved Joseph, measure for measure, for he stirred up love first, to love his brothers and take the blame for their faults upon himself. "His brethren saw that their father loved him"... *therefore* they hated him.... *For whom the one loves, the other hates.*"[63]

It is the zaddik who cries out, " 'I am lovesick,' that is, 'sick' from the hatred I bear... because of the 'love' I share with You."[64]

Sometimes the jealousy which rankled in many breasts and the hatred which poured forth into harsh words and cruel deeds rose to such heights that it affected the inner life of the zaddik. So bitter was the persecution that his worship and service to God was affected. "One hesitates to give free expression to religious joy for fear of the scoffers.... Great is the power of the wicked who prevent the zaddikim from doing the will of the Lord."[65] "They mocked them, shaming them to their face in front of the people—as King David (peace be to him) said: 'Many are those who hate me falsely, and render me evil for good; they oppose me because I follow after good' (Ps. 38:20, 21)—until they could no longer endure the mockery and relinquished their piety!"[66]

The lives of the zaddik and his followers in their communities were by no means secure, because of the fierce hatred of the communal leaders. In the war which was waged against them, "it actually happened that those who cleave to the Lord have been beaten."[67] "...the zaddikim wander homelessly from place to place, for they cannot stand up in the thick of the battle, while the other warriors are taken captive from their land, where they had a special place for themselves [to pray and study], to another land. The intention of the [enemy] is to divide those who cleave to the Lord, that they be unable to join for battle."[68] "They are not permitted to settle in one place but go from city to city, as I heard from my teacher:

'People say that truth travels throughout the world, that is, *it is driven out* from place to place!"[69] The government-appointed rabbi and his delegated officials once tried "to drive [the zaddik] out of the city and to abolish his *minyan*...." They schemed how "to break the bonds of love between them and the Lord, for they had established a separate place to pray and study...." *"For my own eyes have seen"* it. Because of the unrelenting severity of persecution, "the Lord is concerned over the honor of the zaddikim more than over His own honor, that they should not exclaim: 'There is neither justice nor Judge!' "[71]

The humility of the zaddik, his concern for the people and his closeness to God allowed him to withstand persecution, for "when a man cleaves to Him whose Name is blessed, no fear of men or mockery will reach him. But this is not true of him who descends from his rung of *devekut*; for then he becomes ashamed and afraid of mocking men. Experience testifies to this."[72] So long as the zaddik lived in the presence of God and with the fear of God, he need have no fear of men nor of their scorn.

While persecution served to discourage some from following the new group, it also served to strengthen others in their decisions. "When Korah and his company scoffed and mocked Moses, certainly, many Israelites fell away from following the way of *hasidut*, which was the way of Torah and the custom of Moses, for the scoffers mocked them. However, after the earth opened up and swallowed the scoffers, then they realized that a little truth can conquer much falsehood."[73] This is a message for "all generations: Do not follow the multitude to do evil, but follow the single man who follows the path of truth, and stands against the many."[74] Thus, though he may at times become discouraged by it, humiliation does not destroy the zaddik. To the contrary, what was said of Israel in Egypt can be said of him: " 'When they afflicted them, to humble them, the more did they multiply.' He who is despised is in reality exalted. Thus, because of their humiliation, the zaddikim rose to even greater heights...."[75]

The zaddik must be strong in the midst of the opposition and persecution he may encounter. He must be certain of himself and able to withstand whatever attacks are leveled against him. It may sometimes happen that unbounded humility can be a handicap. Too much humility can be a danger to any man, for man is a creature composed of heaven and earth; if he bows too often and too low toward the earth, he may forget to lift his head to the heavens, as the Baal Shem Tov testified. "I heard from my teacher [the Baal Shem] that too much humility removes a man from the service of the Lord."[76] This is a danger which every man faces. But it is a greater danger to the zaddik since his task is greater. Thus for him there is not only the danger of too much pride, but also that of too much humility.[77]

The zaddik must be humble yet proud, meek yet strong. He must be "like Moses our teacher (peace be to him) of whom it is written: 'And the man Moses was very humble.' He was a brave and powerful man, even though he was humble and meek... for the humble man is really the mighty man."[78] "Because Moses was the most humble of all men, he merited ascending on high, as it is written, 'and Moses went up to God.' However, the Holy One, blessed be He, desires to make it known that *occasionally it is necessary for the zaddik to seize the way of pride*."[79] There are times when the people tend to take advantage of their leaders. The leaders, therefore, must be strong from within and from without when they are the object of scorn, and at such times the power of pride may be an asset and not a liability. "If one is in the category of 'men,' such as the Men of the Great Synagogue, then pride is fitting for him, for it is necessary to lead the people thus, *that he [the leader] not become as something to be trampled upon*."[80] There are times when he must act with pride "in relation to the people."[81]

The natural need of the leader of the people to occasionally display that dignity of authority which is akin to pride, does not mean that the zaddik must adopt this quality as central to his personality. Still, since the position of the zaddik is one of leadership, and leadership often requires a proud demeanor, how can the zaddik remain humble? The answer is clear: Even though it may be necessary for the zaddik to *seem* proud in the way he conducts himself in order to gain the respect of the people, yet, *in his heart*, he remains humble. "Inwardly he must be humble, while outwardly he may conduct himself with pride."[82]

"There is no people without a king and Moses was the king in Israel. 'Moses took the bones [*atzemot*] of Joseph with him' (Ex. 13:19). That is, he took the essence [*atzmut*] and character of Joseph with him, to be a garment of royalty for him, outwardly, in order to lead the people. But, inwardly, Moses was meek above all men, for he humbled himself."[83] "I heard an explanation of the verse of Psalms, 'The Lord reigns; He is clothed in pride' (Ps. 93:1). [How can it be written in Scriptures that God 'is clothed in pride,'] since pride is a discreditable quality? Therefore he [the Baal Shem Tov] explained that the clothing of pride is necessary in ruling the kingdom."[84] Rabbi Moshe Hayim Ephraim, the grandson of the Besht, adds to this: "I heard in the name of my grandfather and master an explanation of the verse 'The Lord reigns; He is clothed in pride.' He asked, 'Is it not written: "In every place where you find the greatness of the Holy One, blessed be He, there you find His lowliness?"[85] But where is His lowliness indicated in that verse?' The answer, he said, is this: 'The Lord reigns; He is clothed in pride.' That is, only the *clothing* is pride, but, in truth, within Him (if you can so speak) you find His humility."[86]

A better understanding of the zaddik's relation to the people follows from this discussion. For while humility is the mold in which he is shaped, allowing him to feel that concern which leads him out beyond himself and down to the people, one qualification is necessary. He must not possess the kind of humility which brings him to self-abasement, inaction or weakness. Furthermore, as a ruler—for the zaddik is the ruler of the people just as Joseph or Moses were in their age—it is sometimes necessary to retain an aspect of dignity and authority which resembles pride. But this is only an outward appearance, a "garment" which the ruler must wear in his office; deep within him is humbleness of heart, gentleness of soul and meekness of spirit.

THE ZADDIK'S CONCERN FOR THE POVERTY OF THE PEOPLE

The concern of the zaddik is again expressed in his sympathy for the poverty of the people. He knows their misery. "Because of the pressure of the time, the people are caught [in the net of searching] for a livelihood and bread.... Consequently, Torah and prayer lie in the corner with no one to care for them."[87] "In the past the *yetzer hara* endeavored only to drive people out of the future world. But now it has acquired a certain cunning and drives them from both the present and the future worlds. The burden of making a living permits no rest in this world day or night; therefore, since there is no time to devote to matters of the future world [Torah and prayer], the poor are driven out from both worlds."[88] "The source of causeless hatred is poverty."[89]

The zaddik does not condemn such people. He neither ignores them nor expects the impossible from them. Rather, he tries to understand their plight and to help them, "removing worry and anxiety, which is the source of all *kelipot*" and bringing joy to them. "Even if you yearn for Torah and the service of the Lord, you should nevertheless join yourself with... the poor of your people... those who are poor in spirit... for they are overburdened, resting neither day nor night in the task of providing a livelihood. *You must not condemn them because they do not act as you do, but rather should you give praise and thanks to Him whose Name is blessed, that He has bestowed more light upon you*" so that you might illumine their way and lead them out of their darkness.[91]

THE ZADDIK'S INSIGHT INTO THE PEOPLE'S SITUATION AS REFLECTED IN THE PRINCIPLES OF FREE WILL AND "RUNG"

When the zaddik "goes out to do battle,"[92] to win over the people, he must not demand the impossible from them nor be impatient or belligerent, but instead must try to understand their predicament and slowly lead them in the right direction. He relies always on the freely rendered decision of the individual. "When you [the zaddik] see the common people in captivity [of the Evil Desire] and want to bring them close to the service of the Lord, do not urge them to accept *hasidut*, the wholly pious way, since they were until now completely free from piety, and you may overburden them with the yoke of service."[93] Do not insist on complete devotion, complete inward purity or even the highest of motives from such a person, at the beginning. If necessary, let their service be, at first, "not for its own sake. For the *power of decision is his*, whether he will act without integrity, yearn for material desires and 'beautify' himself with Torah and mitzvot in order that others may admire him. But in the end, the upright path will be clear to him, and *he will choose [to serve God] for its own sake*."[94] Then desire for pleasure and pride will vanish "and what was in his mind until now—base and foreign motives and 'speaking with a double heart'—will disappear. Then [his words will all be] for the sake of heaven, inwardly and outwardly the same; his mouth and his heart will be joined, which is a *yihud* of the Holy One, blessed be He.... As it is written in the Zohar: '*Adonai* in heart and the *Shem Hameforash* in mouth,' and just as his heart and his mouth are the same so are the two names of the Lord."[95]

This remarkable quotation reflects the mature attitude toward the people which had evidently been reached. Such an attitude does not betray a hasty decision whereby the zaddik is sent out to conquer, come what may, but the wise counsel of one who knows the workings of the human heart and the inner machinery of society. The selflessness of the zaddik which flowed into concern for the people made him sensitive to their needs and hurts, but it did not take on the kind of emotional abundance that sometimes prejudices good judgment. Love for the people manifested itself in an understanding heart which comprehended the situation of the people and the possibilities which existed for helping them. In the above quotation there can be discerned two principles which are central to the zaddik's relationship to the people. One is the belief in the importance of free will, and the second is the conviction that each man dwells on his own "rung" of existence. We will first treat the principle of free will.

The belief in freedom of choice lies deep within the thought of Rabbi Yaakov Yosef. "Creation was so intended that free will should be given to man to do good or evil.... Therefore it was necessary for there to be both a Jacob and an Esau in the world."[96] Indeed, man's freedom affects him more than he thinks. Man has "the choice to perform evil deeds or good deeds... and even the upper worlds depend upon the deeds of the lower worlds."[97] The choice is put into the hand of man to stir up "above" through his stirring "below." From this belief in man's free nature it follows that the people must not be forced into a new way of life, but be allowed to make their own decision. Therefore not only the words of the zaddik are important, to convince, but likewise his life, to exemplify.

The second principle involved is that of *madregah*, or rung. We shall not attempt a complete study of this principle here, but limit ourselves to its significance for the zaddik-people relationship. The soul of every man stands upon a special rung, some higher, some lower, and it is the duty of man to serve God from the particular rung upon which he stands. "Man is able to stand upon his own particular station, for on whatever rung he may be, there is need for him. This is an important principle. The wise man will understand."[98] The zaddik did understand and taught each man to serve God as he was, that he could find God and serve Him in whatever station of life he might find himself. " 'It is not in heaven that thou shouldst say: "Who shall go up for us to heaven, and bring it unto us and make us to hear it that we may do it?... But the word is very nigh unto you, in your mouth and in your heart, that thou mayest do it" ' (Deut. 30:11-14). I have explained this passage as follows: Man should not say, 'If I were in a city of righteous men, devoted to heaven, then I would be able to serve God....' For 'the word is very nigh unto you,' that is, *from whatever rung you are on, you are able to serve the Lord,* for everything resides within the *Shechinah.*"[99]

Related to the principle of "rung" is the importance given to the words from the Book of Proverbs, "In all thy ways know Him" (Prov. 3:6). These words can be considered almost as a motto for the entire hasidic movement. Hasidism taught that there is no area of life in which God cannot be served, that there is no final division between the holy and the profane. There is a holy and there is a profane, of course, but their independence must never be considered conclusive. It is the task of man to overcome this division, to raise up all of life to God, to interpenetrate the profane with the holy, to hallow the everyday, to know and serve God in all of our ways. It follows from this that every man, regardless of his station, his learning or his trade, can serve God. He can serve God because all of life—buying merchandise, speaking with one's neighbor, eating and drinking—all become opportunities to hallow: to buy in such a fashion, to speak in such a fashion, to eat in such a fashion that this buying and speaking and eating—seemingly profane acts—become holy acts, because they are hallowed acts. And only man can hallow. A disciple approached a zaddik and asked him what was the best way he could serve God. He expected to be told, prayer or Torah. But, instead, the zaddik told him that he could serve God best with whatever he was doing at the moment.

God can be served from any rung, but this does not mean that man should not strive to ascend from the rung upon which he stands to a higher one. "There are different rungs for each man according to his nature and his faith, and no man must feel that he cannot serve on his rung, for from the very rung upon which he is located, he should join himself to the world of many rungs, all of which are the limbs of the community of Israel. From there he should pray and God will be with him and raise him."[100] This rise must not be a sudden one, however; it must proceed slowly and gradually. "It is necessary to begin from the bottom upward, leaving out no rung, for if one begins at the bottom and rises from rung to rung, gradually, then he can add to his wholeness."[101] But "if he steps two or three rungs at a time, he may fall, God forbid."[102] If one "tries to seize hold immediately upon spiritual perfection (*shelemut* and *hasidut*), he may fail completely. Not only will he not add to his *shelemut*, but he may even lose what he had already achieved."[103] "I heard from the rabbi and preacher, Menahem, a parable explaining the passage, 'Your walking should be slow.' Two rich brothers lost their fortune. One regained it gradually, the other immediately. The difference was that the former enjoyed great pleasures at each step which the latter did not. Furthermore, if the first fell again, he would know how to slowly reascend each rung, which would not be true of the second."[104]

Since men are composed of different natures and reside on different rungs, each man must be careful not to go beyond his potentiality: Danger threatens when too much is expected. "I heard from my teacher the following explanation of the passage, 'Many acted like Rabbi Shimon ben Yohai, but few succeeded:'[105] it is a general rule regarding each of the three pillars of the world, Torah, prayer and good deeds, that a man should not go beyond his own rung, lest he fail completely...."[106] "The zaddik should lead the common people with true understanding... in a manner conforming with nature, that they do not stumble from their rung.... But he who wants to lift them above their rung may upset them altogether.... *For one should not be overly strict with the people....* This is not the case with the select, the exalted ones, who are few,"[107] who go beyond nature.[108]

This difference in standards may sometimes appear to be a paradox, for, since men inhabit different rungs, it follows that their standards must likewise be different. What is beneficial and should be encouraged for those on a lower rung may be detrimental and should be opposed for those on a higher rung. Scripture tells us that while the ashes of the red heifer were used by the priest to purify those of the people who had become impure, these same ashes rendered the priest himself impure! A paradox! But the ancient mystery had its contemporary counterpart. " 'The red heifer purifies the impure,' that is, the simple people, 'and makes impure the pure,' that is, the faithful ones of Israel."[109] What this statement, seen in its context, means is that the common people may be permitted to study the Torah and fulfill the mitzvot even though it be for bad motives, as the Talmud says, "By all means let a man engage himself in the study of Torah and in good deeds, even if not for its own sake; because through the work of a selfish purpose, he will eventually arrive at observing it for its own sake."[110] Thus the selfish purpose or bad motive, in the case of the simple people, serves "to purify the impure," leading them to serve God eventually for the proper motive. But in the case of the learned and pious it is just the reverse. The study of Torah and the performance of the mitzvot which are carried out for base motives—for pride, vainglory and the like—serve to destroy such a man and must by no means be tolerated. They "make impure the pure."

Some of Rabbi Yaakov Yosef's contemporaries misunderstood the harsh criticism he directed toward the Torah study of his time as a falling away from the traditional emphasis on the study of Torah, and attacked him because of this. They failed to perceive that his sharp words were addressed exclusively to the learned class, to the scholars and rabbis, from whom he demanded inward dedication as well as outward learning and held the latter achievement up to the bitterest scorn if the former virtue was lacking. Indeed, he even went so far, in some cases, as to advise them to cease studying until they had purified themselves.[111] But this harsh criticism, this bitter scorn and these same sharp words did not at all apply to the common people whom he urged to study Torah, whatever the reason may be. It was a double standard which he employed and can only be properly understood in terms of his principle of "rung."

This double standard which applies to different classes of people and which may appear paradoxical at first, actually reflects a profound understanding of the human situation and served to bring near those who were remote and maintain the nearness of those who had already arrived. The zaddik is told to have patience with the people, bearing in mind constantly that his task is to meet the people as they are and lead them on, somewhat like the Almighty Himself. "It is the custom of a father to teach the child to walk between his legs, and when he is able to walk by himself, then the father releases him that he might walk without help. So it is with the service of God. At the beginning the Holy One, blessed be He, helps a man, holding his hand. Then he becomes inflamed with fervor, and God lets him go that he might walk by himself."[112]

The zaddik's constant awareness of the people, his willingness to undergo persecution for their sake, his sympathy for their economic predicament and his insight into their human situation as reflected in the principles of free will and of "rung" are all mainfestations of his concern for the people. With this preliminary examination behind us, we are better prepared to enter into a detailed discussion of that manifestation of this concern which was its most valuable expression and which is most central to the character of the zaddik—his descent to the people.

CHAPTER 8

The Descent of the Zaddik (continued)

ORIGINS OF THE DOCTRINE OF DESCENT

The hasidic doctrine of the descent of the zaddik has its origins in the earlier teachings of Jewish mysticism. While the similarities are striking, the differences, as we shall see, are decisive.

According to Lurianic Kabbalah, the harmony which once existed in the universe was disrupted by *shevirat hakelim*, the "breaking of the vessels" which contained the divine light of grace. As a result of this "breaking of the vessels," the *Shechinah* was cast into exile and part of the divine light flowed downward and entered into the cosmological process. Thus sparks from the divine light are to be found in all aspects of creation. But these sparks, which yearn to reunite with their source, are mixed now with the evil elements that surround and imprison them with isolating shells called *kelipot*. The purpose of all existence, therefore, is to restore the original harmony which was the goal of creation and reintegrate the original whole. This is the meaning of redemption. The hebrew term for it is *tikkun*. Man has the power to help in the great process of *tikkun*. He is able through *kavannot*—special types of mystical intention which he brings to his prayers and his deeds—to liberate the imprisoned sparks and rejoin them to their source. Thus will the *Shechinah* be returned, a divine outpouring will descend from on high in the form of the messiah, and man and the world be redeemed.

Rabbi Yaakov Yosef speaks of sparks of holiness which even the evil man possesses and of the duty of the zaddik who, by liberating these sparks, raises that man. "There is no man so wicked that thoughts of repentance do not come to him each day."[1] With these words his master the Baal Shem explained the Mishnah: "Every day a heavenly voice resounds from Mount Horeb."[2] The zaddik is sent to those who dwell in darkness, but in whom sparks of the divine light still are hidden, to draw them out of the pit. This is his task and his genius. "It is well known that the goal of everything—of all our labors in Torah and prayer, and our *kavannot* in eating and in the performance of other mitzvot—is to redeem the sparks of holiness from the depths of the *kelipot*. An example of this *in the affairs of men* is the raising of the man of matter to the rung of the man of spirit.... In order to raise a lower rung to a higher one it is necessary that he [the zaddik] join himself to that lower rung; only then he will be able to raise those who dwell upon it."[3]

The Lurianic doctrine of the redemption of the sparks provided the idealogical mold out of which the hasidic teaching of the zaddik's descent was fashioned. What happened in Hasidism was that those aspects of Kabbalah which were related most directly to the affairs of men—both in relation to God and in relation to one's fellow man—were seized upon and developed with a profundity and a richness that is to be marveled at. The "descent of the zaddik" is an example of this. In the above quotation from Rabbi Yaakov Yosef, it is important to note how he first repeats the kabbalistic doctrine of the redemption of the sparks much as it was repeated in countless books before him. But after he has stated the doctrine in its classical form, he turns his attention to what interests him—"an example of this in the affairs of men"—raising man out of the pit of temptation and transgression. Mystical *kavannot* which sometimes border on the magical are not the goal, but the leader's going down to the rung of the people and raising them. Thus a purely spiritual doctrine was transformed by Hasidism into a far-reaching social-religious program. The hasidic movement was, in Buber's pregnant phrase, "Kabbalah become ethos."

In Hasidism, writes Gershom Scholem, "Kabbalism appears no longer in a theosophical guise, or to be more exact, theosophy with all its complicated theories, if it is not entirely dropped, is at least no longer the focal point of the religious consciousness. Where it continues to play a prominent part... it is bound up with some belated offshoot of the older Kabbalah within the framework of Hasidism. What has really become important is the direction, the mysticism of the personal life. Almost all the Kabbalistic ideas are now placed in relation to values peculiar to the individual life, and those which are not remain empty and ineffective. Hasidism is practical mysticism at its highest."

A further example of the similarity and the difference between the two teachings, the Hasidic and the older Jewish mysticism, can be found by comparing a passage from the Zohar with Rabbi Yaakov Yosef's comment on the same passage:

The Zohar: "'Whatsoever thy hand findeth to do, do it with all thy might, for there is no work, nor device, nor knowledge, nor wisdom, in Sheol, whither thou goest' (Eccl. 9:10). Do all men go down to Sheol? Yes, but they come up again at once, as it is written, 'He bringeth down to Sheol and bringeth up' (I Sam. 2:6); save for those sinners who never harbored thoughts of repentance who go down and do not come up. *Even the completely righteous (the zaddikim) go down there.* Why do they descend there? In order to bring up certain sinners. Who are they? Those who thought of repenting in this world, but were not able to do so before they departed from it. The zaddikim go down to Gehinnom, to the sinners who are in Sheol, and bring them up from there."[4]

Rabbi Yaakov Yosef's comment: "It seems to me that I heard in the name of the rabbi and preacher from Bar the following interpretation of the verse 'Those who pass through the valley of weeping...' (Ps. 84:7). Just as the zaddik descends to the doors of Gehinnom to bring up the souls of the wicked who, because of him, had previously harbored thoughts of repentance; so it is that *in this world* every day or at certain times the zaddik descends from his rung in order to join himself with those lesser in degree... for when he again ascends to his rung, he brings them up as well. But it is only possible for one to ascend with him if he too joins himself to the zaddik, for he who does not wish to join himself to him surely will not ascend with him. Thus the Talmud teaches, 'He who despises a scholar has no remedy for his wounds.' "[5]

The difference which strikes us immediately between the passage from the Zohar and that quoted in the name of Rabbi Mendel of Bar, which was accepted, developed and taught by Yaakov Yosef, is *"a change of the place of action from Gehinnom to this world."*[6] According to the passage from the Zohar, before the soul of the zaddik rises to paradise, it must first go down to Gehinnom in order to bring up the souls of some of the sinners. While this must have been a source for the later teaching, how different they are. The descent of the soul of the zaddik as described in the Zohar is a purely spiritual activity, portraying the movement of the zaddik's soul after death down to Gehinnom before rising to Paradise. All this transpires in the world of spirit. But the quotation of Rabbi Mendel teaches something altogether different. Here the action changes to the affairs of men, to what goes on, as he says, "in this world." Gehinnom is no longer stituated in the lower recesses of the universe, a cosmological location, but now assumes a human garb in earthly form, "for man is called a world-in-miniature and he posseses within himself Paradise and Gehinnom... and just as the zaddik passes by the door of Gehinnom in order to raise souls, so there is a parallel in this world."[7] It is "the parallel in this world" which opens up under the pen of our author into a richly detailed doctrine which determined in large measure the nature as well as the ultimate destiny of the zaddik.

THE PARABLE OF THE KING'S SON

As Abraham is the symbol *in history* of the zaddik who descends to the people, so the story of the lost prince who is returned to his father is the symbol *in parable*. This story, told and retold, altered and transfigured, alluded to and hinted at, becomes in many ways the single most important image in understanding the zaddik's task with the people. This simple tale, though its meaning seems, at first reading, quite obvious, was made the object of detailed exposition and analysis by Yaakov Yosef. Every aspect of it was understood to have a special significance, the implications of which are, therefore, not always apparent.

The parable: A king sent his only son away from the royal palace to a village so that he might afterward yearn all the more for the table of his father. Because of his foolishness, the prince mingled with the strangers in the village, learned their ways and, after a time, forgot the royal pleasures. The king sent one of his nobles after the prince to bring him back, but he failed. Another was sent, and then another and another, but none succeeded. At last, one of the nobles discovered the secret. He removed his elegant clothing and put on plain clothes like those of the villagers, in order that he might have something in common with the prince and enter into conversation with him. He succeeded, and returned him to his father.[8]

The apparent meaning of this parable is clear. The son whom the king—the King of kings—has sent away is the man who has turned from the ways of the Lord and fallen in with men of low repute. He should desire to return to the way of righteousness, but instead becomes sunk in the life around him and forgets what he should desire. In a sense, every man's story is contained in this parable. Man is put in the world, away from His Father in heaven, amidst temptation and evil so that he might distinguish between good and evil, and yearn all the more for the table of his Father, the King. Life is a trial in which man is tested that he might taste both good and evil, and desire the good. But there are some, weaker than others, who, instead of yearning for the holy and the good, from which they stemmed and to which they should strive to return, become lost in the treachery of worldly living. To save them, the King sends his nobles.[9] The first nobles sent are the rabbis, whose task is to lead the wayward son back to his father. They fail because they remain aloof, having no way of coming close to the prince. The last noble is the zaddik who succeeds because he goes down to the level of the prince in the village. He wears his clothes, speaks his language, and wins the confidence of the prince, so that his helpful words are finally heeded. He neither forgets his task nor becomes lost in the village life of the prince. But in order to raise him, he must first himself descend. *Aliyah tzrichah yeridah*, "Ascent requires descent." "Thus Caleb joined himself to the spies, saying that he agreed with them, so that in the end, he was able to silence them."[10] "It is necessary for one to descend from his rung to raise up him who dwells in the valley, for, except he does this, it is not possible to raise him."[11] The zaddik is compared to a broom: it sweeps clean, but in doing so it cannot avoid coming in contact with dirt.

The message of this classic parable then is that the zaddik must descend to the people in order to raise them.

"It is not given to every man,"[12] nor even to every leader to act as the zaddik does. Not every leader has the strength, the humility and the concern to go down to the level of the lost prince, to live his life outwardly while remaining inwardly bound up with God. "There are seventy peoples and the people of Israel; few are those who are close to the oneness of God. And among the people of Israel there are many who do the mitzvot for show and fame, and study Torah in a like manner; few are those who are truly devout. The closer one comes to the oneness of God, the fewer there are."[13] "It seems to me that this is the explanation of the passage, 'I have seen the exalted ones and they are few.'[14] It refers to one who is able to raise himself along with his generation, causing them, through prayer or Musar to cleave to Him Who is blessed: men such as this are few.''[15]

The above parable about the lost prince distinguished between two kinds of leaders while the following parable, somewhat similar in nature, delineates three kinds. "There is the tale of a king who lost a precious stone which fell into the depths of the sea. Because of his love for the precious stone, he sent his three sons to the sea's bottom to bring up the gem. Each of these sons represents a different type of leader. First, the wise one who struggles, finds the stone and returns it to his father in peace. Second, the one who says: 'Let it come out of the sea by itself.' And the third, who remains down in the depths of the sea.''[16] With the third type we shall deal later, but the first two are clearly identical with the nobles in the parable of the lost prince. Both are sent by the king, both are leaders of the people. But here the resemblance ends. One is aloof and distant, never coming into real contact with the problem. His attitude is one of contempt: "Let the fallen Jew, who is a precious stone which his Father in heaven dropped, rise from his ignorance, transgression, and anxiety by himself[33] —the attitude of contempt of Noah. The other son succeeds not because of miracles, but through laborious effort, overcoming obstacles and working with great patience; diving to the bottom of the sea, living with the villagers, descending below his rung in order to return to God what is precious and fallen—the attitude of concern of Abraham.

Rabbi Levi Yitzhak of Berditchev, a disciple of the Maggid of Mezritch, makes a striking observation. "Why did the Lord create this situation—that the zaddik should fall from his rung? Would it not be better for the zaddik always to remain in his station, serving the Lord (may He be blessed) with

perfect wisdom and loving Him with perfect love? The Baal
Shem Tov (may his memory be for a blessing) and my master
zaddik, Dov Baer, explained this: from the zaddik's fall and
his strengthening himself and returning to his first strength,
new souls are made. *One who intends to raise his friend from the
mire and refuse, must himself go down to that mire and refuse, in order
to bring him up.*"[17]

THE PROBLEM OF EVIL

One would think that the scholar, immersed in prayer and
Torah, who remains cloistered in his study away from the
people and far from worldly temptation, would serve God better
than the one who disturbs his study and his contemplation
to go out and down to the people. Such is not the case, for
the problem of the zaddik and the people is, in a sense, a part
of the problem of evil, and evil must not be avoided by the
zaddik. Evil must be met and conquered in a manner which
involves both deception and inner strength. But this manner
of action is not permitted to every man, not even to every
leader.

It is a fundamental principle that there are two different ways in
the service of the Lord. One way is for a man to first purify his
thoughts and afterward perform the mitzvah of prayer or study,
so that it might be clean and pure, without ulterior motives....
There is, however, a second way, more profound than the first. The
Mishnah in *Avot* says: "Do not say, 'When I am free I shall study.'
Perhaps you will not be free."[18] This means: When I am free from
strange thoughts I shall study, but not now when I am filled with
strange thoughts. Do not say this, for perhaps you will not be free
and your study and prayer will be interrupted.... "Let a man
engage in Torah and mitzvot for ulterior motives, for from this he
may come to engage in them for true motives...." It follows from

this that one must deceive the *yetzer hara,* attaching oneself to it at first, but afterward becoming strong as a lion and acting sincerely... as it is written, "Your brother came in guile, and hath taken away thy blessing" (Gen. 27:35). Even though there is greater danger in entering the *galut* of the *yetzer hara* and joining oneself with it—for who knows which side will prevail or if one will be able to separate himself from it afterward... in order to ascend —nevertheless, he should understand that he has the power to ascend and should pray to the Lord to help him overcome the *yetzer hara.* This second way, then, is superior to the first. Consider this well, for it is the secret of "coming in and going out," which is a higher state than never having "come in" at all.[19]

There are two paths for the zaddik, the servant of the Lord: one is to seclude himself and worship the Lord without the *yetzer hara;* the other is to serve the Lord with the *yetzer hara....* When a man is about to commit a sin, God forbid, or is tempted by the evil impulse to physical pleasures and, afterward, because of the glory of the Lord and his awe of Him, he controls his passion and turns to the way of the Lord, behold, he subdues the left pillar with the right pillar and a complete *yihud* is achieved on high. This means that *the goal of the zaddik who serves the Lord with the* yetzer hara [i.e. *with the fallen people] is greater than the one who worships him simply, without the* yetzer hara. The latter is concerned with the right pillar alone, while the other zaddik unites all three pillars through the middle pillar....[20]

This statement is a clear declaration of a basic motive which runs throughout the thinking of Yaakov Yosef: *the radical conquest of all of life.* It is expressed here in kabbalistic terminology in which the left and right pillars are united by the mediating force of the middle pillar. Applying this to human society the zaddik serves God both with Torah and prayer, and with those who have fallen away from the service of God. This is a greater achievement than simply dividing the two and identifying himself with the right pillar, for the element of evil is present in the world, uncontrolled, running rampant. Not to escape evil, but to conquer it is the attitude which Yaakov Yosef adopts, an ancient Jewish attitude which denies both the flight from evil and the submission to it. To be in the world, but a little above it, is the goal. Not to escape the evil thought or the evil man, but to take issue with them both, and turn them to the Lord.[21]

Though the zaddik may at first be repulsed when he descends to raise those who have transgressed, he persists in his task. He leaves the security of his studies for the perils of the "world," but this does not mean that his mission is applauded or even accepted by those whom he seeks to help. On the contrary, it may happen that "the sinners do not join themselves to the zaddikim so that they might be raised, for they mock the learned and think it of little consequence that they be raised.... But the zaddikim must be as the disciples of Aaron, loving the people and drawing them to Torah, as did Aaron.... The wicked act as if they are ignorant of their wickedness, and so Aaron had to join himself to the wicked, until they were ashamed and cried out: 'Woe unto us!' "[22]

THE PARADOX: TO BE AMONG THE PEOPLE, YET IN THE PRESENCE OF GOD

The descent is fraught with peril, but there is yet a way. "When Jacob went out from Beer Sheba and dwelt in Haran... he was among the counsel of the wicked, as was Caleb in his day, and among sinners, as was the prophet Samuel in his day, and among scoffers where danger threatened. The Hebrew letters in the name Haran (*h r n*) imply sinners (*hataim*), evildoers (*reshaim*), and adulterers (*noafim*), among whom Jacob dwelled. So that he not be caught in their snare, he prayed to the Lord, and was delivered. He spent the night there among the wicked whose deeds are dark as night, among the sinners and scoffers who are ignorant of Torah. He lay himself down to sleep and dreamed of the ladder.... For the 'complete man' is called a ladder, fixed in the earth among evildoers, sinners and scoffers, but, nevertheless, whose head and thoughts reach the heavens, because his heart is toward heaven."[23]

"When a [zaddik] is on a lofty rung—for example, when he secludes himself with his Creator—nothing foreign can approach him, for he is immersed in the Torah. Because of this, he is delivered from the *yetzer hara*, bad thoughts and the like, for the Torah is an antidote for the *yetzer hara*. However, he knows that afterward he must depart from his book and go into the midst of the city to engage in business or for some other matter, and, as soon as he departs from his book, 'sin croucheth at the door' (Gen. 4:7). For in the city 'the well is empty of the water of Torah and filled with snakes and scorpions'[24] of slander, idleness, looking at women and the like.... What can he do to be delivered from sin? He must bind himself to God while still in seclusion, so that *the four letters of the divine name are before his eyes even when he walks among men*, as it says, 'I shall set the Lord before me at *all* times' (Ps. 16:8). *This is a fundamental principle for zaddikim.* And this is what was revealed to our father Jacob [in his dream], a ladder fixed in the earth whose head reached the heavens, which means—even when the zaddik is fixed in the earth, with the lowly, common people of the earth, among scoffers and gossips and the like, nevertheless his head, his thoughts, reach the heavens, joining his thoughts to his Creator. For the Divine Name is before him. In this manner, the angels of the Lord—those who come into this world to do the bidding of the Lord [the zaddikim]—are called messengers of the Lord (*malach* means both "angel" and "messenger") and ascend the ladder"[25] of the world.

"Jacob's ladder, according to the rabbis, had four rungs. And why precisely four rungs? In the book *Olelot Efrayim* it is explained that this world is a preparation or 'ladder' by which to mount to the world to come. But it seems to me [Rabbi Yaakov Yosef] that the ladder is needed *in this very world,* that men might rise from rung to rung.... The four rungs of the ladder are the four letters of God's name" which when kept before the mind's eye assure one of rising upon the ladder of life, and not falling.[26]

Some fail to understand why the zaddik emerges from holy seclusion and enters into mundane affairs of the world. They must be taught that it is false to believe one can serve God only in a formal manner; the reverse may at times be the case. " 'The Merciful One desires the heart....' While one who is occupied with worldly affairs may cleave to the Lord with his mind and heart, which is complete worship of the Lord, another who is occupied with Torah or prayer, may not cleave to the Lord with his mind and heart, which is rebellion against God, as it is written, 'They draw near me with their mouth and honor me with their lips, but their heart is far from me' (Isa. 29:13).... There are some who when they see the pious engaged in worldly affairs (like the patriarchs sowing seed, etc.), criticize them unjustly.... *Woe to such people who see but do not know what they see, for they look only upon the outward actions and not the inward intention. The zaddikim perform all their actions for a higher purpose.*"[27]

All of life is a battle against the *yetzer hara* which stalks man at every turn of the road. It is a battle no man can avoid. The zaddik must be victorious in this battle, and then lead others to victory. The zaddik can do this because he is able to sense the presence of God in the midst of daily living. It is his constant awareness of God's presence which gives him strength to teach others to feel the nearness of God, for only His presence can help them. He fights for them, if only they permit him. This is the meaning given to a passage from Scripture.

Scripture: "When thou goest forth to do battle against thine enemies and seest horses and chariots and a people more than thou, thou shalt not be afraid of them; for the Lord, thy God, is with thee, Who brought thee up out of the land of Egypt. And it shall be, when ye draw nigh unto battle, that the priest shall approach and speak unto the people, and shall say unto them: 'Hear, O Israel, ye draw nigh this day unto battle against your enemies; let not your heart be faint; fear not; nor be alarmed, neither be ye affrighted at them; for the Lord your God is He that goeth with you to fight for you against your enemies, to save you" (Deut. 20:1-4).

The interpretation: "'When you draw nigh unto battle'; that is, when you go out from the study of Torah to the city to undertake your business, immediately there is the battle with the *yetzer hara*, who tries to entice you with glancing at women, gossip, cynicism and the like. Therefore you should not trust in the Torah which you have just learned for protection from the *yetzer hara*. Rather, 'the priest [the zaddik] shall approach and speak unto the people,' for he is a priest anointed for battle [i.e., he is 'anointed' because he keeps the name of God before him].... 'For the Lord your God is He that goeth with you to fight for you.' This refers to the name of God which always goes with him, for *it is the nature of the zaddik to fulfill the verse, 'I have set the Lord before me at all times'—he will fight for you to save you.'* "[28] It is God's presence which permits the zaddik to give comfort and assurance to the people. They need not fear, for the Lord is close to the zaddik and through him will fight for them also.

One of the principal characteristics of the zaddik is to live in the presence of God even when he leaves his seclusion and moves about in the affairs of the world. "First he is alone with God, binding and cleaving himself to the Lord before he goes out into the midst of the city.... But even afterward when he mingles with the people, he is not separated from *devekut* with God.... *For when he is among the common people in the midst of the city, he must also be a zaddik.*"[29] Indeed it is his constant cleaving to God which gives him the right to be a leader.[30] Without *devekut* he cannot be a zaddik. This is the meaning given to the verse "The zaddik liveth by his faith" (Hab. 2:4): "While the zaddik has faith, he liveth; which is not so when faith leaves him."[31] Faith, the Baal Shem taught, is cleaving to God: "*emunah is devekut.*"[32] Only if he possesses faith—which is *devekut*, cleaving to God—does the zaddik possess that manner of life which must be his, the life that permits him to go out and down into the pit of the world and raise those who have fallen. But if he is lacking faith—which is *devekut*, cleaving to God—then it is as if he no longer possesses life. His task, his destiny, his very essence has perished.

Two statements are quoted by our author in the name of Rabbi Nahman Kossover which reveal the inner struggle to achieve God's presence which went on among the zaddikim. "I heard from Rabbi Nahman of Kossover that one should have the name of God engraved before him, even though it does not occur of itself, as a result of the exile of the *Shechinah*. But the Name, Who is blessed, should always be in one's mind, once in this verse, which he can delve into, and again in another verse; until the Name *of itself* is engraved before him."[33] But Rabbi Nahman was not satisfied with such general advice when it came to his own person, for here he employed a remarkable device. "I heard that the hasid, Rabbi Nahman Kossover, paid a fixed sum of money each week to a certain man to remind him, when he was among people, that he should not forget the Name of God before him!"[34]

The zaddik is close to God in *devekut*, but he is at the same time close to the people. "Again we see," writes Gershom Scholem, "the ancient paradox of solitude and communion. He who has attained the highest degree of spiritual solitude, who is capable of being alone with God, is the true center of the community, because he has reached the stage at which true communion becomes possible.... To live among ordinary men and yet be alone with God, to speak profane language and yet draw the strength to live from the source of existence, from the 'upper root' of the soul—that is a paradox which only the mystical devotee is able to realize in his life and which makes him the center of the community of men."[35]

HOW TO SPEAK TO AND PRAY WITH THE PEOPLE

One of the ways in which the "descent of the zaddik" expressed itself was in his ability to speak to the people. While in the market place the zaddik might, for example, engage in conversation with a peddler. To the casual observer this conversation had no apparent significance, but in meeting the simple Jew on his own level, the zaddik, through homely analogies, simple parables and gentle words of reproof, may find a way to unlock the gates to his heart and open the windows of his mind, to turn him from the path of sin and reveal to him a way of righteousness. The power of the word, of the simple tale, is great. Not only are the words of the Torah or the *siddur* holy; any words can be holy—if they are used in the proper way. "I heard that the verse 'In all thy ways know Him' (Prov. 3:6), applies to simple stories, for if by such parables one tries to draw another man close to him, afterward, if he asks him to do a certain mitzvah, he may be ready to do his bidding, because he has already drawn close to him through these simple tales. This is the mystery of the *vav* of the Divine Name bending beneath the *he* of the Divine Name, to raise it, and this is a great *yihud*."[36]

"The rabbi and preacher of the holy community of Bar said that through conversation with the common people one becomes friendly with them and is able to draw them to Torah and mitzvot."[37] For the zaddik to know how to speak to the people, however, is by no means a simple task. The Baal Shem

Tov, we are told, joined himself so firmly to God in *devekut* that he could not join himself to the people at all to talk with them. It was only after Ahijah the prophet (his teacher) showed him certain verses of the Psalms to recite each day that he learned how to speak to the people while all the time remaining bound up with the Almighty. The grandson of the Besht, in the latter's name, divides into two categories those whom the zaddik raises. "There are those whom the zaddik raises through his Torah and prayer, and there are those whom he is only able to raise by conversing with them. This latter case is as the rabbis have explained the verse, 'and its leaf shall not wither' (Ps. 1:3), to mean there is need even for his [the zaddik's] ordinary conversation.[38] Though they seem to be wasted words, in reality the zaddik raises a man through the words he speaks to him."[39] For "even the word which a man speaks in the street must be spoken with fear and love."[40] "The essence of the matter is to realize that He Who is blessed is to be found in every place and every deed. Thus even in *simple stories one should be able to feel the presence of the Creator (may His Name be blessed) just as in one's study and prayer.*"[41] Indeed, "*there are men who can pray while speaking with a friend about plain things.*"[42]

The people were no longer to be in despair of reaching God, for the zaddik reached down to them and showed them the way. He did not engage solely in the narrow legalistic discussion of the scholars and scoff at all those who were not learned enough to partake in such a discussion, but tried to shape a mold which could contain all the people, even those who were not deeply learned. When speaking to the common people he was able to express profound thoughts with plain words in a way they could understand and were subsequently influenced by. A parable used in another connection by a later writer, Rabbi Eliezer Horovitz of Tarnegrad, tells us how the Torah was brought to the people. "A golden vessel encrusted with precious stones, a delight to behold, stood high up on the top of a mountain and, because of the great height, it could not be brought down. Everyone yearned to see it clearly, but because of the great height it was impossible, for the hand of no one could reach it. A wise man came along and in his wisdom, brought it down and set it on the table. Afterward, everyone could take the precious vessel in his hands...."[43]

The zaddik believed that the spoken word was one of the keys which could unlock the treasure-house of the human spirit, banishing despair, overcoming evil and crushing pride. Because of his concern for the people, he went out to them, attempting to break through the barriers which surround each man so that he might raise him out of the dark pit. That he was able to succeed was in some measure due to his mastery of the spoken word, for through parable, story and simple conversation, he was able to bring the Torah to all men. But this mastery of the spoken word meant more than creating an attractive and effective form in which to express one's thoughts. It meant knowing how to fashion each sentence with the gift of the artist of the soul, so that it should not be uttered in vain, a lonely if lovely monologue which reaches only the speaker's ear, but will melt all resistance and force itself into the innermost heart of the listener. The zaddik knew the "situation" of the people: felt their sorrow, their fears, their sufferings; understood their question, their doubts, their ambitions. And it was to this "situation" that he spoke.

Every evening after prayer the Baal Shem went to his room. Two candles were set in front of him and the mysterious Book of Creation put on the table among other books. Then all those who needed his counsel were admitted in a body, and he spoke with them until the eleventh hour.

One evening when the people left, one of them said to the man beside him how much good the words which the Baal Shem had directed to him had done him. But the other told him not to talk such nonsense, that they had entered the room together and from that moment on the master had spoken to no one except himself. A third, who heard this, joined in the conversation with a smile, saying how curious that both were mistaken, for the rabbi had carried on an intimate conversation with him the entire evening. Then a fourth and a fifth made the same claim, and finally all began to talk at once and tell what they had experienced. But the next instant they all fell silent.

Just as there is a way to bring Torah to the people by simplifying its words and applying its meaning to their lives in a manner they can understand, so there is a way of bringing prayer to the people, kindling their souls with the awareness of God's presence and God's concern and God's love. The zaddik separates himself from impure worship and may even establish a new community of prayer, but he does not exclude himself from nor avoid praying with the simple people. In his prayer, as in his Torah, he joins with them to raise them. The Talmud says, " 'Let him who prays cast his eyes downward, but turn his heart upward.'[44] That is, he should cast his eyes down upon and concern himself with the simple folk—for they are 'downward'—to join himself in prayer with them; but during this union he must 'turn his heart upward' in order to raise them... for the center of his prayer should not be for himself, but out of compassion he should join himself to the common people, even though they may not know the meaning of the prayers."[45]

CHAPTER 9

Transgression and danger

THE PARABLE AGAIN: CONCERN IMPLIES INVOLVEMENT

Let us recall the favorite parable of Rabbi Yaakov Yosef about the banished prince, which we referred to before.[1] The prince, you will remember, is dismissed from the palace by his father the king, and, after much wandering, finds himself among common peasants in a small village. Instead of yearning to return to the palace, he gradually forgets his royal youth, learns the evil ways of the peasants and, in the course of time, becomes one of them. The king, anxious for the welfare of his son, sends many nobles to return the prince to the royal palace; but all fail. Until one noble, wiser than the rest, exchanges his costly clothes for the simple garments of the peasant. Thus he wins the confidence of the prince and brings him safely home.[2]

We have already seen that this tale teaches that in order to help the people the zaddik—who is the noble-that-succeeds of the parable—must not remain aloof from them like the proud scholars—who are the nobles-that-fail of the parable—but must descend to their rung. It is necessary to look a bit deeper into the meaning of this story. By virtue of what is the noble able to help the prince? The other nobles were also sent by the king, and they also descend. How does their descent differ from the descent of the one who, at last, succeeds? The answer, of course, is in his *change of clothes*. The others only seem to go down, for, in reality, they remain as they were before. They have been sent by the king, it is true, but they do not take their mission seriously. A wall stands between them and the fallen prince. They have no common denominator. The zaddik, however, has put on the likeness of the people, for the peasant "clothes" which he dons symbolize the life of the people, the transgression of the people. He involves himself in their lives and takes their guilt upon himself. He understands that their guilt is, in part, his guilt as well, since he is to some extent responsible for them, and this becomes the bond which unites them. Only then can he redeem the lost prince, the people of Israel, and return him to the king, who is the King of all kings.

"This is the general principle: 'One who is not himself guilty cannot help to remove the guilt of others....'³ It is impossible to join two opposites except through a third element. So it is that when the leader of the generation who is a perfect man wishes to join himself to the common man, he must find in himself some small transgression, an aspect of worldly sin by means of which a bond can be formed...."⁴ When the zaddik finds within himself such a fault and becomes aware of his real kinship to the others, there is no longer an endless distance between them. They no longer stand separated by an unbridge-able chasm which only stray glances cross, but a bridge leaps the void, joins one to the other and permits passage.

The prophet Hosea had to undergo the consummate pain of being wedded to a harlot before he could truly comprehend the harlotry of his people Israel, the wedded one of God. The sage Hillel said: "Judge not thy neighbor until thou art come into his place."⁵ "How can the zaddik understand anything of the transgressions of the wicked if no glimpse of that trans-gression has crossed his mind?"⁶ "The Baal Shem Tov once remarked to a zaddik who was given to preaching sermons of chastisement: 'What do you know about chastising? You yourself have remained unacquainted with sin all the days of your life, and you have nothing to do with the people around you—how should you know what their sinning is?'"⁷

"Only he who is himself guilty can help remove the guilt of others."⁸

If the people, who are wanting in Torah and weak in faith, have come to transgression—"for the imagination of man is evil from his youth"—then the zaddik must know that the wants and weaknesses of the people are his responsibility and, therefore, his own wants and weaknesses as well. He must understand that the sin he sees in others is in himself too. This is the meaning given to the verse "If you lend [*talveh*] money [*kesef*] to my people, to any poor person among you, thou shalt not be to him as a creditor, neither shall ye lay upon him interest" (Ex. 22:24): "If you yearn [*kosef*] to join yourself [*tillaveh*] and bind yourself to my people, that is, to the common people, to raise them—for they are 'the poor among you'—do not act the 'creditor,' that is, as if he is guilty and you are not. Rather, be like the wise man who learns from all men, for there is an aspect of his guilt in you as well. Only thereby are you able to join yourself to him and raise him with yourself. 'Do not lay upon him interest.'"[9]

Similarly, the following passage from Deuteronomy is explained:

Text: "...thou shalt not defile thy land, which the Lord thy God giveth thee for an inheritance. Thou shalt not see the *hamor*[10] of thy brother or his sheep driven away and hide thyself from them; thou shalt surely return them unto thy brother. And if thy brother be not nigh unto thee, and thou know him not, then thou shalt bring it home to thy house, and it shall be with thee until thy brother inquire for it, and thou shalt return it to him.... And so shalt thou do with every lost thing of thy brother's, which he hath lost and thou hast found; thou mayest not hide thyself" (Deut. 21.23-22.3).

Explanation: "Thou shalt not defile thy land"—that is, the *am ha'aretz*, the people of the land, who are called "*thy* land"—"which the Lord thy God giveth *thee* for an inheritance." "Thou shalt not see the *hamor* [donkey] of thy brother driven away and hide thyself from them" —that is, you, the chosen one [the zaddik] should not see that the common people [*homer*], who are indeed your brothers for there is in you an aspect of them, are driven from the path of righteousness to the path of evil, and then hide yourself from them. You should not hide yourself from them as if all this had no relation to you. For it does. Because of the underlying unity there is an aspect of their transgression in you as well, and, as it were, you [do not simply *see* their transgression, *but*] *are being shown* it with a finger in order that you might feel your own failing. Therefore, good counsel is given: first you must yourself turn to God, that this failing of yours be no longer in you. Then you will return your brother too.

"But if thy brother be not nigh unto thee and thou know him not"—that is, you search yourself to find an aspect of the transgression which you see in your brother, but "you know him not," because you do not find this fault in yourself since he is "not nigh unto you" as your brother, in this sin. "Then thou shalt bring it home to thy house"—that is, you should turn away from all other concerns, seclude yourself in meditation within your house, and "bring it"—the sin which you have seen in your brother—constantly before your eyes.... Until after this self-examination you "find" that he is your brother in that sin, and you turn in repentance from that taint of the sin which is in you. Then you will return him as well.

"And so shalt thou do with every lost thing of thy brother's which he hath lost"—for sin is called a lack or loss—"and you have found,"—that is, have found *in yourself also*. Therefore, "Thou mayest not hide thyself," in order to fulfill the commandment: "Thou shalt love thy neighbor as thyself," which is a great principle of the Torah.[11]

"Only he who is himself guilty can help to remove the guilt of others."

Earlier[12] we mentioned the discussion which took place between Rabbi Yaakov Shimshon of Shpetivka, the defender of Yaakov Yosef, and Rabbi Ezekiel Landau, the famous scholar of Prague who opposed the teachings of the book *Toldot Yaakov Yosef*. According to one authority, this discussion revolved around the problem of the descent and transgression of the zaddik.

If you will ask me, dear reader, behold I say to you that his [Rabbi Landau's] intention [in opposing the teachings of Rabbi Yaakov Yosef's book] was well meant, for he found written in the *Toldot* that the zaddik cannot atone for those who would find shelter in his care unless he descends to their rung, that is, into their wicked deeds. This view was supported by the statement of our sages: "Only he who is himself guilty can help to remove the guilt of others." Now at that time there existed the sect of the wicked one, Yaakov Frank (may the name of the evil one rot!) and Rabbi Landau suspected that perhaps, God forbid, the holy of holies, the author of the book, *Toldot Yaakov Yosef*, was one of them, God forbid, for there are members of the sect who reveal their identity and others who conceal it.

Therefore the *rav*, gaon and zaddik, Rabbi Yaakov Shimshon, the *av bet din* of Shpetivka [attempted to remove Rabbi Landau's suspicions]. He told him that he must have forgotten that which was explained in the Midrash[13] regarding the golden calf. The Holy One, blessed be He, was angered at the incident of the golden calf, as Scripture says: "And the Lord said unto Moses: 'I have seen this people, and, behold, it is a stiff-necked people. Now therefore, let Me alone, that My wrath may wax hot against them, and that I may consume them; and I will make of thee a great nation.'"

But Moses our teacher (peace be to him), the lover of Israel, he who was beloved and trusted, who brought himself into mortal danger for the sake of the community of Israel, wishing to save them from the harsh decree, began to descend to the rung of the sinners and said: "What does it matter to You, O Holy and Awful One, Who is unique in all the world, if they make an image of an ox which eats grass? Will anyone say that *it* has made the earth? Does not everyone thank *Thee*, and praise *Thee*? Does not everyone declare: There is no one holy as the Lord, the Creator of sun, moon and stars and all their hosts? Creator of darkness and light, all exalt Thee, for You are He Who bringeth forth the sun from its place and the moon from its dwelling, giving light to the world and all who dwell therein."

The Holy One, blessed be He, replied to him: "Moses, thou dost err as they do, for surely it [the golden calf] possesses no reality."

Then Moses, he who loves us, the trusted one, our souls' beloved, he who offered his life out of a compassion for Israel which was fixed deep in his heart—for there has not risen another like unto Moses—he had the opportunity to answer that he had sought. He said: "If it [the calf] possesses no reality, then how are the people deserving of punishment?"[14]

Thus Moses made himself appear guilty in order to be able to remove the people's guilt. So it must be for the zaddik.

We have defined the zaddik's descent to the people as an attitude of concern.

But what is the nature of true concern? Can it be produced on order, the result of duty or propriety? It must mean more than simply walking among the people in the market place, chatting with them and possessing intimations of pity and the desire to help, just because that is the proper thing to do. One may be close to the people in the sense that he has forsaken the solitude of his study for the spectacle of the streets, and still remain apart from them, unable to help, to grasp their hand. He is pure and they are impure. How shall he reach them? How shall he hope to understand them, when there is still no bond between them?

True concern, which is the concern of the zaddik, is not the required result of duty, which is no concern at all, but the inevitable consequence of involvement. The zaddik is concerned because he is *involved* in the life of the people. He is included in their life and problems, and can no longer distinguish between their anxieties and his own. The zaddik manifests concern in descending to the people, because "he dons the clothes of the peasant."[15] He puts himself in the place of the sinner in such a manner that he considers himself to be the sinner and the sin which he sees, and wishes to remove his own sin as well.[16] Then, indeed, he not only stands beside the sinner but reaches for his hand. He is able at last to touch it

and to hold it firmly in his grip, ready to begin the long climb
upward, half of his perilous journey completed, for, in the
Zohar's words, "Happy is the one who can grasp the hand of
the guilty."[17]

Gershom Scholem writes that Sabbatai Zevi's conversion to
Islam, the apostasy of the false messiah, "happened to recall
an idea of entirely different historic origin, namely the Lurianic
theory of restitution through 'the uplifting of the sparks....'
This doctrine was capable of being given a turn of which
nobody had thought before Sabbatai Zevi's apostasy, but
which from then on quickly became only too fashionable.
According to its recognized orthodox kabbalistic interpretation,
Israel has been dispersed among the nations in order that
it may gather together the sparks of souls and divine light
which are themselves dispersed and diffused throughout the
world, and through pious acts and prayers 'lift them up' from
their respective prisons. When this process is complete, the
Messiah appears and gathers the last sparks, thereby depriving
the power of evil of the element through which it acts. The
spheres of good and evil, of pure and impure, are from then on
separated for all eternity. The heretical version of this doctrine,
as expounded by Nathan of Gaza, differs from the orthodox
mainly in its conclusions: the attraction of saintliness is not
always sufficient to liberate the sparks from their prisons, the
kelipot, or shells. There are stages of the great process of *tikkun*,
more particularly its last and most difficult ones, when in order
to liberate the hidden sparks from their captivity, or to use
another image, in order to force open the prison door from
within, the Messiah himself must descend into the realm of evil."[18]

"Just as Christianity emerged as the justification of a

crucified messiah, so Sabbatianism originated in the justification of an apostatized messiah. It leads from the vindication of his sinful act as the necessary entrance of the messiah into the realm of evil in order to redeem it, to the adoration of these acts on the part of the people and the desire to imitate them, culminating finally in the devilish doctrine of the 'holiness of sin' as expounded by Jacob Frank and his followers. For Sabbatianism is built upon the tragic paradox of an apostate Savior and it thrives upon paradoxes of which one implies the other.... Israel Baal Shem, the founder of the hasidic movement, began at a time when Sabbatianism, incessantly persecuted by rabbinical orthodoxy, had steadily become more and more nihilistic. Toward the end of his life there occurred the great outburst of antinomianism which found its expression in the Frankist movement. The founder of Hasidism and his first disciples, therefore, must have been fully aware of the destructive power inherent in extreme mystical Messianism, and from this experience they undoubtedly drew certain consequences."[19]

The catastrophic consequences which the Sabbatian movement provoked rocked Jewish life to its very foundations, implanting seeds of poison from which weeds grew that had to be rooted out time and again in later years. It caused Rabbi Yaakov Yosef[20] to treat with especial care and devote many pages in his books to explaining in unmistakable fashion precisely what he meant by the "guilt of the zaddik" or the "transgression of the zaddik" which must exist in order for him to raise the people, and how it differed radically from the Sabbatian doctrines. Hasidism denied that, because the Sabbatians, in order to find a source for their newly conceived beliefs, seized upon and perverted an aspect of Kabbalah, the study of Kabbalah itself should therefore be forbidden, as was done in certain parts of Europe.[21] Some communities, shocked at Sabbatian and Frankist heresies, even eliminated all customs which had their basis in Kabbalah and pruned the liturgy of such influences.[22] A fearful blow against the religious life of the people had been struck by the Sabbatians. The answer, however, was not to be found in withdrawing from the study of Kabbalah, that treasure house of the spirit which had served to nourish the souls of generations of Jews, but in recultivating it so that it might again give forth its precious fruit. (According to tradition the Baal Shem Tov was one of the three representatives chosen to defend Polish Jewry against the Frankists in the infamous disputation of Lemberg in 1751.[23]) The answer to the Sabbatians and the Frankists was rather to be found in refuting their claims[24] and in retaining and developing those aspects of Kabbalistic thought which were most humanistic. The doctrine of the guilt of the zaddik in Hasidism, then, would seem to be a clear example of how the hasidic movement, emerging in the middle of the eighteenth century, less than one hundred years after the death of Sabbatai Zevi and contemporaneous with Jacob Frank, recaptured one of the most profound ideas of Lurianic Kabbalah, denied the perversion it suffered at the hands of the Sabbatians and Frankists and, giving it a new meaning, turned it into a bold philosophy of action for the good of society. Hasidism was "Kabbalah become ethos."

THE NATURE OF THE ZADDIK'S TRANSGRESSION

While there is no mention of them by name, we can be fairly certain that it is with the Sabbatians in mind that the guarded language and careful formulation of this central doctrine of the "guilt of the zaddik" is generally employed. "In every descent of the zaddik he must take special care how he will again ascend, and not, God forbid, remain below. For I heard from my teacher that there are *many who did remain*."[25] Who were the "many who did remain" if not the Sabbatians? The venture is for the few, the dangers are great and the warnings, therefore, are many. *"One may perhaps err and transgress intentionally to join oneself to the lower realms in order to raise them as the heretics* [Sabbatians?] *have done ... for this, God forbid, is complete denial of God."*[26]

Often when the guilt or sin of the zaddik is mentioned, the words "sin" or "transgression" are qualified so that the reader might be certain not take them literally.[27] The classic source in the Zohar regarding the zaddik's descent reads: "The zaddikim go down to Gehinnom, to the sinners who are in Sheol, to bring them up from there."[28] But when Rabbi Yaakov Yosef refers to this source, several words are carefully added. He writes of it as: "The zaddik's descending to the *doors* of Gehinnom,"[29] or "The zaddik descends *on the way* to Gehinnom,"[30] or, most striking, "The zaddik *passes by* the doors of Gehinnom."[31] These careful distinctions in language are by no means accidental, but represent deliberate formulations which were meant to distinguish the hasidic doctrine of the zaddik's descent from that of the Sabbatian heresy.

The zaddik must know the taste of sin and must feel the pang of guilt, but he is forbidden to transgress in the full sense of that word, to enter directly into the depths. It must only be "as if" he had transgressed. If this be true, precisely how does transgression come to the zaddik? Several answers are given to this question.

Transgression may come to the zaddik by virtue of his *finite nature*. No man is perfect, not even the zaddik. Every man is a "rising and falling creature,"[32] inferior to the angels in that angels never fall, but superior to them in that angels never rise. The angels are static; man is dynamic. And when the zaddik falls into a lower spiritual state, as all men do, he must not despair, but turn this falling into a creative act. By having fallen himself, he can better know what fallen men are. Now that the thought of sin has crossed his mind he better under-

stands what that sin is and can help those who are entangled
in its meshes; now that transgression has touched him, he can
better raise others who are enslaved by it. "By means of the
defect in the zaddik, he is able to join himself with the wicked
ones, and to raise them."[33]

The guilt of the zaddik, on the other hand, may be a guilt
of *complete fiction*, an imaginary guilt, which he claims to find
after searching his inner self in his desire to cast his lot with
the people. He is guilty in his own eyes, but in the eyes of God
he is innocent.[34] It is a guilt which in fact does not exist at all.
But there are times when the zaddik must go beyond what is
just and in love accept the plight of the people as his own,
though no fault of his own is involved. God wants it so and
sometimes tries him to see if he is worthy. The Biblical Joseph
is a symbol of the zaddik, and thus when Scripture relates that
he spoke ill of his brothers, "brought an evil report of them to
their father" (Gen. 37:2), he included himself in that evil, even
though he was quite innocent. "And Joseph brought an evil
report of them to their Father in heaven; for everything evil
which he saw in them, he found an aspect of in himself and
confessed before their Father in heaven, joining himself with
them. *This is the mystery of the zaddik.*"[35] At the "waters of
Meribah" so serious a transgression was committed that Moses,
Aaron and Miriam were denied entrance into the holy land
because of it. But "certainly Miriam and Aaron did not sin.
Moses alone sinned [in smiting the rock] and, according to the
sages' explanation, even he did not sin.... It was the Israelites
who sinned, not Moses nor Aaron. Nevertheless 'God was
sanctified through them,' for *He accused them falsely and they
went beyond the letter of the law* [in taking the guilt upon them-
selves]... rising to the occasion for the sake of [the zaddikim]
of the future generations." Though Moses and Aaron were
falsely accused, they accepted their lot, which is the lot of the
zaddik, for now they were joined to the people and could render

them help. Indeed, the whole incident at the waters of Me-ribah, according to Rabbi Yaakov Yosef, was a test, and the way in which Moses or Aaron responded to it was a sign for all future zaddikim who may likewise be tested. This is the meaning of the passage "I shall try you according to the waters of Meribah": I, the Lord, shall try and test each zaddik of the generations to come in the same manner as I have tried and tested Miriam, Aaron and Moses at the waters of Meribah, ac-cusing them falsely for the sake of the people.[36]

The transgression of the zaddik most commonly referred to, however, is the one which *simply befalls him.* An example will best illustrate what is meant by this. Suppose that a zaddik plans to travel to a certain town to spend the Sabbath, and due to an accident to his carriage, is forced to pass the holy Sabbath day in the open field. He has no Sabbath bread or wine, no *minyan* to pray with, and no means of hearing the Torah read. He is not able to observe the Sabbath properly. But his transgression is not a conscious act; it is simply the result of forces beyond his control. He is the unfortunate victim of circumstance.

Whether the zaddik transgresses by virtue of his finite nature in a fictional act or through something which "befalls him," the point upon which emphasis must be laid is that the trans-gression is *unintentional* and not premeditated. The zaddik does not initiate the sin; it is not the product of conscious action. "If it happens that unintentionally the zaddik commits a transgression, he should join himself with the common man to raise him. *But this is not so if he intentionally sins in order to join himself with the common man and raise him....* Accordingly we can explain the Mishnah, 'If a man said, I will sin and repent, and sin again and repent, he will be given no chance to repent.'[37] This means that it is of no avail to say, 'I will sin and repent,' implying that he will sin in order to bring others to re-pentance...."[38]

The Talmud states: " 'One who repents brings forgiveness to himself and to the world.'[39] That is, when he joins himself with their realms.... But the sin which befalls him [the zaddik] is not a sin which he is responsible for of himself. It befalls him only that he might find a common bond with the world, as it says, 'He who is not himself guilty cannot help remove others from guilt.' " The zaddik understands this, and when he falls into sin "he immediately realizes that this has befallen him because of the people and for the sake of the people, in order that he might repent and raise them. However, one may perhaps err and sin intentionally for the sake of joining with the lower realms in order to raise them.... This, Heaven forbid, is complete denial of God."[40]

We can comprehend how the zaddik might unintentionally transgress—for example, by not being able to observe the Sabbath properly—and, further, how through this act he may thus be better able to understand and help the man who consciously profanes the Sabbath. But how is he able to understand and help more serious and dangerous sins, such as idolatry or adultery? Though this problem is dealt with in the writings of Yaakov Yosef, it is formulated more clearly in a later work which expands his words. "Sometimes the zaddik needs must fall from his height for the good of the evildoer in order to raise him; still the transgression he commits is not a real transgression, God forbid, but only *as if* [he had transgressed], as it is said, 'He who bears himself haughtily is *as if* he had committed adultery,'[42] and 'He who is of an angry nature is *as if* he had worshiped an idol.'[43] In this manner the zaddik stands with the transgressor on the same rung in the depths, and when the zaddik repents for himself, he raises the wicked as well."[44]

"It may well be that his 'as if' transgression is more serious for him than the 'real' transgression is for the evildoers."[45]

"The disciples of the Besht reported that once the Besht saw a man profane the Sabbath publicly. He stood dumfounded. Why had he *been shown* this? He searched his deeds, but it was not possible that he had committed a sin such as this. He searched further and, at last, remembered that once he had kept silent when he heard a friend defame a scholar." [In the Zohar the scholar is sometimes referred to as "Sabbath."][46]

Another point in the development of the "as if" nature of the zaddik's guilt is the distinction drawn between thought and deed. "There are two kinds of 'rising' and 'descending.' The descending of the people comes about by means of a transgression in deed through which they sin. This is not the case with the descent of the faithful ones [the zaddikim], for it is only by means of *thought and not deed*."[47] Even in the case of an evil thought it is clearly stated that this is not to be brought about consciously. "Certainly one has not the right to think impure thoughts in order to join oneself to the people.... But if an impure thought *happens* to occur to him unintentionally, he should understand that it is for the benefit of the people that he might join himself with them."[48]

Three examples from Rabbi Yaakov Yosef's writings expressing opposition to the idea of the zaddik's intentional sin should be mentioned. The first concerns the parable of the lost prince, the second a passage in the Palestinian Talmud, and the third the Biblical incident of the golden calf.

1. We have already dealt with the parable[49] of the king's son who returned only when one noble "removed his clothing and put on peasant clothing like the other townspeople."[50] Just as the noble had to simulate the peasants to come close to the prince and save him, so the zaddik must simulate the people to come close to them and deliver them. The king represents the heights and goodness, the peasants the depths and sin. Many nobles are sent. They all fail because they remain pure, unchanged, clothed in their royal robes. Only

the wise noble succeeds because he changes his clothes and dons theirs. What do these clothes signify? "The royal clothes are good deeds,"[51] while the peasants' clothes are wicked deeds or "clothing of filth."[52] The zaddik, in changing clothes, exchanges good deeds for bad deeds. Does not this parable, then, imply that the zaddik must consciously commit wicked deeds? This is emphatically denied. "The noble puts on a *likeness* of clothing of filth, and *not real* clothing of filth, God forbid."[53] They are only a "likeness' because the zaddik does not sin intentionally. "The zaddik sins because of the sins of the people, for the generations and its leaders have the same source, and the sin of the generation brings sin to the leaders in order that the one might join and raise the other."[54] The evil of the age brings error to even a good man.

2. "And Samuel exclaimed: 'We have sinned against the Lord' (I Sam. 7:6). Rabbi Samuel bar Yitzhak said, 'Samuel clothed himself with the garment of all Israel.'"[55] The commentary to this passage from the Palestinian Talmud remarks that "since Samuel was without sin, he could not utter a falsehood and say *we* have sinned.... Therefore it was necessary for him to make a slight change in himself by removing his pure garments and putting on other garments, garments of filth, so that all (Samuel included) could say as one, 'We have sinned.'"[56] Still, even this implies intentional sin, and therefore, Yaakov Yosef at once objects, for "since he [Samuel] is without sin how can it be said that he deliberately put on clothes of filth, God forbid? But just as 'Moses was the most faithful in all his house' (Num. 12:7) and, nevertheless, when Israel sinned, Moses came into sin also—for Moses was the source of Israel—so it is with each generation and its leaders. Through the sin of Israel a portion of sin reached Samuel also. It was *as if* he sinned the same sin which the people committed."[57] Thus putting on the clothes of the people means entering into the sin of the people, unintentionally. It means

that when the zaddik is affected by the spiritual life of the people, when he descends to their level and "dons their clothes," so to speak, "he understands that all this is for the purpose of repenting and raising all the realms into which he had descended."[58] So it was that Samuel could say, "*We* have sinned" (I Sam 7:6). It was "as if" he had sinned.

3. The deepest rebellion against God which the people of Israel perpetrated is that of the golden calf. Here we find the people of Israel at the nadir of their spiritual career. Many times they had acted wrongly, but building an idol of gold below while God was giving the tablets to Moses on high—no treachery could be greater than this.

Rabbi Yaakov Yosef writes that "the main responsibility for the sin of the golden calf came, as the Zohar says, from the 'mixed multitude.' By virtue of their association with the mixed multitude, a small number of Israelites also took part, but only in *thought* [not in deed]. Aaron too was caught in this sin but only *unintentionally*."[59] "Israel was not guilty of this sin of itself, even though some Israelites did indeed transgress, for the 'mixed multitude' were the actual perpetrators of the crime, and because of their proximity and common origin (for Moses was their common origin) the blemish touched Israel as well...." It must be made clear that regarding those few Hebrews who were involved in this sin, it was "only to teach repentance; that is, that they might don the garments of the mixed multitude so that when those who were to some extent caught in this sin repented, then all the realms would be raised.... And from this the future generations may learn the great way in the service of God. This is what I remembered and received from my teacher *mouth to mouth*, and it is not possible to explain in a book, but consider and understand."[60]

This is the most decisive statement on the subject in Rabbi Yaakov Yosef's works.[61] Its implications are apparent. The few Israelites are the zaddikim, who are caught in sin but do not initiate it. The mixed multitude are the common people. They initiate the action, and by virtue of their common relationship involve the zaddik too, but only in thought and unintentionally, in order that he might be joined to them and help raise them. This is clearly the task of the zaddik in all generations, but a perilous task, to be sure. So we see that the worst of all sins, the sin of the golden calf, was no sin at all, at least not a conscious one.[62]

The above quotation is all the more impressive since Rabbi Yaakov Yosef concludes it by telling us that he heard it from his teacher, the Baal Shem Tov, "mouth to mouth." This phrase occurs nowhere else in his writings,[63] and is used to confirm unmistakably the fact that only this is the Besht's teaching on the subject.

THE CAUSAL RELATIONSHIP BETWEEN THE ZADDIK AND THE PEOPLE

Underlying much of what has been said about the transgression of the zaddik and the manner in which it reaches him is the belief that the zaddik and the people form a basic unity, though one that can at any time be broken.[64] Each, being a part of the other, is, in the deepest sense, responsible for the other. "I have heard in the name of the deceased Leib Pistener... that when the pious man [the zaddik] sees a wicked act on the part of the people, he must blame himself... and when the people see an improper action on the part of the zaddik, they must blame themselves.... Each must judge leniently: the leader should correct himself in order that the people might be corrected, and the people must correct themselves in order that the leader might be corrected."[65]

The basic unity implies a causal relationship which moves back and forward between the zaddik and the people. "The leaders of the generation are punished for the people of the generation."[66] "Because of the unity which exists, the sinful deeds of the people cause sinful thoughts in the zaddik."[67] "The intentional sin of the people causes the zaddik to transgress unintentionally."[68] "A blemish in the thoughts of the pious causes a blemish in the deeds of the people."[69] Such statements remind us that society is a matrix from which a man, though he may desire it, can rarely remove himself. The thoughts and deeds of men are dependent, to some extent, upon the thoughts and deeds which surround them day by day. Rarely can a man isolate himself from the influence of other men. What happens to one man, in a sense, reveals what happens to all men. The zaddik, when an evil thought crosses his mind, knows that this thought is not his alone but may be the product of many evil deeds involving a combination of persons and places far beyond his immediate circle and may have reached him only for the sake of making him aware of the deeds of others.[70] Thus, when he repents, his repentance is not limited to the narrowness of his own ego, but expands to embrace many men.

INTENTIONAL TRANSGRESSION—WHO MAY UNDERTAKE IT

Despite the denunciations against and warnings about intentional transgression, if the doctrine of the "descent of the zaddik" is to be understood properly, it must imply deliberate action, at certain times and under certain conditions. There is a place for it in the thinking of Rabbi Yaakov Yosef of Polnoy, albeit a carefully circumscribed place. The zaddik may fall into sin unintentionally due to his finite nature, for every man is a "rising and falling creature," or due to the sin of the people, for their transgression has its effect on him: in either case allowing him to join the people and thus raise them. But there are times in the life of the zaddik when he himself is called upon to initiate the action, going down deliberately to the rung of the people.[71] Still, even the intentional transgression of the zaddik is to be compared to the unintentional act in that both are, in a greater or smaller sense, "as if" transgressions. The zaddik must himself be guilty to help others from guilt, but *serious* sin is, in all cases, forbidden. Unintentional transgression is "as if," because it is virtually no transgression at all. Intentional transgression is also "as if," because the sins involved are so mild and the conditions under which they may be performed are so carefully circumscribed as to greatly reduce the element of danger. We can best understand this by referring to specific cases.

If the zaddik, animated by the desire to help the people, leaves the quiet of his room where he can engage in the undisturbed study of the Torah in order to mingle with the people and raise them, he commits the transgression of *bitul Torah*, "neglect of Torah." Or if the zaddik goes to a certain inn where there is a man caught in the web of sin, and, while winning the confidence of the man to raise him, becomes aware that the time for the *minhah* prayer is passing but chooses, nevertheless, to remain with this man, he commits the transgression of not praying at the proper time. Or if the zaddik is about to preach to the people, he may first begin with an intricate display of learning, *pilpul* (a custom he ordinarily condemns in other scholars because it leads to the pride of ostentatious display). He does this precisely because he knows it is wrong and will lead to the transgression of pride, for once having transgressed he will no longer be above the people but at one with them and therefore can the more easily include himself in his own preaching. Being at one with the people, he is able to raise them with himself.[72]

These three cases [73] are examples of deliberate sin, but there are qualifications which must at once be added. First of all, it is imperative to pay attention to the fact that the *only* intentional sins which are mentioned in the writings of Yaakov Yosef are: "neglect of Torah" (*bitul Torah*),[74] "praying later than the prescribed time" (*over zeman tefilah*), "idle talk" (*devarim betelim*), "anger" (*ka'as*),[77] "pride" (*ga'avah*)[78] and "falsehood" (*sheker*).[79] Furthermore, even these conscious acts cannot be undertaken by every self-styled leader, but "only the select few may enter into this danger."[80] "It is only permitted to the wise men of the generation to make use of the *yetzer hara*, pride and falsehood for the sake of heaven. This is not permitted to the people."[81] Even the wise "select few" are given an additional warning. "He must derive no personal pleasure from the transgression, nor must it benefit him in any possible way; indeed it is a calamity to him. He is ashamed of it, and must suffer on its account, but is compelled to do it for the final good.... If he derives pleasure from it, however, he must desist from it."[82] Finally, there must be a clear possibility of helping the fallen. The case of Elisha the Prophet and the dead child is cited. Since Elisha was a priest and it is forbidden for a priest to touch a dead person, how did he permit himself to raise the boy from the dead as he did? Because he felt certain he could succeed. But if there had been a serious doubt in his mind, he could not have acted in such a manner.[83] The zaddik, likewise, must act in wisdom, aware of his limited power. He must not enter into danger upon every occasion regardless of the circumstances, but only when there are conditions which promise hope. If those to be helped are sunk so deeply in the depths that helping them is a grave doubt, if they are completely "dead in spirit," then the zaddik must not put his own soul into danger. Conscious transgression is in such case forbidden.[84]

"I heard a parable from my teacher regarding the need of the one who preaches Musar to preach Musar to himself as well. A pious man once entered a village reputed for its houses of ill fame. He wanted to learn something about the people of the town and said to himself, 'I shall go to the tavern where many people congregate. From their conversation and stories I can learn about them, for the tongue is the pen of the heart.' Thus it happened that he listened to one man tell what he did with a certain prostitute and similarly another man and another and another, so that he burned with rage. When the people discovered who he was, that he was well known for his piety, each one presented him with a substantial sum of money to seek forgiveness from him by means of their gift. The following day he cunningly arranged that the same people should be again gathered together there, in order that he might again receive gifts from them—until, after a time, he too conducted himself like them...."[85]

This parable speaks of the temptation of sin, the weakness of human flesh and the falseness of human motives. The stranger was pious, but he was a man, finite and fallible. In addition, we see that his motive was not to save the people from sin, but "to learn something about them." His curiosity was aroused, not his concern—though he may have justified his curiosity, no doubt, by labeling it concern. The opportunity to acquire easy money drew him down closer to the bottom, until, at last, sunk in the mire which he had touched through curiosity and drawn on by cupidity, he was conquered with lust. A striking story it is, aiming at the frailty of humanity and the potential corruption of the so-called pious. It was meant to stand as a stark example of what must be avoided, of what the "descent of the zaddik" does *not* mean.

To mix with the sinner is an undertaking fraught with danger. None, therefore, but the purest and the most faithful dare accept it; and then only if they are fully prepared, cleaving to the Lord in *devekut* and banishing all thought of personal gain or pleasure from their mind. It must not be their own desire, something they *want to do*, but the desire of God, something they *must do*. Even then, not every journey is to be embarked upon, but only those which give some good evidence of eventual success. The man must be selfless, the Lord must be with him, and the way must be open. Otherwise the dangers are too great.

THE PARABLE ONCE MORE: THE DESCENT OF THE ZADDIK IMPLIES DANGER

Rabbi Yaakov Yosef derives still another lesson from the oft-repeated parable of the prince who lived among the peasants and was rescued only by the noble who dressed and acted like the peasants. We have seen, first of all, that this tale teaches descent and not aloofness, concern and not contempt; secondly, that true concern implies involvement; and, thirdly, that the "clothes of filth" donned by the noble and the wicked deeds which he committed in order to come close to the prince had no real existence, since he put on only the "likeness" of clothes of filth and acted only "as if" he were performing wicked deeds. Now the final lesson of the parable is made manifest: the danger of the zaddik's descent. Perhaps the prince has sunk so deeply into the pit of darkness and become so attached to his new life that the noble, wise and concerned though he may be, not only cannot retrieve him, but, what is worse, because of his closeness to the lost prince and the peasants, is in danger of not being able to retrieve himself.

I have heard a parable concerning a prince whose father banished him to a distant village so that he might yearn for the table of his father, the king, but the prince, because of his folly, mixed with the strangers in the village, learned their deeds and forgot the royal pleasures. So the king sent one of his nobles to bring the prince back but he failed, until finally one clever noble removed his royal clothing and dressed in peasant clothing like the villagers. He succeeded....

By this deed he [the zaddik] is able to join with the people who are of lowly deed in order to speak to their hearts, to stir them into the realization that they are far from the table of the King of kings and that they should return to Him as in the tale above. Now, surely, the wise man acts for the love of the King and may indeed bring the son back to his father. Nonetheless *he enters into danger*. It is possible that, after speaking in an intimate manner with the prince once or twice, he may return him; it is also possible that the prince, though reared in royal fashion, has become so accustomed to the evil ways of the villagers as to have become one of them, forgetting all the pleasures of his youth.[86]

The zaddik's descent, whether it be deliberate or not, "as if" or accidental, implies contact with sin, regardless of all precautions, conditions and qualifications—and therefore, *danger*. So it is that we fear for the zaddik.

"To help the people the zaddik joins himself to them, sitting, standing or walking with them, in order to raise them.... However, in order to attach himself to their rung, he must neither sit nor stand nor walk with them too much, for an excess of this is dangerous."[87] We have mentioned "the parable of a king who lost a precious stone in the depths of the sea and because of his love for it, sent his sons to bring it up. Now there are three kinds [of sons]. The first is the wise one who struggles, labors, finds the precious stone and returns it to his father in safety. The second is the one who says: 'Let the stone come up from below by itself!' *The third one remains below in the depths of the sea*. The Lord wanted all of them to be like the first son, but they reply: 'Would that we *ourselves* could emerge [even without saving the stone, that is, the sinners], so that we will not be like the third son, remaining, God forbid, in the depths of the sea!"[88]

Tradition tells us that both Noah and Abraham were righteous men; yet they were different. As we have seen above, Noah saved himself and his family while the rest of the generation was destroyed. Abraham was not only concerned with his own well-being but with the well-being of others too, and so it is said that if Abraham had lived in the time of Noah, the entire generation would have been saved and the flood would never have come. Abraham was clearly superior to Noah. But he was also in greater danger. If the task was greater, so was the risk. While Abraham achieved more than Noah, his position was more perilous. Noah wanted to be assured of his own safety; he took no risk. But Abraham went down to the others who lived on a lower rung than he, and there was always the possibility not only that he would fail to raise them but that he himself might remain among the fallen.

So it is with the zaddik. He is superior to the rabbi who, in contempt for the people and concerned only with his own spiritual well-being, secludes himself in the haven of his room. However, in leaving his shelter to redeem the people, the zaddik immediately exposes himself to dangers which the one who remains within is protected from, for "sin croucheth at the door"[89] (Gen. 4:7), and he himself may be caught in its lair. A terrible warning is issued: "Descent is certain while ascent is not!"[90] "The zaddik is fearful lest he descend below too far, and, God forbid, the *kelipot* seize him!"[91] When the zaddik descends from his rung to join with the people and raise them, "he must beware lest they refuse to join themselves to him except he clothe himself with their wicked ways, until he is at one with them on their own rung... lest he become accustomed to clothing himself in wicked ways *even when it is not for the sake of joining himself to the people!*"[92] "In every descent one must take great care how to ascend again and not remain, God forbid, below, for I have heard from my teacher that many did remain!"[93] The zaddik is like one who goes down into a pit, descending into the darkness of the world, meeting temptation, slander and wickedness. Perhaps in his descent to bring up the fallen he himself will be drawn down deep into the pit, never to ascend again. One who lends a helping hand is always in danger, for, to change the metaphor, "The man who seeks to save his drowning friend may himself be pulled in."[94]

It is the paradox of the zaddik's descent that even "when he joins himself to the people, he must not fall from his own rung."[95] Even when he seems outwardly to be on the people's level, inwardly he never leaves his own station. To use Rabbi Yaakov Yosef's analogy, just as the glowing flame of one candle may light many candles while losing nothing of its own brightness, so the zaddik must kindle a spark in the people, keeping his own flame burning brightly all the while.[96] We shall now see how this paradox of remaining with God even while going down to the people is to be achieved.

PREPARATION FOR THE DESCENT: CLEAVING TO GOD

The zaddik must realize the danger of his position. He should not be impressed with the glory of the task to be done, but should always bear in mind that he is nothing more than the channel of God's bounty. He must possess the quality of humility which alone teaches him how to stand at a distance from himself and how to understand the plight of others. "After the zaddik ascends on high, he descends again to raise the lower realms.... But when he descends to help others, it is not because he wants to go down, for he fears, God forbid, that he may never again return, and will come to sin."[97] "He knows the bitterness of his own soul which comes from having to deal all the day in the midst of mockery, derision and frivolity."[98]

The zaddik, in all humbleness, aware of his frailty and of the dangers involved, does not immediately descend to the people. He must make the proper preparation first, and it is this preparation which on the one hand helps to qualify him for the task and on the other hand assures its success. "The one who is truly wise, before he descends into Egypt, going below the rung upon which he previously stood, must first join himself closely to God—binding himself in cleaving and yearning and love to Him Who is blessed—so that even when he descends... to raise others... he will not be cleft from God... but will be worthy of again ascending. This is just as it is with one who goes down into a pit and ties himself with a rope so that he may once more arise from that pit."[99] Before the zaddik can dare go to the people and raise them, before he can bind himself to the people, "he must first bind himself to Him Who is all-blessed."[100] The binding of the soul to God is the earnest task of the zaddik and the prime prerequisite for his descent, that which indeed makes of it a holy task. He must undertake this through prayer and Torah study, striving to sustain that cord of the spirit which binds him to God and whose strength and elasticity depend largely on his efforts. With all his might he must seek to come close to God, to be firm in faith and to live as if the Lord were near him at all times, so that even when he leaves his Torah and his prayer, God will be with him.

Another striking metaphor, similar in content, is used to describe the descent to the people in the presence of God. "I heard a parable from the Rabbi and Preacher Menahem Mendel of Bar. Once a child was advised that if he fell into a pit and was unable to get out, he should go home and bring a ladder that he might climb out." But if he is in the pit already, how can he go home to get the ladder? "Rabbi Mendel explained the parable as meaning that *before* he goes into the pit, he should bring the ladder so that later he might be able to emerge."[101] This parable is further developed by Ephraim, the grandson of the Baal Shem. "Just as Abraham went down into Egypt and came up out of Egypt, so every man, according to his nature, descends and ascends. Abraham... was afraid of going down into Egypt, the Zohar says, until he had first bound his soul to the *Shechinah* (if one may say that).... But when he had bound himself in a strong and lasting bond with the *Shechinah*, he no longer needed to fear. A parable: When a man wishes to go down deeply into a pit, he is afraid lest he not be able to come up when he wishes. Therefore he takes a ladder with him into the pit so that he may ascend. The meaning of the parable: The *Shechinah* is, as it were, the ladder. And this is what the Lord said to Jacob: 'Fear not to go down into Egypt.' For Jacob was afraid to descend into Egypt, into that deep pit, since he might be lost there with no hope of returning; and truly, his fear was an inner fear, lest he might sink into the depths of the *kelipot*. But when he bound himself to that most inner awe, which is the *Shechinah*, then he cleaved with all his strength to the *Shechinah*. This is what is meant by the words 'He said to him, do not fear,' for I, the *Shechinah*, which you hold in awe, will surely go down with you—lest you slip from your rung." And this is the meaning of the verse "I [the Shechinah] shall go down with you to Egypt and I shall surely bring you up" (Gen. 46:4).[102]

Cleaving to God is the preparation for the descent, that the *Shechinah* might remain close to the zaddik wherever he may go. "Purify yourself; afterward purify others."[103] To help the people the zaddik must first attach himself firmly to the cord of heaven. This cleaving or attachment requires *seclusion*. For while the zaddik is opposed to the seclusion of the leader which flows from contempt for the people and the desire to secure only his own perfection, he feels the absolute need of the seclusion which is the result of concern for the people, during which time he strengthens himself through Torah and prayer for the task which lies ahead. Indeed this seems to be the pattern for many great spiritual figures in history. Before Moses went to Egypt to bring Israel out of bondage, he lived the lonely life of a shepherd and encountered God at the burning bush. Before the Baal Shem revealed himself to his people, he dwelt in the mountains preparing himself.

It is necessary that he [the zaddik] first shut himself up with God... that he might receive the heavenly bounty... and afterward descend below, bestowing it upon others. Therefore he busies himself with communal needs.... It seems to me that this is the meaning of the verse which tells us that Jacob our father looked "and behold a ladder was fixed in the earth, and its head reached the heavens; and angels of the Lord were ascending and descending on it." It would seem that "descending" should have been mentioned first. But actually the order is correct, for [the zaddikim] are God's messengers sent to this world to do his bidding and are called the angels* of God. It is necessary that they seclude themselves each day to first receive for themselves heavenly bounty, and so it is written first "ascending" and only afterwards "descending."[104]

CARE REGARDING THE PEOPLE

The dangers which await the zaddik are first met by the preparation which he undertakes in the seclusion of his room through prayer and Torah, seeking to secure the cord of his soul in the Lord, that he may cling to it during his perilous journey. The zaddik's action in relation to God is clear, but what of his action in relation to the people? Rabbi Yaakov Yosef taught that just as the zaddik's mission requires a certain course of conduct regarding God, so it requires a certain course of conduct regarding man. Thus, to minimize the danger of the descent, he is told not only to cleave to God but, when he moves among the people to save them, *to come only as close as necessity requires.*

"I heard an explananation of the passage, 'At the time Thou mayest be found, let every hasid pray that when the great

* The Hebrew word *Malach* means both "angel" and "messenger."

waters overflow, they shall not reach unto him' (Ps. 32:6). This means that when you endeavor to save a drowning man, *take care to seize some small part of him, his hair for example, but do not seize him by his body, because of the danger that you may drown with him.*"[105] And another explanation of the same passage: "If you attempt to pull out a drowning man, you yourself may be pulled in, therefore care is necessary... and the proper advice is to save him *at a distance.*"[106] When the zaddik descends, he does not enter into the *kelipot*, as the Sabbatians taught, but he passes only as near to the evil as is necessary, to redeem it. Here we see a significant distinction, reflecting the fundamental difference between these two doctrines of descent, the Sabbatian and the hasidic. One teaches the forced entrance into evil, the other minimal association with it. One plunges into the depths, the other merely passes by. One throws caution to the winds, exposing itself to the lurking dangers, the other retains the maximum security in a precarious situation. The zaddik is situated between God and the people, attempting to return one to the other. To accomplish his task he adopts a double attitude: standing as close to God and as far from the people as possible under the circumstances.

DIVINE AID

The zaddik must solemnly attempt to fulfill all the preparations for the descent—drawing close to God—and, during the descent, to take all possible precautions with the people—keeping a proper distance from them. But even then the matter is still not at an end. That is, the human aspect of it may be ended, but not the divine. It represents all the zaddik can do, but man is not alone in the world. God is with him. He too has a stake in this venture, for it is more than a human venture. God too lends a hand. The zaddik knows this and looks to the

Lord for aid. "... It is necessary for such a man [the zaddik] to pray and seek help from God when he wants to undertake such a task, for without God's help it is easy to stray from the path. He must gird his loins in prayer that he should not, God forbid, come to the stumbling block of sin. This is the meaning of the verse, 'Oh Lord, teach me Thy paths and lead me along the way straightforwardly' (Ps. 27:11): I beg that You grant me help, aid and support that I go along the way straightforwardly and not crookedly, for without Your succor I may stray, God forbid."[107]

Caleb went along with the spies saying, "I am with you in counsel," and because of this the people trusted him, as it is written, "And Caleb stilled the people toward Moses" (Num. 13:30). He told them to be silent because he was going to speak to them about Moses, proclaiming: "Has the son of Amram done this alone to us?" Thinking that he was about to speak against Moses... all the people kept silent to hear. Instead, he said: "Did he not also divide the Red Sea for us and bring down the manna for us?"[108]

The danger in all this, however, is that he [the zaddik] *really* may be caught up in their [the sinners'] "counsel," just as one who wishes to save a drowning man enters into danger: he may save the drowning man or he may drown with him. Because of this danger we understand why Caleb had to go to Hebron and prostrate himself upon the graves of the patriarchs and pray that he might be delivered from the counsel of the spies. So it was that Moses our teacher (peace be to him) prayed for Joshua: "May the Lord deliver you out of the counsel of the spies."[109]

We are told that when Jacob dreamed his dream about the angels ascending and descending upon the ladder which reached to heaven, "the Lord stood beside him" (Gen. 28:13). The Lord was nearby, reassuring him and giving him the promise of His presence. So it is with the zaddik, the Lord's messenger,[110] who descends the ladder of life in order to raise the people. "Wherever his descent may lead him, he must be aware that the Glory of God's Presence is also there. This is the mystery of the verse 'His dominion ruleth over all' (Ps. 103: 19)."[111] "The Lord stands beside him [the zaddik], guarding him from transgression in his descent to join the common people, that he learn not from their deeds as did the king's son who mixed with the strangers and adopted their ways. This will not be true of the zaddik, because he comes in order to help others; and *the Lord will deliver him from transgression.*"[112]

The ladder is placed in the pit, which is our world, and the zaddik descends. He has done his task, seeking first to cleave to God with his innermost soul, and then taking care how he approaches the sinner. Now God grants His promise that He will guard him and watch over him while he is on his way, even more, that His *Shechinah* will accompany him wherever he may go, shielding him from sin and permitting him to once again rise from the black pit of the world's darkness, bearing aloft into the light the fallen souls which he carries with him.

CHAPTER 10

The Circle of Musar

The Hebrew word *Musar* means "to preach in a strong manner." It implies moral exhortation: condemning the unjust and enjoining the just, revealing what is crooked and demanding that it be set straight. To "speak Musar" is a phrase which has had a long history in the annals of Jewish preaching, but seldom was it treated in such a profound and comprehensive manner, seldom was the note sounded by Rabbi Yaakov Yosef heard before.[1] To him, Musar takes place not only between the preacher and the people but between the preacher and his ego, and, ultimately, between the preacher and his Creator. It is a dynamic, changing relationship which seems almost to have a life of its own, and occupies a significant place in the picture of the ideal religious leader which is sketched by Rabbi Yaakov Yosef.

The renewed concern in Musar followed naturally from the renewed concern of Hasidism in the people. The typical discourses of the rabbis of the time were given only twice a year, on *Shabbat Hagadol* and *Shabbat Shuvah*, were concerned mainly with complicated details of halachah, and were in many cases hairsplitting and merely opportunities for the speaker to display subtlety of thought, cleverness in juxtaposition of ideas and range of knowledge. Such preaching is bitterly condemned by our author, who claims that it serves little purpose other than demonstrating the ability of the speaker as "one that hath a pleasant voice and can play well on an instrument" (Ezek. 33:32). He appeals for the kind of preaching which took place among the Hasidim each Sabbath afternoon at the "third meal,"[2] preaching which is bound up with spiritual and moral issues, which speaks to the heart of the people about pride and humility, hatred and love, ignorance and knowledge of Torah, jealousy and compassion and the observance of the mitzvot with joy and Kavannah. A revival of the spirit is called for, and Musar is one of the main weapons in the arsenal of the zealot.[3] It must be used wisely and justly, it must be used lovingly and understandingly. It is not that the teaching of Torah is opposed, for Torah and Musar go hand in hand. Musar itself is an aspect of Torah. But *pilpul*, far-fetched dialectics which are understood by few and are delivered in pride, is decried. To teach the people the practical law is a different matter. "In any event, the leader or the sage of the city or the generation must speak these two things to the people: laws of the Torah and Musar."[4]

CRITICISM OF RABBI AND MAGGID FOR FAILURE TO PREACH MUSAR

The new emphasis on Musar expressed the concern of the zaddik for the people in the sense of popular preaching, seeking to "subdue the hearts" of the people with words they could understand instead of secluding oneself from them or preaching in pride. It also expressed concern for the people in the sense of a bold and courageous speaking out, a fearless denunciation of the evils of the time. It was not unusual to find among the rabbis an attitude of subservience before the rich in an effort to sue for their favor and thus guarantee their own personal security. In holding their peace, they not only tolerated but encouraged the spiritual degeneration which was going on all about them. "The land is destroyed because the zaddik does not pour Musar upon it."[5]

" 'The people look with favor upon a rabbi not because of

his excellent qualities but because he does not reprove them with words of heaven....'[6] 'Noah walked with God' (Gen. 6:9), that is, he did not reprove the people of his generation but withdrew from them and secluded himself with God."[7] To stay in the good graces of the people it was naturally the more clever course not to reprove them and incur their enmity. "There are two kinds of holy men: the one who secludes himself, like Noah... and the one who wants to purify others, like Abraham our father (peace be to him), who spoke out openly. The difference between them was that one was beloved and the other hated."[8] And to be hated by the people, by the rich among the people in particular, meant a loss in status, in position, in personal security.

Apart from the rabbi who preached but twice a year and then only *pilpul*, there was also the itinerant preacher, the *maggid* or *mochiah*, whose task it was not to teach Torah or decide cases of Law, but to travel from town to town, preaching the word of the Lord to the people. It seemed to Rabbi Yaakov Yosef that many of these roving preachers were more interested in their own finances than in the spiritual well-being of the community. "I heard from my teacher that the people say one should not listen to the Musar of the preachers because their real purpose is to be given money. Thus it is written, 'They were not able to drink from the waters of Musar because they were bitter' (Ex. 15:23); that is, [because the words of Musar are only spoken] *'far gelt'* " [*fargalt* means "bitter as gall"].[9] Sometimes, with eloquent sentences and telling parables, the preachers would stir up the emotions of the people so that, in a perverted way, the words of the Psalmist, "My tears have become my food day and night" (Ps. 42:4), applied to them. For the tears they themselves shed and the tears they would wring from the eyes of their listeners during their sermons were too often nothing more than the means of acquiring a daily livelihood.[10] "Tears" had indeed become their "food." Instead of reproving and correcting, they did not hesitate to flatter the people to insure receiving a generous gift from the community when they were about to depart.[11] In any case, the maggid rarely preached Musar. He usually delivered a "pleasant discourse,"[12] designed to offend no one, for he desired "to be beloved of the people, thinking that in this way he would receive money.... How then could he give Musar, which implies criticism? The people might take a dislike to him and give him nothing, and 'if there is no bread there is no Torah.'[13]

"In truth, however, the opposite is the case. 'If there is no Torah'—no showing of the way to the sinners—'then there is no bread.' "[14] For the sake of a few coins will the maggid cease to speak the truth, twisting his words, sweetening them, dulling them so that truth can no longer be found in them? Will he pander the very words of God just so he may have a bit of comfort? To place matter above spirit is to court disaster. "The land is destroyed because the zaddik does not pour Musar upon it."[15]

In many cases both rabbi and maggid were concerned with their own personal security first and the people last. Both were filled with ambition and pride. When they did speak, they spoke to impress others, not to correct them. Therefore, Yaakov Yosef condemned both of them: the rabbi, for not preaching often enough, but secluding himself to avoid controversy; the maggid, though preaching often enough, for not preaching the truth. Neither the one nor the other spoke Musar to the people.

Concern for the people must precede concern for the self.

THE APPEAL FOR MUSAR

The quality of humility which is to characterize the zaddik must not render him passive and prevent him from speaking Musar. Too much humility can sometimes weaken a man and make him lose confidence in himself. But true humility is not a weakness. It is not the lack of something, but the presence of something; not weakness but a strength from that which is higher than the self. True humility gives strength to a man; so it did to the zaddik. As the channel from God to the people, he was filled with power which knew no self-interest. It was the power of courage which a humble man, dedicated to a cause more vital than his own life, feels in the midst of a great battle.

So Rabbi Yaakov Yosef issues a fervent appeal for Musar. He tells the zaddik to put aside all concern for personal security; to be strong and take courage to speak the truth and not shun it, even though it means that he who speaks it may suffer. Although a sickness of soul has spread among the people making the learned proud, the rich arrogant and the masses afraid, "nevertheless, there is a remedy: not to withhold from the people the rod of Musar."[16] "'Command Aaron and his sons to say' (Levit. 6:2); that is, the essence of commanding and urging is 'to say,' for one should say to the people words of Musar."[17] "You must denounce in public with words of heaven even though you will be hated."[18] "Do not be trampled upon by the people," but "'in a place where there are no men, be thou a man,' to chastise and reprove."[19] If many of the rabbis and maggidim are like the fox which follows the people subserviently, "the zaddikim are mighty like the lion to do the will of their Father in heaven... for the lion has no fear of any creature...."[20] The zaddik must not be afraid of the rich and powerful who rise up before the people to tyrannize them. As with the "pillar of cloud" which led the weakened Israelites amidst the dangers of the wilderness, "leveling the mountains and the valleys and removing the thorns, so shall it be with the zaddik.... Through the ruling rod in his hand, he shall level the great and the small and uproot the thorns from the vineyard of the Lord of Hosts...."[21]

"While there is chastisement in the world... there is blessing in the world."[22] This talmudic dictum is frequently quoted in the works of our author, for he believed that a war must be waged against evil through preaching the word of the Lord, a war which only rarely knows armistice and which, by the very nature of the enemy, can never hope to achieve final victory. "Just as it is a mitzvah to circumcise one's own heart, so is it a mitzvah to circumcise the hearts of others through the reproving of Musar... as it says, 'Better open chastisement than hidden love'" (Prov. 27:5). Now we understand why the Talmud teaches circumcision of the heart, which is the preaching of Musar, and causes grief to the people, pushing aside the joy of the Sabbath, "for when one grieves and weeps over his sins, he will be overcome with contrition."[23] The zaddik preaches to the people "in order to speak to their hearts and stir them, to remind them how far they have strayed from the table of the King—that they should return to it. [24] He preaches "to arouse, with words of admonition, the hearts of Israel that they turn in penitence to our Father in heaven."[25] For "through Musar the sins of the generation are forgiven."[26]

There may be a time preceding the giving of Musar when the heart is sealed shut and will not receive words of admonition. In such a case it must first be opened so that the stream of Musar can enter. Just as it is not possible for a physician to heal if he does not open the wound and lay it bare, "so is it when one wants to heal the sickness of a soul to whom sweet tastes as bitter and thus does not accept the healing of wisdom and Musar. One must open every wound and failing a man has and lay them bare before him.... Thus he will get himself a broken heart... which is the cure, as it is written, 'The sacrifices of the Lord are a broken spirit.' *This* is the sacrifice which atones for man... for Musar breaks the heart of man."[27]

And yet, important as Musar is, it must be used with caution and applied as the situation warrants; it cannot be used indiscriminately. In certain situations it should not be used at all.[28] The wise man must know how to wield the rod of reproof: gently on some, firmly on others; at times like a heavy stick, at times like a wand of feathers. The art of speaking to men is as infinitely complicated as man himself. To speak to all men in one manner is folly; to speak to each man in the manner suited to his peculiar needs is wisdom. One of the tasks of the zaddik is to know how to preach to different kinds of men.[29] "The *mochiah* should not say: 'I shall preach in public: whoever wants to may listen, and whoever does not want to may not listen!' But, at first, let him preach in public, and then, afterward, let him speak again to each one of the people individually."[30] "Joseph is the one who chastises in public, for it is written, 'He shepherded his brothers among the flocks' (Gen. 37:2). This means that he shepherded his brothers as the shepherd does his flock—and just as the shepherd treats the lambs in the way proper for them and the ewes in the way proper for them... so it is that he who is a true shepherd of his people must say Musar to each man in the way proper for him."[31]

"There are two kinds of Musar, one for the learned and one for the simple people, and to each one must speak according to his character and rung."[32] There should be "harsh words for the learned and mild words for the simple."[33] "To the wise man who loves reproach and Musar—for it is written, 'Reprove the wise man and he will love you' (Prov. 9:8)—one can speak Musar openly without cloaking it with fine phrases; but to the common people and certainly to the wicked one must cloak it with fine words and stories so that it seems like wine or milk."[34] "There is a difference between the words of Musar given to the righteous and pure who love Musar... and those given to the wicked, to whom one must speak in allusion lest they be angry from chastisement."[35] The wise preacher is like "the physician who, when he sees that his patient is not able to take his medicine because it seems too bitter, must mix it with various kinds of sweet herbs so that he will accept it."[36]

On the one hand the zaddik has the duty of speaking Musar to the people. On the other hand the people have the duty to listen. Without their acceptance and response, his preaching is of little avail. The ear is as important as the mouth. Three kinds of people are described who do not respond as they should. One class, after learning that a preacher has arrived, come to hear him out of a sense of shame, but do not listen to his words. They are the deaf. A second class do listen while the sermon is being given and even take what they hear to heart, "but when they leave the synagogue, 'sin croucheth at the door' (Gen. 4:7). The evil impulse tempts them, saying: 'It is enough that you have listened; it is not necessary that you do what you heard, for you have your own problems to worry about.' They are the fools who destroy what is given them. (They should heed the admonition of the hasid, the deceased Rabbi Pistener, who said, 'Take the words *with you* and return to the Lord' (Hosea 14:3); that is, listening *and* doing.)" The members of the third class run from the synagogue when they hear that someone has come to preach.[37] They are the infants who do not yet know how to hold their father's hand. And "when, in a time of desolation, the people close their ears from listening to the rebuke of Musar, then the preacher, too, is unable to open his mouth to speak."[38] The people's neglect brings despair to the zaddik.

However, even when the people refuse to listen, there is still a way. It is true that the preacher who reproves simply to fulfill his formal obligation will seek any opportunity to excuse himself. If he sees that the people do not want to be preached at, he will refrain from preaching with no sense of guilt. This is not the case, however, with "the preacher who reproves not from the fear of punishment but from love of the King, who preaches in order to return the son to his Father—even if he knows that he will not listen. He dresses himself like the prince who is lost among the wicked, to come close to him and speak to his heart, so that he might restore him to his Father, the King. The preacher thinks to himself: 'Though the people do not accept my words now, perhaps afterward they will perceive and repent.' "[39] The zaddik, filled with concern for the people, will not be balked at a light refusal, at their turning aside from him, but will follow after them as the Zohar prescribes: "One must pursue after the guilty." "Even though the people were separated from Moses, he was not separated from them."[40] There can be no separation as long as love for the people burns in the zaddik's heart. He will pursue after all who will listen. If the learned will not listen, he will speak to the simple people. "If there are only a few, even a single one who wants to receive Musar, [the zaddik] must preach to him."[41]

"It is not easy for the zaddik, who is the leader of the generation, to bestow the heavenly outpouring upon others; it is easier for him to retire from the world and receive the outpouring of heaven for himself. But when the people make ready to accept the outpouring from the zaddik, desiring to hear from his mouth Torah and Musar, then he is likewise stirred to bestow his spirit upon them.... But, at first, when the people neither know of this, nor wish this, it is necessary that he bestir *himself*, as in the beginning of creation. So it is at the beginning of the leadership of a city for each generation and its leaders."[42]

The ideal situation is one in which the people and the preacher remove all barriers between them—all hatred, suspicion and desire for honor—and meet one another in that *devekut* of preacher and congregation, of mouth and ear, which is the ultimate goal of Musar. This is the highest hope which the preacher possesses, not only to subdue their hearts and turn them to contrition, but to join with them and raise them in *devekut*. He can hope to achieve this with only a few. "Words of Musar are not enough... for there is a higher rung... that of raising them in spirit.... But this cannot apply to everyone, for it is difficult to raise them in spirit, except for a single man or woman."[43] " 'Happy is the one who seizes the hand of the guilty.' I heard in the name of the rabbi and preacher from Bar that words of Musar which one speaks with his mouth to the people are not enough, but he must join himself to them, to raise them."[44]

The preacher, having achieved *devekut*, preaches to the people, and, in the midst of his words, tries to raise them as he speaks. Not only his words but his heart and soul are bound up with God, and seek to be bound up as well with the people, so that they may rise together. Thus Musar becomes not only a matter of moral exhortation, but a spiritual moment when souls join, when the people, in utter faith and acceptance, give themselves to the preacher, and the preacher, in utter love and concern, gives himself to the people. A holy union is then formed which touches the very heavens. "... at the same moment when he utters words of chastisement to them which break their hearts... they cleave to him and are included in him, for there remains only one who speaks and one who listens, both of whose hearts are directed to heaven. The one preaches—not for self-glory or for benefit—but for the sake of heaven; the other listens—suspecting him of no evil thing—also for the sake of heaven. Then a heavenly *yihud* is fashioned and an outpouring descends upon each from above."[45] "When there is reproving in the world, that is, there is one who preaches and one who listens, then a *yihud* takes place in heaven, and this causes 'blessing in the world.' "[46]

There are occasional moments when the giving and receiving of Musar may reach the exalted goals of *devekut* and *yihud*, but the preacher is regularly required to speak strong words, to reprove, reproach and admonish, to break the hearts of those who listen. And herein lies a problem. For is it not a fearful duty to preach Musar to the people of Israel, the chosen of God, who are called the "children of the Lord" and bear His tidings for all mankind? To accuse the people of Israel falsely may widen the abyss between God and His people, cause anger and strife, bring punishment and calamity.[47] Some preachers chastise freely with no sense of responsibility. They are to be reviled, for they speak harshly, cruelly, often just to hear themselves talk. But even the zaddik whose motives are honorable must hesitate in giving Musar, since it is possible that, in a spell of self-righteous anger or an outburst of uncontrollable rage, he might condemn the people unjustly. "It is necessary to warn the one who chastises the people lest he transgress the command, 'Thou shalt not go up and down as a tale-bearer among thy people.'"[48] What then is he to do— keep silent?

The answer is that he should chastise the people *out of love*. Chastise them he must, but never in a spirit of anger, bitterness or indignation, only in a spirit of compassion.[49] Concern for the people and their plight flows over into love for them, a going out toward them, an embracing of them, a feeling of tender compassion and clement dismay for a dear one who has done wrong. "No man who merely speaks from his mouth may dare to chastise the people.... His silence is better than his word."[50] He must speak "from the innermost chambers of his heart."[51] "The scholar who preaches in public to the people must be certain that in the very moment he admonishes them he loves them and that he admonishes them out of love, as a loving father admonished his son, as it is written, 'Whom the Lord loveth He admonisheth.' "[52] "He should say Musar out of love for God and love for Israel, even though they have not acted properly, for it is all because of the exile.... 'You shall not stand by the blood of your neighbor,' but 'love your neighbor as yourself' (Lev. 19:16, 18) and out of love reprove him."[53] Thus the verse "Better open reproof than hidden love" (Prov. 27:5) is ingeniously read, "How good is open reproof when it comes *out of* hidden love."[54]* Musar must be given, but it comes from the love for the people which is hidden in the zaddik's heart.

"There are two kinds of preachers, as in the parable I heard from my teacher. A king sent his only son away from him, selecting two servants to go with him. One returned and spoke evil of the prince to his father. The second one returned and spoke similarly. But the latter spoke out of the anguish he felt at the anguish of the king and the anguish of his son, who had been sent away for such a long time... that he forgot the royal customs and was mocked by the nobles. Then the king was filled with pity...."[55] Rabbi Yaakov Yosef pleads for the second kind of preacher and chastiser, one who loves his people with a love as deep as the love with which the second servant loved the prince. He speaks the truth about the people, but it is a truth surrounded with understanding and compassion. He feels both the anguish of the king and the anguish of the people "How good is open reproof when it comes out of hidden love."

THE ZADDIK MUST HEARKEN TO HIS OWN MUSAR

Since Musar is an act of condemnation and reproof, is it not implied that the one who gives Musar is innocent while the

---

* *Tovah tochahat megulah* me *ahavah mesuteret.*

one to whom it is given is guilty? Does it not follow that the judgment which the zaddik utters falls upon the people and places him as judge and admonisher—even though he judges and admonishes out of love—above the people?

The answer is that the zaddik is partially *responsible* for the sin of the people and must himself hearken to the very Musar which he preaches. If the concern and the love which the zaddik feels for the people joins him to them, it is because he understands that he is, in part, one of them. They are not two separate units, but portions of a larger unity. The head may be wiser than the body, but it is no less a part of it; the heart is more centrally located than the limbs, but each is joined to the other. When the zaddik judges the people, he does not set himself above them, for he is not their judge apart from the judgment he utters and must, therefore, himself be judged by that very judgment. He is not the Judge, but His messenger; he is not the source, but the channel of God's chastisements. The responsibility for the situation is his as well as the people's, for they are—people and leader, hasid and zaddik—in essence, one. If the people do not study Torah, should he not have taught them; if they are jealous, does he not feel envy for other scholars; if they do not pray with devotion, may it not be due to his lack of kavannah; if they clamor for money, does he not yearn for security? "How can the preacher, who is the leader of the city or the generation, open his mouth to condemn the people for doing this or that? Will they not say: 'You are the cause,' even though you say they are the cause? If so, who can give Musar? Apparently it is better to keep silent. Therefore the verse teaches, 'rebuke' yourself and afterward 'rebuke your neighbor.'"[56] For the zaddik this means that "he must not separate himself from Musar in the hour when he gives Musar to others, but should include himself in that very Musar."[57]

He who speaks Musar stands in a relation of unity with and

therefore of responsibility for all those whom he would have listen to him. Thus, he is warned: "Do not cast the blame upon others and exclude yourself. But join yourself with them. This is the meaning of the verse, 'Moses went and he spoke' (Deut. 31:1)—when he *spoke* reproachfully, Moses himself *went* with them, joining himself with them."[58] The preacher should join himself to the people to whom he preaches. His ears should hear the words which his mouth utters, and his soul should hearken to them. He should feel the failing of the people and his share in that failing, for he and they are one.

The Scriptural passage to which Rabbi Yaakov Yosef would have us turn to best understand his message is from the holiness chapter of the Book of Leviticus. In these words he finds, hidden and revealed, much of his doctrine of Musar.

Text: In righteousness shall you judge your neighbor. You shall not go up and down as a talebearer among your people; neither shall you stand by the blood of your people: I am the Lord. You shall not hate your brother in your heart; rebuke, rebuke your neighbor, and do not bear sin because of him. You shall not take vengeance, nor bear hatred against the children of your people, but you shall love your neighbor as yourself (Lev. 19:15-18).

Explanation: "In righteousness shall you judge your neighbor." When you give Musar, you should bear in mind that he is "your neighbor," for all his faults are yours as well. Then surely you must judge him "in righteousness." "You shall not go up and down as a talebearer among your people," that is, you should not act the false accuser of your people, so that "you do not stand by the blood of your neighbor." For you and he are one. "For I am the Lord," full of mercy, and you may not, God forbid, change mercy to harsh judgment. "You shall not hate your brother." How can you hate him since he is your brother? Even if he has committed a sin worthy of hatred, this fault which is in him, is in you also, for you are one Divine Countenance.... Hatred is brought about because of the two impulses in man, the good impulse and the evil impulse, which are in you as well as in him. "Rebuke, rebuke your neighbor," that is, when you rebuke your neighbor, rebuke yourself *with him* since he is your neighbor. "Do not put sin upon him," that is, you should not heap sin on him alone, for the two of you are as one. Thus "You shall not take vengeance nor bear hatred, against the children of your people, but you shall love your neighbor as yourself."[59]

One further consideration must be added. Not only must the zaddik join himself to the people, rebuking himself *at the same time* he rebukes the people, he must "rebuke himself *first* and afterward rebuke the people."[60] He must be worthy to rebuke the people, having fulfilled the talmudic dictum: "Purify yourself and afterward purify others."[61] "One may extend a hand to raise his friend out of a pit... filled with snakes and scorpions, but if his friend does not want to grasp his hand *because he finds some fault in him,* how can he pull him out? He can only draw out one who will seize his hand."[62] There must be no fault in the one who gives Musar, no cause for suspicion, no double standard separating what he does from what he says. He must be one in word and deed, in heart and lips. His very life must be a confirmation of the words he dares to speak, "for the true effect of the words of rebuke do not depend upon the word of the preacher, but upon his deed."[63]

GOD'S RESPONSIBILITY

Rabbi Yaakov Yosef is not content with issuing a call for Musar, with denouncing the preacher who sets himself over the people for his own profit and with laying down the principles of love and responsibility as the characteristics of the one who would give Musar. He goes a step further. There are times when the zaddik pleads for the people and holds not only himself responsible, but God as well! This view is clearly implied in a slightly different version of the above-mentioned story. "A king sent his son to another land and dispatched two servants with him. After a time, the prince forgot the royal ways, committed adultery, murder, robbery and became like the wicked people among whom he lived. One of the servants fled from the prince and spoke ill of him to his father. Afterward, the second servant fled and entreated the king: 'How could you not have mercy upon your son who has fallen to such a low estate, *because you have expelled him?*'"[64] Still more striking is the manner in which a third version of the tale ends. "The second servant said the same things as the first, but *he put the blame on the prince's father* who sent him away, so that he mingled with the nations and learned their ways."[65]

The deep concern for the people which animated the zaddik and cast a glow of compassion on his every deed made it impossible to complete the doctrine of Musar with the demand that the preacher speak out courageously against the evils of the time, sparing no one, not even the rich and the mighty. This was one significant level of the doctrine, which brought the strength and wisdom to lay bare those very evils, to condemn openly the persons at whose door lay the responsibility for the degeneration of spiritual life, which silence on the part of the leaders had fostered. At this point most doctrines of Musar have ended: The wrong is denounced and the right demanded. But concern, which grows into compassion and love and is filled with the selflessness of humility, burst through such an ending with the question: Is he who rebukes himself innocent? Does he have a right to hold himself above the people? Surely he does not. It is precisely because he is one of the people that he feels concern for them at all. He is the soul for their limbs, the heart for their body. Since he is ultimately responsible for whatever he condemns, the words he utters are meant for himself as well as the people. He cannot speak to the people if he does not also listen. Indeed, he must hear them first and then hope that the people will hear them too. His actions must be the living symbol of his words. This is the next level of the doctrine—involvement of the preacher in the sin of the people, whom he rebukes out of love. Unity implies concern; criticism implies self-criticism; judgment implies responsibility.

Even at this level, the love which burns within the zaddik will not give him ease. So great is his compassion for the people and so deep the anguish he feels for their anguish that he comes near to blasphemy. True, the people are sinful and full of impurity. They are not what the kingdom of priests and the holy nation should be. Bad thoughts, jealousy, pride, a hardening of the heart, exist. All this must be admitted and dealt with. But has not the long arm of the exile weighed heavily upon a defenseless multitude, driving them from land to land, exposing them to suffering without end, crushing their spirit, grinding them into the muck of every age? This is the reason why the prince has become as the common peasants around him, why Israel, once a nation chosen of the Lord, royal in the glory of its holiness, has become like all the nations.

And who sent the prince away from the table of the king into a foreign land where he was oppressed and abused, if not the king himself? Who sent Israel into exile if not the King of all kings, their Father in heaven? With Him then lies part of the blame. It is not enough to hold the people *and* the leader responsible—*God too is responsible!* The people must repent, the leader must purify himself, but God also must take pity. Still more, this exile that Israel suffers amidst the nations is only the outer exile which reveals within a yet deeper exile, an inner exile of the spirit, an exile that has the power to bring moments of desolation and despair to the wandering, princely people; "for there is no greater exile of the *Shechinah* than this: that every Israelite strives to cling to Him Who is blessed, by any manner of subterfuge, but the 'leaven in the dough prevents.'"[66] Who is it that has set the course of humanity so that it could be written, "The imagination of man's heart is evil from its youth" (Gen. 8:21)? The reign of the evil desire over the individual and the reign of the nations over the people of Israel spell a twofold exile. God is involved in both. It is against the Creator of the universe and the Lord of history that accusation must be hurled. Ultimately, the exile—in body and in spirit—is His doing. Ultimately, therefore, He must take mercy. This is the most passionate word the zaddik can utter.

Thus the circle of Musar is completed. The zaddik rebukes the people, rebukes himself and, if one may speak so, rebukes the Almighty. He pleads for repentance from all three—that the people may turn to the Lord with a broken heart, that he who speaks Musar should only do so in love, listening to his own words and, finally, that the Lord Himself should turn to the people and grant them mercy. The responsibility rests upon all three: the people, the zaddik and the Lord. One bond binds them all.

Conclusion

Let us attempt to briefly sum up Rabbi Yaakov Yosef's doctrine of the zaddik.

The spiritual decline of the inner life of eighteenth-century East-European Jewry, while blamed in part upon the failure of the people, was due mainly to the shortcomings of the rabbis and scholars of the time. The sin of pride had three primary effects upon them. First, it perverted their Torah study into a form of vain display which engendered jealousy, hatred and self-seeking; second, it promoted a desire for personal security which led to an attitude of obsequiousness toward the rich that destroyed effective rabbinic leadership; third, it fostered a craving for spiritual security which resulted in the seeking of personal salvation for themselves through a meticulous observance of the details of the law, while at the same time ignoring the needs of the people. Thus the general attitude of the scholars toward the masses, most of whom were without learning (and also without means), was one of contempt for and seclusion from them and contributed to the disastrous condition of *perud*—that fearful breach which divides man within himself, from his fellow man and from his God.

The crisis of the age was brought about by corrupted leadership. The solution lay in the same area. The solution demanded an uprooting of the old and the development of a new kind of leader, one who was both dedicated and selfless, strong in conviction, humble in character and fearless in action —the zaddik. He is the "foundation of the world," for around him the ruins of the time could be rebuilt into a dedicated community of the faithful.

The zaddik stands between heaven and earth. He is the "channel" which brings heaven to earth and the means (through *devekut*) for earth reaching heaven. As pride characterizes the rabbi and scholar, placing blinders over their eyes so that they looked only inwardly toward their own needs and desires, so humility characterizes the zaddik who sees the needs of others even before he sees his own. He moves between two poles: God and Israel. To the *Shechinah* he owes all his powers, for the root of his soul is in the *Shechinah*, the deepest source of his "I"; to Israel he belongs, since it is only for their sake that he lives, to serve them, to lead and watch over them as a shepherd his flock. It is not for his own sake that he labors but for the sake of the people; it is not from his own powers that he draws strength but from the *Shechinah*. His task is to heal the breach, to make whole the broken, to bring heaven down to earth and raise earth up to heaven: to bring God and Israel together. He joins his own effort to the drive for *ahdut* which surges throughout the universe—that wholeness which unites man within himself, with his fellow man and with his God.

While pride fostered contempt for the people and seclusion from them, humility permitted concern for the people and a going down to them. The doctrine of the zaddik is in its most profound sense a doctrine of concern. He is willing to suffer for them, since they are "the limbs of the *Shechinah*"; his life is bound up with theirs, for they are the body of which he is the soul and the matter of which he is the form, a portion of his own self without which he is only half. He strives to save the people, for in each of them, no matter how dark the pit into which they have fallen, are sparks of holiness which wait to be redeemed. The concern of the zaddik expresses itself best in what is described as his "descent" to the people. For if he is to help the people by raising earth to heaven, he must locate that earth, he must reach out toward the people, find them and meet them. He does not wait for them to come to him but goes out and down to their level, speaking with them, praying with them, preaching to them, trying to find some way to reach them so that he may return them on high. This is the task of the zaddik.

The classic example of the "descent of the zaddik" is the parable of the banished king's son who, after many nobles (the aloof rabbis) have been sent and failed, is at last brought back to the table of his father by the wise noble (the zaddik). To save the prince, the zaddik must descend to his level and become involved in his life—for concern implies involvement, that is, feeling, at least in part, responsible for the sins of the prince and even, in a sense, guilty of them as well. Only then can he know the way to reach him and bring him up. But herein lies the danger: perhaps the zaddik's very proximity to sin and his familiarity with the ways of the world may entice him, and instead of raising the sinner from the dark pit of the world, he himself will be drawn into it.

The answer is manifold. Not every self-styled leader is permitted or able to descend, and he who does undertake the perilous venture must take care regarding his relationship to the people. He must be close to them, but not too close. Above all, before he goes out to the people in the market place or the tavern, away from the security of house of study, he must first bind the root of his soul to God, like the man who, before descending into a pit to raise up one who lies at the bottom, must first fasten a rope about himself and secure it at the top of the pit. Thus, even when going out to the people, the zaddik somehow remains bound up with God; and this is the paradox of the zaddik, a paradox of solitude and communion, of being among the people and yet all the while standing in the presence of God, of going "into the midst of the city" and yet, at the very same time, cleaving to the Lord and fulfilling literally the verse, "I have set the Lord before me at *all* times."

ABBREVIATIONS

THE TITLES OF RABBI YAAKOV YOSEF'S BOOKS

T. = תולדות יעקב יוסף, Lemberg, Stand. ed. 1863.
P. Y. = בן פורת יוסף, Lemberg, Balaban ed. S. D.
K. P. = כתנת פסים, Lemberg, Photo-offset ed. 1866.
Z. P. = צפנת פענח, Lemberg, Druker ed. 1866.

OTHER ABBREVIATIONS OCCURRING IN THE NOTES

אא"כ — אלא אם כן.

אא"ה — אברהם אבינו עליו השלום.

אא"ז — אדוני אבי זקני.

אב"ד — אב בית דין.

אבע"א — איבעית אימא.

אדמו"ר — אדוננו מורנו ורבנו.

א"ה — אי הכי: אומות העולם.

אה"ע — [אברהם] אבינו עליו השלום.

או"ח — אורח חיים.

אח"כ — אחר כן, אחר כך, אחרי כן.

א"נ — [פרק] אלו נאמרין [סוטה].

אנס"ו — אמן נצח סלה ועד.

א"ע — את עצמו, את עצמם.

אר"א — אמר רבי אלעזר.

אר"י — [האר"י] אשכנזי רבי יצחק לוריא [=האלהי אשכנזי ר' יצחק לוריא]:
אמר רבי יצחק; אמר רבי יוחנן.

אר"ע — אמר רבי עקיבא.

א"ש — אתי שפיר.

א"ת — אם תאמר.

ב"א — בני אדם.

ב"ב — במהרה בימינו.

בה"מ — בית המדרש.

בזה"ז — בזמן הזה.

ב"ח — בעלי חיים: בעלי חוב.

בל"א — בלשון אשכנז.

בלא"ה — בלאו הכי.

במ"א — במקום אחר.

בע"ת — בעל תורה, בעלי תורה.

ב"פ — ב' פעמים.

בפ"ע — בפני עצמו.

בפ"ק — בפרק קמא.

בשהרז"ל — בשם הרב זכרונו [זכרון] לברכה.

ג"כ — גם כן.

דהל"ו — דהוי ליה למימר.

דהע"ה — דוד המלך עליו השלום.

דק"ל — דקשה ליה.

ה"ה — הלא הוא.

הו"ת — הלכה ותוספות.

הל"ל — הוי ליה למימר.

ה"נ — הכי נמי.

הנ"ל — הנזכר לעיל.

הרה"ק — הרב הקדוש.

השי"ת — השם יתברך.

התו' — התוספות.

וג', וגו' — וגומר.

ודפח"ח — ודברי פי חכם חן.

וה"נ — והכי נמי.

וז"ל — וזה לשונו.

וז"ש — וזה שאמר, וזה שכתב.

וכו' — וכוליה.

וכ"כ — וכן כתוב.

וי"ל — ויש לומר, ויש ליישב.

ולענ"ד, ולפענ"ד — ולפי עניות דעתי.

ומש"ה — ומשום הכי.
וע"כ — ועל כן.
וק"ל — וקל להבין:

ז"א — זאת אומרת.
זה"ז — זמן הזה.
זי"ע — זכותו יגן עלינו.
[זללה"ה] זלה"ה — זכרונו [זכרו] [לברכה]
לחיי העולם הבא.
ז"ש — זה שאמר; זה שכתב.

ח"ה — [פרק] חזקת הבתים [בבא בתרא].
ח"ו, חו"ש — חס ושלום.
חז"ל — חכמינו זכרם [זכרונם] לברכה.

טו"ר — טוב ורע.

י"ל — יש לומר, יש ליישב.
יעוי"ש, יעו"ש — יעויין שם.
[יצ"ט] יצה"ט — יצר [טוב] הטוב.
יצה"ר — יצר הרע.
ית' — יתברך.
יח"ש — יתברך שמו.

כ' — כלומר.
כ"א — כי אם; כל אחד.
כד"א — כמה דאת אומר.
כדק' — כדקאמר.
כ"י — כל ישראל; כתב יד.
כ"כ — כן כתוב.
בנ"ל, כנ"ל — כנזכר לעיל.
כנ"ל — כן [כך] נראה לי.
כ"ת — כתב תורה; כתר תורה.

ל"ה — לשון הדיוט.
לענ"ד, לפענ"ד — לפי עניות דעתי.
לש"ש — לשם שמים.
ל"ת — לשון תורה.

מ"א — מקום אחר.
מא"ה — מאומות העולם.
מחו' — מחותני.
מ"ט — מאי טעמא.

מכ"ש — מכל שכן.
מ"מ — מכל מקום.
מ"צ, מ"ץ — מורה צדק.
משא"כ — מה שאין כן.
מש"ה — משום הכי.
משרע"ה — משה רבנו עליו השלום.

ני"ו — נדו יאיר ויזרח.
נר"ו — נטריה רחמנא ופרקיה.

ס"מ — סמאל.
ס"ת — ספר תורה.

ע"ד — על דבר, על דרך.
ע"ה, עה"ש — עליו השלום.
עוה"ב — עולם הבא.
עוה"ז — עולם הזה.
ע"י — על ידי.
עי"ז — על ידי זה.
ע"כ — על כן; על כרחך.
עע"ז — עובד עבודה זרה.
עפ"ז, עפי"ז — על פי זה.

פ' — פרק [פ' א"נ=פרק אלו נאמרין
בסוטה]; פרשה.
פ"א — פעם אחת.

קב"ה, קוב"ה — קודשא בריך הוא.

רז"ל — רבותינו זכרם [זכרונם] לברכה.
ריב"ל — רבי יהושע בן לוי.
ר"ל — רצוני [רצונו] לומר; רחמנא ליצלן.
ר"מ, ר"ס — ריש מתיבתא.
רשב"י — רבי שמעון בר יוחai.
ר"ת — ראשי תבות.

שו"ת — שאלות ותשובות.
ש"מ — שמע מניה.
ש"ש — שם שמים.

תו' — תוספות.
תוב"ב — תבנה ותכונן במהרה בימינו.
ת"ח — תא חזי; תלמיד חכם.

APPENDIX

Rabbi Yaakov Yosef's Books

Even though the *Toldot*, the earliest of his books, was published in 1780, toward the end of his life (c. 1782),[1] there is every indication that he commenced writing them many years before. The evidences of early material in his books are abundant. Such passages as "... many holy ones were killed for our sins *this year 1752* (תקי״ב) in the land of Ukraina";[2] "the occurrence that I was told of which took place in the city of Begrad *this year 1768* (תקכ״ח)";[3] "... *last year 1755* (תקט״ו)";[4] the several sermons which are prefaced by the dates when they were preached, ranging from 1761 (תקכ״א) to 1767 (תקכ״ז);[5] and the fact that several times in the *Toldot* we find the phrase: "I heard from my teacher *may he live forever*"[6] (indicating that the Besht was still living at the time — he died c. 1760)[7] — are all indicative of the period of time, at least twenty-seven years,[8] which was spent in the writing of his books.

In the process of recording what his master said, Rabbi Yaakov Yosef was well aware that his would be the responsibility of preserving for the generations the words of his master. He, therefore, took great pains to report them as accurately as possible, clearly indicating to the reader whether he heard each particular statement from the Besht himself or from a third party. Thus the expressions: "I *heard* from my teacher" (which occurs 394 times), or: "I *received* from my teacher" (nineteen times), represent *direct* quotations from the Besht. (In addition to these two forms of direct quotations there is a possible third form "ביאר מורי." Frequently he simply writes "שמעתי," but, in all probability, refers to the Besht.) Even here he sometimes changes the wording for emphasis, and so we find: "I heard *explicitly* from my teacher" (*P. Y.* 70b), "I heard from the *mouth* of my teacher" (*T.* 28d, 63a; *P. Y.* 55c), "I heard *explicitly from the mouth* of my teacher" (*T.* 23b, 100a. The last mentioned reference in the Lemberg edition, 1863, is printed "מפרש," which is an error for "מפורש." See Koretz edition, *loc. cit.*), and "I heard from my teacher *mouth to mouth.*" (*T.* 131a).

But often he presents *indirect* quotations, which fact he is particular to call to one's attention. Thus: "I heard *in the name of* my teacher" (ninety nine times). And when he is not certain himself of the authenticity of what he quotes or the manner in which he heard it, he tells us so expressly. Thus we find: "*It seems to me* that I heard from my teacher" (*T.* 50c, 75a; *P. Y.* 53c, 54c), or: "The above is the *style of my teacher*" (*P. Y.* 71a), or: "It appears to me that I heard this line of thought from my teacher (*Z. P.* 20b), or: "It is possible that I heard this also from my teacher, the Lord knows." (*P. Y.* 64c), or: "This is *not his exact language*, for I have added somewhat to it" (*Z. P.* 25b).

In other respects too, the wording of the opening phrase of quotations from the Besht are significant. Some examples of these phrases are: "I heard from my teacher in the name of *his teacher*" (Aḥiyah ha-Shiloni);[9] "I heard from my teacher in the name of the Ramban";[10] "I heard from my teacher in the name of Saʿadia";[11] "My teacher explained *according to his method*";[12] "I heard from my teacher *regarding himself.*"[13]

Introducing a number of quotations from the Besht toward the end of the *Toldot*, our author remarks, "These are the words which I heard from my teacher (may his memory live on in the future world), and I have written only 'headings of chapters' (ראשי פרקים) *because I am afraid of revealing secrets and because of forgetfulness.*"[14] It would seem that here we have two of the principles which guided his writing: first, "forget-fulness" of what the exact words of the Besht were as well as the manner in which he heard them, and, second, his fear of revealing mysteries which were best kept secret. "I am afraid to write down the wonderful things I heard from my teacher ..., but I put down the chapter headings on a separate sheet of paper ... May God forgive me."[15] This fear not only characterized his attitude to some of the quotations from the Besht but applied to his writings in general: "I have written of this in another place in the briefest fashion, for I have no right to enlarge upon it."[16] "This is a great principle, but it is not given to me to write more ...."[17] "I have written out of necessity .... May the Lord who is blessed forgive me ...."[18] May the Lord who is blessed forgive me if I have erred."[19] "It is for the sake of the Lord's glory to conceal the matter."[20]

Four books of Rabbi Yaakov Yosef were published. *Toldot Yaakov Yosef* appeared first in 1780 both in Meziboz[21] and Koretz, and in numerous later editions. *Ben Porat Yosef* was first published in Koretz in 1781 and *Zafnat Paneah* in the same city in 1782. *Ketonet Passim* appeared years after his death, in 1866.

Toldot Yaakov Yosef was the first and by far the most important. It appeared (as did all the others) without the customary *haskamah*, or encomium, of contemporary authorities. This was explained by the publishers, Rabbi Abraham Samson Katz, head of the *bet din* in Rashkov, and Rabbi Abraham Dov-Baer, head of the *bet din* in Hmelnick (both sons-in-law of the author): "Because of preoccupation with the printing, we have not been able to acquire 'encomiums' from the great scholars of the land, but we are certain that all of them would give their assent to this precious book."[22] That all of them did not give their approval was soon evident from the storm which the publication of the *Toldot* aroused.

The book itself is arranged as a commentary on the Torah whose divisions, or *parshiot*, it follows. Its stated purpose is to explain how each of the commandments are eternal and meaningful for all times: "Since the Torah is eternal, it must be [true] in every place, for every man .... But one will raise objections regarding many *mitzvot* which do not seem to be

applicable to everyone, everywhere. Therefore I have come
now with the help of the Creator to explain how it is that not
one of the 613 *mitzvot* lacks meaning for any man, wherever
he may be ....'' [23] If the *mitzvot* were not eternal, but only
true under certain historical conditions which no longer
exist, then one might well say, ''... what is past history is
past history. Why should they be written in the Torah,
except to indicate that they, indeed, have meaning in the
present and in the future as in the past, for the Torah is
eternal?'' [24] Taking a specific example, our author writes: ''We
intend to explain the chapter of the golden calf, which is
written in the eternal Torah, because of the question, 'what is
past is past, what does it (the golden calf) teach *us*?' ... For
it is my method of writing to ask this question of each mitzvah *which
does not [seem true] for every age.*'' [25] Perhaps the best statement
as to the purpose of the book is to be found in the introduction.
After raising questions of time and place that would seem to
render many *mitzvot* inapplicable, he states: ''... because of
the above questions and doubts, my heart is full to explain
with the help of the Lord the 613 *mitzvot*, showing how they
[apply] to every age and time and to each man, and how each
mitzvah is a means whereby to cleave to the Lord. May the
Lord help me to complete [this book] for good and teach the
wonders of His Torah, that we may be worthy of cleaving to
Him, for 'the righteous man liveth by faith.' '' [26]

In the course of analyzing the *mitzvot* he moves across many
areas of thought and life. Some of the subjects he treats in
some detail are: the inner meaning of the Torah; the proper
study of the Torah for its own sake; prayer as a means of
helping the *Shekhinah*; the dynamic nature of man who ''rises
and falls'' and is, in truth, more than man; the paradox of
the transcendence and immanence of God; God's providence
and the consequent need for man's trust in Him; man's
ability and duty to ''know God in all His ways''; exile and
redemption as spiritual rather than merely physical conditions; continuous revelation; Israel, the Sabbath and the

Torah as the three inner aspects of creation; the underlying unity of each man, mankind and God, which has been sundered by pride and sin; the social and spiritual evils of the day; the relation between the scholar and the people, and between the scholar and the rich; the call for the new leader and the new community. This is a brief outline of several of the topics with which our author deals, albeit in an unsystematic manner, sometimes cryptically, occasionally stretching over many pages filled with striking quotations from the widest reaches of Jewish literature, but always with the burning desire of revealing the eternal message of the Torah to the Jew of his day.

The other three books of Rabbi Yaakov Yosef are smaller in size, less significant and often repeat ideas which had been treated in the *Toldot*, though often developing them more completely or along different lines. *Ben Porat Yosef* is divided into two sections, the first of which is a commentary to Genesis. It deals at times with the *mitzvot*,[27] but more often with the story of Genesis itself. Characteristic of the book is its manner of analyzing an idea or verse in several ways and listing these, "first manner" of explanation, "second manner,"[28] etc. It is, however, unsystematic and poorly organized. The second part of the book contains legalistic material: a talmudic pilpul,[28] and a number of responsa,[30] most of which are addressed to Rabbi Shabtai. Following this are some sermons delivered on *Shabbat Shuvah* or *Shabbat Hagadol*.[31] At the end of the volume is the famous letter of the Baal Shem to his brother-in-law, Rabbi Gershon Kitover, which was sent through Rabbi Yaakov Yosef.[32]

Zafnat Paneah is a commentary to Exodus and, like *Ben Porat Yosef*, has the tendency to analyze a subject in a number of different ways, which are listed: a, b, c, etc. It too is poorly organized and rarely brings a complete statement from the author's contemporaries, assuming that the reader is familiar with the quotation in its entirety. It is somewhat richer in content than *Porat Yosef* but still not equal to the *Toldot*.

Ketonet Passim is the last of his works, published posthumously. Dubnow considers it a forgery, but fails to cite any conclusive evidence for his opinion. A careful reading of the text in comparison with his other three volumes leads to the conclusion that it is an authentic work, edited by a later hand.

Dubnow writes: ספר מאוחר „כתונת פסים" (לבוב תרכ"ו) המיוחס לר' יעקב יוסף, חשוד בזיוף: אין בו אלא צירופים של דרשות שנדפסו בספר התולדות ובשאר ספרי הרב מפולנאה. (Dubnow, p. 97, note 1). While many of the thoughts and much of the language of *K. P.* can be found in his other books, the same can be said for *P. Y.* and *Z. P.* What is more important is the fact that several names mentioned in *K. P.* are not found in the other volumes: המנוח החסיד מוהר"ר חיים צאנזיר, 12b; מחותני ר"ח מוה', 12b; המנוח החסיד מוהר"ר צבי מבראד, 8a. *K. P.* is certainly not *simply* a collection of quotations from his other works (See chapter 10, note 2).

There are, for example, several early dates in the book. כתבתי אשתקד שנת תקט"ו, *K. P.* 1a. Cf. 22d. (See note 5 to this chapter.). Furthermore it is a commentary to Leviticus and Numbers which follows the pattern set by *P. Y.* (1781) which is a commentary on Genesis, followed by *Z. P.* (1782) which is a commentary on Exodus. So that it would seem that these volumes were all parts of a second commentary to the Torah the author had planned after the *Toldot*, which is a commentary to the complete Torah. However, *K. P.* does not possess the characteristic of *P. Y.* and *Z. P.* of listing different interpretations numerically, nor does it deal with the *mitzvot* as does the *Toldot*.

We have already endeavored to prove that Rabbi Yaakov Yosef's concern in reporting accurately what he heard from his master led him to choose expressions which inform the reader in what category of authenticity the quotation which he brought was. There is now another factor to be considered which, apart from supporting this thesis, sheds light on the number of years he spent writing each of his books and, also, on the authenticity of *K. P.* Whenever he quotes his teacher, the Baal Shem, either the abbreviation זלה״ה (may his memory live in the future world) or ז״ל (may his memory be for a blessing) appears afterwards, indicating that the Besht was already dead; or no abbreviation at all, indicating, perhaps, that he was still alive. Now it may well be that our author was not exact in this matter and that even when no abbreviation follows, his teacher may likewise have been dead. But if we assume the contrary, namely, that he was careful in the use of the abbreviations, זלה״ה and ז״ל, just as he was careful in the use of other phrases (as we have already indicated), some striking implications follow. In the *Toldot* the Besht is quoted 213 times without the above abbreviations and 36 times with them; in *P. Y.* he is quoted 59 times without abbreviations and 55 times with them; in *Z. P.* 29 times without and 78 with; in *K. P.* twice with and 64 without. To put it more clearly:

date of publication	ממורי (וכו׳) ממורי זלה״ה, ז״ל	שמעתי (וכו׳) שמעתי ממורי זלה״ה, ז״ל
1780 *Toldot*	36	213
1781 *P. Y.*	55	59
1782 *Z. P.*	78	29
1866 *K. P.*	2	64

Granting that there is evidence of material written at an early period in all of Rabbi Yaakov Yosef's books, the above figures allow us to draw the following conclusions:

1) The later the book published the higher percentage of quotations with זלה״ה and ז״ל, generally indicating, therefore, what percentage was written after the death of the Besht (c. 1760).

2) The material of the *Toldot* was written in good part *before* the death of the Besht, while that of *P. Y.* and *Z. P.* was written in good part *after* his death.

3) *K. P.* displays features which distinguish it from *P. Y.* and *Z. P.* not only in its not listing different interpretations,

but in reversing the rising percentage of the use of the abbreviations זלה״ה and ז״ל to a point less frequent even than in the *Toldot*. This indicates that either a different hand edited the volume or that the material was drawn from a pre-*Toldot* period and compiled by Rabbi Yaakov Yosef himself. The former alternative seems the more logical since, in addition to the percentage factor, *K. P.* does not possess the literary characteristics of both *P. Y.* and *Z. P.*, namely, analyzing a subject in a number of different ways which are listed numerically. An editor, in all probability, using material which our author had left in rough form as a commentary to Leviticus and Numbers, reworked it into its present form.

In addition to his four published works, Rabbi Yaakov Yosef had other manuscripts[33] which, for reasons unknown to us, he did not publish. This explains passages such as: "as is written in the preface of my Siddur,"[34] ". . . regarding this matter, see my other book,"[35] or "look toward the end of my large book (ספרי הגדול)"[36] or "I wrote regarding this matter, in my book."[37] We conclude that the books which we possess represent only a portion of what Rabbi Yaakov Yosef meant to publish. Is it possible, however, since in the *Toldot* he writes of his "book" and even tells the reader to "see" or "look" into "my book," apparently implying that it was in print and available, that another volume or volumes had actually been published?[38]

His Teachers

While the Besht was the master of Rabbi Yaakov Yosef, there were other contemporaries whom he also mentions in his works as his teachers. Several times he writes: "I heard from my *teachers*,"[39] and, thus, since the word "teachers" is used in the plural, we know he was not referring to the Besht alone. It may be significant to note that he never calls them "my masters" (מורי) but "my teachers" (רבותי). The word "master" (מורה) seems to have been used only in reference to the Besht himself. Rabbi Yaakov Yosef had a number of "teachers," but only one "master."

Many of the men he quotes by name are little known to us from other sources, at least so far as their teachings are concerned. Among those he mentions are the Mokhiaḥ Aryeh Leib Gliner of Polnoy, R. Barukh Mokhiaḥ, R. Gershon Kitover, R. Efraim, the Maggid I. of Meziboz, the Maggid Menaḥem Mendel of Bar, R. Moshe of Kutov, R. Noaḥ of Rashkov, R. Naḥman Kossover, R. Naḥman of Horodenka, R. Leib Pistener, R. Naftali and R. Shabtai of Rashkov. But which of these men, if any, he meant when he speaks of "my teachers" is nowhere indicated, since when he quotes someone by name, he never calls him "teacher" or "master"; and when he writes "I heard from my teachers," he never mentions a specific name. Rabbi Naḥman Kossover is the one exception to this generalization, since in one place he is quoted by name as "the ḥasid, *my teacher*, . . . Naḥman Kossover."[40] Elsewhere he is spoken of as "the distinguished ḥasid,"[41] and is quoted many times. In view of this, he may be considered one of the "teachers" referred to; but who are the others?

If we assume that Rabbi Yaakov Yosef was precise in his manner of quoting the Besht, as we have endeavored to demonstrate, then an examination of the way in which other persons are quoted or referred to, can be of aid to us. For example, scattered through Rabbi Yaakov Yosef's works are three funeral addresses.[42] One is for Rabbi Leib Pistener. "He who was unique among the zaddikim, who was a shield for many thousands of Israel, Rabbi Leib Pistener, has been snatched from this world."[43] He is the only person to be called "zaddik"[44] by name and is also referred to as "the holy one"[45] and "the ḥasid" and is frequently quoted. A second eulogy is for Rabbi Menaḥem Mendel, the Maggid of Bar, who, apart from the Besht himself, is quoted more often than any other single person.[46] "I shall write here in *parashat Bo*' of the year 1760 a eulogy for a distinguished rav, the deceased I. (?)[47] and the Rav, Menaḥem Mendel. The prophet Jeremiah says, 'O my soul, my soul! I writhe in anguish! O agony of my heart! My heart beats wildly within me, I cannot keep silent! For I hear the sound of the trumpet, the alarm of war. Crash follows crash, for the whole land is ruined . . . . (Jer. 4.19–20).' Rashi refers this to the destruction of Jerusalem . . . . But it refers also to the death of the zaddikim, which is equal to the burning of the house of our God . . . . And if you should think that it is enough for the people of his city to mourn the death of a zaddik, the Talmud says that when a zaddik dies, evil comes to the world. This means that the whole world suffers in the death of a zaddik; therefore he should be mourned in every place."[48] The third eulogy is for Rabbi Aryeh Leib, the Mokhiaḥ of Polnoy, to whose position Rabbi Yaakov Yosef succeeded after his death, and who helped to win him over as a disciple for the Besht.[49] Though in later years he may have continued ω exert an influence over him,[50] it should be added that he is rarely quoted by name.[51] In addition to the persons already dealt with there are others, most prominent among whom is Rabbi Naḥman of Horodenka,[52] who are called by the titles חסיד, ותיק ישיש or רבני. Mention of these occurs several times and they too may have been among Rabbi Yaakov Yosef's "teachers."[53]

Rabbi Yaakov Yosef's books, though the truest record of the teachings of the Besht and the source of the doctrines of a number of the Besht's circle which are known to us only from his work, are, nevertheless, something more than all this. Not only did he lean upon the exposition of his teachers but at times went beyond them and even disagreed: "I heard from my teacher . . . ., but I say,[54] or "The Rav and Maggid Menaḥem explained . . ., but I explained . . . ."[55] More important, however, than these few citations, are the wide areas of his thought which find no counterpart in that of the Besht or his "teachers."

NOTES

NOTES TO INTRODUCTION

[1] M. Buber, *Hasidism*, Philosophical Library, New York, 1948, Foreword, p. 4.

[2] *Ibid.*

[3] S. Baron, "Steinschneider's Contribution to Historiography, *Alexander Marx Jubilee Volume*, English Section, New York, 1950, p. 95.

[4] H. Graetz, *History of the Jews*, Philadelphia, 1898, Vol. 5, chapter 9, pp. 375–81.

[5] G. Scholem, *Major Trends in Jewish Mysticism*, New York, 1946, p. 337.

CHAPTER 1

THE CONDITIONS OF THE TIME

[1] S. Dubnow, *History of the Jews in Russia and Poland*, Philadelphia, 1916, vol. 1, pp. 156–57.

[2] Dubnow, "תולדות החסידות," Vol. 1, pp. 10–11

[3] *Ibid.*

[4] *Ibid.*, pp. 13–14.

[5] *Ibid.*, p. 21.

[6] *Ibid.*, p. 17.

[7] See *T.* pp. 27d, 28a, 85d.

[8] *T.* 85b.

[9] Yoma 9b.

[10] *T.* 28a.

[11] *Ibid.*

[12] Quoted by Kamelhar, "דור דעה," New York, 1952, Vol. 1, p. 114.

[13] *T.* 28a.

[14] *T.* 33d.

[15] *T.* 28a.

[16] *K. P.* 3b.

[17] *T.* 46a.

[18] *T.* 28a; cf. *Z. P.* 49a.

[19] Sotah 49a.

[20] *T.* 85c.

[21] See *T.* 127b, c.

[22] *T.* 58c.
[23] *K. P.* 7b.
[24] Zohar III, p. 203a.
[25] *T.* 127d.
[26] *T.* 80b.
[27] *K. P.* 7b.
[28] *Ibid.*
[29] *T.* 127b.
[30] *T.* 127c.
[31] See *Z. P.* 16a, *P. Y.* 17d, 99c.
[32] *P. Y.* 17d.

CHAPTER 2

THE LIFE OF RABBI YAAKOV YOSEF

[1] Our author speaks in the first person in his own books only rarely. See *T.* 99a and 102a.

[2] Preface to *T.*

[3] הבעש'ט זללה'ה אומר: הש'י וועט מיר דאנקין :41 .p ,1876 ,Warsaw ",מדרש פנחס"
.וואס איך האב איהם צו גישטעליט אזוי אייז יוסלי

[4] According to Dubnow, "תולדות החסידות," Vol. 1, p. 94, note 3, he was driven from Sharograd about 1748, resided in Rashkov from 1748–1752, in Nemirov from 1752–1770 and in Polnoy from 1770 until the time of his death, about 1782.

[5] למשפחת המקובל ר' שמשון מאוסטרופולי והמקובל ר' יוסף כ'ץ מחבר .יסוד יוסף',
ולמשפחת הגאון ר' יום טוב ליפמאן העלער מחבר .תוספות יום טוב' — נולד ר' יעקב יוסף
הכהן. Horodetzky, "החסידות והחסידים," Vol. 1, p. 105. See the second part of
P. Y. in which are printed a number of his responsa and a halakhic discourse
prefaced by: *P. Y.* חילוק של כבוד ה ר ב המחבר בימי חורפו בלימוד הישיבה לחידודי
78a. On the title page of *T.* (Koretz edition, 1780, only) are printed the names
of Rabbi Yaakov Yosef's son and son-in-law: הובא לבית הדפוס ע'י כבוד הרב
המאור הגדול המופלג בתורה וביראה ובחסידות החכם השלם כבוד מו' א ב ר ה ם ש מ ש ו ן
כ'ץ אשר ה' אב'ד בק'ק ראשקוב ה'ה בן הגאון המחבר נר'ו אשר תקע אהלו לשבת
בארץ הקדושה תוב'ב כי שם ביתו וע'י כבוד הרב המאור הגדו' החריף ובקי המופלג בתורה
ובחסידות כבוד מוהר'ר א ב ר ה ם ד ו ב נר'ו אב'ד ור'ם ום'ץ דק'ק חמעלניק ה'ה חתן
הגאון המחבר הנ'ל.
Further references to Rabbi Yaakov Yosef's family are as follows: *K. P.* 8a:
לא נחתי ולא שקטתי ויבא רוגז ליוסף'.* *P. Y.* 84a: שמעתי בשם מ ח ו ת נ י מוה' ר'ח
שנענשתי ב פ ט י ר ת א ח י הנחמד ז'ל ואנה אני בא מצערו של אבא אשר כל מנמתו
חפצו וישעו היה אליו . . . This latter remark is contained in a responsum

written from Rashkov, where he lived circa 1748–1752, to R. Shabtai. *P. Y.* 99d: בשם גיסי החסיד המפו' מוהר"ן זלה"ה שמעתי. Is it possible that we should read instead of גיסי, גיסו, thus identifying מוהר"ן as ר' גרשון, the brother-in-law of the Baal Shem? See also *P. Y.* 88a.

[6] א. כהנא, ספר החסידות", Warsaw, 1922, p. 105.

[7] Kidushin 4.14.

[8] י. ל. מימון, מדי חודש בחדשו", Jerusalem, 1955, pp. 176–77

[9] Cahana, *op. cit.*, p. 106.

[10] הרב המוכיח אריה ליב גלינר מפולנאה. He was the predecessor of R. Yaakov Yosef in Polnoy. See Horodetsky, "החסידות והחסידים," Vol. 1, pp. 136–38

[11] שבחי הבעש"ט," ed. Horodetsky, Tel Aviv, 1947, p. 61.

[12] *Ibid.*

[13] Yaakov Yosef's opinion of the Besht is reflected in the following quotations: שמעתי מן הרב המנוח מו"ה יעקב יוסף הכהן זללה"ה ששמע מן אדוני אבי זקיני [הבעל שם טוב] זלה"ה שאמר .לפעמים יש שהעולם עומד במעלות הרוממות ולפעמים העולם עומד במדריגות התחתונות. ועתה שאני בעולם העולם עומד במדרגות הרוממות. עד כאן לשון הטהור אא"ז זלה"ה. .דגל מחנה אפרים", פ' בלק

שמעתי ממורי שהראו לו כשהוליכו אותו תחת תחת עץ הדעת טו"ר [=טוב ורע] *P. Y.* 14c: היו עמו אנשים הרבה מישראל, ואחר כך כשהכניסו אותו תחת עץ החיים היו מועטים, ואחר כך כשהכניסו אותו בגן עדן הפנימי נתמעט עוד עד שנשארו מעט מזעיר ודפה"ח [=ודברי פי חכם חן].

[14] שבחי הבעש"ט," p. 61.

[15] *Ibid.*, p. 62.

[16] *Ibid.*, p. 65.

[17] *Ibid.*

[18] *Ibid.*, Avot 1.4.

[19] Cahana, *op. cit.*, p. 111: תלמידי הבעש"ט היו נוהגין לישון בחדר הסמוך לחדר משכבו, כל אחד לילו. פעם בליל שבת קדש לילו של ר' דוד לאה"קס היה. שומע הוא באמצע הלילה שני קולות מדברים בחדרו של הבעש"ט. הטה אזנו, והנה קולו של הבעש"ט אומר: .נו יצחק, הלא תודה לדעתי בעניין כוונת שמע ישראל"? האר"י: .לא"! הבעש"ט: .ואני עומד על דעתי. שהכוונה היא כך. ידעת מה? נעלה ונשאל בעליונים". האר"י: .טוב, נכנס להיכלו של משיח". הבעש"ט: .ואני רוצה ליכנס דוקא להיכלו של רשב"י". אחר כך נשתתקו הקולות לזמן מה. ושוב נשמע קולו של הבעש"ט: .נו, יצחק, עכשיו רואה אתה שהכוונות הן לשיטתי. מחר אדרוש ואטעים כוונתי בניגוד לכוונתך. ר' יעקב יוסף הקפדן יצא וישיג עלי כי יהא עומד על צדך. אולם איני חושש לו, שהרי דוד שלי שמע הכל והוא יבא ויסהיד עלי". כך הוה: למחר בשעת הסעודה השלישית דרש הבעש"ט על כוונת שמע ישראל נגד שיטת האר"י, יצא ר' יעקב יוסף והקפיד כנגדו. בא ר' דוד והסהיד שהסכים הר"י לדעת הבעש"ט.

[20] See *T.* 52d, 54b.

[21] שבחי הבעש"ט," p. 62.

[22] *Ibid.*

[23] *T.* 174b; cf. *T.* 58c, 69d, 80d, 139a, 135c, 195c.

[24] בוצינא דנהורא השלם," (Bilgoray 1920), pp. 9, 10.

[25] שבחי הבעש"ט," p. 64.

[26] ...‏גם בקשתי מאוד ומאוד אוד' מחו' הרב המפורסם החסיד מ' יוסף :P. Y. 106b
‏כ"ץ עובד ה' לקרבו אותו בשתי ידים ובכל מיני הנייתא, כי מעשיו רצוים לפני השי"ת וכל מעשיו
‏לש"ש וגם לכתוב בעדו להגבירים לעשות לו הספקה טובה ולתמכו אותו ישיבה שיש בה סמיכה
‏כי בודאי יה' לך נחת אם יהיה אתך עמך במחיצתך.

[27] ‏ר' שלמה לוצקר, „דברת שלמה" according to Horodetzky.

[28] ‏"פאר לישרים" (Jerusalem, 1921), 14a.

[29] ‏"שבחי הבעש"ט," p. 61.

[30] Ibid., p. 65.

[31] ‏"פאר לישרים," p. 14b.

[32] ‏"שבחי הבעש"ט," p. 64.

[33] Ibid., p. 65.

[34] Ibid.

[34a] ‏מ. ש. גשורי, „אנציקלופדיה של החסידות, הניגון והריקוד", כרך ראשון, ר ו ס י ה
‏ה ג ד ו ל ה, pp. 63–68. ‏תל אביב, תשט"ו

[35] ...‏ובענין מאכלות אסורות להעביר שוחטים טובים ולהעמיד רעים לפי :T. 129d
‏רצונו, וכיוצא בזה, לפי מה שראתה עיני...לגרש מהעיר ולבטל מנין
‏[‏של הלומדים העוסקים בתורה ועבודה]...

[36] ‏ואני הכותב בדידן הוי עובדא הנ"ל מרישא לסיפא, ומרומז למה דווקא זה :T. 127c
‏וכאשר עיני ראו ולא זר מלחמה :See also T. 127b. ‏האיש צוה לעשות בה"מ בשארי גראד
‏זו תמיד במי שרוצה להתקדש ולהיות פרוש להתפלל במנין בפ"ע מאחר שאי אפשר להתפלל
...‏בציבור שעושין מצות אנשים מלומדה וכמה טעמים כיוצא בזה, ובענין אכילה.

[37] T. 87c.

[38] P. Y. 67a.

[39] T. 163d, 167c.

[40] K. P. 15b.

[41] T. 37c.

[42] T. 33c.   [43] K. P. 4a.

[44] T. 100a.

[45] T. 46a, 129d.

[46] T. 129d.

[47] One of the שאלות ‏מוהר"ה יוסף הכהן אב"ד דק"ק is explicitly addressed to:
‏ר א ש ק ו ב." P. Y. 88a.

[48] Ibid.

[49] See Bereshit Rabbah 84.3.

[50] ...‏וברוב הטירדא אשר אנכי עמוס התלאות אשר לא שקפתי :P. Y. 84a. P. Y. 82c
‏ולא שלותי מאז ועד עתה לא אוכל לצאת ולבוא לטייל ארוכות וקצרות ולדבר צחות ולארוג
‏מליצות לעייל לעייל שפה ולהוציא שפה ואף גם היה מהראוי למנוע עט ידי.

[51] P. Y. 74a.

[52] ‏"פאר לישרים," 11b, 12a.

[53] ‏"שבחי הבעש"ט," p. 63.

[54] ‏וגם חתנו [‏של הבעש"ט] כבנו הוא הקדוש ר' יחיאל ‏"בוצינא דנהורא השלם" p. 3:
‏מטולטשין זצ"ל היה מעולמא דאתכסיא שלא יכלו לעמוד על תרומת מדותיו, וזה דרכו לאלקיו,
‏הצנע לכת כל ימותיו. טרם לקח אותו מרן הבעש"ט זצ"ל לחתן בתו הצדקת ‏אדל ע"ה ‏ש ל ח

את תלמידו הרה'׳ק בעל התולדות יעקב יוסף זי'׳ע לבחון
אותו...

[55] ,,רשימות ר׳ שלמה בן ר׳ אברהם יעקב מסדיגורה'׳, כ'׳י אדמו'׳ר מקופיטשיניץ, quoted
by Dr. A. Heschel, ,,לתולדות ר׳ פנחס מקוריץ׳׳ in מנחת דברים לשלמה , ע ל י ע י '׳ ן ,
זלמן שוקן, (Jerusalem, 1948–52), p. 221.

[56] ,,שבחי הבעש'׳ט,׳׳ p. 72.

[57] See Heschel, *op. cit.*, p. 221, note 78.

[58] See *ibid.*, p. 221.

[59] Gutman, ,,ר׳, פנחס מקוריץ׳׳ quoted by A. Heschel, *op. cit.*, p. 223.

[60] ,,רשימות ר׳ שלמה מסדיגורה'׳,,׳׳ p. 118b, quoted by A. Heschel, *op. cit.*, p. 221.

[61] *Ibid.*

[62] *P. Y.* 98a, quoted by A. Heschel, *op. cit.*, p. 222; cf. p. 238, notes 81, 82.
See also Cahana, *op. cit.*, pp. 111–12..

CHAPTER 3

THE WRITINGS OF RABBI YAAKOV YOSEF

[1] See appendix for a detailed analysis of his books.

[2] Dubnow, *op. cit.*, pp. 107–125.

[3] Cahana, *op. cit.*, p. 112. Cf. J. Bloch, "A Legendary Edition of the Toldot
Yaakov Yosef by Jacob Josef Ha-Kohen of Polonnoye," *Jewish Quarterly
Review*, N. S., Vol. XXXI, 3, p. 255.

[4] Cahana, *op. cit.*, p. 116. These quotations were soon collected and published in a separate volume ,,כתר שם טוב,, זאלקווא, תקנ'׳ד..

[5] ,,ר׳ מענדל בורק, סדר הדורות החדש'׳ (place and date of printing missing),
pp. 21, 22. Regarding this book itself see Dubnow, ,,תולדות החסידות,׳׳ p. 102,
note 21.

[6] Rabbi Jacob Joseph of Ostro (1738–1798). See Horodetzky, Vol. 2, pp.
99 ff.

[7] ,,סדר הדורות החדש'׳,׳׳ p. 22.

[8] *P. Y.*, 106a.

[9] The author of ,,אור המאיר, קאריץ, תקנ'׳ה..

[10] Cahana, *op. cit.*, p. 113.

[11] See the recent critical edition by M. Wilensky, ,,בקורת על ספר תולדות,׳׳
The Joshua Starr Memorial Volume, New York, 1953, pp. 183–189.

[12] Wilensky, *op. cit.*, p. 185. Dubnow, *op. cit.*, p. 140, note 1, writes: לדעתי
נשלחה אגרת זו מאוקריינא כעין תשובה על שאלת הרבנים מליטה ע'׳ד מוצאו ואופן פרסומו
של הספר ,תולדות יעקב יוסף'..

[13] He quotes from *T.* the statement: לא ירגיל להיות מתמיד בלימודו רק יתערב
עם בני אדם ולא ילמוד כלל כי הלימוד מביא לידי גדלות The text, *T.* 28c–d, actually

. . . לא ירגיל בזה להיות מתמיד בלימודו בלימודו תמיד רק יתערב עם בני אדם   ג ם   כ ן. reads
ושם יהיה נ״כ יראת ה׳ על פניו לקיים שויתי ה׳ לנגדי תמיד גם שהוא נגדיות, ביטול תורה או
תפלה, מ״מ יתן לב שיש שם   ג ם   כ ן   מוסר ועבודת ה׳. . . שהש״י עם כל המדריגות של
בני אדם. See Dubnow, *op. cit.*, p. 140.

[14] See above, pp. 58–59.

[15] "פאר לישרים," p. 14a.

[16] See Dubnow, *op. cit.*, pp. 144–47. Instead of the words קול השופר which
would herald a ḥerem, the words: קול הספר, referring to the book, *T.*, were
substituted.

[17] See M. Teitlebaum, "הרב מלאדי" (Warsaw, 1910), p. 36; and Graetz,
Geschichte der Juden, 1900, vol. XI, p. 560.

[18] Graetz, *op. cit.*, pp. 114 and 559.

[19] J. Perl, "מגלה טמירין," (Lemberg, 1864), p. 3, note 4.

[20] *Ibid.*

[21] *Ibid.*

[22] משה המגיד מקאוניץ, .דעת משה׳, (לבוב, תרל״ט), פ׳ וינש.

[23] "שבחי הבעש״ט," p. 66.

[24] Cahana, *op. cit.*, p. 115.

[25] Cahana, *op. cit.*, p. 117, note 2, reports an incident reflecting Rabbi
Yaakov Shimshon's learning, without giving his source. Rabbi Yaakov
Shimshon was once visiting the Maggid of Mezritch. An *'agunah*, whom the
Vilna Gaon was unable to release was present. She had been advised that the
Maggid and his circle might herself release her. She was unable to find the Maggid
or any of his circle, except Rabbi Yaakov Shimshon who was at that moment
eating breakfast. The testimony of evidence was shown to him. He then took
a piece of paper and wrote down the reference to a responsum which indicated
that this woman could indeed be released. The Maggid told him that if he
had known that during a scant breakfast he could release an *'agunah*, he would
have prepared a better meal for him. R. Yaakov Shimshon replied that it had
been thirty-four years since he had seen the responsum.

[26] אין לי עסק בנסתרות, והלואי שאוכל לצאת ידי חובתי בתלמוד ופוסקים הנחוצים למעשה,
והם חיינו ובהם נהגה. (.נודע ביהודה״, או׳ח, סי׳ ק״ט). בדורנו זה כי עזבו את תורת ה׳ ומקור
מים חיים שני תלמודים בבלי וירושלמי לחצוב להם בורות נשברים ומתנשאים ברום לבבם.
כל אחד אומר, אנכי הרואה ולי נפתחו שערי שמים ובעבורי העולם מתקיים. אלו הם מחריבי
הדור, ועל דור יתום אני אומר ישרים דרכי ה׳ צדיקים ילכו בם   ו ח ס י ד י ם   יכשלו בם
(נודע ביהודה״ מהדורא קמא יו״ד סי׳ צ׳ו), quoted by Cahana, *op. cit.*, p. 118,
note 3.

[27] Sanhedrin 56b.

[28] "דברי נועם," Warsaw, 1892. See below, pp. 194–95.

[27] Sanhedrin 56b.

[29] Personal communication from Moses Marx, Hebrew Union College
Library.

[30] "פאר לישרים", p. 20b: כל הספרים החדשים שנתחברו בתוך שבעים שנה .בשהרז״ל:

אינם עפ״י אמת לבד ספרי הרב דפולנאה״, שאמר עליהם שאין ספר כמותם בעולם ולבד מספר
..אור החיים״ (לר׳ חיים נ׳ עטר)
p. 21. ,״מדרש פנחס״ [31]

CHAPTER 4

A CRITIQUE OF LEADERSHIP

[1] *T.* 47d.
[2] *P. Y.* 76b.
[3] *T.* 29b.
[4] *T.* 141c.
[5] *T.* 34a.
[6] *K. P.* 25a; cf. *Z. P.* 30b.
[7] *Z. P.* 90c.
[8] *T.* 191d.
[9] See *T.* 103c.
[10] Horayot 14.
[11] Shabbat 119b, *T.* 48b; cf. *T.* 96, 47d.
[12] *T.* 49d.
[13] *Ibid.*
[14] Sotah 49b.
[15] *T.* 47d. See Zohar III, 119b. Cf. *T.* 129c: ,(י״א ,תה׳ פ״ה׳) ״חסד ואמת נפגשו״.
ר״ל כשעושין להשפיע זה לזה החכמים מקבלים ״חסד״ מהעושר והעשירים שומעים חכמה ומוסר
הנקרא ״אמת״ מהחכמים שהוא עיקר התכלית כמ״ש ״חסד ואמת מן ינצרוהו״ כנ״ל. אז גורמים
ליחד ב׳ מדות הגורמין שפע וברכה בעולם וזהו ״צדק ושלום נשקו״ (שם), שהוא יסוד ומלכות
שחבורם הוא ע״י יחוד בעלי חכמה עם בעלי עושר להשפיע זה לזה. ״אמת מארץ תצמח וצדק
משמים נשקף״ (שם י״ב), ר״ל עד עכשיו היו משליכים ״אמת״ ארצה שהם בעלי תורה והחכמה
שהיתה חכמת סופרים סרוחה בעיני בעלי עושר והיו החכמים שפלי מושחים עד לעפר, ו״צדק״
שהיא בעלי עושר שאינם בעלי חכמה היו עולין ברום המעלות עד לשמים שזה גורם חורבן
ואיבוד הבית והארץ. Cf. *P. Y.* 60b.
[16] *T.* 41b; cf. 46d, 131d; *K. P.* 45c.
[17] Berakhot 3b.
[18] *T.* 45c; cf. *K. P.* 25a.
[19] *T.* 75c.
[20] *Ibid.*
[21] *Ibid.*
[22] *T.* 42c.
[23] *T.* 42d.
[24] *T.* 131c.
[25] *T.* 46d; cf. *K. P.* 45c.
[26] See appendix.

[27] *T.* 40c: שמעתי מהרב המנוח מהרי"ל פיסטנר ביאור פסוק .הושיעה ה' כי גמר חסיד
כי פסו אמונים מבני אדם', דלכך גמר חסיד לפי שפסו אמונים מבני אדם שזה מושך לזה מצד
אחדות. ונאמר לו בחלום שמא הפירוש הוא איפכא: לפי
cf. ;שנגמר חסיד לכך פסו אמונים מבני אדם וכו' ודפח"ח
10c, 15a, 63b, 97b, 100a, 130b, 160b; *Z. P.* 14a; *K. P.* 42a.

[28] רגילים היו בעלי המוסר שבישראל, המטיפים ומגידים, להטיף מוסר ביחוד להמון העם.
על עמי הארץ, על פשוטי העם והדיוטות המטירו גפרית ומלח, כאלו הם דוחקים רגלי השכינה
והמעכבים את הגאולה. בא הבעש"ט, הפך את הקערה על פיה וטען: וכי אלה הצאן מה פשעו?!
אם בארזים נפלה שלהבת, מה יעשו איזובי קיר?! גדול פשעם של הרועים מחטאותיהם של
הצאן. הבעש"ט העביר הקולר מצואר העם ונתנו בצואר המנהיגים, החרש והמסגר, הרבנים
והפרנסים. לא הפיץ הבעש"ט את תורתו כי אם לצרף בה את הבריות, וביחוד לצרף כצרף
כסף יחידי סגולה, מתי מספר. הוא חזה מכל העם אנשי חיל, יראי אלקים, אנשי אמת, שונאי
בצע, ופקד אותם על העדה אשר יצאו לפניהם ואשר יבואו לפניהם ולא תהיה עדת ה' כצאן
אשר אין להם רועים נאמנים. בשטה זו הלך ר' גרשון [קוטובר]. דרש הוא את דברי הנביא:
.החרשים שמעו והעורים הביטו לראות" (ישעיהו, מ"ב, י"ח), והקשה: .אם הוא חרש איך ישמע
ואם הוא עוד איך יוכל לראות?" ופירש: .החרשים" הם תלמידי חכמים .החרש והמסגר", שהם
ישמעו. כי .העורים" שהם המוני העם .הביטו לראות" על התלמידי חכמים. אם ייטיב בעיני
התלמידי חכמים או גם הוא נוטה אזנו לשמוע בלמודים, ואם לא וכו' (תולדות יעקב
יוסף, קוריץ, תקמ"א, קצ"ה, ב', קפ"ו, ג'), A. Heschel, "ר' גרשון קוטובר," *The He-*
brew Union College Annual, Vol. XXIII, part two, Cincinnati, 1950–51, p. 29
(Hebrew section).

[29] One must not overlook the correlative nature of the interpretation, which
does not place the blame solely on the leaders, but declares the leaders and the
people interdependent, each the cause of the other's sin. It is the leader's
part in this responsibility, however, which is the new element, the element
which Rabbi L. Pistener emphasizes.

[30] *T.* 127b; cf. *T.* 155a. See below, chapt., 5, note 5.

[31] *Ibid.*

[32] *T.* 188b; cf. *P. Y.* 95b: יש שני סוני מוכיחים ומתפללים בימים נוראים: אחד המקפיד
שיהיה לו חיתוך הדיבור טוב ויפה שבזה ישא חן בעיני המוני עם והנשים ואינו יוצא מפנימיות
הלב כמו שכתבתי במקום אחר ... ובחינה ב' המקפיד על תוכן הדברים מיוסדים על שרשים
.טובים והוא מפנימיות הלב ... ואין לו חיתוך הדיבור

[33] This quotation is actually from Maimonides, משנה תורה, הלכות ת"ח פ"א, ה"ז.
See also Berakhot 29a and Nedarim 37a.

[34] See Ketuvot 111b.

[35] *T.* 85b, c.

[36] *T.* 158d.

[37] *Z. P.* 15c.

[38] *P. Y.* 60c.

[39] *Z. P.* 71d.

[40] According to Rashi.

[41] *K. P.* 8c.

[42] *T.* 10b: אר"י לא היה צריך להתחיל התורה אלא מ.החודש הזה לכם' שהיא מצוה ראשונה

שנצטוו ישראל (בעלי שררה) שצריך לתת לב למצוה זו, החודש הזה לכם, שתהיו דוגמתה כמו הלבנה המקטינה את עצמה בתחלה ולסוף נתמלאה, כך ישראל [התלמידי חכמים] צריכים להקטין א"ע... .ומה טעם פתח בבראשית? משום ,כה מעשיו הגיד לעמו' ', ר"ל, ת"ח שנקרא .עמו' כמ"ש .הגיד לעמי פשעם", הם הת"ח והם הנקראים ישראל שהם עלולים להיות נסי הרוח ע"י לימוד הרבה כמעשה דתענית [לעולם יהא אדם רך כקנה ולא יהא קשה כארז. מעשה שבא רבי אלעזר ברבי שמעון ממגדול גדור מבית רבו והיה רוכב על חמור ומטייל על שפת הנהר ושמח שמחה גדולה והיתה דעתו גסה עליו מפני שלמד תורה הרבה. נזדמן לו אדם אחד שהיה מכוער ביותר. אמר לו: שלום עליך רבי. ולא החזיר לו. אמר לו: ריקה כמה מכוער אותו האיש שמא כל בני עירך מכוערים כמותך? אמר לו: איני יודע אלא לך ואמור לאומן שעשאני כמה מכוער כלי זה שעשית! כיון שידע בעצמו שחטא, ירד מן החמור ונשתטח לפניו ואמר לו: נעניתי לך מחול לי. אמר לו: איני מוחל לך עד שתלך לאומן שעשאני ואמור לו: כמה מכוער כלי זה שעשית. היה מטייל אחריו עד שהגיע לעירו. יצאו בני עירו לקראתו והיו אומרים לו: שלום עליך רבי רבי מורי מורי. אמר להם: למי אתם קורים רבי רבי? אמרו לו לזה שמטייל אחריך. אמר להם: אם זה רבי, אל ירבו כמותו בישראל. אמרו לו: מפני מה? אמר להם: כך וכך עשה לי. אמרו לו: אף על פי כן מחול לו שאדם גדול הוא בתורה. אמר להם: בשבילכם הריני מוחל לו ובלבד שלא יהא רגיל לעשות כן. מיד נכנס רבי אלעזר ברבי שמעון ודרש: לעולם יהי אדם רך כקנה ואל יהא קשה כארז. תענית כ' ע"א-ב]. לכך פתח בבראשית שהיא היראה הנקרא .ראשית חכמה יראת ה'', ובזה יבוא לענוה ושפלות.
According to the Tosafot to Taanit 20b the ugly man whom R. Elazar met was Elijah. ולטוב נתכוין כדי ירגיל בדבר.

[43] *Z. P.* 8d.

[44] *P. Y.* 75a.

[45] *P. Y.* 68c.

[46] *T.* 104a.

[47] *T.* 10b, c. See note 42.

[48] *T.* 10a.

[49] Sotah 5a.

[50] *T.* 38d, 39a: וכמ"ש כל התורה והמצות לא נתנו אלא כדי שיזכה לידבק בו ית' וכמ"ש .ובו תדבק', וכמ"ש המפרש להרמב"ם בפרק ב' מהלכות יסודי התורה וז"ל: כשיתבונן בהם תתאוה נפשו להדבק בו. ולא נתנו כל המצות אלא כדי שנגיע לזאת המדרינה שנ' .ובחרת בחיים למען תחיי באהבה את ה' וכו' '. יעו"ש. וברבות השנים נתמעטו הלבבות להבין ולהשכיל ע"ד הנ"ל רק לעשות מהתורה עטרה להתהדל בהם ולהתפאר בהם וגם בעלי תשובה הוא להראות מעלתו וכשלומד הלכה הלכה א' מתפאר מעט וכשלומד יותר מתפאר יותר וכשלומד פוסקים או קבלה מתנאה יותר ונתרחק מהש"י כמ"ש בש"ס דסוטה על גסי הרוח אין אני והוא יכולין לדור בעולם וכו' והנה התלמידי חכמים המכתתין רגליהם לילך מעיר לעיר כמ"ש בפ' וזאת הברכה .והם תכו לרגליך וכו' '. ובזה יובן .על מה תכו' יותר שמכתתין רגליהם לילך בישיבה ללמוד .עוד תוסיפו סרה' להתרחק ולסור מהש"י וק"ל.

This was one of the passages which aroused the ire of the *mitnagdim* and was especially attacked in "עמיר עריצים". See the critical edition by Wilensky, *The Joshua Starr Memorial Volume*, p. 186: על מה תכו עוד תוסיפו סרה' (ישעיהו א', ה'). דרשו חז"ל (בבא בתרא, דף ח' ע"א): אלו ת"ח מכתתי רגליהם ללכת מעיר לעיר".

וּפירש הנ"ל (תולדות יעקב יוסף דף ל"ט, ע"א): „על מה תכו ללמוד תורה בישיבוח? הלא
עוד בזה תוסיפו סרה?" אף אם נצדד בזכותם שהם כוונו ללמוד תורה שלא לשמה רק להתנאות,
הוא נ"כ נגד חז"ל שאמרו: „לעולם ילמוד אדם". וכו' (נזיר דף כ"ג ע"א). והמאור שבה מחזירה
למוטב (איכה רבתי, פתיחתא) ומכ"ש שאינו מוסיף סרה ח"ו.

Our author treats this subject in detail. *T.* 3a: שוגם במתק ז"ל חכמינו אמרו
(מגילה דף ג' ע"ב). „מבטלין ת"ת להוצאת המת". „להוציא הקליפה הנקרא „מת". ולהכנסת
„כלה", להשראת השכינה ברמ"ח אבריו וש"ה גידין ששורש כולם ד' אותיות הוי"ה.

In certain cases it is necessary להתפאר יהיה שלא שלא ה' ועבודת תורה מעסק להרחיק
הנאה לשאר או שאור כמו „ולהתנשא", *T.* 80a; cf. *T.* 31c, 80a, 109a, 151a. However, this
advice is not meant as a general principle but is true only for some of the
scholars and not the people. *T.* 64a: ואותך אותי והרגו המצרים אותך יראו כי „ויהיה
„יחיו", כי ע"י עסק התורה ועבודה שלא לשמה וע"י פניות הצניעות יהרגו הנשמה שנק' אברם.
T. 80a: ואותך, אנשי החומר, יחיו, כי ע"י פניות ולימוד שלא לשמה יחיו ויתקרבו אליו ית' יותר
לשמה. Cf. *T.* 146c, „הלוואי שילמוד אפילו לאיזו פניה שהיא שלא לשמה שמתוך שלא לשמה בא
184a; *Z. P.* 70b; *P. Y.* 34d. See below, pp. 170–72.

51 Ḥagigah 9b.
52 *T.* 195a.
53 *T.* 60b.
54 See *Z. P.* וארא 'פ.
55 *T.* 167c: שלא התח' שבין המחלקת להשוות... העקוב מלב מכשול להסיר וכדי
יבוא זה את זה רק שיהיה מחלוקתן לש"ש ונ"ש עתיד להנחיל לכל צדיק וכו' שנא' להנחיל
או ה ב י יש, ר"ל שיאהוב את השם יתברך בפלפול ולא את עצמו, דהיינו שיקשט את עצמו
בפלפול שיהיה לו יד ושם בין התלמידי חכמים ח"ו.

Compare the quotation of the Besht in ממעזריטש' מהמגיד אמרים' ליקוטי.
קארעץ, תקע"ד, דף כ"ט: „וירא את ישראל שוכן לשבטיו" (במד' כ"ד, ב'): ופירש רש"י „ראה
שאין פתחיהן מכוונין זה כנגד זה". שמעתי בשם הבעש"ט: ראה שאין פתחיהן מכוונין זה כנגד
זה. אמר: ראוי שתשרה עליהן שכינה (ב"ב דף ס' ע"א), ר"ל כי שני לומדים שמתפלפלים זה
עם זה ולפעמים אינם מודים על האמת רק הם מכוונים לסתור
דברי חבירו אף שיודע בעצמו שצדקו דברי חבירו אעפ"כ
כוונתו בפלפול לקנטר, ר"ל, אבל עיקר הכוונה בפלפול הוא להודית אל האמת ויקויים בהם
מה שאמרו חכמינו ז"ל (אבות ג':ב') „שנים שיושבים ויש ביניהם דברי תורה שכינה שרויה
ביניהם", והנה הפה נקרא פתח שמשם הדיבור יוצא וזהו שאמרו שאין פתחיהן מכוונים זה נגד
זה, ר"ל שאין כוונתם בפלפול להתנגד ולקנטר זה כנגד זה רק כוונתם להודות על האמת אמר
שראוי שתשרה שכינה עליהם, ודפ"ח.

56 *T.* 167c.   57 *T.* 20d.
58 *T.* 105b: דברי איזה ובשמעו עצמו של רק זולתן של התורה מחבבין שאינן מרבנן יש
...תורה מזולתן מעבירין כלאחר יד.
59 *Ibid.*
60 *Z. P.* 20a. Dr. A. Heschel believes the city here referred to by the Besht
is Brody.
61 *T.* 44c: בור תרגום וכן נובא ותרנומו ארבה מכת עד המכות שאר לפרש יש וכן...
כי הוא לשון רבוי כמ"ש „ארבה את זרעך" וכו' והענין שהוא רבי המנהיגים שלא יהיה דָּבָר
אחד לדור רק ההיפך שיהיה כולם ראשים מנהיגים... ואז נהפך מן דבר א' לְדָבָר ח"ו לברד

ומכח זה .וכסה את עין הארץ", מי שהוא עין הארץ כמו עיני העדה שהיה ראוי להשגיח על
הארץ נעשו אלו הרבה מנהיגים נעשו כסה אל עין הארץ ולא יוכל לראות את הארץ להשגיח
עליהם כמו שכתבתי בפסוק .ועיני ישראל כבדו מזוקן ולא יוכל לראות" וה'נ כך וזה שאמר
.ואכל את יתר הפליטה הנשארת לכם מן הברד" כשהיה דָבָר א' לדור היה ברכה וכשנהפך
.ונעשה הרבה מנהיגים נעשה מן דָבָר, ברד, וזהו הנורם חורבן ליתר הפליטה, וק"ל.

[62] *T.* 30c.

[63] *T.* 44c. See above note 61.

[64] *T.* 179a: .כי תבוא אל הארץ ואמרת אשימה עלי מלך" ...יובן על דבר הלצה:
(דב' י"ז, י"ד). כשיתישב איזה ארץ שהוא עיר חדשה ואמרת .אשימה עלי מלך' לקבל איזה
רב (מאן מלכי רבנן), לכך תהיה זהיר .שום תשים עליך מלך", ר"ל, ק ו ד ם ש י ע מ ו ד
א ח ד מ ע צ מ ו, וזה שאמר שים מעצמו תשים עליך מלך מי שאינו רודף אחר זה שהוא
איש בליעל .בודאי ירא שמים אבל מי שהוא רודף אחר זה בודאי Cf. *T.* 178d; *Z. P.* 2b.

[65] Pesaḥim 49b.

[66] *T.* 173d.

[67] Mekhilta, Beshallaḥ, parashah 7 (Lauterbach ed., p. 252). This midrash is
often quoted and is central to our author's analysis of the zaddik. See
T. 56b; cf. עקב, נשא, צו, פ'.

[68] *T.* 184c; *T.* 184b, c: סוני ישראל הם ב': א' הם המוני עם בסוד ז; סונ ב' הצדיקים
נקראה ן. והם החומר והצורה וכשהם בחיבור אחד גורמים יחוד למעלה ג'כ שיהיה אחד
וח'ו בהיפך גורמים פירוד וז"ש בזוהר ותיקונים שהערב רב גורמים להפריש בין ש ש
לשבע, והבן . . . ובזה יובן .עם זו יצרתי" (ישעיהו מ'ג, כ"א). ב' סוני ישראל: אנשי
החומר ואנשי הצורה, אות ן ז יצרתי שיתחברון ז עם ן גימטריה א ח"ד שיכנע החומר
אל הצורה לשמוע מהם תורה ומוסר וז"ש .תהלתי יספרו" ...הלא ה' זו חטאנו לו', שהפרישו
בין שש לשבע שיש בין אנשי החומר לאנשי הצורה פירוד ועי"ז נורם מה שהיה ז ו גי' אחד
וע"י הפירוד ח"ו גרמו למעלה כך Cf. *T.* 181d, 184b, c, d.

[69] Shabbat 119b.

[70] *T.* 184c. That the scholars were responsible for the death of Zechariah
is also mentioned in *T.* 167c and 184c. An interesting reference to this is found
in ר' יצחק אייזק מקאמארנא, .נוצר חסד" (לבוב, תרט"ז), פרק ד' אות ה': כמו שסיפר מרן
אלק' הריב"ש זצ"ל, שבעָרי אשכנז היה צדיק אחד, ואמר קודם פטירתו שימות מיתה משונה
ר"ל על ידי רוצחים. וכבר היה מאה פעמים בעולם הזה ובכל פעם נהרג, שהוא היה בזמן המקדש
ראש הסנהדרין, חריף וחכם ו ל מ ד ב ס ם ה מ ו ת ש ל ת ו ר ה ו ה ו א ה י ה
ה ר א ש ו ן ש ה כ ה ע ל ל ח י ו פ נ י ם ש ל ז כ ר י ה ה נ ב י א: .אתה עם הארץ
מתנבא בנביאות!" ועל ידו נפלו עליו עמי הארץ רשעים גמורים והרגו אותו. וצוה שיכתבו על
מצבתו פ"נ מי שהרג זכריה הנביא. ואמר שכבר הוא מתוקן. והיה מספר
מרן זה לתוכחת מוסר היאך יזהר מלימוד תורה שלא לשמה ומסם המות מים מרים של לומד
תורה לקנטר.

[71] *K. P.* 7d, 8a.

[72] *T.* 181d; cf. *T.* 179c.

[73] *Ibid.*

[74] *T.* 49c; cf. *K. P.* 25a.

[75] *T.* 167c.

[76] *T.* 30c.

[77] Taanit 20a, **Eruvin 55a.**

[78] Yoma 72b.

[79] See Jer. 4.22.

[80] *T.* 181d; cf. *T.* 180a; *P. Y.* 6a. A further difference between the חכם and שמעתי אומרים בשם גדול א' הלצה. .שיחת חולין של *T.* 106d–107a: ,תלמיד חכם the תלמידי חכמים צריכין לימוד" (ע"ז דף י"ט ע"ב) כי מן שיחת חולין, שנקרא ת ל מ י ד חכם, ולא תואר ח כ ם. מזה נשמע ש צ ר י כ י ן ל י מ ו ד מ א ח ר י ם...אנחנו אומרים לו שצריך לימוד אבל הוא עצמו אינו סובר כך אלא מחליט בדעתו שא"צ לימוד משום אדם. א"כ מאחר שאינו מכיר ערך מעלתו, א י נ ו ב ג ד ר ח כ ם

[81] *K. P.* 30b. See Eruvin 55a; Maimonides to Avot 2.5.

[82] *K. P.* 18d; cf. *P. Y.* 90b; *K. P.* 8c.

[83] *T.* 85a; cf. 85b, *P. Y.* 45a: מגלה עמוקות" כי סולם בגימטריא' שמעתי בשם ס' ממון, כי על ידי חימוד ממון גם הצדיקים שנקראים ,מלאכי אלהים", ,עולים ויורדים בו'.

[84] *T.* 56c.

[85] *P. Y.* 68d.

[86] *T.* 103c.

[87] At the same time a serious economic problem did confront the rabbis, as R. Yaakov Yosef mentions in the same parashah. הסיבה לשנאת חנם היא מיעוט פרנסה, *T.* 103a. See C. Reines, "Public Support of Rabbis and Scholars," *Yivo Annual of Jewish Social Science*, Vol. VII, pp. 99–102; *T.* 13b, d, 79d, 45c, 103a, 185a, 188a.

[88] *T.* 103d.

[89] *T.* 188a.

[90] *T.* 49b. On the same page we find: .על אשר עזבו את תורתי אשר נתתי ובזה יובן לפניהם" (רב' כ"ט, כ"ד cf.). ר"ל, שילמדו מזה שהולך בדרכי התורה לפניהם ולא כמו השועל המביט לאחוריו. והטעם ביאר רב שלא בירכו בתורה תחלה שלא היה חשובין בעלי תורה שיברכו תחלה אמרו שוא עבוד ה' היה שפלים בעיניהם ע"י ש ר א ו ד ר ך ר ש ע י ם צלחה ב ח ד ו ב ד ר כ י ה ם.

[91] *K. P.* 32a.

[92] *K. P.* 30c: .אהוב את המלאכה וח"ש ,בה' הידיעה' עסק התורה נקרא מלאכה... שהיא עיין את התורה, שיהנה מן המלאכה עצמה ולא מן השכר שיתגדל ויזכה לרבנות, רק .שנא את הרבנות. והיינו .שאל התודע לרשות' ופי' הר"ב: כ ד י ל ק ב ל ר ב נ ו ת ע" י [על =]. Cf. *T.* 129d. [על ידה]

[93] Sanhedrin 7b.

[94] It is significant to read the complete statement of *Maharsha* to Sanhedrin בשביל כסף וזהב כו'. יש לפרש בשתים רעות שעשו: כי הם מתמנין בשביל הזהב וכסף :7b שנותנין למלך או לנשיא: גם מה שעושין כן הוא בשביל הכסף וזהב שרוצין לאסוף ע"י הרבנות והדיינות ולמלאות חסרון כסף וזהב שכבר יצא מידם שנתנו לאותן שמינו אותן והוא קודם לו לאכול ממנו ולהתעשר מרבנות. והנה חטא ואשמה זו נשתרבב עתה בקרוב בימינו וכבר באו רבותינו כמה פעמים בהתחלת המון (זה) ואשמה זו בנזירה ובעונשים חמורות וחרמות וממון בדבר הזה שלא יתמנה שום רב ומורה בכסף וזהב הן ליתן ליחידים הן לרבים. אבל אין איש שם על לב העונש הנזכר בשמעתין. דעתיד הקב"ה ליפרע ממעמידין. גם דימה העון הזה לעע"ז ויצא הדבר לנו בדור הזה למכשול ולמזכרת עון דכמה תקלות וקלקולים אשר באו לנו בדור

הזה עי"ז. ואתה המעיין ראה איך ברחו חז"ל מן השררה כההיא דהוריות שהיה ר"נ רצה להושיב
בראש ר"א חסמא ור"י בן נודגדא ואף שלא היה להם פת לאכול ובגד ללבוש ולא רצו להתמנות
עד שא"ל ר"נ וכי שררה אני נותן לכם, עבדות אני נותן לכם כו'. גם מ"ש בסוטה פ' א"נ בעונותניתה
דרבי אבהו דאימנו רבנן עליה לממניה ברישא כיון דחזייה לר' אבא דמן עכו דנפישי עליה
ב"ח, א"ל איכא רבה. ויש לדקדק בזה מאי ענותיה שלא רצה להיות ראש? הרי אמרו דאינו
אלא עבדות. ויש להשיב בזה דלא חשיב מינוי הראשית והרבנות לעבדות אלא למי שנתמנה
לצרכו, כמו ר' אבא דמן עכו בשביל חובבתיו וכמו ר"א חסמא ור"י בן גודגדא משום פרנסתן,
דה"ל מינוי ראשית שלהן כעבד וכפועל בדמלאכתו הוא עוסק שיהיה לו זה לצורך פרנסה,
אבל ר' אבהו שהיה עשיר כבר לא היה נחשב לו מינוי הראשית לעבדות שהרי אינו צריך לו,
אלא לשררה היה נחשב לו אילו היה מתרצה בכך, וכשלא נתרצה נחשב לו לענוה, הרי שאלו
החכמים המפורסמים בורחים היו מן השררה אם לא לצורך פרנסתם שהיה נחשב להן כעבדות.
ועתה בדור הזה החכמים בעיניהם ולהיטיב לא ידעו רק באים להשתחרר על הצבור שלא לשם
שמים ורודפים אחר השררה בממונם לענוש ולהתכבד ולהכשיל המקבל ממנו בכל עונשין המוזכר ולפי
שהם אינם עושין כן אלא להתגדל ולהקל בכבודן. וז"ש ר' מנא מיקל לאלין דמתמנין בכספא ר' אמי
ס"ה ע"ד) דראוי לבזותן ולהקל בכבודן. וז"ש ר' מנא מיקל לאלין דמתמנין בכספא ר' אמי
קרא עליהם אלהי כסף וגו' אין עומדין מפניו ואין קורין אותו רבי והטלית שעליו כמרדעת
של חמור, ע"כ מ"ש אין עומדין מפניו ואין קורין כו' הוא מבואר דעמידה מפני התח"ח אינה אלא
מפני התורה שיש בו כמ"ש בסוף מכות כמה טפשאי אינשי דקיימי מקמי מקמי ס"ת ולא קיימי מקמי
גברא רבה, גם שקורין לבעל תורה רבי ע"ש בי מלכים ימלוכו ושרים וגו', וזה שנתמנה בכסף
ואין לו ריח תורה אין ראוי לעמוד מפניו ולא לקראו רבי אבל מה שדימה הטלית שעליו למרדעת
של חמור צריך ביאור, ויש לפרש בו כי הטלית של תח הוא משונה כדאמרי' פ' ח"ה: טלית
של תח כיצד כו', כל שאין חלוקו נראית מתחתיו ובפ' המוכר פירות אמרי כל המתנאה בטלית
של תח אין מכניסין אותו כו' והנה זה המתמנה בכסף וזהב ועושה לו טלית של תח להנאות
בו הוא לובש אותו תמיד כדי שיהא ניכר שהוא א' מכלל החכמים תמיד עליו ובזולת הטלית שעליו לא
יהיה לתח בעיניו מאומה וחזי הוה טליתו דומה למרדעת של חמור שהוא תמיד עליו ולא ינטל ממנו כמ"ש חמור
אפי' בתקופת תמז קרירא ליה ובעי מרדעת.

⁹⁵ *T.* 127b; Jerusalem Talmud, Bikurim 65d.

⁹⁶ *T.* 49b; cf. *T.* 85d.

⁹⁷ *T.* 127c.

⁹⁸ *T.* 49b. Compare the following: *T.* 46a: שמעתי בשם גדול אחד הלצה להבין
שאלה: מפני מה ראשיהם של בבליים סגלגלים? (שבת דף ל"א ע"א) שהם תלמידי חכמים
ראשי' שבבבל סגלגלים, שאינם יכולים לישב במקום אחד ומחגלגלין מעיר לעיר . . . והשיבו
מפני שאין להם חיות פקחות. דאיתא משל בס' בן סירא שפעם אחד היה הארי רעב ופגע בצבי
וכו' ואחר כך כבש וכו' עד שפגע בשועל פיקח שבחיות ואמר שאין לו חוש הריח וניצל וזהו
שאמר מפני מה שאין להם חיות פקחות ליקח מוסר ממנו כג"ל ודפח"ח.

This rather cryptic explanation, especially the parable about the fox, is
presented in full with the implicit criticism more clearly expressed in a later
work, "אהבת דודאים" (לבוב, תקנ"ה), comment to Song of Songs 3.1:

שמעתי אומרים בשם הרב הנדול מ' יוסף קאלמאנקיס ז"ל אב"ד דק"ק קראקא על הא דאיתא
בנמרא: מפני מה ראשיהם של בבליים סגלגלות, מפני שאין להם חיות פקחות, על פי דאיתא
משל אחד. דפעם אחד היה הארי רעב מאוד שלא היה לו לאכול מכמה ימים והיה ריח רע יוצא
מפיו, ופגע בזאב ואמר לו שריח בתוך פיו. והשיב לו שמרגיש ריח רע. ואמר לו הארי שהוא
חייב מיתה מורד במלכות מורד שאמרת על הארי שהוא מלך החיות שריח רע יוצא מפיו, ומיד

טרפו ואכלו. לאחר ימים פגע בחיה אחרת וציוה לו גם כן שיריח בתוך פיו והיה מתירא לומר
האמת. לכן אמר שיוצא מפיו ריח טוב. ואמר לו הארי שהוא מורד במלכות שאמרת שקר בפני
המלך, כי אני יודע שמחמת שלא אכלתי כמה ימים יש ריח רע בפי ואתה אמרת שקר וחייב
מיתה, ומיד טרפו ואכלו. לימים פגע ארי זה בשועל שהוא פיקח שבחיות וציוהו שיריחו לתוך
פיו. ואמר לו השועל: אדוני המלך זה כמה ימים שאין לי חוש הריח כלל וגם אם אריח אצלך
כל היום לא אדניש שום ריח. ובזה ניצול מן הארי.

והנמשל כי יש כמה לומדים שהם עובדים להבורא ית"ש באמת ובמסירת נפש ומריחים מכל
חטא שנמצא בעיר וממלאים פיהם תוכחות ומתקוטטים עמהם כל בני העיר ומדחים אותם מעליהם,
וצריכים לילך לעיר אחרת, וכשיושבין שם איזה זמן וכשמרנישים בבני העיר איזה עברה, גם
שם הם מוכיחים את החוטאים ואז גם שם מתקוטטים עמהם ואומרים איש אחד בא לנור וישפוט
שפוט ומדחים אותן ונם מעליהם וצריכים אותן המוכיחים לילך מדחי אל דחי מעיר לעיר ואין
להם מנוחה כלל. משא"כ מי שאינו ירא שמים באמת לאמיתו ואין
לו חוש הריח שירית בדבר עברה שבעיר. ונם כמה שרואה
דבר עברה בעיר אין לבו דוה עליו, ומראה עצמו כאלו
אינו רואה ואינו שומע. וזהו ,מפני מה ראשיהם של בבליים", היינו הת"ח ראשי
הנולה, ,סנלנלות", שמתגוללים מעיר לעיר? מפני שאין להם המדה של חיות פקחות, היינו השועל
שאין לו חוש הריח, רק הם מריחים ולכן אין נותנים להם מנוחה.

[99] T. 49b.

[100] T. 152c; cf. T. 128a, T. 41c.

[101] T. 41c.

[102] T. 85d.

[103] T. 131d.

[104] T. 13c. Ketuvot 105b. Cf. P. Y. 18c, d; T. 103d.

[105] T. 194b.

[106] P. Y. 34a; cf. Z. P. 44a. K. P. 30d: ונם הלומדים שעוסקים בתורה ובמצות
להתנדל ויבוא תועלת לגוף נקרא גם כן עמי הארץ.

[107] K. P. 48b.

[108] K. P. 44b.

[109] K. P. 4d.

[110] Z. P. 16b.

[111] See T. 10c.

[112] Regarding the poverty of the people, see T. 13b, 79d, 103a.

[113] T. 10c.

[114] T. 85c; cf. T. 127b: היו כמה מוכיחים דורשים הלכות מליחה לנשים בפרטות ולא
כן עתה.

[115] T. 179a. Compare the following Midrashim, Shemot Rabbah 30.10: מלך
במשפט יעמיד ארץ" (משלי כ"ט, ד'), זה יהושפט, שנאמר (דהי"ב י"ט, ו'), ,ויאמר אל השופטים:
ראו מה אתם עושים"; ,ואיש תרומות יהרסנה" (משלי כ"ט, ד'), זה חכם שהוא יודע הלכות ומדרשות
ואנדרות ויתום ואלמנה הולכין אצלו שיעשה דין ביניהם והוא אומר להן: עסוק אני במשנתי
איני פנוי. א"ל ה': מעלה אני עליך כאלו החרבת את העולם, לכך נאמר ,ואיש תרומות
יהרסנה".

Tanhuma Mishpatim: ,מלך במשפט יעמיד ארץ ואיש תרומות יהרסנה" (משלי כ"ט, ד').
מלכה של תורה במשפט שהוא מעמיד את הארץ. ,ואיש תרומות יהרסנה". אם משים אדם

עצמו כתרומה הזו שמושלכת בזוית הבית ואומר: מה לי בטורח הצבור? מה לי בדיניהם? מה
לי לשמוע קולם? שלום עליך נפשי! הרי זה מחריב את העולם. הוי, ‏‎,‎ואיש תרומות יהרסנה‎‏:

מעשה בר׳ אסי, כשהיה מסתלק מן העולם, נכנס בן אחותו אצלו מצאו בוכה. אמר לו:
רבי, מפני מה אתה בוכה? יש תורה שלא למדת ולימדת? הרי תלמידיך יושבים לפניך. יש
גמילות חסדים שלא עשית? ועל כל מדות שהיו בך, היית מתרחק מן הדינין ולא נתת רשות על
עצמך להתמנות על צרכי צבור. אמר לו: בני, עליה אני בוכה: שמא אתן דין וחשבון על
שהייתי יכול לעשות דיניהם של ישראל [ולא עשיתי].

[116] *T.* 29c. See *T.* 30c.

[117] *T.* 30c.

[118] *T.* 97c.

[119] See Rashi to Genesis 6.9, cf. Bereshit Rabbah 30.11: ‏‎את האלהים התהלך‎‏.
נח׳. ר׳ יהודה ור׳ נחמיה: ר״י אמר משל למלך שהיו לו שני בנים. א׳ גדול וא׳ קטן. אמר לקטן
הלך עמי. ואמר לגדול בא והלך לפני. כך אברהם שהיה כחו יפה ‏‎(בר׳ י״ז, א׳)‎‏ ‏‎.‎התהלך לפני
‏‎.‎והיה תמים״, אבל נח שהיה כחו רע, ‏‎את האלהים התהלך נח״‎‏

[120] *P. Y.* 16a. Cf. Devarim Rabbah 11.3: ‏‎שניצלתי‎‏ ‏‎נח אמר למשה אני גדול ממך‎‏ ‏‎והיה
מדור המבול א״ל משה אני נתעליתי יותר ממך. אתה הצלת את עצמך ולא היה
בך כח להציל את דורך, אבל אני הצלתי את עצמי והצלתי את דורי כשנתחייבו
כלייה בעגל. מנין, שנא׳ ‏‎(שמות ל״ב, י״ד)‎‏, ‏‎וינחם ה׳ על הרעה אשר דבר לעשות לעמו׳‎‏. למה״ד?
לב׳ ספינות שהיו בים והיו בתוכם שני קברניטין. אחד הציל את עצמו ולא הציל את ספינתו.
ואחד הציל את עצמו ואת ספינתו. למי היו מקלסין, לא לאותו שהציל את עצמו ואת ספינתו?
‏‎.‎כך נח לא הציל אלא את עצמו אבל משה הציל את עצמו ואת דורו

[121] *T.* 13c.

[122] R. Yaakov Yosef does not advocate the abolition of ‏‎התבודדות‎‏. He understood not only the value of "seclusion" but its utter necessity: firstly, as a
means of achieving ‏‎דביקות‎‏, thus qualifying the zaddik to go out to the people,
for ‏‎נבואתא כלה אם אינו מתבודד תחלה‎‏ (see *T.* 194b). [We know that R. Yaakov
Yosef himself practiced ‏‎התבודדות‎‏. See above pp. 52–53.]; secondly, as a benefit
to be fought for when the people either overburdened the zaddik with communal responsibilities (see *T.* 46c) or paid him so poorly that he was forced
to spend much of his time seeking a livelihood (see *T.* 46c). See also *T.* 56c:
‏‎ויוצא לן מוסר השכל לדור דור ודורשיו שאם יסכימו ויתנו מקום לראשי הדור הבוחרים
בבדידות להדבק א״ע בו ית׳ בתורה ובתפלה ושיהיה פנוי מצרכי ציבור שיפקחו הן בעסק צרכי
‏‎י׳‎‏ ‏‎העיר בבדידות, אזי טוב לו ולהן שיוכלו הן ג״כ לידבק ע״י בו ית׳‎‏; and, finally, as a per-
manent requirement for those leaders too weak in spirit to mingle with the
people. *T.* 51c: ‏‎לפתח חטאת‎‏ ‏‎ואם יראה בעצמו כי מיד שנתרחק מפתח בית מדרשו מיד‎‏.
‏‎רובץ׳ אזי יבחור בבדידות‎‏. In all this, it must be noted, the middle way is advised:
neither an excess of seclusion nor of mingling. ‏‎גם כשירצה להתבודד לוכות לעלמין‎‏
‏‎שרי הצורך לפי אבל ,ירבה לא נ״כ דכטיפין‎‏ (*T.* 179b). See below, pp. 215–17; cf.
K. P. 15a, *T.* 51c, 179b.

[123] Avot 5.2.

[124] *P. Y.* 18c: ‏‎,‎ובזה יובן ‎.‎עשרה דורות מאדם ועד נח להודיע כמה ארך אפים לפניו״‎‏
‏‎ר״ל מצדו ית׳ היה כח יכול להאריך אפו עוד, רק מצד נח שהיה מעורר דינים עליהם, וז״ש שהרי
‏‎כל הדורות היו מכעיסין לפניו ולא נענשו עד דורו של נח ש ה ב י א נ ח ע ל י ה ן מ י‎‏

ה מ ב ו ל וש"ש הפסוק ,כי מי נח זאת לי' וגו', שהוא הגורם. וזש"ה ,את האלהים התהלך נח',‎
שנהג עם דורו ב מ ד ת ה ג ב ו ר ה לעורר עליהן דינין הנקרא אלהים כמו רשב"י כשיצא
מהמערה, והטעם משום שהיה עוסק בבדידה שנאמר את האלהים התהלך נח וסבר מאחר
שהם אינם עושין כן ומניחין חיי עולם וכו'. משא"כ אברהם היה במעלה ב' הנ"ל והיה מעורר
רחמים בעונם וזש"ה אלה תולדות השמים והארץ בהבראם באברהם. ג ם ש ה י ו ע ו ל ם
ה ת ה ו ה י ה מ ק י י ם ב ר ח מ י ם וש"ש ,עשרה דורות מנח עד אברהם להודיע כמה
ארך אפים לפניו שכל הדורות היו מכעיסים לפניו עד שבא אברהם אבינו וקבל שכר כולם',‎
,ר"ל כנגד כולם כמאמר חז"ל בעשרה שבא לבה"כ וכו' וק"ל.‎

¹²⁵ T. 17b; cf. Bereshit Rabbah 34.1 and Tanḥumah, Noah 9. R. Yaakov
Yosef refers to a passage from the אלשיך (parashah Noah, Warsaw 1861, 15c)
which is here given in full. והנה בב"ר (פ' ל"ד, א') ובתנחומא (נח פ', ט') אמרו שהיה
[נח] כמונח בבית הסוהר והיה צועק ואומר הוציאה ממסגר נפשי וכו'. ולא הרשהו הוא יתברך
עד י"ב חדש. וכן ספרו רז"ל מרוב צער שהיה לו שם ואשר נדדה שנתו מעיניו להאכיל גם בלילה
למי שדרכו לאכול בלילה, ולא היה לו מנוח כלל. ע"כ אין ספק כי מה' היה לו לכפרת עון.‎
למה היה הוצרך לימרק שם י"ב הודש? נגד משפט הרשעים בגיהנים י"ב חדש ויחיה ולא ימות.‎
וזהו מאמר מדת הדין אליו עשה לך תיבת כו' לומר אל יעלה על רוחך שבשביל הבעלי חיים
אצוך לעשות תיבה... כי לא כן רק עשה לך בעבורך תיבה כו' כי אתה צריך אליה לכפרת
עון. וע"פ דרכך ,קנים תעשה את התיבה' הנזכר בעד הבעלי חיים שהיו המינים נפרדים בל
ידקקו לשאינם מינם, ובזה יתכן מאמרם ז"ל שהקשו למה במשה נאמר בחמר ובזפת ופה כולה
זפת מבית ומחוץ? ואמרו כי במשה היה חומר מבפנים כדי שלא יריח אותו צדיק ריח רע. והנה
קשה על זה כי הלא גם נח איש צדיק תמים היה? אך במה שכתבנו יתכן שנח לא הושם שם רק
למרק עון ועל כן יריח וירית. וזהו מאמרם ז"ל באומרם ,אותו צדיק" כלומר א ו ת ו צ ד י ק
ולא זה צדיק. ובזה מצאנו ראינו טוב טעם אל שנות הכתוב את טעמו לומר בכופר ולא אמר
בזפת כמו שאמר במשה, אך הוא לרמוז היות הזפת גם מבית לכפרת עון. ע"כ הוציאו בלשון
כופר ואמר מבית מבית ומחוץ בכופר. עוד ידוקדק אומר עשה לך על דרך זה. והוא כי ה' חפץ
דכאו בתיבה י"ב חודש מדה כנגד מדה. לומר אתה לא יצאת לישע עמך להיישירים ולהדריכם
בעבודת קונם רק נסגרת בתוך ביתך מה שלא עשה אברהם, לכן תסגר תוך התיבה גם אתה
ותצטער. ואשר לא היתה רועה ומנהיג את בני אדם ומנדד שינה מעיניך לרודפם להיישירם
להטיבם, עתה תרעה בהמות וחיות ומנדד שינה מעיניך להאכילם. וזהו ,עשה לך" כלומר כי
לך צריך אתה לעשות תיבה להנצל לעומת מדתך.‎

¹²⁶ T. 44c.

¹²⁷ T. 164a.

¹²⁸ T. 52a: ועיני ישראל כבדו מזוקן, כי אלה החשובים שהם עיני העדה שהיה להם לראות
ולהשגיח על העדה ולא די שלא השגיחו על זולתן אלא גם על עצמן לא השגיחו לראות שילכו
בדרך הישר וש"ש ועיני ישראל כבדו מזוקן, לכך לא יוכל לראות אח"כ גם על עצמו, שהוא
,עין א', מפני שיבה תקום ולא אחר שנתיישן הדבר וק"ל.‎

¹²⁹ T. 179c; cf. T. 58c.

¹³⁰ T. 132a: ובזה יובן ,והשיב לב אבות על בנים', תחילה שהת"ח, שנק' אבות, יעובו
ה ש ב : א ה ש ב ל ב ם תחלה על בנים שהם המון עם. Cf. T. 10c.

¹³¹ Kohelet Rabbah 1.10.

¹³² T. 46b. See above note 125.

CHAPTER 5

THE ZADDIK

¹ *T.* 132a: הנני שולח לכם את אליהו הנביא... והשיב לב אבות על בנים [.ובזה יובן
ולב בנים על אבותם] והשיב לב אבות על בנים תחילה שהתלמידי חכמים שנק' אבות יעזבו
השנאה שבלבם תחלה על בנים שהם המון עם ועי"ז השיב לב המון עם אל אבותם שהם ת"ח
שיהי' אחדות אחד בעולם... See *T.* 10; *Z. P.* 21d, 72d.

² See *T.* 85, 103.

³ See *T.* 137c; cf. *T.* 9d, 13d, 14a, 30c, 45d, 46, 47, 49, 65c, 81b, 100b, 129d,
131c, 133c; *K. P.* 4d, 25a; *Z. P.* 30c.

⁴ *T.* 137b, c: אמר ר' שמעון בן חלפתא לא מצא ה' כלי מחזיק ברכה. ובזה יובן כוונת התנא
לישראל אלא השלום וכו' ", כי הת"ח נקרא שלום וכמ"ש חז"ל: ת"ח מרבים שלום בעולם, שנא'
"וכל בניך למודי ה' ורב שלום בניך' ". וגם הצדק' נקרא שלום שנאמר "הי' מעשה הצדקה שלום",
והטעם מבואר בסוד "ונתתי שלום בארץ", כי הוא משפיע לארץ. לכך הת"ח המשפיע בתורה
והמוני עם משפיעים בצדקה, לכך כל א' נקרא שלום .... השלום שהוא בין בת"ח בין באנשי
המונים שישפיעו זה לזה בתורה וזה לזה בעושר .... ובזה יובן כוונת ריב"ל .עתיד הקב"ה
להנחיל לכל צדיק וצדיק וכו' ", ר"ל, כי יש ב' מיני צדיק הנ"ל, שכל א' נקרא צדיק המשפיע
לזולתו, זה בתורה וזה בצדקה ...

⁵ We quote the complete context of this and the following quotations,
T. 127b, c, d: העולה מזה לפי שהיו ישראל נבדלים ומפורשין מן ערב רב בתרי גווני: באכילה,
שלא היו אוכלין מאכל א' וגם שלא היו מעורבים עמהם רק שהיו מתבודדים בתוך ענני ישראל
ולא ערב רב. מזה יצא העגל בטענה: או נהוני בכללא עמכון, ר"ל, למה תעשו התבודדות חוץ
ממנו להתפלל וללמוד בפני עצמיכן וגם שלא לאכול מאכל שלנו? **וכאשר עיני ראו**
ולא זר מלחמה זו תמיד במי שרוצה להתקדש ולהיות פרוש להתפלל
במנין בפני עצמו מאחר שאי אפשר להתפלל בציבור שעושין
מצות אנשים מלומדה וכמה טעמים כיוצא בזה. ובענין **אכילה לא אכשיר**
דרי שהכל שוחטים אפילו שאינו בקי בהלכות שחיטה ואינו ירא שמים והוא נגד רבותינו
הקדושים שהזהירו הפוסקים ראשונים ואחרונים שיהי' השוחט ירא את ה' מרבים ובפרט
בענין חוש מישוש והרגשת בדיקת הסכין שהוא לפי כוונת יראת הלב וכמ"ש רבינו יונה יעו"ש.
ובודאי הפורש ממאכלי העולם קדוש יאמר לו כי הרבה אינן
בקיאין בה' מליחה ושחיטה שהרבה דינין מסתעפים ממנו. ובזמנינו היו כמה מוכיחים דורשים
הלכות מליחה לנשים בפרטות ולא כן עתה ובודאי **מי שרוצה להתקדש לא יסב**
במסיבתן וכאשר מוהרש"ל הזהיר לתלמידו בעל של"ה: במאכל יותר מכל" יעו"ש.

וכן שמעתי מחכם א', כי עתה התחכם היצה"ר שלא יצטרך לילך לפתות וללכוד ברשותו
כל יחיד ויחיד, רק כל עצמו ללכוד את היחיד אשר רבים נכשלים בו והוא שמעמיד שוחט
בעיר א' מסטרא דילי' המאכיל טרפות לרבים וכולם נלכדים ברשתו עבור זה. וכן הש"ץ
שהוא סרסור בין ישראל לאבינו שבשמים להוציא רבים ידי חובתן. ורבותינו הזהירו בפוסקים
ראשונים ואחרונים שיהיה הש"ץ המובחר שבעם לא כן עתה שבוחרין הגרוע שבעם כנודע,
ואין להאריך בזה. ובודאי צריך לעשות כמ"ש הרמב"ם עד "מי יתנו מלון מדבר" וכו' יעו"ש.
ואהרן שראה רוע כוונתם להתערב עם ישראל כדי למשוך את ישראל למדינתו לכך א' אם
ישתתפו עם עמא קדישא אתי אלקי רב אלהי זהב. ומזה יצא העגל שיעשו הערב רב אלהי זהב.
בפ"ק מלא תעשון אתי אלקי זהב. בתמיה. הא דעך שרי? אלא א"ר אשי אלקי הבא בשביל

זהב, ופי' מוהרש"א ב' אופנים וז"ל: כי שתים רעות עשו שהם מתמנין בשביל
זהב שנתנו לשדרה וגם שרוצין לאסוף זהב וכסף ע"י הרבנות
למלאות חסרונן וכו' וכבר באו רבותינו וכו' עד ובירושלמי אמר ר' מנא מיקל
לאילין דמתמנין בכספא ר' אמי קרא עליהון אלוקי זהב אין קורין אותו רבי ואין עומדין
בפניו והטלית שעליו כמרדעת של חמור וכו', יעו"ש.

ובזה יובן פרשה הנ"ל שהיא היה במדבר והיא נוהגת בכל זמן עד ביאת משיחנו ב"ב. וז"ש
"וירא העם כי בושש משה' שהוא רמז מוסר בזמן ההוא לדורות בענין הנהגת המוני עם רבניהם
שיש כשירי ראשי הדור העוסק בתורה ועבודת ה' עד שש שעות ביום שאז הוא זמן סעודת
ח"ח המאוחר לכולם, כמ"ש בפ"ק דשבת. וכמו שהיה משה ראש לכל דורו שהיה דור דיעה
כך בכל דור ודור הראש שבהם הכשירים הם מניצוצי משה רבינו ע"ה, וכמ"ש בתיקונים
ובמדרש וז"ש "מה שהיה הוא שיהיה וכו' ". וכ"כ בל"ת שש מאות אלף רגלי וגו', וגם
בל"ה מי שיש לו דעה נקרא משה, וכאשר היה בדורו של משה כך היא בכל דור דור כי
גם הוא הערב רב שיש בכל דור ודור כמ"ש בכתבים וז"ש "וירא העם כי בושש משה'
שהרב כשר שבעירם שוהה לבוא לפקח בעסק הקהל גם כי ב א ש ש שעדיין עוסק
בהתבודדות שהיה הזמן צריך לזה מיד קמו בתרעומת ואמרו עשה לנו אלקים שילכו
לפנינו כי אנחנו כבירה בלא מנהיג שהוא עוסק תמיד במלאכתו מלאכת ה' ואנחנו בני
העיר כצאן בלא רועה. וכאשר בזמנינו היה מסירה לפני השררה וצריכין אנו למנהיג ובאירו
דבריהם ואמרו כי "זה משה האיש לא ידענו מה היה לו'. ור"ל כי זה משה שהיה איש נבר
בוגברין להיות מנהיג עתה לא ידענו מה היה לו שלקח דרך אחרת, לבחור בבדידה ומעתה
אין ראוי להיות רב זמננו לנו גם כי יבוא אח"כ כי צריכין אנו לראש כזה שנהיה
עמו בכללות א' במאכל ובתפלה שלא יפרוש ממנו בכל עת, וז"ש אשר ילכו לפנינו, משא"כ משה
וישראל שהם נפרדין ממנו ע"י עניני יקר ובאכילת מן וכו'. והרמז לדורות ע"י שעושה עם
אנשים יחידי מנין בפני עצמו וגם אינו אוכל עמהם במסבה כלל שזה היה סיבה לערב רב
לעשות עגל זהב וכמ"ש בזוהר הנ"ל וכן לדורות מצד זה יצא עגל זהב שהיא א ל ק י זה ב
שנתמנה עפ"י השדרה בשביל זהב וכשאין סיפק בידו
עושה שידוכין בעיר. וכמו ששמעתי פי' הש"ס משה רבכם גנב או קביוסטוס
שגונב נפשות כדי להתחתן עם ס' רבוא ישראל וכו', ומ"ש עתה רבים הם הרבנים בעיר
וז"ש אשר ילכו לפנינו שאינו לאלהות הרבה שהוא הרב והמחותנים
עד שמצד זה נעשה קטטות ומריבות בעיר, וז"ש "וישמע יהושע
וגו' ויאמר אל משה קול מלחמה במחנה וגו' " שהיא קול מלחמת קטטות ומריבות ומצד זה
נשתברו הלוחות שנסתלקה תורה מהעיר עד שברחמי השם ית' חזר ושלח את משה וטחן
העגל לעפר כדי להראותו שאין בו ממש אף שילכו לפניו וחזרו וקבלו אותו לרב, ונתברר
הטוב מן הרע שמתו מתו בחרב מהם במגפה מהם בהדרוקן, ובסוף כשנעמד משה בתפלה
ונמחל לישראל וצוה לעשות משכן מכסף של ישראל לבד ולא מערב רב וכמ"ש בזוהר ויקהל
משה את כל עדת בני ישראל קחו מאתכם תרומה וגו', והרמז לדורות שיעשו בית
המדרש ליחידי ישראל שיהיו נפרדים מהמוני עם כי א י
אפשר שיהיו בכללות א' והיא תיקון מה שקלקלו תחלה
להתרעם בזה וכאשר היה במקדש עזרת כהנים ועזרת ישראל לבד.

ובזה יבואר מה ענין פרשת שבת אלה הדברים למשכן וכו' ודרשת חז"ל ידוע, ולדברינו
א"ש כי התח"ח נקרא שבת, וכשם שיש הבדל ושינוי בין חול לעשות ל"ט מלאכות משא"כ בשבת
כך יש הבדל בין שחיטה ומליחה שהוא מן ל"ט מלאכות כמ"ש בפ"ז דשבת .השוחט והמפשיטו
המולחו וכו' " הנוהג בחול שהם המוני עם ובין התח"ח הנקרא שבת שהרשות נתונה להוסיף לו
תוספת פרישות בזה כנ"ל והיא תיקון קלקול שני ואז הוי מחילת עון לישראל

אחר שתקנו וקיבלו על עצמן לתקן ב' דברים שקלקלו וק"ל. ואני הכותב בדידן
הוי עובדא הנ"ל מרישא לסיפא ומרומז למה דווקא זה
האיש צוה לעשות בה"מ בשארי גראד...

מה ענין אזהרת שבת למלאכת המשכן ונ"ל דכ' בזוהר (דף כ"ג) פ' ויקהל משה:
כניש לן למימר שבת לון בדבקדמיתא לא נטרו ערב רב כיון דשמעו ביני ובין בני ישראל
אמרו מלה דאתמנע מינן מיד ויקהל העם על אהרן וכו' ואתמשכו סגיאן אבהריהן לבתר
דמיתו כניש משה ב"י בלחוד ויהב לון שבת וכו' יעו"ש. וענין חילול שבת מבואר שם אח"כ
דף ר"ה ע"ב וז"ל: ומאן דאשתדל במילין אחרנין ובמילין דעלמא בשבת דא איהו בר נש דמחלל
שבתא ליה לי' חולקא בעמא קדישא דישראל תרין מלאכים שוו ידיהון על רישא ואמרי ווי
לפלניא דלית לי' חולקא בהקב"ה יעו"ש. מעתה תראה ענין חילול שבת בדורות הללו שהיא
עקבות משיחא אשר היו צריה לראש מן ערב רב כמבואר בכתבים ובר"מ פרשת נשא יעו"ש,
דלא די דמשתדלין במילין דעלמא שאינן צרכי צבור צרכי מצוה אף גם שטטריחין להמתין
בציבור עם ברכו דשבת עד שיבוא הראש ובשארית להמתין עם שוכן עד להפסיק בין הדבקים
לכך נתן משה שבת לישראל לחוד ונתחזק ע"י עשיית
המשכן עזרת כהנים לחוד דהיינו ל'כהן ולשרת להש"י
ועזרת ישראל שהם להמוני עם שבהם הראשים לחוד
והם יעשו מה שלבם חפץ עד שירחם הש"י על עמו לקבץ
נדחינו ורועה אחד לכולנו ב'ב אנס'ו.

[6] T. 127b. See note 5. In P. Y. 82c–84a a תשובה of R. Yaakov Yosef is
brought in answer to the question: ..בנידון השוחט שלא בדק סכינו תחילה.

[7] T. 127c. See note 5. The source for this is a passage from the Zohar II, 195a:
אלמלי ההוא ערבובייא דאתחברו בהו בישראל לא אתענשו ישראל על עובדא דעגלא. ותא חזי
מה כתיב בקדמיתא .מאת כל אשר ידבנו לבו' (שמ' כ"ה, ב'), לאכללא כלא בנין דבעא
קב"ה למעבד עובדא דמשכנא מכל סטרין במוחא וקליפה. ובנין דהוו אינון ערב רב בנוייהו
אתמר .מאת כל איש אשר ידבנו לבו' לאכללא לון בנייהו דישראל דאינון מוחא. וכלהו אתפקדו.
לבתר סטא זינא לוניה דאתו אינון ערב רב ועבדו ית' עגלא וסטו אבהרייהו אינון דמיתו וגרמו
לון לישראל מותא וקטולא. אמר קב"ה, מכאן ולהלאה עובדא דמשכנא לא יהא אלא מסטרא
דישראל בלחודייהו. מיד .ויקהל משה את כל עדת בני ישראל וגו' " וכתיב בתריה .קחו מאתכם
תרומה לה''. מאתכם ודאי ולא בקדמיתא דכתיב .מאת כל איש אשר ידבנו לבו'. .ויקהל
משה וגו' " מאן אתר כניש לון אלא בנין דהוו אינון ערב רב בינייהו אצטריך משה
.לאכנשא לון וליחדא לון מבינייהו

The Soncino translation follows: "If it had not been for the riff-raff that
became associated with Israel, the Israelites would not have incurred punishment for the sin of the golden calf. For, observe that first it is written here,
"of *every man* whose heart makes him willing ye shall take my offering"
(Exodus 25.2); to wit, of the whole body of the people including the mixed
multitude, as the Holy One, blessed be He, desired to have in the work of the
tabernacle the co-operation of all sections of the people, both the "brain"
category and the "shell" category: all were charged with the performance of
the work. Subsequently, however, the sections separated, each betaking itself
to its own affinity, and so the mixed multitude made the golden calf and led
astray numbers who afterwards died, and thus brought upon Israel death and
slaughter. The Holy One, blessed be He, then said: "Henceforth the work of

the Tabernacle shall be performed from the side of Israel only." Straightway "Moses assembled all the congregation of the *children Israel ... Take ye from among you* an offering unto the Lord" (*ibid.* 35.1–5). "From among you" emphatically, but not "from every man whose heart maketh him willing," as in the previous injunction. Furthermore, as no place of assembly is mentioned, the words, "and Moses assembled," etc., signify that, as the mixed multitude were mingled among the Israelites, Moses found it necessary to assemble the latter on one side so as to segregate them from the former." (Zohar, Sonc. ed. Vol. IV, p. 156.).

[8] *T.* 127c; see note 5.

[9] *Ibid.* See note 5. Elsewhere he complains bitterly how the separate מנין was destroyed and may refer to Sharegrad, from which town he himself was driven. *T.* 100a: ‏...ושאר צדיקים ונאונים נדים ונעים מדוך לדוך שאין להם לעמוד בקשרי מלחמה ושאר אנשי המלחמה הנשארים לקחם בשבי ממדינתם שהיה להם מקום מיוחד אל מדינה אחרת וכל כוונתו לעשות פירוד בין הדביקים שלא יעשו קשר וחיבור להלחם בו ועתה אין לנו על מי להשען‏...

Verses 1–4 of Psalm 2, ‏למה רגשו גוים‏ ... ‏יתיצבו מלכי ארץ על ה' ועל משיחו, ננתקה את מוסרותימו ונשליכה ממנו עבותימו‏, are interpreted to mean that the nations hate Israel because the rabbis, who have bought their positions, and their appointed officials destroy the private מנין of the hasidim. ‏ננתקה את מוסרותימו ונשליכה ממנו עבותימו, ר"ל, כי עצתם להשליך עבותת האהבה שבינם לבינו יתברך ע"י שיש להם מקום להתלמד ולהתפלל‏ ... ‏לפי מה שראתה עיני, ואל משיחו' שהם הלומדים העוסקים בתורה ועבודה, איך לגרש מהעיר ולבטל מנין שלו‏ (*T.* 129d). This separate מנין is not to be established out of hate or pride, and this is sometimes misunderstood by others. See *T.* 25b: ‏וע"ד הלכה נראה לי הרוצה להשתמש בתנא לעשות מנין לעצמו בשבת שהוא לכבוד ולתפארת שידעו שהוא איש נכבד וכשיש בו יראת שמים שאינו רוצה לטלטל ס"ת בשבת ומטלטל בעש"ק וז"ש ויריבו רעי גרד גי' חנא ע"ה [= עם הכולל] מי שרוצה להיות רועה נקר' רועה גרר ויאמר לנו המים שאנחנו ז"כ יכולין להראות תורה ומוסר הנק' מים בסעודה שלישית או בשחרית בב"הם המגיד' לקחו ס"ת עש"ק לכך ויקר' עשק ר"ת ערב שבת קודש ובפירוד הנופות נפרד הנפשות והשנאה גוברת ונק' שטנה ואח"כ שראו שמאריכים בתפלתם ונק' רחובות. על שמרחיבים ומאריכין בתפלתן אז נתרצו לפטור מהם ובחרו במעוטן ואז אמרו כי עתה הרחיב ה' לנו ופרינו בארץ ור"ת ג' בארות עשק שטנה רחובות הוא עשר דקאי על מנין שהוא בעשרה רמז על האמונה וכפי המאורע למי שאינו סובל בתפלת בית הכנסת שמקצרין. ‏ובהלכו לבית המדרש ויריבו רועי גרד תנא והלכו משם לעשות מנין לעצמו אז נק' שטנה שסברו שעשו שנאה מחמת שנאה ליפרד מהם ואחר המשך הזמן שהוא הרחבה וריבוי זמן תפלה שמחו ובחרו בשלהן ונק' רחובות והוא ענין אחר. סן האמור למעלה והכל בקנה אחד עולה והשם ית' ירחיב לנו ופרינו בארץ אנס"ו.‏ Cf. *T.* 9d, 123; Dinabourg, "The Origins of Hasidism," *Zion*, Year IX, p. 103. See below Chapter 7, note 71.

[10] Dubnow calls R. Yaakov Yosef "the prophet of religious separation" [‏נביא הפירוד הדתי‏] (Dubnow, *op. cit.*, p. 98). This, however, is not true, or, to be more exact, only partially true; for while he pleads for separation, as we

have seen, it is only for the sake of a final unity. The zaddik separates himself to be able once again to join himself with his fellow man; the hasidic community separates itself in order once again to purify itself and to, eventually, unite all of Israel. If we are to give any title to R. Yaakov Yosef it would not be that of the prophet of separation, but rather the prophet of unity. See pp. 108–10, 124, 137–41.

[11] *T.* 127c. See note 4, 5.

[12] *P. Y.* 67a.

[13] *T.* 19b, 63d, 168a.

[14] *T.* 100a; cf. *T.* 52a.

[15] *T.* 158d: מי שאוהב אותו ית' בתכלית נותן נפשו בכפו כי צר לו מאד על צער וגלות השכינה הגולה בסבת עונותינו ואין מנהל ולא מחזיק בידינו ותועלת השכינה הוא בידינו ע"י תשובותינו להוציא מבית האסורין ולהוציא ממסגר אסיר, ע"כ במקום שאין אנשים השתדל להיות איש להשיב רבים מעון ולעשות נחת רוח ליוצרו ולכף .... רגלי היונה ההולכת נדוד עד יערה עלינו רוח ממרום.

[16] *T.* 100a: ועתה אין לנו על מי להשען כי אנחנו אלה פה היום כולנו נצא במלחמה זו לעורר משינת התרדמה לעורר לבבינו הטהור עד פור התפורר' על העדר הצדיקים וגלות השכינה ולשתף בצער המדולדלים והמטורפי' ולעוק טרה וצרה כמבכירה וקול תשובתינו יעלה עם קול השופר לעורר אדם העליון משינתו ולהמשיך חסד ורחמים מעיני פקיחא דלא נים תדיר ואחר עשות תשובה...שלא יהיה מסך מבדיל כי יש עוד תקנה כי גם שהנפשות .... רחוקים מ"מ הלבבות קרובים.

[17] *T.* 170c: ...ובזה מבואר ששוקל גם במדת הענוה ותופס מדת בינוני חכם יחשב כי הוא תועלת וחכמה נפלאה רענין עבודת הבורא שלא יהיה נמאס בעיני עצמו רק יאמר מתי יגיע מעשי למעשי אבות הראשונים ובפרט בזמן הזה שהשכינה בגלות שלא מצא' היונ' מנוח לכף רגל' כי מיד בהכין אדם מעשיו לשם שמים בכל דרכיו מיד נעשה כסא להשכינה שתשרה בו והוא נקרא יותר מדורות הראשונים שהיו הרבה צדיקים בעולם משא"כ בזה"ז כי נגמר חסיד עם קונו ודאי ראוי לאיש לאזור כגבר חלציו לגמול חסד עם השכינה ואז נעשה כסא אל מדת החסד כמו בדורו של אברהם שלא היה עזר לשכינה כי אם ע"י אברהם כך עתה שאין איש שם על לב לעשות עזר וסמך לשכינה בגלות הזה כי אם מיעוט דמעוטא, השם נפשו בכפו ודאי נעשה כסא אל השכינה במדת החסד והש"י יעזרנו לעבדו באמת ובתמים, שיהיה דרוש .... הזה יוצא ממעשינו להיות נאה דורש ונאה מקיים.

[18] The meaning of the word "zaddik" and its use in the works of Rabbi Yaakov Yosef are often confusing and contradictory. In later hasidic literature the term zaddik has the specific meaning of the hasidic rabbi; but in these early writings, while the term may sometimes have this clear meaning also, it is often used in a broader sense. Originally the term ḥasid referred to a person superior to the zaddik: the latter being the one who fulfilled the law, the former being the one who went beyond it. Even in Rabbi Yaakov Yosef's works there are examples of this; *T.* 21c: והנה זכרנו אחר שהסיר מדות רעות וקנה מדות טובות, אז יכנס בנדר צדיק לקיים כל התרי"ג מצות ו' דרבנן, וא ח"כ יכנס בנדר חסיד להתחסד עם קונו לגמול חסד עם השכינה.

On the other hand, in the next statement we see a distinction made between the one who fulfills the commandments (here called תלמיד חכם) and the

‎בשבת... ידבק מחשבתו את האלהים או חסיד‎, who is now joined with the ‎צדיק‎
‎במחשבה או בדיבור או במעשה. עכ"פ לכל א' לפי בחינתו: לאיש המוני במעשה, ולתלמיד‎
‎חכם תלמיד‎ (T. 13a). The terms ‎חכם בדיבור, ולצדיק וחסיד גם במחשבה‎
and ‎צדיק‎ are sometimes opposed to one another and then again used inter-
changeably. But what is usually meant is that the ‎צדיק‎ is the good ‎תלמיד‎
‎חכם‎. Thus: ‎שהוא הבריות להצדיק שרוצים לת"ח הצדיקים, את אוהב‎
‎צדיקים שהם ת"ח ומישרים, הוכחות אוהב‎, (T. 180a, b). In the Zohar the
distinction between the ‎חכם להטיב תלמיד‎ and the ‎חכם להרע תלמיד‎ (see Jeremiah
4.22) is common, while in our author's writings "‎לומדים‎" and usually "‎חכם‎"
are used in the sense of ‎להרע ת"ח‎. T. 184c: ‎להרע חכמים הלומדים שהם רב ערב‎;
T. 36d: ‎הצדיקים את הלומדים שונאים‎. In addition, "‎צדיק‎" is sometimes used in
the sense of a leader in general. ‎הש"י לפני מתבודד שהוא צדיק בין הפרש יש כי‎
‎ומחזירין העיר תוך שהולך בצדיק כ"כ משא עצמו, את אם כי דורו להציל יכול אינו לבדו‎
‎למוטב‎ (P. Y. 16a). Or: ‎הצדיק להם השפיע שלא הארץ אבדה מה על‎. ‎לפרש הפסוק כונת‎
‎מוסר‎ (Z. P. 17c). In these two quotations ‎צדיק‎ is used in the sense of a leader,
but not necessarily the new hasidic leader. Thus, we see that in the earliest
hasidic literature the term ‎צדיק‎ is used in a number of different meanings, the
context alone telling us which particular meaning is meant. Nevertheless, as
a general rule, we may say that the term ‎צדיק‎ usually means the good leader,
the true leader, the ‎להטיב חכם תלמיד‎, the one who tries ‎הבריות את להצדיק‎.

[19] Z. P. 87d.

[20] T. 73d. Compare Zohar III, 114a: ‎משתיזבן עמא כל טב, הוא דעמא רישא אי‎
‎בחוביה אתפסן עמא כל אתכשר לא דעמא רישא אי בגיניה;‎.

[21] Ibid.

[22] T. 49d; Shabbat 88a.

[23] T. 74a: ‎והיה יתן מי ?לי אתה המקנא מרע"ה. דאמר והענין תהיו' קדושים....‎
‎אינו כי מרע"ה שזכה למדרינה ישראל כל שיזכו מרע"ה שכוונת באופן ',וגו נביאים ה' עם כל‎
‎שנתבאו משה עליהם ונסף מרע"ה. מעלת ומעלת למדרינת שיזכה עד חומרו לכך האדם ביד חפשית שהבחירה הנמנע מן‎
‎איש לכל אפשר המדרינה לזה וגם בכה'. נתבאו שהם הנביאים כל על למרע"ה נוסף מעלה מצינו‎
‎בהקהל. קדושים פ' נאמרו דלכך האלשיך כמ"ש וכמ' בקדושה דברה גרנון של משה מתוך עצמם השכינה שה, הדבר. בזה‎
‎סגולה.... ליחידי ולא קדושים יהיו שכולם ית' שכוונתו‎.

[24] Z. P. 88b: ‎חכמים בתלמידי ,.... בתוכם' ושכנתי :המשכן תכלית זהו‎
‎שלאחרי' בפרשה וז"ש המשכן. של ואבנים בעצים ולא ה' היכל שהם‎
‎רק הכוונה תכלית זהו הכנסת ובית המשכן בבנין תאמרו שלא ר"ל תשמרו, שבתותי את אך.‎
‎העיקר תעשו ולא בתוכם. ושכנתי נאמר עליהם כי תשמרו, שבתותי כנודע נקראים שהם ח"תת‎
‎את לדחות בעיניך יקל אל המשכן מלאכת על שהזהרתי אע"פי חז"ל שאמרו וזהו טפל.‎
‎כי הוא בהיפך ובאמת ח"ח, בכבוד ומקילין הכנסת בית לבנות העולם מנהג כי ר"ל השבת,‎
‎תורה ידו שעל ,וביניכם ביני היא אות כי. וז"ש לכך. הראוים חכמים בתלמידי בתוכם, ושכנתי‎
‎כ"ש משא ליחרב עתיד והמקדש המשכן ר"ל .... בישראל שכינה‎
‎קיים המקדש שאין נם לעולם מקדש הוא חכם, התלמיד.‎
Cf. Z. P. 50d.

[25] ‎נצבים פרשה‎, "‎שלמה תפארת‎," R. Solomon of Radomsk (Warsaw, 1867),

This quotation is found in the midst of a general statement on the zaddik by a writer living almost one hundred years after R. Yaakov Yosef and reflects the "institution" which the zaddik had already become during that period.

בזמנינו העיקר לעבודת השם ית', הוא, להתדבק אל הצדיקים, כל אחד לפי מדריגתו, וזה
העניין פרסם הבעל שם טוב ז'ל בעולם, שכל מי שמפריד את עצמו מהצדיק ואומר בלבבו מ ה
ל י   ל נ ס ו ע   ל צ ד י ק   ה ד ו ר   ו ל ב ק ש   ת ו ר ה   מ פ י ו   ה ל א   כ מ ה   ס פ ר י ם
ק ד ו ש י ם   ב מ ו ס ר   ה ש כ ל   ד ר ו ש י ם   ל כ ל   ח פ צ י ה ם   ב ת ו ר ה   ו ב י ד א ת
ש מ י ם,   אבל באמת אין זה כלום כי ראית פני הצדיק הוא מבטל ממנו כל מדות רעות,
דהיינו העצלות והעצבות וכל האוות רעות ר'ל וגם בצדקה מה שנותן לצדיק זוכה למדות
טובות וכל חסרונו ישלים על ידי דיבוק חכמים וגם הצדיק מעלה תפלתו למעלה כי הקב'ה
מתאווה לתפלתן של צדיקים (יבמות דף ס'ד ע'א) שמגלים אלהותו יתברך שמו בעולם ובזה
יבוא לשלימות האמיתי וכמשל בן כפר שרוצה לבא אל המלך ולבקש מלפניו על אבותיו ועל
עניניו אבל א'א לו בעצמו לדבר אל המלך כי כבד לשון הוא לדבר עם המלך דברים מועטים
הסובלים פירוש הרבה ועיין גדול והמלך אינו סובל רוב דיבוריו של בן כפר לכן העצה בזה
.לבא אל שר אחד משרי המלך המבין בלשון בן כפר וגם כן יכול לדבר עם המלך כראוי

Rabbi Yaakov Yosef by contrast does not speak of traveling *to* the zaddik, but of the zaddik going to the people. See Heschel, "לתולדות ר' פנחס מקוריץ," *op. cit.*, pp. 221, 2; also Weiss, *op. cit.*, pp. 103–5.

[26] "The new ideal of the religious leader, the zaddik, differs from the traditional leader of rabbinical Judaism, the Talmid Ḥakham or student of the Torah, mainly in that he himself 'has become Torah.' It is no longer his knowledge but his life which lends a religious value to his personality. He is the living incarnation of the Torah ... A tale is told of a famous saint who said: 'I did not go to the Maggid of Mezeritz to learn Torah from him but to watch him tie his boot-laces.'" Scholem, *Major Trends in Jewish Mysticism* (New York, 1946), p. 344. See "סדר הדורות החדש," *op. cit.*, p. 35.

[27] *Z. P.* 86d.

[28] *P. Y.* Introduction.

[29] *T.* 99a.

[30] *T.* 137c. In *T.* 94d an almost identical statement is quoted as "ששמעתי ממורי," while in *P. Y.* 35a (פ' חיי שרה דף ד') the same idea is quoted "כמ'ש [כמו ששמעתי] בשם הרב מו' יצחק פיסטנר." Cf. *T.* 24c.

The idea of the zaddik as the foundation (יסוד) is closely allied to his action as the mediator between the two extremes. Since he is the foundation of the world, he is able to reach those forces which have drawn apart and join them in peace.

[31] Avot 6.2.

[32] Taanit 24b.

[33] *Z. P.* 74d. Compare the following quotations: משה רבינו עליו השלום פתח
צינור הירדאה בעולם, ואהרן פתח צינור האהבה, כמו ר' חנינא שפתח שביל וצינור פרנסה
בני" חנינא בשביל ניזון העולם .כל וזלה'ה ממורי ששמעתי כמו שבעולם ומזון (*T.* 96c).
שמעתי ממורי .כל העולם ניזון בשביל חנינא בני" שהוא פתח הצינור ושביל השפע לעולם
ורפח'ה. וכמו שהוא בעניין השפע מזונות, כך הוא לפתוח צינורות החכמה הוא   ע ' י   ה צ ד י ק

מ ו מ ח ה   ש ב ד ו ר   כמ"ש במקום אחר ביאר הש"ס (בר' ל"ג, ע"ב): ‎.אטו יראה מלתא
זוטרתי‎ .אין'‎, ומשני ‎?זוטרתי'?‎ ‎(T. 84b, c). Cf. T. 72b, 73b, 100a; Z. P.
39a, 86c, 86d, 87a; P. Y. 67c, 74a.‎ וכמו ‎...‎ צינור היראה ‎...‎ פתח להם [לדורו] ‎...‎ משה
ש ה י ה   מ ש ה   ר ב י נ ו   ע ה " ש   ע ם   ד ו ר ו   כ ך   ה ו א   ב כ ל   ד ו ר   ד ו ר
‎(Z. P. 86c).

‎[34] כל‎ .‎ובשם מורי ר' חנינא בני עשה שביל וצנור להמשיך שפע בעולם וזה שאמר‎
העולם ניזון בשביל חנינא בני"‎, ודברי פי חכם חן‎. ‎ולי נראה לא מלבד שעשה
ש ב י ל   ו צ נ ו ר   ו כ ו'   א ל א   ש ה ו א   ע צ מ ו   נ ק ר א   ש ב י ל   ו צ י נ ו ר   שהשפע
התלמיד חכם‎ :125c .T. Cf. ‎(P. Y. 67d).‎ ‎.עובר על ידו בסוד‎ .ברכות לראש צדיק"
ה ו א   ש ב י ל   ו צ י נ ו ר   להריק השפע כמו שאמרו חכמינו ז"ל‎ .כל העולם ניזון בשביל
חנינא בני"‎.

‎[35] T. 100a:‎ הצדיק נקרא לב אל שאר‎.‎ איברים כי הצדיק הוא צינור להמשיך שפע החיים
מן חיי החיים אל שאר איברים שהם בני דורו‎.

‎[36] Mishnah Shabbat 3.6.

‎[37] T. 73b.

‎[38] Berakhot 33b.

‎[39] T. 96c.

‎[40] M. Buber, *The Tales of the Hasidim* (New York, 1947), vol. 1, p. 76.

‎[41] Z. P. 86c.

‎[42] Z. P. 87a. See Z. P. 86c.

‎[43] T. 127b:‎ וכמו שהיה משה ראש לכל דורו שהוא דור דעה‎, כך בכל דור ודור הראש
שבהם, הכשרים, הם מנצוצי משה רבינו ע"ה‎. Cf. Z. P. 86c.

‎[44] T. 72b:‎ אם זה המקבל השפע אינו משפיע לאחרים, נמנע השפע ממנו כיון שאין מעבר
וצינור להשפיע. וזה סוד גלות השכינה שנמנע השפע ממנה שאין לה להשפיע בסבת עוונתינו
המבדילים בינינו, וז"ש‎ .כי תשא את ראש"‎, כשתרצה לקבל, אז‎ .ונתנו"‎, שתתן לאחרים באופן
שיהיה מעבר לשפע, וק"ל‎.

‎[45] Rabbi Barukh of Meziboz, grandson of the Besht, wrote, in his grandfather's name: ‎(...)‎ היינו‎ .(תה' קי"ח, כ')‎ צדיקים"‎ .זה השער לה',‎ :זקיני הבעש"ט אמר‎
ל ה'‎ .ה צ ד י ק י ם   ה ם   ש ע ר‎ Rabbi Barukh of Meziboz, "‎בוצינא דנהורא"‎,
‎(לבוב, תר"מ)‎ 25a.

‎[46] For an analysis of this concept in hasidic literature, see G. Scholem,
"Devekuth," *The Review of Religion*, January 1950, pp. 115–139.

‎[47] T. 144a.

‎[48] T. 55b.

‎[49] T. 54d:‎ כתב הרמב"ם בספר‎ .י"ד שרשים"‎ וז"ל: מצוה א' היא אשר צונו בהאמונות
אלהות שנאמין שיש עלה וסבה הוא פועל לכל הנמצאים והוא אומר‎ .אנכי ה' אלהיך"‎.
But according to Rabbi Yaakov Yosef "‎האמונה היא הדביקות,"‎ (T. 54c, 56b).
To Maimonides אמונה meant commitment to the first cause, a mental acceptance of a dogma or creed, an intellectual attitude; while to Rabbi Yaakov
Yosef אמונה is דביקות, an attachment of the whole person — mind, heart and
spirit — to the Lord of creation, a cleaving to God. Since only one מצוה was
given by God Himself to the people which is דביקות=אמונה (אנכי affirms it,
while לא יהיה לך denies it's denial), one may fulfil the whole Torah by

fulfilling it. Cf. Makot 24a, Maimonides to the end of Mishnah Makot.
בקיים מצוה אחד כראוי סגיא...כי בכל מקום שאני תופס ואוחז בקצה וחלק מחלק
האחדותו, הרי אני תופס כולו, וכן שמעתי ממורי...והנה מאחר שהתורה והמצות נאצלו
מעצמותו ית' שהוא אחדות האמתי, א"כ כשקיים מצוה א' על מכונה ובאהבה שהוא ה ד ב י ק ו ת
ב ו ותפס במצוה זה חלק האחדות, א"כ כולו בידו כאלו קיים כל המצות שהם כללות
אחדותו פרצוף שלם כביכול וכ"כ בזוהר (פ' נשא דף קכ"ד) דמקיים מצוה א' על מחכונתו
כמו T. 55b: .(T. 55a) סני רתי"ג מצות T. 56c: .(T. 55a). דבוק אל שורש האמונה כאלו קיים כל הרי"ג מצות
הלב חיות כל האברים כך מצות האמונה מקור ושורש לכל רמ"ח מצות עשה דהוא השרוש
איך :בא חבקוק והעמידן על T. 55b: לכולם וממנו יוצאין המצות, שהוא לב של כל המצות
אחת' (מכות דף כ"ד ע"א), דכתב מהרש"א (שם) כי ,רבי תרי"ג מצות הוא מצד
המקבל אבל מצד הנותן שהוא הש"י אינם רק כמצוה אחת'.
Cf. T. 56c.

[50] T. 74a.

[51] T. 79c. See Sifre to Deut. 11.22.

[52] Z. P. 30b: יש ב' סוגי דביקות: א' סוג האיש הוא הת"ח שדביקים בו ית' ממש, ב' המוני
עם שאינם יודעים לדבק בו ית' וצוה התורה .ובו תדבק' לדבק בת"ח וכאלו דבוק בו ית'
ואם א י נ ו ב ר ה כי שיוכל לדבק בו ית', עשה לך רב לדבקבו. Cf. K. P. 15b:
וראה והבן מעלה זו (דביקות) על כל המעלות .הדבק בת"ח וכמ"ש. Cf. also T. 125c:
שתכלית כל המצות לא נתנו אלא כדי לידבק בו ית', ואם א י נ ו י ו ד ע ס ד ר
ה ד ב י ק ו ת ב ו י ת' שפיר ציותה התורה .הדבק בת"ח. It would
seem then that only if one cannot himself achieve devekut with God should he
seek to achieve it through the zaddik. Absolute dependency upon the zaddik
is not part of the doctrine presented here by Rabbi Yaakov Yosef.

[53] T. 58b. Mishnah, Rosh Hashanah 3.8.

[54] T. 58d.

[55] Oraḥ Ḥayyim 6.

[56] P. Y. 7c.

[57] Z. P. 50d; Mekhilta, ed. Lauterbach, Vol. 1, p. 252.

[58] Sifre to Deut. 11.22.

[59] See Taanit 22a.

[60] T. 125c.

[61] Mekhilta, loc. cit.

[62] ומעתה מה שאמרו חז"ל על מצוה .ובו תדבק' הדבק בת"ח אינו מוציאו מהפשוטו :T. 56c
כי ע"י שידבק את עצמו לת"ח הדבקים בו ית' ע"י תורתו ועבודתו או ע"י דביקותו בו יכול
להגיע למדרינת דביקות בו ית'.

[63] Pesaḥim 22b, Baba Kama 41b.

[64] Z. P. 39a.

[65] Bemidbar Rabbah 18.2.

[66] T. 191d. See Rashi and Targum to Num. 16.1; also Tanḥuma, parashah
Koraḥ 1.5.

[67] Shabbat 105b.

[68] Z. P. 30b.

[69] T. 87c.

[70] E.g., R. Elimelekh of Lizensk in his book "נועם אלימלך." See above note 25.

[71] T. 86b. See also T. 86a.

[72] Mishnah, Sanhedrin 4.5.

[73] T. 110d: משל שמעתי ממורי. למדינה שהיה להם גבור א' ובטחו עליו כל בני המדינה ולא למדו נמוסי המלחמה כי סמכו א"ע על גבור המלחמה שהיה בתוכם ביניהם, ואח"כ בעת המלחמה שרצה הגבור להכין כלי זיינו והשונא נתחכם ונגב ממנו כלי זיינו אחד לאחד עד שלא נשאר לו במה להלחם, ונם אנשי המדינה שסמכו עליו נלכדו עמו וכו', ודפח"ח. ובזה יובן "אשרי העם יודעי תרועה", ר"ל כשהעם אינם סומכים על הגבור רק הם עצמם יודעי תרועת המלחמה ואז "באור פניך יהלכון". . . "העולה מזה דודאי אשרי לעם שמקדימין עצמן באמת אבל לפי המשל חסד ה' יתברך הוא שנתרצה לעם בקדימת פנים של הגדולים לבד, וז"ש משרע"ה, כי שם ה' אקרא". "אבל אתם הבו גודל לאלהינו", וק"ל. While this version of the story seems to apply to the zaddik or leader in general, other versions apply to the בעלי התפלה who were unworthy and should not be relied upon. See P. Y. 37a: שמעתי ממורי זלה"ה משל על בעלי תפלות בימים נוראים, שלא יסמוך עליהם בני העולם רק ישתדל כל אחד להתפלל עבור עצמו אמר משל פעם אחד היו שני מלכים נלחמים יחד, ומלך אחד היה אדיר ותקיף שהיו לו גבורי חיל מלובשים בשריון וקשקשים וכו' וזה המלך שכנגדו הלך למצוא אנשים גבורים כאלו ולא עלתה לו וכו' עד שאמר לחילו שלא יסמכו על הגבורים וכו', ודפח"ח.

The following two passages likewise reflect the lack of absolute dependency upon the zaddik. P. Y. 64b: ואם המוני עם אינם יודעים לקשר הגשמי ברוחני, אז יחברו עצמם אנשי החומר והגשמי אל אנשי הרוחני והצורה, וז"ש חז"ל, זכור ושמור בדיבור אחד נאמרו, שהם אנשי החומר והגשמי הנכלל בשמור יתחברו עם אנשי הצורה הנכלל בזכור ויהיה הכל רוחני, וזהו מצוה הכולל, ובו תדבק", ודרשו חז"ל, הדבק בת"ח" שנקרא שבת, והבן: כי ת"ח ויחידי סגולה מקשר בימי החול הגשמי ברוחני, כמו כנסת ישראל וטע"ז יש לבאר מ"ש חז"ל, עשה שבתך חול ואל תצטרך לבריות", ר"ל, שתעשה שבתך בחול לקשר ערב עם בוקר ולא תצטרך לבריות להתחבר לת"ח שנקרא שבת ואם אינך עושה בחול כך אזי עכ"פ בשבת לוו עלי, להתחבר ולקשר הגשמי ברוחני עלי או לת"ח.

Z. P. 69a: שמעתי מהרב המנוח מוהר"ם שיש בעניני בני אדם ד' מיני זיווגים: אחד, זיווג פנים בפנים, כשלומד ומתפלל בתכלית השלימות. בחינה ב', בחינת זיווג אחור בפנים, דהיינו כשהוא טרוד בעסקיו ואין לו פנאי ללמוד וט"מ חושק תמיד שימצא עת הפנוי שיוכל ללמוד. בחינה ג', היא זיווג פנים באחור, נם שילמד ומתפלל מבלבלים אותו מחשבות זרות מחמת טרדתו. ויש עוד בחינה ד', בחי' זיווג אחור באחור הגרוע מכל ג' בחינות הנ"ל. והנה בחי' ג' זיווני הראשונים נ"ל שיש לרמזם בג' בחי' שיש בו לאכל על שולחן אחד, משא"כ בחי' ד' בחי' זיווג אחור באחור, אין בזה תקנה כ"א במה ששמעתי ממורי זלה"ה, ואשר יוציאם ואשר יביאם וכו' ", ודפח"ח. Only the last category is in absolute need of help. Cf. Z. P. 25d, 19c; chapt. 5, note 25.

[74] Buber, Tales of the Hasidim, Vol. 1.

[75] R. Yaakov Yosef in treating the doctrine of חומר וצורה refers several times to the אלשיך (see T. 81d, P. Y. 7c) in whose writings we find a similar idea. See particularly אלשיך to parashah Pinḥas.

[76] T. 5c. The division into חומר and צורה runs throughout three categories: the individual, divided into body and soul; Israel, divided into the people and

the zaddikim; the world, divided into the seventy nations and Israel. In each case it is the form (צורה) — the soul, the zaddik and Israel respectively.— whose task it is to conquer and spiritualize the matter (חומר) — the body, the people and the seventy nations respectively. ונ׳ל כי האדם נברא מן החומר וצורה,

והם ב׳ הפכים: כי החומר הולך אחר שרירות חומר הגופני שהוא קליפות, והצורה הומד ומתאוה לדברים רוחניים ותכלית בריאת האדם שיעשה מן חומר צורה ויהיה אחדות אחד ולא שיהיה דברים נפרדים. וכמו שזה התכלית באדם פרטי כך בכללו אומה ישראלית שנקראו אנשי ההמוני העמי הארץ, לפי שעיקר עסקיהם בארציות החומר ולכך הם החומר, משא׳׳כ הצדיקים העוסקים בתורה ועבודת ה׳ הם הצורה, ועיקר התכלית שיעשו מחומר צורה כמו שנאמר .שפתי כהן וגו׳ ורבים השיב מעון וג׳׳. וכמו שהוא בפרטי׳ האומה ישראלית כך הוא בכללות העולם שיש ע׳ אומות האוחזין בענפי האילן הקדוש וישראל אחיזתן בשורש האילן וצריכין ישראל להמשיך שפע לכל ע׳ אומות וזה ענין ע׳ פרים בחג וע׳׳י שמקבלין ע׳ שרים שפען ע׳׳י ישראל נכנעין תחת יד הקדושה ונכנע החומר תחת הצורה וכל אנפין נהירין ואז הם אומה ישראל דבקים בשמו הגדול שהוא אילן הנ׳׳ל עץ החיים אשר ממנו נמשך השפע לכולם, ואז ישראל הם במדריגה עליונה למעלה מהטבע... וישראל ואומות נכללין בתואר א׳ אדם שלם כי זה חומר בשר אדם וזה אדם טלנאו צורה אל החומר וזהו האדם המיוחד, ר׳׳ל שנתייחדו העולם החומר והצורה להיות החומר מוכנע תחת הצורה שהיא תכלית בריאת העולם (.T. 5c).

[77] *T.* 99a.

[78] See *T.* 5c.

[79] *T.* 72b. See *T.* 5c: אין הנשמה פועלת כי אם על ידי כלי ואיברי הגוף. בכל עניני המצוה; cf. *T.* 41b.

[80] Buber, *Tales of the Hasidim*, Vol. 1, p. 7.

[81] *T.* 36d.

[82] See Pesaḥim 50a.

[83] *Z. P.* 48d.

CHAPTER 6

HUMILITY

[1] *P. Y.* 67d. While this interpretation is quoted here in the name of the "ד יוסף," it is mentioned in the name of the אלשיך in *P. Y.* 60a. See also *T.* 161c.

[2] *T.* 40a.

[3] *T.* 40a; J. Emden "פירוש על אבות." 4.4.

[4] *Ibid.*

[5] *P. Y.* 71a, b.

[6] *T.* 19c.

[7] *P. Y.* 27c.

[8] *Ibid.*

[9] ‏K. P.‏ 18b: ‏כי הצדיק כל טומאתו וחטאתו לנגדו תמיד, משא"כ הרשע מראה סימן‬
‏טהרה שבעצמו כמו החזיר וכו' . . . האדם שסובר שהוא טהור הוא סימן טומאה, משא"כ מי‬
‏שסובר שהוא טמא וכמ"ש ,וחטאתי נגדי תמיד", הוא סימן טהרה . . . ובזה יובן ,קדושים תהיו",‬
‏ר"ל שתכלית הידיעה שידע שאינו יודע וגם במעלת השלימות ידע שלא הגיע לגדר הקדושים,‬
‏גם שהוא במעלה עליונה ידע שהי' למעלה מועט אלא שיהי' מכל המצפים לישועה. אימתי יזכה‬
‏לגדר ,קדושים תהיו'? לעתיד ולא בהווה. ,כי קדוש אני ה". הוא לבדו ית' הוא בתכלית‬
‏השלימות הקדושה אבל אדם אי אפשר בזה. לכך יראה עצמו תמיד חסר מגדר הקדושה‬
‏והשלימות. Cf. ‏T.‏ 106b.

[10] ‏T.‏ 17c: ‏האדם הוא ,סולם מוצב ארצה וראשו מגיע השמימה" ,ומלאכי אלהים עולים‬
‏ויורדים בו'. ר"ל כשהוא סובר שהוא רחוק מהש"י והוא מוצב ארצה והוא מן היורדים, הוא‬
‏קרוב להש"י וראשו מגיע השמימה. וכשסובר שהוא קרוב להש"י וראשו מגיע השמימה והוא מן‬
‏העולים, אז הוא רחוק מהש"י ומוצב ארצה והוא מן היורדים וכו', וק"ל. Cf. ‏K. P.‏ 12c.

Compare the following remark in the name of the Besht:
‏שמעתי בשם מורי:‬
‏,אתה הוא אלהינו", דתחילה אמר לנוכח ואח"כ נסתר כו', שאם סובר האדם שהוא דבוק בו ית'‬
‏והוא נוכח פני ית', אז הוא רחוק ממנו; ואם סובר שהוא רחוק, אז הוא קרוב. ואם כן זהו שאמר‬
‏מ י   ש ס ו ב ר   ,א ת ה"   א י נ ו   א ל א   ,ה ו א",   ו מ י   ש ס ו ב ר   ,ה ו א"   א ז‬
‏,א ל ה י נ ו",   ודפח"ה (‏T.‏ 107b).

[11] ‏K. P.‏ 30b. See also ‏P. Y.‏ 64c.

[12] ‏Z. P.‏ 69d.

[13] Avot 4.1.

[14] ‏K. P.‏ 18b.

[15] ‏T.‏ 81d.

[16] ‏T.‏ 74a.

[17] Horayot 10a, b.

[18] ‏P. Y.‏ 90b.

[19] ‏P. Y.‏ 74a: ‏צדיק התחתון ראש הדור . . . אינו נוח לו להשפיע לזולתו כי נוח לו יותר‬
‏להתבודד שהוא יקבל השפע מלמעלה.

[20] An early hasidic attitude towards the rabbinate is revealed in the following story: ‏כמו שנודע המעשה מהבעש"ט, זכותו יגן עלינו, שפעם אחת הפציר מאוד באחד‬
‏מגדולי תלמידיו, הוא רב הקדוש הצדיק ר' מיכל ז"ל, אשר בני העיר מאחת הערים החשובות‬
‏הפצירו מאוד בהבעש"ט על ככה לומר לו לקבל הרבנות, ולא רצה בשום אופן, עד שכעס‬
‏עליו הבעש"ט ואמר לו, אם לא תשמע לדברי אלו הנה תדע כי אבדת עולמך בזה ובבא. והשיב‬
‏לו, אף אם יהיה נאבד ח"ו משני עולמות, מכל מקום לא אקבל שררות הרבנות עלי אשר לא‬
‏נכון לי. אז ענהו הבעל שם טוב בשמחה. ברוך אתה לה' וברוך טעךְ, זכאה חולקךְ בגן עדן‬
‏כאשר לא התנשא רוחךְ ולבך על כל דברי אלו כי אנוכי אךְ לנסותךְ באתי, ולדעת את אשר‬
‏בלבבך להטיבךְ באחריתךְ. R. Shelomo of Radomsk, "‏תפארת שלמה‬" (Warsaw 1867)
parashah Devarim.

[21] ‏K. P.‏ 30c: ‏. . . ,אהוב את המלאכה" . . . שעסק התורה נקרא מלאכה וז"ש ,אהוב את‬
‏המלאכה": בה' הידיעה שהיא עיין התורה שיהנה מן המלאכה עצמה ולא מן השכר שיתגדל ויזכה‬
‏לרבנות רק ,שנא את הרבנות" והיינו ש,אל תתודע לרשות" ופ' הר"ב כדי לקבל רבנות ע"י.‬
‏הכוונה ע"ד שאמרו בש"ס ,שלא רצו לקבל הרבנות ואמר להם כלום שררה אני נותן לכם‬
‏עבדות אני נותן לכם וכו'." וה"נ קאמר ,שנא את הרבנות," אם שנחשב לו שררה שיתודע לרשות‬
‏לקבל תקיפות ושררה מן השררה שנקרא רשות שיהיה תקיף ושליט, זה ישנא; אבל אם נחשב לו‬

לעבדות שאינו רוצה לנהוג רבנות ושררה רק ע"י הרבנות יפקח בצרכי ציבור. אין ראוי לשנוא זה.

²² *T.* 130a; cf. *T.* 129d.

²³ *T.* 144c; cf. *P. Y.* 64c.

²⁴ *Ibid.*

²⁵ *Ibid.*

²⁶ See *T.* 97b.

²⁷ See *T.* 144c; *P. Y.* 64c.

²⁸ Avot 3.7.

²⁹ Berakhot 32a.

³⁰ Avot 3.7.

³¹ *T.* 97c.

³² *Z. P.* 79d.

CHAPTER 7

THE DESCENT OF THE ZADDIK

¹ *P. Y.* 74a.

² Zohar III 128b. See chapter 9, note 17.

³ *K. P.* 26d. See אלשיך to Exodus 19.10.

⁴ Avot 1.12.

⁵ *Ibid.*

⁶ *Z. P.* 39a.

⁷ *T.* 125c.

⁸ *Ibid.*

⁹ Cf. ‏תחילה‎ . . . . . ‏ובזה יובן והשיב לב אבות על בנים (מלאכי ג', כ"ד)‎ :*T.* 132a. *T.* 10c.

¹⁰ See *T.* 132a; also *T.* 46a, 173c; *Z. P.* 49a.

¹¹ *T.* 22a: ‏ויהי ערב ויהי בקר יום אחד," שצריך להחזיר הרשעים למוטב עד שיעשו אחד עם הצדיקים, וז"ש .אם לא בריתי יומם ולילה חוקות שמים וארץ לא שמתי", ר"ל לחבר על ידי הצדיק הנקרא ברית יומם ולילה ב' סוגים הנזכר לעיל שהוא תכלית בריאת שמים וארץ נגד ב' סוגים לחברן להיותן אחד, וק"ל.‎

¹² *Ibid.*

¹³ *T.* 60c; cf. *T.* 60b.

¹⁴ See *T.* 107d: ‏לא בלבד שיקשטו גדולי וראשי הדור את עצמן רק להזהיר גדולים על הקטנים שהם הרשעים שהם מקטני אמונה להזהיר הגדולים שיחזירו למוטב את הקטנים ג"כ.‎

¹⁵ *T.* 60c.

¹⁶ *T.* 17b; cf. *P. Y.* parashah Noah.

¹⁷ Rashi to Gen. 24.7: ‏ה' אלהי השמים אשר לקחני מבית אבי", ולא אמר ואלהי הארץ ולמעלה אמר .ואשביעך וגו'". אמר לו עכשיו הוא אלהי השמים ואלהי הארץ שהרגלתיו בפי‎

הבריות. אבל כשלקחני מבית אבי היה אלהי השמים ולא אלהי הארץ שלא היו באי עולם
מכירים בו ושמו לא היה רגיל בארץ. Cf. Genesis Rabbah 39. *T.* 60c.

[18] See Genesis Rabbah 39.14. Cf. *T.* 18d.

[19] See *T.* 60c.

[20] See *T.* 18, 19.

[21] *T.* 19a: . . . ואף אם ירצה אברהם לפרסם אלוהו' ית' בעולם להחזיר בני עולם
לאלוהו ית' לא ישמעו לו שאין לו התחברות עמהם שהיה במדרינה עליונה תואר אברם . . .
והם במדרינה תחתונה ולחוס על כבודו ית' צריך שירד ממדרינותו, סוד ו' כורע לגבי ה'
להעלותו וסוד .שבע יפול צדיק וקם., כדי שיתחבר עם בני העולם ואז יוכל להעלותן. וז"ש
.התהלך לפני והיה תמים., ר"ל ע"י תואר הילוך בסוד .לכי ומעטי עצמך" שהוא .לפני. תוכל
להתחבר עם המוני עם להעלותן, ואז יהיה תמים. אחר שזיכה את עצמו ואת אחרים נקרא שלם
.ותמים, משא"כ בלא"ה נקרא מחצה בסוד מחצית השקל . . . Cf. *Z. P.* 87b. See chapter 8,
note 36 for an explanation of "ן כורע לגבי ה'."

[22] *T.* 18d.

[23] *T.* 60c: יש ב' סוגי צדיקים: א'. ההולך בתום לבבו בקרב ביתו להתבודד. לקיים
.והצנע לכת עם אלהיך" וכמ"ש בנח .את האלהים התהלך נח". סוג ב', שקיפשט עצמו ואחרים
גם כן כמו אברהם אבינו שנאמר. ויקרא שם בשם ה' וגו'." ודרשו חז"ל שהיה מרניל שם שמים
בפי הבריות וכמו שביארתי פסוק .אם אמצא חמישים צדיקים בתוך העיר", שהוא צדיק
יש ב' סוגי צדיקים: אחד ההולך .בתוך העיר. Cf. *P. Y.* 77c: להשיב רבים מעון
בתום לבבו בקרב ביתו להתבודד לקיים .והצנע לכת עם אלהיך", וכמ"ש בנח .את האלהים
כי יש הפרש .התהלך נח". סוג ב' שקיפשט א"ע ואחרים נ"כ Cf. also *P. Y.* 16a:
בין צדיק שהוא מתבודד לפני הש"י לבדו ואינו יכול להציל דורו כי אם את עצמו, משא"כ
.בצדיק שהולך תוך העיר ומחזירן למוטב מציל דורו גם כן See also *P. Y.*
19a.

[24] *T.* 39a; cf. *P. Y.* 18c.

[25] *P. Y.* 18c. "Briefly, the originality of Hasidism lies in the fact that the
mystics who had attained their spiritual aim — who, in kabbalistic parlance,
had discovered the secret of true *Devekut* — turned to the people with their
mystical knowledge, then 'Kabbalism became Ethos', and, instead of cherish-
ing as a mystery the most personal of all experiences, undertook to teach its
secrets to all men of good will." Scholem, *op. cit.*, p. 342.

[26] *Z. P.* 87b: ומ"ל דיש ב' סוגי עבודת השי"ת במין האדם: א' במעשה, ב' במחשבה ודביקות
בו ית'. אך דאי אפשר שיזכה לטהר מחשבתו . . . כי אם שיקדש את עצמו במעשה תחלה
באברים הנגלים, ואח"כ במחשבה, שהיא באיברים הנסתרים . . . וכמו שהוא בפרטות אדם אחד
כך הוא בכללות, שיש אנשים הנקרא צורה ויש אנשים הנקרא חומר, ואי אפשר לאנשי
הצורה לטהר מחשבתם לדבק בו ית' כי אם אחר שהרתם
אנשי החומר במעשה.

[27] *T.* 158d: .עיקר תשובה להשיב אחרים.

[28] *T.* 19c: .חושב הצדיק שכל א' מבני ישראל הוא [מ]אברי השכינה.

[29] *T.* 48c: משל א' שמעתי שאמרה אשה אחת מק"ק מעזביז בלשון רוסיא: .יפה בחרנו
לנו את אלהינו, אבל גם הש"י יפה בחר בישראל שהרי פייבוש איש קל ומקדש את הש"י". . . .

[30] *T.* 59c.

[31] *P. Y.* 18c: מדריגת נח היה ירא לחוד, שנאמר .את האלהים התהלך נח". לכך גרם

שהביא עליהם מי המבול שהיה תהו ובהו וחשך. משא״כ אברהם. היה מדריגתו בעבודת השי׳
מאהבה . . .

[32] Z. P. 90c: שהוצרך החכם לחזור אחר הרשע ולפשוט לו יד אולי יחזור בתשובה. Cf. 90d.

[33] T. 66a: ומי לנו גדול ממשה רבן רבן של ישראל? בודאי כל מעשה תפלתו ותורתו ומוסר
היה בענין זה: שפשט ידו להם לישראל שיאחזו בו להעלותן.

[34] T. 180a; cf. chapter 5, note 18.

[35] Baba Mezi'a' 107b.

[36] T. 97d, 98a, 100c.

[37] T. 100c.

[38] T. 98b.

[39] See T. 145a, Zohar III, 220b. See also pp. 147–50, 198–200.

[40] Berakhot 63b. Z. P. 80a.

[41] T. 151b.

[42] Z. P. 30.

[43] Z. P. 54a: אל תבכו למת׳ ר״ל כשמת ממש אל תבכו. ובזה יובן ש״ס דמ״ק (דף כ״ז ע״ב)
מצד שמת, ונסתלק מן חיי עוה״ז לעלות לחיי עוה״ב, כי אדרבה מיתת הצדיק נקרא הלולא כי
נעשה יחוד עליון עי״ז, כמפורש בזהר, מלבד שנפטר מצרות העולם הזה והולך למנוחת לחיי
עוה״ב. לכך נקרא פטירה וכו׳. רק .בכו בכה להולך׳, שיש צדיק שאינו מת ממש. רק יורד
ממדריגתו שנקרא .ה ו ל ך ׳ כדי שיתחבר עם מדרינת המוני׳ עם להעלותם . . . וכאשר
הם אינם רוצים להתחבר אליו להעלותן, א״כ בחנם הלך ממדריגתו, וז״ש כפול .בכו בכה׳:
א׳ על ירידת הצדיק בכה, הב׳ על ירידתן של המוני״עם שנשארו למטה ואינם יכולים לעלות . . .
(זה היה הספד להרב המוכיח זלה״ה מפולנאי).

[44] Z. P. 14a.

[45] T. 107d.

[46] T. 190b: הצדיק, עובד ה׳, יודע ממלחמות היצר הרע ומלסטים שבדרך עובד ה׳, שהוא
מסוכן ותמיד חיי צער יחי׳ — איך להנצל ממצדתו — ויודע להזהיר אחרים מסכנת לסטים,
זה .יוסף דעת יוסיף מכאוב . . .׳. Cf. 190a, b.

T. 148c: וחטאתי נגדי תמיד׳ הצדיק הוא המשים אל לבו חטאתו ומריו כמ״ש דוד.

[47] The Besht finds justification for opposition to the zaddik: שמעתי בשם
בעל שם טוב, פירש הכתוב .מה רב טובך אשר צפנת ליראיך׳ (תהל׳ ל״א, כ׳), כי ל פ ע מ י ם
מ ד ב ר י ם ד ב ר י נ ב ל ה ע ל ה צ ד י ק ואמר הבעל שם טוב ש ז ה ח ס ד ה ש ם
י ת ב ר ך שרואה שהס״ם מתקנא הרבה בהצדיק ורוצה להחטיאו. לזה עושה השם יתברך
שידברו בני אדם על הצדיק. וכשרואה הס״ם שהעולם מרננים על הצדיק אינו מתקנא בו כל
כך, וזה שאמר הכתוב .מה רב טובך אשר צפנת ליראיך׳. ר״ל שהצפנת והסתרת הצדיקים שלך,
שהעולם אינם יודעים שהם צדיקים גדולים ומרננים עליהם וזה .רב טובך׳, שבזה סרה קנאת
הס״ם, ודפח״ח. — ר׳ ראובן הלוי הורוויץ מזיאראנאוועצ, .דודאים בשדה׳, (לבוב תרי״ט), פ׳
שמעתי בשם מורי שצריך להתפלל על שונאיו, שהם רוחו של נח; and see also P. Y. 19c:
צדיק בגלגול וכו׳.

[48] T. 141c.

[49] T. 87c.

[50] T. 58c.

[51] P. Y. 67a.

[52] T. 163d.

[53] *T.* 167c.

[54] *T.* 174c.

[55] *K. P.* 15b.

[56] *T.* 58c.

[57] *T.* 34a.

[58] *T.* 104a.

[59] *T.* 37c.

[60] *T.* 104a.

[61] *T.* 173c: הכל מכירין ויודעין מעלת הצדיק ומכבדין אותו ואפילו הרשעים יודעין מעלתו,
רק שאין אומרים בפיהם שבח מעלת הצדיק פן יאמרו להם למה לא תעשו כמעשיו?

[62] The name יוסף is taken here to be derived from אסף which means "to gather."

[63] *T.* 33c.

[64] *T.* 36d.

[65] *P. Y.* 19b.

[66] *T.* 101b, c: ונ"ל דאיתא במד' איכה .על עזבו את תורתי" שהם הת'ח. ול'נ כפשוטו
דדריש .את ה' אלהיך תירא'. לרבות ת'ח וכו', וה 'נ .עזבו את ת' " שהם הת'ח שלא החזיקו
בידם, ועפ'ו בארתי קושיה התוס' בהא .דשואלין תחלה נשאת ונתת באמונה? ואח"כ .קבעת
עתים לתורה? וכו' יעו'ש. ואחר שעזבו את ה' הרשיעו עוד יותר שנאצו קדוש ישראל הם שלומי
אמוני ישראל המקדשין עצמן למטה וכו' ונקראו קדוש ישראל והם מנאצים אותם לספר גנות
בפניהם ובפני כל עם כמ"ש דהע"ה, .ישמונוני תחת רדפי טוב' ומכח זו נזורו אחור, שלא
יוכלו לעמוד בפני המלעיגים ושבקו לחסידותן וקדושתן
ואחרים שהיו ג'כ רוצין להתקדש נזורו אחור וכאשר שמעתי
כמה בע"ת (בעלי תורה) נסוגו אחור. וגדול עונם מנשוא שהוא חוטא ומחטיא ... Cf. *P.* 104a.

[67] *T.* 100a.

[68] *T.* 100a. See chapter 5, note 5.

[69] *T.* 46a. See chapter 4, note 98 for a similar statement from a later work.

[70] *T.* 129d. The context of this passage is given here in full, interpreting
Psalm 2: .למה רגשו גוים ולאומים יהגו ריק יתיצבו מלכי ארץ וגו' " ור"ל, שלא אמר זה דרך
תרעומות להתרעם למה למה רגשו וכו' רק שא' דרך מוסר לעמו ישראל בטוב טעם ודעת להבינם למה
רגשו נוים ולאומים יהגו ריק להתעולל עלילות בריק והבל על בחירי אומה ישראלית כאשר
באזנינו שמענו עלילות שונאינו בכמה מיני תחבולות אין מספר להעלותן אשר האומות מעלילין
והם המוני האמונות הנקרא .גוים' שרגשו וגם השרים של המדיניות מא"ה הנקרא .לאומים' יהגו
ריק. היאומן [היאמן] כי יסופר להאמין מחכמי א"ה על דברי הבל וריק כזה, אבל זה נמשך
מצד .כי יתיצבו מלכי ארץ'. מאן מלכי? רבנן, שמעמידין עפ'י השר שאר ץ
שלו וזה שנצב לרב שנק' מלך על פי מלכי ארץ, שהארץ והעיר שלו אחר חורבן
הבית (ותיבת מלכי משמש לכאן ולכאן), ויתיצבו מלכי ארץ ורוזנים, שהם המנהיגים
של הרב הנ'ל. .נוסדו יחדו על ה' ועל משיחו', כי מיד יועצים עצות על ה' בענין
מאכלות אסורות להעביר שוחטים טובים ולהעמיד רעים לפי
רצונו וכיוצא בזה לפי מה שראתה עיני. .ואל [ועל] משיחו'. שהם הלומדים
העוסקים בתורה ועבודה איך לגרשם מעיר ולבטל מנין שלו יעשו
כעובדא דאחז המלך שאחז בתי כנסיות ובתי מדרשות וא' אם אין חכמה אין הקב'ה ישרה
שכינתו בישראל שנאמר .חתום תורה בלימודי' וכו'. .ננתקה את מוסרותימו ונשליכה ממנו

עבותימו" ור"ל כי עצמם איך להשליך עבותת האהבה שבינם לבינו
ית' ע"י שיש להם מקום מיוחד להתלמד ולהתפלל ולהסיר
מוסרותימו שע"י תורה ומוסר כולם נכנסים לפניהם ולהסיר עול מעלינו, זהו תוכן עצתן. והנה
כאלו יש ב' כתות הנ"ל שיש יראי השם לש"ש וכנ"ל ובזה א' "יושב בשמים ישחק", ר"ל כי זהו
שהוא ברום המעלות בשמים שכבר נתקשר באהבה ית' גם עתה ישחק וישמח ולא יחוש כלל
לעצתם משא"כ "אדני ילענ למו" כי כת ב' הנ"ל שהיה במדרגה התחונה הנק' 'אד' כנודע שלא
היה לש"ש רק ליטול את השם שהוא מחסידי ארץ ובעת שראוה שיועצים עליהם הרוזנים וכו'
מיד הוא עצמו ילענ למו על יראים כדי שלא ימצא בו שום דבר מחסידים שלא ילכד בעצ'
רוונים וזה הוא השמיר' של מעל' לבל יכנס פנימה כל מי שהיה כי מי שאינו הגון אז "ידבר
אלימו באפו ובחרונו יבהלמו" כדי שיהיה נרפים מהתורה והעבודה לכוונה הנ"ל. אבל "אני
נסכתי מלכי על ציון הר קדשי" ור"ל שדוד אמר על עצמו ואני "שעמדתי בנסיון כל
הבזיונות והשפלות וכעת אני נסכתי מלכי שאינו נצב ממלכי ארץ עפ"י השררה
רק ואני נסכתי מלכי שהוא אלהי עולם על ציון הר הלומדים המצויינים בהלכה
שעיקר מלכותי ונסיכותי הוא על הלומדים העוסקים בתורת ה' ועבודתי כמ"ש "חבר אני לכל
אשר יראוך וכו'" ועל זה הוא סמוך לשון חיבור כמו ועליו מטה משנה כי הם נטורי קרתא, ואין
צריך לומר שלא ינרשם מהעיר רק שהם עיקר ממשלתי. וגם על
הר קדשי שהם ראשי קציני אלופי ישראל שהם נק' הר והם גורמים קדושתן כמ"ש "ויהי כאשר
תמו . . . וידבר ה' אלי" שאין קדושת שמו על נביאים כי אם לזכות ישראל ומה שהעמיד ית'
אותי לנסיך ומלך הוא בזכות ישראל שהם נקראים "קודש ישראל לה' ראשית תבואתו" וחס על
כבודם שיהיה להם רועה נאמן לבל יגיס דעתו עליהם כמ"ש אין ממנים פרנס על הציבור אלא
אם כן קופה של שרצים תלוין אחריו. See further *T.* 129d, 130a. Cf. *T.* 100a:
קורת הזמן אשר קרה מקרה לעובדי ה' אשר אלו הלוקין
בה' הדבקים, אמרתי שלוה נחכוין ג"כ כי הניבור הוא ראש הדור צדיק יסוד עולם
היודע בקשרי מלחמה לעמוד נגד הצורר אותנו תמיד וכלי זיינו הם תלמידיו הלומדים טכסיסי
מלחמה ושימשו אותו או שאר צדיקים שבדור הנטפלי' עמו שע"י קישור ואיסור תפלתם יחד
לזרוק חיצים ובליסטראות אל חויא כונדע. משא"כ השונא בתחבולת נגב כלי זיינו שאחד המיוחד
שבעדר הצדיקים חטפו מהעולם הוא מהור"ר ליב פיסטנר זלה"ה שהיה מגן בעד כמה אלפים
מישראל. ושאר צדיקים וגאונים נדים ונעים מדוך לדוך,
שאין להם לעמוד בקשרי מלחמה הנשארים לקחם בשבי
ממדינתם שהיה להם מקום מיוחד אל מדינה אחרת וכל כוונתם לעשות
פירוד בין הדבקים שלא יעשו קשר וחיבור להלחם בו.

[71] *T.* 58c.
[72] *T. parashah* Ḥukat.
[73] *K. P.* 41a.
[74] *Ibid.*
[75] *Z. P.* 6b.
[76] *T.* 170b. Cf. *Z. P.* 47b, c, d, 49c.
[77] *Z. P.* 47d: ובזה נ"ל פירוש הפסוק, ורבים מישני אדמת עפר יקיצו אלה לחיי
עולם (דניאל י"ב, ב'), ר"ל, שיקיצו מן מדת השפלות שוכני עפר כמ"ש "ונפשי כעפר לכל
תהיה", וירצו לאחוז במדת הגאוה אם הוא לשם שמים נגד היצה"ר הרוצה להשפיל
ותופס חרב הגאוה נגדו, ואז הוא "לחיי עולם". משא"כ אינך המשתמשים במדת הגאוה לכבוד
עצמו ולא לכבוד שמים אזי יהיו "לחרפת לדראון עולם" . This advice, however, would
seem to be limited to the zaddik. *Z. P.* 48a: דרך הצדיק שיאחז לפעמים

הגאוה נגד היצה"ר היפך השפלות שיהיה עזר כנגדו . . . משא"כ אצל הרשעים או אפילו המוני
עם, המשתמשים בגאוה רק לכבודם ולא לכבוד שמים, אצלם אינה רק בחינה אחת
[שפלות].

While outwardly pride may be necessary, inwardly there must be humility:
משל למלך שביקש רפואה מהרופאים שיחיה לעולם ונתנו לו רפואה שיתרחב ויתקרב
לענוה ושפלות. וכל מה שנהג יותר שפלות נכנס בו עצם הגאוה — איך נוהג בענוה ושפלות
יתירה. עד לבסוף הודיעו שינהג נשיאתו ברמה, רק בקרבו ישמור [הענוה] שלא
ינבה לבו בזה. כמ"ש ה' לא גבה לבי" וכו' יעיו"ש. וזה ענין עמלק שהוא היצה"ר שמתגאה יותר
בו שפלות לומר לו: "תמה אני עליך על שפלותך?" וז"ש "זכור לא [אל] תשכח" וגו', ר"ל,
בתחלה מוזהר להרחיק מנסות הרוח הגורם שכחה כמ"ש "רם לבבך ושכחת את ה' אלהיך"
וכשיתרחק מנסות רוח לא ינהוג שפלות יתירה, זכור את אשר עשה לך עמלק ע"י שפלות יתירה.
וזהו שאמרו מאד מאד הוי שפל רוח (אבות ד':ד'), ר"ל, רוח שבקרבו יהיה שפל ולא שפלות
מגולה כמה שהיה מעשה עמלק, והבן. (Z. P. 49c.) This parable is quoted in the name
of the Besht in Z. P. 39d and occurs many times in Rabbi Yaakov Yosef's
works. In T. 187d it is quoted from "כפתור ופרח."

[78] K. P. 4a.

[79] Z. P. 48a. See above note 77.

[80] K. P. 4a.

[81] Z. P. 42c.

[82] Z. P. 42d. See "נוצר חסד," 4.4; 6.4. See above note 77.

[83] Z. P. 40a.

[84] Z. P. 39c. Cf. K. P. 4a.

[85] Megilah 31a.

[68] "דגל מחנה אפרים", דרשה לפורים.

[87] T. parashah Emor.

[88] T. 13b: שמעתי כי לשעבר היה היצה"ר רק לדחותו מעה"ב משא"כ עתה נחכם לדחות
האדם מעה"ז וטעה"ב כגון טרדת הפרנסה אשר יומם ולילה לא ישקוט ואין לו מנוחה בעה"ז
וכמ"ש שאין לו פנאי לפקח בעסקי עה"ב ונדחה משניהם . . . לכך אני מתפלל "לא אמות"
בטרדת עה"ז כדי שאוכל לפקח בעסקי עה"ב ובזה "ואחיה" לעה"ב. Compare the following
remark from the Besht in "כתר שם טוב" by אהרן בן צבי הכהן, section II, 12d:
"כה אמר ה' התבוננו' וגו', (ירמ' ט', ט"ו) מקושר פרנסת של שנים אלו משנים קדמונים, על כן
ותשאנה עלינו' דייקא "נהי" וגו', אף על גב דאמר בזוהר (תקוני זוהר תיקון ו') צוווחין הב
פרנסה." זה היה בשנים ההם שפרנסה היה בשופי, מה שאין כן עתה, שעל ידי
מניעת פרנסה אי אפשר לעבוד אותו יתברך שמו. ולהחזיק
בנינו לתלמוד תורה, על כן תינוקות של בית רבן התפללו
עבור אבותיכם ואמותיכם שיזכו לגדל אתהם לתורה
ולחופה ולמעשים טובים.

[89] T. 103a.

[90] T. 69d.

[91] Ibid.

[92] T. 184d.

[93] Ibid.

[94] Ibid.

95 *T.* 184d.

96 *T.* 24c; cf. *T.* 50a.

97 *T.* 111c.

98 *T.* 132b.

99 *T.* 85d, 86a.

100 *T.* 130c.

101 *Z. P.* 23d.

102 *Ibid.*

103 *T.* 85c.

104 *P. Y.* 70b.

105 Berakhot 35b.

106 *T.* 85b.

107 *T.* 62d.

108 But, on the other hand, there may be times when gradual advance is
not sufficient and one great leap is necessary. *Z. P.* 40a: עניין שפסח ודילג
להתלהב ישראל שלא בהדרגה בעבודת ה' ע"י סיוע הקב"ה בהתחלה כדי שיצאו מן נו"ן שערי
טומאה ואח"כ הניח אותם שילכו, מעצמן בהדרגה שהוא סוד ספירת העומר עד נ' יום מ"ת, וזהו
כוונת התוספות מתוך האש הגדולה וסיוע הקב"ה בתחלה אי אפשר שוה יהיה קיים כי יחזרו
אח"כ לילך מעצמן בהדרגה ושמא לא ירצו לילך מעצמן אחר כך והוצרך
כפיית ההר, והבן. א"כ מוכח מזה שאחזו מיד בתחלה בקצה החסידות
שהוא האש הגדולה להתלהב בתורה ועבודת ה' והוא סותר
הנ"ל שילך בהדרגה. אפס שאין זה קושיא כלל כי רק
ביציאת מצרים הוצרכו לאחוז בקצה מדת החסידות
כדי שיצאו מטומאה לטהרה וקדושה.

109 *T.* 66a.

110 Pesaḥim 50b.

111 See chapter 4, note 50.

112 *Z. P.* 40a.

CHAPTER 8

THE DESCENT OF THE ZADDIK (Continued)

1 *T.* 82c.

2 Avot 6:2.

3 *T.* 59b: נודע כי עיקר ותכלית הכל בכל עבודתנו בתורה ותפלה וכוונת המצוות וכוונת
אכילה לברר ולהעלות נצוצי הקדושה מתוך עָמקי הקליפות, ודוגמתן בעניני בני אדם להעלות
אנשי החומר אל מדרגת הצורה וזה סוד .בזאת יבא אהרן אל הקודש", וכדי שיוכל להעלות
מדריגה תחתונה אל העליונה צריך שיתחבר עם מדרנה ההיא ואז יוכל להעלותם.

4 Zohar III, 220b: [כל אשר תמצא ידך לעשות בכחך עשה כי אין מעשה וחשבון].
ודעת וחכמה בשאול] אשר אתה הולך שמה" (קהלת ט', י'). וכי כל בני עלמא אזלי לשאול?
אין. אבל סלקין מיד כדכתיב .מוריד שאול ויעל" (שמואל א' כ', ו'), בר אינון חייבין דלא

ההרהרו תשובה לעלמין, דנחתין ולא סלקין. ואפילו צדיקים גמורים נחתין תמן. אמאי נחתין?
בגין דנטלין כמה חייבין מתגן, וסלקין לון לעילא. (ותמן עבדין לון להרהר בתשובה). ומאן
אינון? דהרהרו בתשובה בהאי עלמא ולא יכילו ואסתלקו מן עלמא וצדיקייא נחתי בגיהנון
לון מן תמן וסלקין לון דחייבין גו שאול, ונטלון לין.

[5] T. 118d: (תה' ז'), עוברי בעמק הבכא פסוק על מבאר המגיד הרב בשם דשמעתי נ"ל
פ"ד, ז') שכמו שענין ירידת הצדיק בפתחי גיהנם הוא להעלות נשמות הרשעים שהרהרו
בתשובה בעה"ז על ידו, כך הענין בעה"ז בכל יום ויום או באיזה זמנים שיורד הצדיק ממדריגתו
כדי שיתחבר את עצמו עם אותן הפחותין במעלה שלא עלו כלל או שעלו וירדו ממדריגתן
ועכשיו כשיורד הצדיק גם כן ממדריגתו ויחבר את עצמו עמהן אזי כשיחזור ויעלה למדריגתו
אזי אגב יעלה עמו וכו'. אך דכל זה שעולה עמו היינו כשרוצה להתחבר עמו אבל מי שאינו
רוצה להתחבר עמו ודאי שאינו עולה עמו ועפ"ז פ' הש"ס ,כל המבזה ת"ח אין רפואה למכתו'
(שבת קי"ט ע"ב) ור"ל שמבוזה בעיניו לאחוז בו שיעלה עמו וכו'.

While Rabbi Mendel of Bar's remarks are quoted several times in varying
fashion: *T.* 86a, 118d, 147a, 151c; *P. Y.* 21d; *Z. P.* 30b, it may be claimed
that the relation of the idea to this world as a day to day principle of action for
the zaddik is not R. Mendel's innovation but R. Yaakov Yosef's. For example
we find in *T.* 151c: כל המבזה ת"ח אין רפואה. מעגדיל פי' הש"ס ,ביאר הרב מוה' . . .
למכתו' (שבת דף קי"ט ע"ב), כי הצדיק יורד דרך הגיהנום להעלות נשמות הרשעים שהרהרו
בתשובה . . . ודפח"ח, והנה יש מדרגה זה גם בעולם הזה שיורד
. . . הצדיק ממדריגתו כדי שיתחבר אל מדריגה פחותה ההוא. In other words, Rabbi
Mendel only explains the Talmudic passage in terms of the Zohar, while the
new idea follows the closing ''דפח"ח'' and is from our author. Still further indication of this fact is found in *T.* 147a: מיתת צדיקים מכפרת, ר"ל, מטהר טמאים,
לכך יורד הצדיק ממדריגתו כדי להעלות הרשעים מטומאה לטהרה. וכמו שכ' במ"א ,כל המבזה
ת"ח אין רפואה למכתו'. וביאר הרב המגיד מהר"מ ע"ד ,עוברי בעמק הבכא' וכו', ואני
ביארתי כי יש דוגמתו בעולם הזה כי ע"י החסרון שיש בצדיק יוכל להתחבר עם הרשעים
להעלותן.

[6] J. Weiss, *op. cit.*, p. 74. See also pp. 73–6.

[7] *P. Y.* 21d; cf. *Z. P.* 30b.

[8] This story is reported here on the basis of the following three versions.
T. 107: שמעתי משל על בן מלך ששלחו אביו מעל פניו בכפר אחד כדי שיתאוה אחר זה
יותר אל שולחן אביו המלך. אבל הבן מחמת טפשותו נתערב בנוים שבכפר ולמד ממעשיהם
ושכח תענוגי המלך. ושלח המלך שר אחד משריו להחזירו ולא עלתה לו. עד שהתחכם שר אחד
.שפשט לבוש השררה ולבש בגדי הדיוט בדמות אנשי הכפר ועלתה לו

כבר כתבתי בענין המשל ששמעתי מרבותי שר אחד יצא להחזיר בן מלך T. 111c:
אל המלך אחר שנתרחק ממנו והוצרך להלביש עצמו בבגדי אנשי הכפר שם היה בן המלך
.כדי שיהיה לו התחברות עם בן המלך לכנוס עמו בדברים ועלתה לו וכו' ודפח"ח

שמעתי משל ממורי למלך ששלח בנו יחידו למרחקים כדי שיהיה לו אחר כך T. 167b:
יותר תענוג. וברבות הימים נשכח מבן המלך כל תענוגי המלך ושלח המלך שרים יותר חשובים.
לא הועיל כלום עד שהיה שר אחד חכם שכסות ושלון שינה כדמות הבן ההוא ונתקרב אליו
.במדרגתו והשיבו אל אביו ודפח"ח

Note that the quotation from *T.* 167b is in the name of מורי
while that from *T.* 111c is in the name of רבותי. See appendix.

⁹ It is significant that this story which would lend itself so readily to a parable of exile and redemption of the people of Israel is applied only to the individual. Hasidism, perhaps, fearful of how the messianic impetus of Lurianic Kabbalism led to Sabbatianism, is careful to avoid messianic speculation and speaks more often of individual redemption. It is concerned less with eschatology than with a practical program of daily living.

¹⁰ *T.* 107c.

¹¹ „בית ישראל‟ (לבוב, תקצ"ד), parashah Yitro.

¹² *T.* 116d.

¹³ *P. Y.* 14c. Quoted in the name of [?פיסטנר = י"ל] הרב המוכיח מוהריי"ל.

¹⁴ Succah 45b.

¹⁵ 66a; cf. 82b.

¹⁶ *T.* 107d: משל למלך שנאבד ונפלה אבן א' או הרבה בעמקי מצולה ולאהבת האבן טוב שלח בניו שמה להעלותה. ויש בזה ג' סוגים: א', חכם שטרח ויגע ומצא האבן טוב ושב אל אביו בשלום. ב', שאמר הלואי שיצא בעצמו מעמקי מצולה. ג', שנשאר בעמקי מצולה.

¹⁷ „קדושת לוי", Jerusalem, 1936, p. 135.

¹⁸ Avot 2.5.

¹⁹ *T.* 31c, d.

²⁰ *T.* 68c: והנה יש ב' דברים לצדיקים עובדי ה', א' המתבודד ועובד הש"י בלי שום יצה"ר, הב' העובד הש"י עם היצה"ר . . . והוא כשאדם הולך לעבור עבירה ח"ו או שאר צרכי תענוגי הגוף מחמת היצה"ר ואח"כ מפני כבודו ית' ומוראו משבר תאותו ויצרו והולך בדרכי עבודת הש"י הרי מכניע שמאל בימין ונעשה יחוד גמור למעלה, והוא ת כ ל י ת ה ש ל י מ ו ת י ו ת ר מ צ ד י ק ה ע ו ב ד ה ש " י ב ת מ י ם ב ל א י צ ה " ר והולך בקו הימין לבד משא"כ בחינה הב' הוא מייחד ג' קוין שמכניע קו השמאל ע"י קו האמצעי המכריעו לימין. א ח " כ מ צ א ת י ב ז ו ה ר פ' תצוה דף ע"א ח"ל: .שלימא דכולא טוב ורע ואסתלקא בטוב"

We quote here the complete passage from the Zohar with the Soncino translation. דלית נהורא אלא ההוא דנפיק מגו חשוכא דכד אתכפיא סטרא דא אסתלק קב"ה לעילא ואתייקר ביקריה. ולית פולחנא דקב"ה אלא מגו חשוכא ולית טובא אלא מגו בישא וכד עאל בר נש באורח בישא ושביק ליה כדין אסתלק קב"ה ביקריה ועל דא שלימו דכלא טוב ורע כחדא ולאסתלקא לבתר בטוב ולית טוב אלא ההוא דנפק מגו בישא. ובהאי טוב אסתלק יקריה ודא איהו פולחנא שלים.

[. . . there is no light except that which issues from darkness, for when "the other side" is subdued the Holy One is exalted in glory. In fact, there can be no true worship except it issue from darkness, and no true good except it proceed from evil. And when a man enters upon an evil way and then forsakes it, the Holy One is exalted in glory. Hence the perfection of all things is attained when good and evil are first of all commingled, and then become all good, for there is no good so perfect as that which issues out of evil. The divine glory is extolled thereby, and therein lies the essence of perfect worship.] Vol. IV, p. 125. See also Zohar I, 67b; *T.* 68c.

²¹ See *T.* 31c.

²² *P. Y.* 51d.

23 *Z. P.* 55c.

24 Shabbat 22a.

25 183a: כי יקרב אליו זר לא קונו לבין בינו שמתבודד כגון עליונה במדרגה כשהוא . . .
עוסק בתורה ועי"ז ניצול מיצה"ר והרהורים וכיוצא, כי התורה היא תבלין ליצה"ר, ויודע
שאח"כ הוצרך לצאת מן הספר אל תוך העיר או לעסוק פרנסתו או לשאר דברים ומיד בצאתו
מהספר לפתח חטאת רובץ, שבתוך העיר הוא בור ריק בלי מים של תורה רק נחשים ועקרבים
של לשון הרע ודברים בטלים והסתכלות נשים וכיוצא בו . . . ומה יעשה וינצל? כל ערום
יעשה בדעת שיקשר את עצמו בעודו מתבודד שיהיה שם הויה של ד' אותיות נגד פניו גם
בלכתו בין אנשים, וכמ"ש הרמב"ם ורמ"א מביאו, שויתי ה' לנגדי תמיד.,
הוא כלל גדול במעלת הצדיקים וכו'.

וזה הענין הראו ליעקב אבינו שהיה סולם מוצב ארצה וראשו מגיע השמימה, ר"ל גם שהוא
מוצב ארצה בדיוטא תחתונה שבארץ, דהיינו בין אנשים לצנים והולכי רכיל וכיוצא, מ"מ
ראשו ומחשבתו מגיע השמימה לדבק מחשבתו בקונו שם הוי' נגד פניו ובמעלות ומדרגה זו
מלאכי אלהים, שהם סוני בני אדם הבאים בעה"ז לעשות שליחותן של הש"י . . . ונקראו מלאכי
אלהים, עולים בו אם נוהגין כנ"ל, ואם לאו יורדים בו, לכך אזהרה יתירה צריך האדם בעודו
מתבודד וכנ"ל. ושמעתי משל מהרב המגיד מ' מענדיל מבאר ששואלין לתינוק אם נפל לבור
ואינו יכול לעלות ילך לביתו ויביא סולם ויעלה ויעלה מהבור והקושיא תמוה! וביאר שהוא משל אל
הנ"ל: קודם שירד לבור יביא סולם לכשירד יוכל לעלות מהבור, ודפח"ח.

26 *Ibid.*

27 *P. Y.* 66b.

28 *T.*183b, and see *T.* 119a, b: לנגדי ה' ושויתי. ה'דרך נקרא התורה . . .
תמיד. היא דרך הצדיקים והיא מהלך בדרך התמידי שהיה דרכו תמיד
לדבק בו ית' וכמו שכתבתי לעיל נפש לא יטמא ממחשבתו בעמיו גם שהוא בתוך עמיו שהם
עם המוני. Cf. *P. Y.* 18d.

29 *P. Y.* 18d.

30 *T.* 51c: ומה הערים אשר הוא יושב בהנה אם במחנים או במבצרים", כי אדם השלם.
צריך לבחון א"ע בטבעו אם דבק בה' תמיד בין בבית בין בחוץ ואין מזיק לו חברותא בני אדם
אז אין צריך בבדידות רק ילך בקרב בני אדם אולי יראה דבר מה שצריך תיקון וגם שיכול
לקרב בני אדם לעבודת ה' כמו שעשה אברהם וכמו שכתבתי בפסוק. אם אמצא בסדום בתוך
העיר חמשים צדיקים' וכו'. ואם יראה בעצמו כי מיד שנתרחק מפתח בית מדרשו מיד לפתח
חטאת רובץ אזי יבחור בבדידות, וז"ש הבמחנים. ופ' רש"י סימן מסר להם אם בפרזים יושבים
חזקים הם שסומכין על גבורתם וכו' ור"ל אם יודע שהוא דבוק בפרזים א"צ בדידות ויושב
במחנים אם לאו במבצרים שהוא בבדידות יבחר.

31 *T.* 31a.

32 *Ibid.*

33 A. Cahana, *op. cit.*, p. 132. See "ספר בעל שם טוב", מנחם מנדל, ר' שמעון, Vol.
2, p. 48, note 2.

34 *T.* 183b.

35 G. Scholem, *op. cit.*, p. 343.

36 *T.* 70b. The meaning of "ו' כורע לנבי ה' להעלותה" is as follows: the letters
ו and ה are the last two letters of the divine name יהוה. It is the symbol of
the zaddik, who is really higher than the people, descending below the people
to raise them as the ו does the ה. Thus a kabbalistic doctrine was transformed

from a theosophical act moving the upper worlds into an act of this world between leader and people.

והנה יש מדריגה זה גם בעולם הזה שיורד הצדיק ממדריגתו כדי שיתחבר עם מדריגה :151c T.
פחותה ההוא כמו שכתוב בכתובים (משלי כ"ד, ט"ז) שבע יפול צדיק וקם, ומבואר שם כי
למדריגה הנקרא שבע, יפול הצדיק, נקרא ו' להקימה, בסוד ו' כורע לגבי ה' להעלותה.
קבלתי מחכם א' שאמר סוד כריעת ו' לגב' ה' שהגדול נכנע לקטן כדי להגבירו וכו' :130c T.
וכבוד ה' הסתר דבר.

[37] T. 40d. Cf. 25b, 65d, 69c.

[38] Succah 21b.

[39] "דגל מחנה אפרים", פ' מצורע.

[40] "אור הגנוז לצדיקים", פ' פקודי.

[41] . . . והעיקר לב להבין שהש"י בכל מקום ובכל עסקיו. א"כ גם בספורי דברים :195c T.
יוכל להרניש עניני הבורא ית' כמו בלימודו ותפלתו.

[42] T. 40d.

[43] "נועם מגידים" (למברג 1807), פ' אמר.

[44] Yevamot 105b.

[45] כשאתה מתפלל אל תעש תפלתך קבע אלא רחמים ותחנונים לפני המקום :2c .K. P.
שנאמר: חנון ורחום הוא ארך אפים ורב חסד ונחם על הרעה . . . ובזה יובן .המתפלל צריך
שיתן עיניו למטה ולבו למעלה". ר"ל שיתן השנחה ועיניו על המוני עם שהם למטה להתחבר
עמהם, ולבו למעלה בזה ההתחברות כדי להעלותן למעלה, וק"ל. ובזה יובן .אל תעש תפלתך
קבע" לתועלת עצמו שתהיה תפלתך" דייקא שיהיה קבע ועיקר כוונתו לעצמו, רק ישתתף עצמו
עם המוני עם אנשי החומר גם שאינם יודעים כונת התפלה מ"מ מצד הרחמים ותחנונים יתפלל
עמהם.

CHAPTER 9

TRANSGRESSION AND DANGER

[1] See above, pp. 177–78.

[2] See T. 107d.

[3] Rosh Hashanah 29a. See below, note 8. Cf. the following remark from
(כידוע מאמר הרי"ב"ש .כל שאינו מחויב :17 .p ,."שארית ישראל" (לעמבערג, תרכ"ד
בדבר אין מוציא את הרבים ידי חובתן". ואמר הוא ז"ל הפירוש: החכם שאינו מחויב בעצמו
שאין שום השתתפות עם המון עם, פי' שאינו נופל ממדרגתו, אין יכול להוציא את הרבים,
פי' הכלל ישראל, מידי חובתן ולתקנם, כמו למשל מי שמונח ברפש ורוצה חבירו להוציאו
מוכרח הוא ללכלך את עצמו מעט ולהתקרב אליו ויכול להוציאו, אבל כשעומד במקומו לא
יוציאנו בשום אופן. Cf. T. 145a.

[4] T. 66a.

[5] Avot 2.5.

[6] "לקוטים יקרים" (Lemberg, 1863) 6a.

7 ‏בנימין ב״ר אהרן, מ״מ בולאזיץ, אמתחת בנימין׳ (מינקאוויץ, תקנ״ו)‏ .pp. 1–2.

8 This passage is explained in a later work, "‏לקוטים יקרים‏" (Lemberg 1863), 6a: ‏ובגמרא (ראש השנה דף כ״ט ע״א) .זה הכלל כל שאינו מחויב בדבר אינו מוציא את הרבים ידי חובתן׳, מ״ש הלשון שאינו מחויב ולא אמר מי שאינו מחייב בדבר, או הלי״ל בסיפא ובריישא אינו מוציא את הרבים ידי חובתן? וי״ל ע״פ מ״ש שידוע כי כאשר הרשע מרבה לחטא הוא גורם בעוונותיו שיבא לידי צדיק הרהור מעבירה מעין אותו עבירה שעבר הרשע וגם זה ידוע שאין דין מתמתק אלא בשרשו ומחמת זה יכול הצדיק לגרום לעלות גם נפש הרשע מן החטא את הטוב מתוך הרע וגם את הרע ממתק בהעלותו אל שורשו וז״ש רז״ל כל שאינו מחויב בדבר ר״ל כל שלא נתחייב בדבר עבירה דהיינו שלא באה לו הרהור עבירה זו שעשה הרשע אינו יכול להוציא את הרבים ידי חובתן דהיינו הרשעים מעוני שלא באה לו הרהור אינו יודע מעין איזה עבירה עבר הרשע שיהא יכול למתקו ולהוציא את הרשע מחובתו אבל מי שמחויב בדבר כלומר שנתחייב בדבר עם הרשע שנגרם לו הרהור כנ״ל יכול להוציא אמר שמחויב ולא אמרו שחייב כי לא מחמתו בא לו ההרהור כ״א ע״י הרשע אבל גבי הרשעים אמרו ידי חובתן שהם חייבין בנפשותם ולא אחרים מחייבים אותם‏.

9 Z. P. 54c.

10 The text actually reads: ‏שור‏; ‏חמור‏ is found in Deut. 22.3.

11 T. 185c.

12 See above, pp. 71–73.

13 See Shemot Rabbah 43.6.

14 "‏שמועות טובות‏" (Warsaw, 1886), pp. 45–6.

15 T. 107d.

16 ‏אמר הרב בוצינא קדישא איש אלקי הבעל שם טוב ז״ל נשמתו בגנזי מרומים שאין במציאות שיהיה אדם רואה לאחר עובר עברה אלא אם כן יש בו שמץ מנהו מאותה עברה עצמה או דוגמתה, על דרך משל אם רואה לאחר שבאה על אשת איש מסתמא שיש בו שמץ מזה מעין אותה עברה והיינו גאוה שאמרו חכמינו ז״ל (סוטה דף ד׳ ע״ב) .כל המתנאה כאילו בא על על אשת איש׳, או שרואה שעובד עבודה זרה, מסתמא יש בו שמץ מזה, והיינו כעס שאמרו ז״ל (זוהר בר׳ דף כ״ז, ע״ב) .כל הכועס כאילו עובד עבודה זרה׳, ועל דרך זה בכל העברות ומראים לו מהשמים כדי שיזכור ויעשה תשובה. ואמרו מנידי אמת שפעם אחת ראה הבעל שם טוב הקדוש נשמתו בגנזי מרומים לאחד שחילל שבת, פשפש ומצא בעצמו ששימש עם צורבא מרבנן טרם שלמד ממנו דבר תורה, והיינו חילל שבת כי תלמיד חכם דומה לשבת (זוהר פ׳ צו, דף כ״ט, ע״א). פנחס לערנער, .שפתי צדיקים׳, (לבוב, תרנ״ג) פ׳ וירא‏.

17 Zohar II, 128b: ‏.זכאה מאן דאחיד בידא דחייבא.׳ לדעת ד״ר תשבי זהו המקום היחיד בזוהר שיוכל להיות חמכוון אליו, למרות העובדה שהמטבע .זכאה מאן וכו׳ ׳ אין בצורה זו במקום הנידון שבזוהר, אלא .מאן דאחיד וכו׳ ׳, ובסוף הדרוש דף קכ״ט ע״ב הטלים המסיימות .זכאה חולקיה׳‏. J. Weiss. Op. cit., p. 72, note 3. The above quotation is found many times in Yaakov Yosef's works in the name of the Zohar.

18 G. Scholem, op. cit., p. 311.

19 Ibid., p. 302.

20 No single work of early hasidic literature deals in such detail with the problem of the sin of the zaddik as T. The interpretations of such key verses as "‏אם הכהן המשיח יחטא‏" (Lev. 4.3) and "‏אשר נשיא יחטא‏" (Lev. 4.22) or the parable

of the lost prince who is returned to his father by the noble's "change of clothes" are found in other hasidic books also, but only in passing and not as a central problem.

[21] The study of Kabbalah was forbidden in Brody when the Frankists were under ḥerem. See D. Cahana, (תל אביב, תרפ"ז) ‏תולדות המקובלים והשבתאים והחסידים. Vol. 2, p. 71.

[22] E. g., Frankfort am Main.

[23] ‏עי' בקונטרס ‏.מעשה נורה בפאדאליע' מר' אברהם משארינראד (דף כ"ט, ע"ב) ‏וזה לשונו: ‏אז נבחרו שלשה מכל צד. מן היהודים היו נבחרים הרב מדינה דלבוב ר' חיים ‏ראפפורט, ‏ור' ישראל מעזיבוש בעל שם ‏ור' בער רב מיאולווטש ‏.ועיין בספר ‏אנשי השם' מאת ר"ש באבער (ע' ס"ט). D. Cahana, op. cit., p. 81, note 1. However, Balaban, "‏לתולדות התנועה הפראנקית," doubts that the Besht was one of the disputants.

That the Baal Shem struggled with the Sabbatians is evidenced from the following ‏ועוד ספר לי ר' יואל הנ"ל): "‏שבחי הבעש"ט," op. cit., p. 80:
‏שבא שבתי צבי לבעש"ט לבקש ממנו תקנה. ואמר ר' יואל בזה"ל, שהתיקון הוא להתקשר נפש ‏בנפש רוח ברוח נשמה בנשמה, והתחיל [הבעש"ט] להתקשר עמו [שבתי צבי] ‏במתון כי ‏היה ירא ‏כי היה רשע גדול. פ"א ישן הבעש"ט ובא ש"ץ ים"ש ופיתה אותו ח"ו. והשליך ‏אותו [הבעש"ט את ש"ץ] בהשלכה גדולה.

[24] See T. 129b.

[25] T. 20a.

[26] T. 95c. See T. 130c–d. Another remark clearly directed against the Sabbatians, though not in regard to the guilt of the zaddik but in regard to the hastening of redemption through prayer:
‏לא יכנס את עצמו בהכרח שיעשה מבוקשו דיש בזה סכנה כמ"ש בפסוק ‏אם תעירו ואם ‏תעוררו את האהבה עד שתחפץ' (שה"ש ב', ז'), ‏ומעשה של ר' יוסף דלרייני ‏יוכיח . . . ‏אין נכנסין לחורבה", ר"ל, גם שנזדמן במעשה עוני ועינוי ועל כרחך הוא כדי ‏שיתפלל, מ"מ איך יתפלל צריך לכלכל הדבר ‏במשפט שיהיה לרצון לו ית' ‏ולא בהכרח ליכנס בעובי הקורה ‏ומ"ש ש‏אין נכנסין בחורבה" דייקא ‏(T. 136a, b). ‏והוא כלל גדול בתפלה כאשר שמעתי כזה ‏מפורש מפי מורי

The expression ‏מפורש מפי מורי is rarely found in Rabbi Yaakov Yosef's writings and is meant for emphasis. The following passage: ‏ובש"ס ‏.לעולם ‏יעסוק . . .שלא לשמה שמתוך שלא לשמה בא לשמה'‏ (פסחים דף נ' ע"ב) ‏אינו ציוי ‏רק רש‏אי לעסוק שלא לשמה שמתוך וכו', אבל ודאי מי שמצא חן בעיני השי' שיקום ‏(T. 192b) ‏בו לב טהור ברא לי אלהים. ודאי יותר נכון המעורר בראש שנותיו ללמוד לשמה may seem at first sight to be directed against a contrary Sabbatian opinion. However we find in T. 9c: ‏אינו רשות אלא חובה ‏וז"ש ‏.לעולם ‏יעסוק שלא לשמה שמתוך שלא לשמה בא לשמה', כי צריך שיהיה בכל מדריגות של שלא ‏לשמה נ"כ כדי שאם אח"כ יבוא לשמה יעלה גם המדרינות הראשונות נ"כ. וז"ש ‏.במקום ‏שבעלי תשובה עומדים אין צדיק גמור יכול לעמוד' (ברכות דף ל"ד ע"ב).

[27] ‏הרהור (T. 60b), ‏שמץ טומאה (T. 130d), ‏כאילו חטא (T. 66a), ‏מעין דוגמת חטא ‏חיוב קצת (T. 141), ‏שמץ מנהו (T. 9 above, note 9), ‏מעבירה ‏."לקוטים יקרים" 6a. See above, ‏קצת חטא (T. 131a).

²⁸ Zohar III, 220b. See above pp. 174–76.

²⁹ *T.* 118d.

³⁰ *T.* 151c.

³¹ *P. Y.* 21d.

³² *P. Y.* 32c: החיות של האדם רצוא ושוב שגם הצדיק אין יכול לעמוד על מדריגה אחת. לפעמים עולה ולפעמים יורד כדי שיתחבר עם אנשי העולם ... This is directly related to the doctrine of קטנות וגדלות; cf. *T.* 18a, 20a, 91c, 109c, 164c, 165c, 194c.

³³ *T.* 147a: ע"י חסרון שיש בצדיק יוכל להתחבר עם הרשעים להעלותן. Cf. *P. Y.* 102c.

³⁴ *T.* 141b: כל שאינו מחויב בדבר אינו מוציא את ע"י חיוב שמצא בעצמו ביאר ש"ס
הרבים ידי חובתן" ע"ד משל שר א' ששינה לבושו ... ע"כ יש בו חיוב קצת ג"כ שמע מנהו שאם
אינו מחויב בדבר אינו יכול להוציא את הרבים ידי חובתן, א"כ יש בו חיוב רק שהוא אנוס (ואינו
בדרך רחוקה) מ"מ פטור כי **אנוס רחמנא פטריה** ... ותרצה לומר על חיוב
כרת קאמר שהוא חייב ובאמת אינו כי אנוס הוא רק **החיוב הוא על כוונה
אחרת.**

³⁵ *T.* 33b: ויבא יוסף את דבתם אל אביהם שבשמים, שכל דבר שראה בה תלה בעצמו
שמץ מנהו והתודה לפני אביהם שבשמים שכלל א"ע עמהם **בסוד צדיק.**

³⁶ *T.* 142c: ... ובזה יובן ענין מי מריבה שהיה ראוי שלא יחטאו בו, ומכ"ש אהרן ומרים
לא חטאו, באמת רק משה לבדו, וגם משה לפי דרשת חז"ל לא חטא, שדיבר אל הסלע ונדמן
לו סלע אחר ולא יצא מים עד שהכה ונדמן אותו סלע וכו'. אלא כדי שיעמדו **בנסיון
זה שלא הרהרו אחר מדתו ית'** ' ובכח נסיון זה יוכלל נסיונות כל צדיק שיוכלו
לעמוד בנסיון וכמ"ש "אבחנך על מי מריבה סלה", (תה' פ"א, ח'). וזה שאמר הכא "הכה מי
מריבה", ר"ל, מ"ש "אבחנך על מי מריבה סלה". היינו מי מריבה זה אשר רבו בני ישראל ולא
משה ואהרן, ומ"מ "ויקדש בם" מצד לפנים משורת הדין עמד
עמם **בעלילה** כדי שיתקדש בם לדורות שיהיה תועלת ופתחון פה לעמוד בנסיון
לדורות. ושפיר אמר תומך ואוריך לאיש חסידך וגו' תריבהו על מי מריבה ועמדו בנסיון
שלא חטא כלל רק לקיים מ"ש "אבחנך על מי מריבה סלה", וכאמור שהוא חסדו ית'
שנוהג בכל דור מכח אבות הראשונים. Cf. *T.* 142b, c; *Z. P.* 8c.

³⁷ Mishnah Yoma 8.9.

³⁸ *T.* 92b.

³⁹ Yoma 86b.

⁴⁰ *T.* 95c, d: מצוה "ואל יבא בכל עת אל הקדש" "בזאת יבא אהרן אל הקדש". והיא כי היא
מבואר בפסוק "אשר נשיא יחטא לאשמת העם" (ויק' ד', כ"ב), והאלשיך פי' יעו"ש. ולענ"ד
ע"ד שכתבתי פי' הש"ס "כל שאינו מחויב בדבר אינו מוציא הרבים ידי חובתן" (ר"ה דף כ"ט ע"א)
וכו' והוא ע"ד הירושלמי (תענית פ' שני דף ס"ה ע"ד) "שמואל הנביא לבש חלוקן של ישראל
ואמר חטאתי" כנזכר במשל השר שינה לבושו וכו', כי אשמת העם שבמזיד
גורם לראשי הדור חטא שונג כדי שיהיה לו איזה חיבור עמהם
להעלותן, וכמו שכתבתי ויקצוף משה וגו' שמא חזרתם לפעור וכו' כי הכועס
כאלו עובד ע"ז ובזה יש לו מקום תפיסה לשוב בתשובה לתקן כל אותן מדריגות בין
של עצמו בין של אחרים וזה אמרו בש"ס (יומא דף פ"א ע"ב) "כי יחיד העושה תשובה מוחלין
לו ולכל העולם" והיינו כשמתחבר עם מדריגתן ... ולפי הנ"ל כי החטא שנזדמן לו
לא היה ראוי לזה מצד עצמו רק כדי שימצא מקום חיבור
עם העולם וכמ"ש "כל שאינו מחויב בדבר וכו'" ו"ש ... ולדברינו א"ש כמי"ד
הרגיש שנזדמן לו זו עבור אחרים להעלותם עם חיבור תשובתו וק"ל.

אך שמא ח"ו יש לטעות שיחטא במזיד כדי להתחבר עם אותן מדריגות להעלותן כאשר פקרו
המינים בזה. לזה בא הכתוב ,ואל יבא בכל עת אל הקודש", ור"ל כי יש
י"ד עתים לטובה ויש י"ד עתים לרעה כי זה לעומת זה עשה וכו' וז"ש ואל יבא
בכוונה בכל עת הכולל גם עתים הרעים לעבור עבירה במזיד ח"ו,
כדי שבזה יתחבר אל אותן מדריגות שם להעלותן אל הקודש כי זה ח"ו כפירה
גמורה, וכאשר שמעתי בשם מורי טעם הגון כי כשחטא בשוגג בלא דעת
אז יש תקנה בעושה תשובה בכוונה שנותן בו דעת להעלותו, מה שאין כן כשחוטא בדעת
במה יתקנה? וזה פ' הש"ס ,האומר אחטא ואשוב'...

[41] See *T.* 130d.
[42] Sotah 4b.
[43] Zohar I, 27b.
[44] שפתי צדיקים," parashah וירא. Cf. *T.* 189c.
[45] כתר שם טוב," part 2, 2b.
[46] בני יששכר, אות ו', מעמד ד', תשרי.

[47] *P. Y.* 91b, also *K. P.* 21a: במעשה הוא עם אנשי של הארץ עליה וירידה
הטוב או רע ח"ו, מה שאין כן עליה וירידה של שלומי אמוני ישראל הוא רק במחשבה
ולא במעשה ח"ו

That the transgression of the zaddik is primarily one of thought is further
indicated in *T.* 118b: שמעתי בשם הרב המגיד מבאר כי בכל יום בא הרהורי תשובה
לאדם על ידי הכרח שמכריזים וכו' ויש שהוא רק ב.סור מרע' ויש ב.סור מרע' וגם ,עשה
טוב', כל אחד לפי בחינתו. ותשובת הצדיק הנקרא אדם כשרואה שאין לו דביקות בו
יתברך שמו לדבק מחשבתו באור אין סוף. ובזה יובן ,אשרי אדם לא יחשוב ה' '
כי זהו ,לו עון' (תה' ל"ב, ב'), ר"ל, שלא נמצא לו [לצדיק] עון אחר
זולת זה שאין מחשבתו דבוקה בו ית' שמו, וזהו שאמר
,לא יחשוב ה' ' לקיים .שויתי ה' ' אצלו נחשב זה לעון, ודפח"ח.

[48] *T.* 152a.
[49] It occurs no less than twenty six times in *T.* alone.
[50] *T.* 107(2)d: . . . . ועיקר העבודה הוא לא בלבד שיקשט א"ע רק גם אחרים . . .
ומעלה זו מצינו באהרן הכהן שנאמר .ורבים השיב מעון' . . . ר"ל לא בלבד שיקשטו גדולי
וראשי הדור את עצמן רק להזהיר גדולים על הקטנים שהם הרשעים שהם מקטני אמונה להזהיר
הגדולים שיחזירו למוטב את הקטנים נ"כ . . . . .

ואחר שהזהרנו בזה אז הוצרך לומר לנפש לא יטמא בעמיו. דשמעתי משל על בן מלך
ששלח אביו מעל פניו בכפר א' כדי שיתאוה אחר זה יותר לשולחן אביו המלך אבל הבן
מחמת טפשותו נתערב בנוים שבכפר ולמד ממעשיהם ושכח תענוגי המלך. ושלח המלך שר א'
מסריו להחזירו ולא עלתה לו, עד שהתחכם שר א' שפשט לבושי השררה ולבש בגדי הדיוט
דמות אנשי כפר ועלתה לו, עיין בכתבי. ולהבין הנמשל מה הוא לבושי הדיוט? ונ"ל כי המדות
נקרא לבוש כמ"ש בתיקונים כמאמר אליהו לבושין תקינת לון וכו' והן המדות יעו"ש. לפעמים
ת"ח צדיק וישר שהוא שר מצד התורה שנק' שר ומלך שנאמר ,בי מלכים ימלוכו', ולובש בגדי
הדיוט שיש בו מדה גרוע שרי, שבזה המדה יהיה לו התחברות עם העם שהם גרוע המדות כדי
לדבר על לבם ולעוררן איך שנתרחק משולחן המלך מלכי המלכים וישובו עדיו כמו במשל
הנ"ל. והנה זה החכם שעושה לאהבת המלך אולי יחזיר הבן לאביו מ"מ נכנס בספק
סכנה אם יחזיר את הבן בהמשך הזמן שידבר עמו אחר שיתחבר עמו בהכרת פנים פעם
ושתים או יש לחוש לחוש שאם בן המלך שהיה מוטבע בנימוסי המלכים מ"מ ע"י שהורגל ברוע

המדות של אנשי הכפר נעשה כמותן ושכח כל נימוסי המלכים וה"ה לשר זה שיש לחוש לזה.
Cf. same ע"כ צריך אזהרה על עצמו יותר למה שהיה בחצר המלך תחלה כמו במשל והנמשל
page.

[51] *T.* 130d: ...שהוצרך משל אחד שנשלח בן מלך מאביו ולא היה יכול להחזירו עד
שר א' לפשוט בגדיו החשובים ולבש בגדי פחותי הערך כדי שיתחבר עם בן המלך שנעשה
הדיוט מן פחותי הערך וכו'. והנמשל הוא פשוט, בגדי החשובים כנוי למעשיו הטובים ובגדים
פחותי הערך הם דוגמת בגדים הצואים ח"ו ולא ממש בגדים צואים. והענין
הוא כמ"ש אשר נשיא יחטא לאשמת העם, כי כל דור ודור ודורשיו הם שורש א' כמו מרע"ה
עם דורו כן כל דור ודור לפי דורשיו ודורשין לפי דורו כמ"ש בש"ס דעירובין וה"נ חטא
הדור גרמו אשמת ראש הדור כנון כאלו ששורש א' להם ואז כשירד
ראש הדור למדריגתן ובלש לבושי הדור שהם בגדי פחותי הערך ואז יש התחברות מה
ביניהם מאא"כ קודם לזה דהוי דבר והפוכו. עתה ע"י חטא זה הוי התחברות לו עמהם בצד
Cf. note 50. .מ ה ואז כשישוב יעלה כולם אתו עמו...

[52] *T.* 130d. Cf. notes 50, 51.

[53] *T.* 130d. Cf. note 51.

[54] *Ibid.*

[55] Jerusalem Talmud, Taanit 65d.

[56] *T.* 130d.

[57] *T.* 130d.

[58] *Ibid.*

[59] *T.* 131a, cf. note 60; Shemot Rabbah 42\6.

[60] *T.* 131a: לא ראוי ישראל לאותו מעשה דכתיב .מי יתן והיה לבבם זה להם...
ליראה אותי כל הימים", אלא למה עשו? לומר לך שאם...חטאו צבור אומרים להו
כלך אצל צבור (ע"ז דף ד' ע"ב) [כדי ליתן פתחון פה לבעלי תשובה שאם יאמר
החוטא לא אשוב שלא יקבלני, אומרים לו צא ולמד ממעשה העגל שכפרו ונתקבלו
בתשובה.]...נודע שעיקר מעשה זה של עגל יצא מערב רב וכמ"ש בזוהר אלא שנשתתפו
קצת ישראל במחשבה וגם אהרן נלכד בחטא זה בשוגג כמ"ש בזוהר שם,
שלא ידע להזהר מהם...וז"ש לא היו ישראל ראוין לאותו חטא, ר"ל שלא היו ראוין
מצד עצמן לחטא זה שחטאו קצת ג"כ כי ערב רב הם שחטאו בפועל
והגיע הפגם לישראל מצד התחברן ושורש א' עם ערב רב
שהיה משה מצד שורשן כמ"ש האר"י זלה"ה כי הם היו חלק רע מקין והבל ומשה היה חלק
הטוב ולכך רצה לגיירן וכו' ומשה היה שורש כל ישראל כנ"ל לכך הגיעו קצת מן החטא
ההוא לאשר בשם בני ישראל יכוונה אבל לא שהיו ראויין ישראל לחטא
זה מצד עצמו ולומר כי מהם נמשך החטא לערב רב כמו שכ' בפסוק .כי נגמר חסיד
כי פסו אמונים מבני אדם' דיש לפרש מרישא לסיפא ומסיפא לרישא וכו' יעו"ש. אבל כאן זה
אינו כי לא היה ישראל ראויין לחטא זה אלא להורות תשובה, ר"ל כדי שילבשו לבוש של הערב
רב ואז כשיעשו תשובה אלו פרטי שלומי אמוני ישראל שנלכדו קצת בחטא זה עם כל אותן
מדריגות, אז יעלה כולם . . . כי אינו להורות תשובה לדורות רק הם עצמם ילמדו לכלול
עצמן עם כל המדריגות...וזהו עיקר תכלית האדם ומזה ילמדו
ג"כ דורות הבאים דרך גדול בעבודת ה'. וזהו שזכרתי
וקבלתי ממורי פה אל פה ואי אפשר לבאר בספר, ודע
.והבן

[61] Cf. the following: *K. P.* 42a: גבאר בפ' חקת ענין אפר פרה שמטהר טמאים...

וטמטא טהורים, וכהבתי מזה במ'א יעו'ש. ביאור ש'ס מה פרה וכו' ונבאר תחלה בפ' קרח
אתם המתם את עם ה',ׄ. ויש להבין ענין תערומות זה שאין לו ביאור כלל כי מה היה למשה
ולאהרן לעשות אחר שנחלק קרח ועדתו על משה ואהרן ונענשו ומה היה למשה ולאהרן לעשות
ואיך יכתוב זה בתורה דבר שאין לו שחר כלל? וא'ת אתון גרמתון דמית עמא דה', גם זה תמוה.
ונ'ל דכהבתי ביאור ש'ס ,הנד לעמי פשעם', אלו ת'ח וכו' ,ולבית יעקב חטאתם', אלו ע'ה
וכו'. וביאור פסוק ,כי פסו אמונים מבני אדם', לכך ,הושיעה ה' כי נמר חסיד', ונאמר לו בחלום
שמא איפכא וכו' יעו'ש. והמסקנא שם כי משה רבינו עליו השלום תלה
גלות ישראל נמשך ממנו שהזהר על מדותיו והקב'ה יודע
האמת כי משרע'ה בכל ביתי נאמן ומה שהזהר על מדותיו נמשך לו מדון ואבירם
רשעי ישראל. ובזה ביארתי וידבר אלהים אל משה ויאמר אליו אני ה' יעו'ש.

[62] This is contrary to both Rashi's and Maharsha's view of the text.

[63] Furthermore the phrase שמעתי מפי מורי מפורש occurs only twice in Rabbi Yaakov Yosef's writings and one of these is in reference to a denial of intentional sin.

[64] See *T.* 144a.

[65] *T.* 97c.

[66] *T.* 87a.

[67] *T.* 153d. Cf. אלשיך, parashah ויקרא. Cf. *ספר חסידים,* קי'נ :מ' ואם ירננו
העולם על צדיק פלוני אחד שבא לו מקרה אחד רע, תאמר להם בעון הדור נתפש,
שהצדיקים נתפשים בעון הדור שנאמר (איכה ד' כ'), רוח אפינו משיח ה' נלכד בשחיתותם'.
This is quoted in *T.* 97c. Cf. 'Arakhin 17b; Bereshit Rabbah 80, 2; Jerusalem Talmud, Sanhedrin, chapter 2.

[68] *T.* 95c.

[69] *T.* 151d. Also: חטא עכן חטא ונאמר חטא ישראל כי הכל אחדות (*T.* 143d). Cf. *T.* 104a, 141c, 144a.

[70] *T.* 189c: וכמו שהפגם של אנשי דורו מגיע קצת לראש הדור דק בהרהור תשובה של
ראש הדור יבואו גם אנשי דורו לשוב במעשה כי מאחר שהם אחדות אחד, אך דכל זה בחטא
שהוא שונג שנזדמן לו . . . משא'כ במזיד לא שייך זה
T. 145a: מה שנזדמן איזה חטא לצדיק כדי שיתחבר עם המוני עם. J. Weiss, *op. cit.*, pp. 69–72 develops the causal relationship between the zaddik and the people in terms of a *magical*-spiritual relationship.

[71] צוואת הריב'ש'', 7b: שהשם ית', ''פעמים שנופל אדם ממדריגתו מחמת עצמו
יודע שהוא צריך לכך, ופעמים העולם נורמים שיפול אדם ממדריגתו, והירידה
הוא צריך עליה כדי לבא למדרגה יותר גדולה. But does this statement apply only to the zaddik or man in general?

[72] *P. Y.* 77a; *T.* 153a.

[73] We quote another example of deliberate sin from a later work ''לקט פנינים אמרי'' (printed at end of ''היכל הברכה'' by Rabbi I. Kamarna, Lemberg 1886), 208c: מחמת שמשה רבינו קירב את הערב רב נכתב עליו כי פנה אל אלהים אחרים
כמבואר בספר ,ליקוטי תורה'. על כן ראה את הענל ומחולות וראה שאין להם תקנה, על כן
שיבר את הלוחות והמשבר כלים בחמתו וכו' (שבת דף ק'ה ע'ב) ובזה הוציא את הרבים ידי
חובתן כיון שהוא גם כן מחתייב בדבר עשו כולם תשובה על ידי אחדות עם משה רבינו עליו
השלום והעלה את כולם. Cf. Avodah Zarah 17a.

[74] *T.* 146c.

[75] ‏דגל מחנה אפרים, פ' מצורע.

[76] *Z. P.* 59d.

[77] *T.* 95c, 189c.

[78] *T.* 153a.

[79] *Z. P.* 91a: ‏צריך הצדיק להתלבש במדת השקר וכוב כדי לעשות שלום כמו אהרן . . . ‏וכיוצא בזה כמו כעם . . .

[80] *P. Y.* 24a.

[81] *K. P.* 4a.

[82] *T.* 185d: ‏. . .איתא בנדרים פרק ד' ארבנ"י [בנזיר פרק ד' דף כ"ג ע"ב,
‏אמר רבי נחמן בר יצחק] גדולה עבירה לשמה ממצוה שלא לשמה שנאמר .תבורך
‏מנשים יעל אשת חבר הקני מנשים באוהל תבורך' מאן נהו נשים באוהל שרה רבקה
‏רחל ולאה וכו'. והנה לפ"ז יש מקום תפיסה ליצה"ר לפתות האדם לעבירה ולומר
‏שמכוין לשמה שהיא גדולה ממצוה שלא לשמה וכאשר באמת כל עושי רשעה אומרין שמכוין
‏לשמה. אמנם יש כלל אחד שהוא יתר קבועה לבל ימוט והוא מ"ש בש"ס שם ובש"ס דיבמות
‏פרק ב' [פרק י"ב דף ק"ג ע"א-ב] א"ר יוחנן ז' בעילות בעל אותו רשע באותו יום
‏שנאמר .בין רגליה כרע נפל וכו', ופריך והא קא מתהניא מעבירא? אר"י משום
‏רשב"י טובתן של רשעים רעה היא אצל צדיקים וכו' דקא שרי בה זוהמא וכו' ולאו
‏הנאה היא? וכו' יעו"ש. א"כ זה הכלל יהיה לאדם: אם אינו נהנה מעבירה עצמו
‏שהיא רעה אצלו ומתבייש מעבירה ומצער עליה רק שצריך לעשותה כדי שיבא מזה
‏.תכלית טוב שהוא לשמה או שרי ואם לאו יעשנה אם נהנה מהעבירה עצמו . . .

[83] *T.* 19a: ‏אך שמא תאמר שאין העליה ודאי כמו הירידה ואין לסכן נפשו בספק לירד
‏ואינו יודע אם יזכה לעלות וכמו שהקשו התוס' בש"ס דב"מ דף קי"ד ע"ב, .אשכחיה רבה בר
‏אבהו לאליהו דקא' בבית הקברות (של עובדי כוכבים) . . . אמר ליה לאו כוהן מר? מאי
‏טעמא קאי מר בבית הקברות' וז"ל תימה לר"י היאך החיה בנה של אלמנה כיון שכוהן היה
‏דכתיב (מלכים א' י"ז) .ויתמודד על הילד וגו'.' ויש לומר שהיה ברור לו שיחייהו לכך היה
‏.מותר משום פקוח נפש . . .

T. 153b: ‏. . . ונראה גם כי דברי התו' כפשטן פ"ס יודע לן רמז מוסר מה לכהן הוא
‏העובד הש"י כנ"ל שאינו רשאי לטמא עצמו על הספק ר"ל שיתערב
‏במדות העם כדי להחזירם כמו במשל הנ"ל כי אם שידוע בבירור שיחזירן למוטב ויחיה אותם
‏.משא"כ בלאו הכי

T. 108a: ‏צריך אזהרה דלא יקדשו העם בבגדיהם ר"ל שלא יתערבון עם עמא בלבושיהן
‏דהיינו במידותיהן דאם אינו בירור לם וכו' יש לחוש שלא יתערב בנים וילמד ממעשיהם
‏ישב ואל תעשה עדיף כמ"ש הרמב"ם .המדינה שאינו נוהגין בדרך הישר התרחק
‏. . . מהם'.

[84] See above note 23.

J. Weiss, *op. cit.,* pp. 75, 6, note 15, asserts that the only "‏אחיזה" which
could join the zaddik to the people is the transgression of the zaddik, while
the possibility of the righteousness of the people acting as the "‏אחיזה" did
not occur until a later period. But the implication here would seem clear
that not only does the zaddik join the people by virtue of some negative
characteristic in the zaddik but that there must likewise be some positive
characteristic in the fallen one as well.

85 *T.* 195c.

86 *T.* 107d.

והנה מלאכי אלהים שהם אנשי החומר וצורה שנשלחו לעה״ז וכג״ל עולים או :11c *T.*
יורדים, לפעמים נודמים כשגובר אנשי החומר ירידה לאנשי
הצורה.

87 *P. Y.* 57b.

88 *Z. P.* 36b.

89 See *T.* 51c.

90 *T.* 19a. **אין העליה ודאי כמו הירידה.**

91 *P. Y.* 21d, 22a.

92 *K. P.* 2c.

93 *T.* 20a. **ובכל ירידה צריך אזהרה איך לחזור ולעלות שלא ישאר ח״ו וכמו ששמעתי**
ממורי ש״ש כמה שנשארו.

94 *K. P.* 49a, cf. *K. P.* 46b.

95 *T.* 141c.

96 See *T.* 141b, d.   97 *T.* 21c.

98 *T.* 37b.

99 *T.* 129b: **ונראה דכתוב בזוהר הקודש (ח׳ א׳ דף פ׳א ע״ב) ,ויהי כאשר הקריב לבוא**
מצרימה״. אר״א כאשר קרב מבעי׳ לי׳, אלא כדכתיב ,ופרעה הקריב לישראל׳ בתיובתא,
אף הכא הקריב דאקריב גרמי׳ להקב׳ה כדק׳ יאות לבוא מצרימה לאשגחא באינן דרגין
ולאתרחקא מנהון מעובדי מצרים וכו׳, ,אמרי אחתי את׳, כד״א ,אמור לחכמה אחותי״. ולהבין
זה נ״ל דק׳ דאם נתיירא למה ירד למצרים בלא רשות כמבואר שם? ואומר שהוא עיקר שורש
הדבר לעבודת ה׳ וסודו ידוע כי הוא דעייל ונפיק כי אדם מצד כללותו מטוב ורעה אי אפשר
שיהיה תמיד במדרינה א׳ אפילו הקדושים בארץ כי לפעמים עולה ולפעמים יורד גם מצד
שנקרא עולם קטן, וכמו שלמעלה יש קטנות וגדלות כנודע כך באדם צריך יש בו מדרינות
אלו והחכם אשר עיניו בראשו קודם שירד מצרימה והו׳ ירידת ממדרינתו שהיה בה תחלה
צריך לקשר א״ע תחלה בדביקות הש״י שגם אם ירד מטה לטעם הנ״ל או להעלות גם מדרינות
התחתונים אשר ירד להם כדי להעלותן בניצוצין או להעלות בני אדם ובני איש שהם במדרינה
תחתונה כאשר זכרתי במשל השר היורד להעלות בן מלך שנעשה הדיוט וכו׳ אם יקשר א״ע
תחלה בדביקות וחשיקה וחפיצה בו ית׳ אז לא תפרד בין הדביקות גם אם ירד לשם שיזכה
לחזור ולעלות וכמו שהיורד לבור קושר א״ע תחלה בחבל כדי שיאחוז בו לעלות מהבור כך
שורש ישראל הם יעקב חבל נחלתו לאחוז בו בחבל זה הקשור בו ית׳ ולעלות בו וזהו סוד
עייל ונפיק וזהו כונת אברהם אע״ה וז״ש כאשר הקריב לבוא מצרימה לאשגחא באינן דרגין
ושלא ישאר שמה ח״ו דק שיזכה לעלות משם ולאתרחק מעובדי מצרים ר״ל לברד הטוב מן
הרע לכך הקריב את עצמו להקב״ה כדקיאות ושוב לא יעלה מורא על ראשו כי גם שירד
מצרימה יהיה דבוק בירדתו ית׳ שהוא ראשית חכמה יראת ה׳. וז״ש אמרי לי אחותי את, כמו
אמור לחכמה אחותי בדביקה כמו אח ואחות כנודע בזוהר דבין איש ואשתו יכול ליפרד ע״י
נט משא״כ באח ואחות . . .

The source of the parable of the pit is found in the Zohar I, 112b: **לבר**
נש דבעי לנחתא גו גובא עמיקא דחיל דלא יכול לסלקא מנו נובא מה עבד? קשר חד קשרא
דחבל לעילא מן נובא אמר נובא הואיל דקשרינא קשרא דא מכאן ולהלאה אעול המן. כך אברהם
בשעתא דבעא לנחתא למצרים עד לא ייחת תמן קשר קשרא דמהימנותא בקדמיתא לאתתקפא
ביה ולבתר נחת.

[100] *T*. 141a: ביאר פסוק .על זאת יתפלל כל חסיד אליך לעת מצוא רק לשטף מים רבים אליו לא יגיעו" (תה' ל"ב ו'), כי הטובע בנהר וחבירו רוצה להצילו מושכו עמו וז"ש רק לשטף מים רבים אליו לא יגיעו וכו'. **והתקנה לזה שיקשר את עצמו תחלה בו יח' וכו'**.

[101] *T*. 183a.

[102] "דגל מחנה אפרים" (Petrekov, 1912) p. 51, parashah שמות. A noteworthy remark in the name of the Besht is likewise quoted in this same book. p. 40, parashah מקץ: אנכי ארד עמך מצרימה על פסוק .אנכי ארד עמך מצרימה: וכדאיתא בזוהר הקדוש (פ' וירא דף קי"ב ע"ב) משל אחד: ירד לבור צריך ליקח לעצמו סולם שיוכל לחזור ולעלות וזהו .אנכי" שהוא השכינה ארד עמך מצרימה. ואנכי אעלה היינו על ידי השכינה תוכל לעלות גם עלה, היינו שיהיה עלייתך **מפל נגד מה שתעלה כמה וכמה נפשות העשוקים**.

[103] Sanhedrin 18a.

[104] *T*. 194a. Cf. 130a.

[105] *P. Y.* 57b.

[106] *K. P.* 14d: . . . עוד י"ל דכתבתי במקום אחר .על זאת יתפלל כל חסיד אליך לעת מצוא [רק שטף מים רבים לא יגיעו]" (תה' ל"ב ו'). משל הטובע בנהר ובא אחד להוציאו והוא מושכו עמו, וצריך זהירות וז"ש .המשכן' .המשכן' ב' פעמים וכו' . . . יעו"ש. ובזה יובן זאת תורת מוציא רע להציל איש הטובע בנהר של יצה"ר בתאוות וחמדת העוה"ז וכמ"ש .זכאה מאן דאחיד ביד דחייבא" להצילו ביום מהרתו ולהביאו לכהן, להש"י, מ"מ יזהר הוא עצמו פן שטף מים רבים אליו יגיעו גם כן, ע"כ ויצא הכהן **מחוץ למחנה הנ"ל, שלא יהא עמו במחנה משכן א'**. פן יבלבל אותו עמו בכל הקליפות המסבבים אותו, לכך משכן ב"פ ואז .וראה הכהן את הרפא נגע הצרעת ולקח למטהר ב' צפרים וכו'" . . .

[107] "צוואת הריב"ש" (Warsaw, 1918), pp. 32, 3: (תה' כ"ז י"א) .הוריני ד' דרכך וכו' " הנה ידוע כי דרך נקרא כבושה וארחז נקרא שאינו כבושה ויכולים לפעמים לטעות מתוכה ולילך למקום סכנה. מה שאין כן בדרך כבושה שאין מקום לתעות מתוכה. כן באדם יש ב' ענינים אלו: יש לאדם דרך כבושה בעבודת הבורא ית' שילך תמיד בזה הדרך בודאי לא יתעה מתוכה דהיינו אדם שפורע א"ע מכל הדברים ואינו עוסק רק בתורה יומם ולילה ואינו מדבר רק דברים ההכרחיים ולא יותר. ויש ג"כ דרך אחר שאינה כבושה ונקרא .אורח", דהיינו אדם שמדבר לפעמים עם בני אדם אם הדיבורים הם לש"ש דהיינו שמדבר אלה הדברים שיבואו מהם איזה מוסר או אהבת השם או יראת השם וכיוצא או אדם שיודע להעלות דיבורים למעלה בקדושה כידוע מכמה ב"א נמצא שבודאי מותר לדבר בדברים כאלו. אך סכנה יש בדיבורים אלה. כי אולי יתעה מדרך הטוב ויתחיל לדבר דברים בטלים נ"כ כדרך המון עם. ועל זה צריך האדם להתפלל ולבקש מאתו ית' שיסייע אותו כשירצה לילך בזה האורח פ' בלתי ס' מאתו ית' בקל יוכל לתעות מתוך דרך הנ"ל לכך צריך האדם לחגור מתניו בתפלה שלא יבוא לידי מכשול עבירה ח"ו. וזה פירוש הפסוק .הוריני ה' דרכך", ר"ל, שתורני שאדע דרך הכבושה ואז אהיה יכול לילך בה בעצמי, .ונחני באורח" שלא אוכל לתעות בה, ובקשתי שתחנני בסיע ועזר וסעד שאלך במישור ולא בעקלתון כי זולת זה העזר שלך ח"ו אוכל לתעות בה כנ"ל.

[108] Sotah 35a.   [109] Sotah 34b; Zohar III, 158b–159a; *T*. 107c.

[110] מלאך =angel or messenger.

[111] *T*. 116d.   [112] *T*. 26d. Cf. *Z. P.* 14a.

CHAPTER 10

THE CIRCLE OF MUSAR

¹ Dubnow finds in Aḥiyah Ha-Shiloni, the so-called teacher of the Besht, the preacher par-excellence who served as a model for Rabbi Yaakov Yosef: הספר. תולדות יעקב יוסף׳ הגדול בכמותו הוא פולמוסי בעקרו. המחבר הוא מטבעו .מוכיח׳, מניד תוכחת מוסר למנהיני הדור. בדרשתו לפרשת בלק הוא חוזר כמה פעמים על הפתגם התלמודי (תענית דף כ׳ ע״א, סנהדרין דף ק״ה ע״ב): .טובה קללה שקילל אחיה השילוני את ישראל יותר מברכת בלעם הרשע׳, ומתאמץ להסביר שהדרשן המגלה פשעי הדור על מנת לתקנם הוא הנביא האמיתי והצבועים החונפים הדורשין בשבח הדור הם נביאי שקר. כאן מנלה ר׳ יעקב יוסף סוד רבו הבעש׳ט, ומעיד ש.אחיה השילוני היה רבו של אליהו הנביא ורבו של מורי [הבעש׳ט]·זכרונו לברכה׳. אפשר למצוא רמז לטבעו של התלמיד יותר מלטבעו של הרב. ר׳ יעקב יוסף היה באמת קרוב ברוחו אל הנביא הזועם. Dubnow, *op. cit.*, p. 97. In the same parashah our author remarks that אחיה השילוני היה מן סוג מוכיחים נאמנים. *T.* 155a.

It is possible that one of the great influences on Yaakov Yosef's doctrine of Musar was the mokhiaḥ of Polnoy. When the Besht wanted to win over the brilliant young rabbi, Yaakov Yosef, who was opposed to his way, it was the mokhiaḥ, Yehudah Leib, who helped him. (See שבחי הבעש׳ט,'' pp. 61, 63). The doctrine of Musar expressed in Yehudah Leib's book "קול אריה" (קורעץ, תקנ׳ה) is in some ways similar to that of Yaakov Yosef's, particularly his denunciation of the proud learned class. Furthermore it was to Polnoy that Yaakov Yosef came as the successor to the deceased R. Yehudah Leib (תק׳ל) who was both מוכיח and רב, and it was in this city which had been under the influence of the mokhiaḥ for many years that Rabbi Yaakov Yosef spent the remaining years of his life. He was buried next to the mokhiaḥ with one "enclosure for the two of them." See Horodetzky, *op. cit.*, pp. 130–138.

It is important to note that the element of fearless condemnation was only one aspect of Rabbi Yaakov Yosef's doctrine of Musar, and cannot be understood apart from his total doctrine, as will be made clear later in this chapter.

² Since, in general, the rabbi preached but twice a year, while the maggid or mokhiaḥ preached more often, it is of some importance to our understanding of the nature of the zaddik, of his relationship to the tasks and office of the rabbi as well as to the tasks and office of the maggid, to know how often and when the zaddik was to preach. For if he was to preach often then there might be no need of a maggid, and the zaddik would, in a sense, combine and infuse new spirit into the principle tasks of both rabbi and maggid. While there is no decisive material to indicate this in the works of Rabbi Yaakov Yosef (indeed, we seem to find the contrary view expressed in *K. P.* 16a), this is the general impression.

That the zaddik himself was to preach Musar seems clear from Rabbi
Yaakov Yosef's repeated insistence. The very chapters of his books are
divided according to the parashot of the week and were sermons most probably
delivered at the "third meal" of the Sabbath. This seems to have been the
custom even at the earliest period of Hasidism, according to an early source.
In a letter שבר פושעים, which Dubnow describes as: נשלחה אגרת זו
מאוקריינא כעין תשובה על שאלת הרבנים ע"ד מוצאו ואופן פרסומו של הספר .תולדות יעקב
יוסף (Dubnow, Vol. I, p. 140, note 1), we find: למשמע אוזן דאבה נפשכם על
דבר הספר שהגיע לאָרצכם בחודש מנחם תקמ"א לספירותיכם, שחיבר הרב דק"ק פולנאה
יעקב יוסף, ואיכוחו ומהותו מוסרים וחידושים שדורשים לפי דרכי התורה פ'
בתור רב [פרשה] בסעודה שלישית בשבת. Thus Dubnow remarks:
הקהלה היה ר' יעקב יוסף דורש ברבים פעמים בשנה על פי המנהג המקובל: בשבת הגדול
ובשבת תשובה. אולם עיקר תורת החסידות היה מוסר לבני חבורתו, על פי מנהג
החסידים בכל שבת ושבת בשיחותו בשעת הסעודה השלישית
(Dubnow, op. cit., p. 95). Evidence that Yaakov Yosef preached each Sabbath
at the "third meal" is stated in "שבחי הבעש"ט," p. 52: שמעתי כמה פעמים מהרב
הנ"ל [ר' יעקב יוסף] זלה"ה שאמר לחמי בדרך מוסר בסעודה שלישית.
Cf. K. P. 15a.

³ In a שאלה addressed to Rabbi Yaakov Yosef, he is called הדרשן המופלא.
P. Y. 102d.

⁴ T. 85a. The discourse delivered before Pesaḥ should not be pilpul, accord-
ing to Rabbi Yaakov Yosef, but should deal with the laws of Pesaḥ and
Musar derived from these laws. See T. 101d, 102a: ונבאר תחלה מה שהקשה . . .
הט"ז באורח חיים סי' תק"ס: שואלים בהלכות פסח קודם הפסח ל' יום . . . הלכך [ל' יום
קודם פסח חל עליו חובת הביעור"] וכו'. והקשה הט"ז מה עניני של הלכך הנז' בש"ס גם כן וכו'
לזה שואלים ל' יום וכו'. ועוד בטור כתב רק שואל"ן ובש"ס פסחים (דף ו' ע"א) שואלין
ודורשין . . . וכבר ביארתי זה בארוכה ע"ד פשט. ועתה נ"ל ע"ד הלצה דקשה ל"ל דורשין
דסגי בשואלין כי הלומדין יודעין ואין צריך לדרוש להם ולהמוני עם שאין יודעין בדיני פסח
ישאלו מה שיצטרכו. וע"כ לומר שלא ידעו המוני עם שיש בזה איסור כדי שישאלו דינו, לכך
דורשין כדי שידעו לשאול. וקשה א"כ הל"ל דורשין ושואלין ודברי הט"ז שכתב בזה יעו"ש.
ונ"ל דדיני פסח כולל ב' ענינים כמו בכל המצות ובכללו הוא מצות
תפלה שיש בו גוף ונשמה ומרגלא בפומי דאינשי תפלה בלא כוונה כגוף בלא נשמה.
כך יש במצות ביעור חמץ גוף ונשמה דהיינו המעשה עם הכוונה השייך
לביעור חמץ הוא דיני מוסר שרמזו קדמונים על ביעור חמץ הוא יצה"ר ובשעת
ביעור חמץ יכוין לבער יצה"ר מקרבו וכו' והגעלת כלים הוא תשובת
המשקל כפי תשמישן בחימום היצה"ר כך הכשירו בחמין ושאר פרטי דינים הנזכרים בספריהם
עד"ז וא"כ זהו שאמר שואלין", ר"ל דיני חמץ במעשה .ודורשין",
הוא דיני מוסר השייך למעשה ביעור שידרוש החכם שיהיה במצות
ביעור חמץ והכשר כלים ואינם שיהיה להם גוף ונשמה. . . הלכך ש"מ דלעולם חל עליו חובת
ביעור ל' יום קודם פסח לפרש להם ביעור חמץ במוסר השכל.

⁵ Z. P. 17c: טעם שאבדה הארץ שלא השפיע להם הצדיק מוסר.

⁶ Ketuvot 105b.

⁷ T. 13c: האי צורבא מרבנן דמרחמין לי' בני מתא לאו משום דמעלי טפי אלא דלא

מוכח להו במילי דשטיא (כתובות דף ק"ה ע"ב) . . . את האלהים התהלך נח שלא היה מוכיח
.את אנשי דורו רק התרחק מהם והתבודד את האלהים

[8] *T.* 25a.

[9] *P. Y.* 95b: שמעתי ממורי זלה"ה דרך הלצה כי דברת בני אדם שלא לשמוע מוסר
המוכיחים מאחר שכוונתם שיתנו להם מעות וז"ש .ולא יכלו לשתות מים מימי המוסר כי מרים
.הם' בל"א [בלשון אשכנז] מר פר נעלט

[10] *T.* 101c.

[11] For a striking example of the corrupting influence of gifts, see above,
pp. 210–11.

[12] See *T.* 101d.

[13] Avot 3.17.

[14] *T.* 153a: '. . . העיקר שטבטל כבודו ורצונו מפני כבוד הבורא שבראו לכבודו ית'
שחדשו יש מאין וכל פועל ה' למענהו. והנה הסוג שיראה להיות אהוב ביניהם וסובר שבזה יקבל
מהם פרנסה בפרט בסעודה אשר הוא מנהגם ליתן מתנות לתלמיד חכם ואיך יאמר מוסר שהם
דברי קנטרין וישנאו אותו ולא יתנו מתנות ואם אין קמח אין תורה? ובאמת ז"א כי איפכא
.מסתברא אם אין תורה דייקא שנק' תורה ע"ש יורה חטאים בדרך, אז אין קמח

[15] *Z. P.* 17c, cf. note 4.

[16] *T.* 85d.

[17] *T.* 85d: ובזה יובן פסוק הפרשה צו את, אהרן ואת בניו לאמר, ר"ל שעיקר הצוי והזירוז
.הוא לאמר, שיאמר לעם דברי מוסר כמ"ש בזוהר על פסוק .כה תאמר לבית יעקב וכו'"

[18] *T.* 84b: אתה צריך להוכיח בשער בת רבים במילי דשמיא גם שלא יאהבם מ"מ אתה
מוזהר .הוי מקבל את כל האדם בשמחה' גם שהוא לא יקבלוך בשמחה כמו שכתבתי בפ'
.ואהבת לרעך' — שיהיה כמוך. Cf. *K. P.* 41a.

[19] *K. P.* 41a.

[20] *T.* 48b.

[21] *K. P.* 15a. Cf. above note 2.

[22] Tamid 28a.

[23] *T.* 24d, 25a: יש לפרש .כל המענג את השבת נותנין לו נחלה בלי מצרים וכו'" והענין
כי שבת נק' ענג' לכך אסור לבכות בשבת וכתב רמ"א בא"ח ס' רפ"ח וז"ל ומי שיש לו ענג אם
יבכה כדי שילך הצער מלבו מותר לבכות בשבת עכ"ל. וכתב הט"ז דוקא מרוב דביקותו
בקב"ה מותר לבכות אבל כדי שיצא מלבו לא וכו' והוא נגד רמ"א דכ' סתם מותר ונ"ל לתרץ
דדברי רמ"א כנים ואמתים דק"ל מילה דוחה שבת ומ"ט להבין דיש להבין מ"ט שופר וללולב שהם מצות
ג"כ ואינו דוחה שבת גם שהיא רק שבות ומ"ט מילה שהיא אב מלאכה ודוחה שבת וכ"ת דכתיב
ביום השמיני ימול אפילו בשבה באמת ק' למה התירה תורה זו דוקא? ונ"ל דודאי
מילת ערלת הלב דוחה שבת לומר מוסר כדי לימול ערלת לבו של בני
אדם דוחה שבת גם שהיא ענג וע"י מוסר מצטער . . . כמצטער על עוונותיו וע"י שבוכה על זה
ומתחרט על עוונותיו שהוא עיקרי התשובה שכ' הרמב"ם אין לך מילת ערלת לב גדול מזה
.וכדי שילך זה הצער מלבו ודאי שרי ומכ"ש מרוב דביקות דשרי וא"ש דברי רמ"א וק"ל

[24] *T.* 107d.

[25] *T.* 100a: .לעורר לבבות ישראל שישובו בתשובה אל אבינו שבשמים בדברי כבושים

[26] *T.* 85d: .ע"י מוסר נמחלין עוונות הדור

[27] *P. Y.* 60c.

[28] *T.* 102: .איברא דבדיני מוסר יש זמן לאמרו ולפזר ויש זמן למנוע ולכנס . . .

[29] *T*. 100a: אף אם מסתיר את עצמו בכל השנה, מכל מקום בראש השנה הזמן גורם לזה
לפתוח פיו במוסר. וכן שמעתי ממורי מפורש רק שיהיה המוסר במדה מטובעת כי הלא יש ג'
בחינות: זהב, כסף, נחשת. והנה נ ח ש ת הם נחשים השרפים אשר נאמר עליהם .וישלח ה'
בעם את הנחשים השרפים', מוכיחים המעוררים ח'ו דין על בני עולם וכאשר כתבתי מזה גם
כן על פסוק .לא תלך רכיל בעמך וכו' " נמצא הם נקראים נחש כמו וכמו שאמרו חכמינו
ז'ל (בראשית רבה פל'א ס' ח' והובא ברש'י) .ויעש משה נחש נחשת' לשון נופל על לשון
ויש בחינה כ ס ף שהוא כולו רחמים מלהתעורר במוסר שהוא קצת דין וכמו שכתוב
.מוסר ה' בני אל תמאס ואל תקוץ בתוכחתו'. אבל בחינה ממוצע הוא זה ב, לומר דברים
נחמדים וכמו שכתבתי .הנחמדים מזהב', גם שהוא זהב .כי מצפון זהב יאתה' והיינו
לעורר לבבות ישראל שישובו בתשובה אל אבינו שבשמים
בדברי כבושים הנכנס בלב כל אחד ואחד לפי בחינתו.
[30] *T*. 59a.

[31] *P. Y*. 57c. The correct reading is "He was shepherding the flock with his brothers," but את is understood here as the sign of the accusative. Thus: He shepherded (את) his brothers."

[32] *T*. 106c: יש שני מיני מוסר: אחד לתלמידי חכמים ואחד להמוני עם, ולכל אחד צריך
.לומר לפי בחינתו

[33] *T*. 105b: .יהיה דברים קשים להלומדים ודברים רכים להמוני עם Cf. 160c.

[34] *T*. 112a: לחכם האוהב תוכחה ומוסר כמו שנאמר (משלי ט' ח') .הוכח לחכם ויאהבך.
יאמר לו דברי מוסר כפשוטו בלי לבוש ומליצה מה שאין כן להמוני עם ומכל שכן לרשעים
ילביש במשל ומליצה ונדמה ליין וחלב For a sterner view see *T*. 80c.

[35] *T*. 85a.

[36] "דגל מחנה אפרים," parashah תצוה.

[37] *T*. 164.

[38] *T*. 13d.

Sometimes lack of interest on the part of the people brought despair to the preacher and kept him from speaking at all. *P. Y*. 70b: ושמעתי מן מוהר'ן
כשהחכם הרוצה להשמיע תורה ומוסר הוא בין בין אוילים אשר חכמה ומוסר אוילים בזו, אז הוא
כבד פה מלהשמיע תורה ומוסר שאין פיו יכול לדבר ולהשמיע, וח'ש, .כבד פה אנכי'. לכך,
.מי אנכי כי אלך אל פרעה', המוני עם, בחי' הערף, שאז אני כבד פה ואין תועלת, ודפ'ח.
ועל פ' זה כתבתי .האזינו השמים ואדברה' לשון עתיד דהל'ל .האזינו השמים
דבר'' כמו בסיפא .אמרי פי', ולפי הנ'ל אתי שפיר, כשאני בין החכמים תואר שמים
שתואר חכם הלומד מכל אדם, וח'ש .האזינו שמים', אז איני כבד פה רק .ואדברה' שפי
יפתח בחכמה להשמיע א ח ר ש י ש ה ת ע ו ר ר ו ת מ ה ם שרוצים לשמוע
משפיעים לי שאוכל להשפיע תורה ומוסר לדבר דברים חדשים משא'כ כשאני בין אנשי
הארץ ששומעים מרחוק, אז אני כבד פה, כי איני מחדש דבר רק מה שכבר אמרתי, וח'ש
..ותשמע הארץ אמרי פי' לשון עתיד

P. Y. 74a: שאינו נוח לו להשפיע לוולתו כי נוח לו יותר להתבודד שהוא יקבל השפע
סלמעלה כי אם . . . שבני דורו מקשטים א'ע להכין לקבל שפע מהצדיק שהם רוצים לשמוע
.מפיו תורה ומוסר אז הוא מתעורד נ'כ לזווג דהיינו להשפיע להם שפעו

[39] *T*. 44b: . . . ונ'ל דיש בענין אמירת תוכחה ומוסר ב' בחינות שונות. א': להנצל מעונש
אם יש לו התנצלות לפטור עצמו מלהוכיחו כגון שידוע לו שלא יקבל וכיוצא שאז אין עליו
אשמה ונמנע מלהוכיחו. בחינה ב': שאינו עושה מיראת עונש רק לאהבת המלך להשיב בן אל

אביו אז גם שיודע שלא יקבל מ"מ עושה תחבולה לשנות מלבושיו החשובים ולובש בגדי פחותי
הערך כמו שהוא לבוש עתה בן המלך שנתערב בין הפחותים ואז לובש השר ג"כ כמותו כדי
שיוכל להתחבר עמו ולדבר על לבו לשוב לאביו המלך. Cf. Shabbat 35a. ...

[40] Z. P. 81a: גם שנפרדו ממשה מ"מ משה לא נפרד מהם. Cf. Z. P. 88c.

[41] Z. P. 17d: אך אם יש איזה יחידים או אף יחיד א' הרוצה לקבל מוסר צריך התלמיד
חכם להשפיע לו מוסר.

[42] P. Y. 74a: דאיתא ב,עץ חיים. דף קצ"ח, פ' המאמר כד סליק ברעותיה למיברי
עלמא וכו' כי צדיק העליון אינו רוצה להזדווג לזולתו. רק רוצה לקבל השפע מלמעלה, כי
אם שהנקבה מקשטת את עצמה ותכין לוויג, אז הוא מתעורר גם כן לזווג וכו'. אמנם בפעם
ראשון נתעורר הזכר מעצמו וז"ש כד סליק ברעותיה וכו' יעו"ש. ולהלביש דבר זה נ"ל
שהוא ג"כ בכל דור ודורשיו, שהראש נקרא איש כמ"ש איש ירושלים, ודורו נקראו נקבה אשה
נגדו, והוא בחינת חומר וצורה משפיע ומקבל השפע. והנה צדיק התחתון ראש הדור
שהוא דוגמת צדיק העליון שאינו נוח לו להשפיע לזולתו כי נוח לו יותר להתבודד שהוא יקבל
השפע מלמעלה! כי אם שהנקבה שהם בני דורו מקשטת את עצמה להכין לקבל שפע מהצדיק
שהם רוצים לשמוע מפיו תורה ומוסר, אז הוא מתעורר גם כן לזווג, דהיינו להשפיע להם
שפעו. וכמו שביארת פסוק ,עקב תשמעון' יעו"ש. אמנם בפעם ראשון שאינם יודעים מזה או
שאינם רוצים בזה צריך להתעורר מעצמו כמו בתחלת בריאת העולם, כך בתחלת הנהגת
העיר דור ודורשיו והבן טעמו של דבר, והשם יכפר.

I have quoted this in full to show once again how a purely kabbalistic
doctrine relating to the upper worlds is transformed into a principle of action
for the zaddik and people in this world.

[43] T. 126a.

[44] T. 104a. See chapter 9, note 17.

[45] T. 65d.

[46] T. 120b. See Tamid 28a.

[47] T. 101c: צריך ליזהר בתוכחת מוסר שיאהב אותם ומצד אהבה מוכיחם כמו אב
האוהב בנו שחרו מוסר וכמ"ש ,את אשר יאהב יוכיח' וכיוציא בזה אבל אלו שרוצין להתגדל
ח"ו עי"ז וכיוצא בזה כגון להנאת ממון וכדומה שאינו לשם שמים ומעורר בקול וכמו ששמעתי
,הי' לי דמעתי לחם' ושמעתי ממורי שח"ו גורם עי"ז וכו' ח"ו גורם מדנים בין ישראל לאביהם
שבשמים. וכמו שזכרתי בביאור ,וידבר העם בה' ובמשה וגו' וישלח ה' בעם את הנחשים השרפים'
שהם ב' מיני מוכיחים והוא ע"פ משל ששמעתי ממורי ששלח המלך בנו ידידו מעל פניו ושילח
את ב' עבדיו וחזר אל אביו וכו' והשני אסר כדברים האלה רק שדיבר מצד
שהיה צער לו בצער המלך ובנו שנשלח מעל פניו זמן רב עד שנשכח ממנו נימוסי המלכות וכל
מכבדו הזילוהו ואז נתמלא המלך רחמים וכו'. כך יש מוכיח בשער שמדבר בגנות ישראל
וח"ו עי"ז גורם נחש נחש הקדמוני וכו' וז"ש ,וישלח ה' בעם הנחשים השרפים' ששורפים בארס
שבפיהם וכו' יעו"ש. וא"כ פיו ולבו אינו שוין שמכוין להנאתו ואומר בפיו שעושה למען כבוד
ית' וח"ו גורם רעה כאמור שנית שמלבין פני חבריו ולא את עצמו שנאמר ,ולא תשא ע ל י ו
חטא' שהוציא עצמו מהכלל ובאמת צריך לכלול עצמו עמהן.

[48] T. 163b: Lev. 19.16. See below, note 67.

[49] שמענו מספרים בשם הרב מוהר"י ז"ל מסקווירא שסיפר בשם פה קודש אביו ז"ל אשר
בימי הבעש"ט דרש פעם אחת איזה דרשן ובתוך דרשתו דיבר על עם בני ישראל דברים לא
טובים ובא הרה"ק ר' דוד ז"ל מתלמידי הבעש"ט זי"ע ודחף אותו מעל הבימה ובא הדרשן
בקובלנא עליו לפני הבעש"ט ושאל הבעש"ט לר"ד למה עשית לו כך ואמר שדיבר גנות על

ישראל. אמר הבעש"ט: כך אמר הקב"ה ,מוסר ה' בני אל תמאס' (משלי ג', י"א), היינו
מוסר יש לך רשות לומר לישראל, אבל .בני אל תמאס',
היינו, שלא תמאס לי את בני. רמ"ם מליבאוויטש, ,צרור החיים' (בילוגריי,
תרע"ג) דף י"א ע"א.

⁵⁰ T. 100c. Cf. below, note 63.

⁵¹ Ibid.

⁵² T. 101c. See above, note 47.

⁵³ T. 101d.

⁵⁴ Z. P. 15c.

⁵⁵ T. 101c. See above, note 47. Cf. the following passage from ,שבחי הבעש"ט",
(Berditchev, תקמ"ה) p. 82: ,דשם? [פרנס חדש] פעם אחת שבת הבעש"ט בק"ק אליק אצל הפ"ח
ובשבת במנחה הלך הפ"ח לבית הכנסת לשמוע דרשת מדרשן מחד אורח. והמתין עליו הבעש"ט
בסעודה שלישית עד שיבא מבית הכנסת ובתוך כך שמע שהדרשן מלבין על ישראל ורגז
הבעש"ט ואמר למשרת שלו שילך ויקרא את הפ"ח לביתו והמשרת גילה לכמה אנשים שרגז
הבעש"ט על הדרשן, וראה הדרשן שהעולם נשמטים אחד אחד ופסק מלדרוש וביום מחר בא
הדרשן להבעש"ט ונתן לו שלום ושאל אותו מי הוא ואמר אני הדרשן, מפני מה רגז מעלתו עלי?
וקפץ הבעש"ט ממקומו ונחזו דמעות מעיניו ואמר: אתה תדבר רע על ישראל. תד ע
שבר ישראל שהולך כל היום על יומא דשוקא ולעת ערב
נחרד והולך בבית אחד ומתפלל מנחה ואינו יודע מה
שאומר ואף על פי כן מזדעזעים שרפים ואופנים מזה.

⁵⁶ T. 104b Lev. 19.17.

⁵⁷ P. Y. 72c.

⁵⁸ T. 191d.

⁵⁹ T. 100d, 101a: ,בצדק תשפוט עמיתך', תחשוב ותשפוט שהוא עמיתך כי כל
החסרונות שבו הוא בך ג"כ אז בודאי תשפוט אותו בצדק. וכך אמר ,לא תלך רכיל בעמך'
ור"ל שלא תלמד קטגור בעמך כדי של.לא תעמוד על דם ר ע ך', כמוך כמוהו, כי אני ה'
רחמים, ולא תעשה שתהפך רחמים למדת הדין ח"ו וז"ש .ולא תשנא את אחיך', ר"ל שאין לך
לשנאותו כי אחיך הוא, אף אם יש בו חטא אשר ראוי לשנאותו מ"מ יש פגם זה בך ג"כ כי
כי [כל ישראל?] הם פרצוף א' קומה שלימה והשנאה הוא מצד ב' לבבות שבך ג"כ
והוא היצה"ר והיצה"ט שבך וגם כן כמוהו רק הוכח תוכיח את עמיתך ור"ל כשתוכיח
לחברך תוכיח את עצמך אתו עמו מאחר שהוא עמיתך ולא תשא עליו חטא ר"ל שלא
תטיל החטא עליו לבדו ולא בך גם כן רק שניהם כאחד שוין ובזה .לא תקום ולא תטור
ואהבת לרעך כמוך', וק"ל.

⁶⁰ T. 58a.

⁶¹ Baba Mez'ia' 107b.

⁶² T. 66a.

⁶³ T. 100c: באומרו דברי קנטורין על ישראל שמחייבין למטה בזכירת עוונתם פן ח"ו
יהיה מקום למדת הדין הנקרא אלהים לקטרג על ישראל למעלה וזה שמצינו ביהושע וישעיה
ואליהו שנענשו שאמרו קנטורין על ישראל ובגדעון חפץ שלמד זכות על ישראל נחשב לו לזכות
גדול כמבואר שם כי הש"י רחמן ואינו חפץ בקטרג מדת הדין המותח תמיד להשגיח בעולם
והם נקראים עיני ה' המשוטטות בארץ, עי' בזוהר פקודי דף רס"ה, וכו'. לכך כשאומר
ברמז בזה אין מקום תפיסה למדת הדין על ישראל וכל איש הרואה נוגעי עצמו וידע מרת נפשו
מרגיש אף ברמז כאיזמל בבשר החי . . . כי כבר זכרנו בש"ס דכריתות אר"ע תמה אני אם יש

בדור הזה מי שיוכל להוכיח וכו'. והעולה משם כי סיבת חטא ראש הדור גורם אשמה לכל
אנשי דורו דאי רישא דעמא טב כולהו טב וכו' ולכך צריך ד ב ר י ת ו כ ח ה ה ת ל ו י ן
ב פ ה ה מ ו כ י ח ר ק ב מ ע ש ה שיתקן את עצמו תחלה ולתקן כל בחינות של דורו
הכלולין בו ו ב מ ע ט ד ב ר י ם נ כ נ ס ב א ז נ י ה ד ו ר וכמ"ש כ ל א ד ם
ש ה ו א י ר א ש מ י ם ד ב ר י ו נ ש מ ע י ם . . . וא"כ מאחר שכל דברי תוכחה שטובים
בשער להעם נוגע גם על עצמו ובשרו בודאי יקצר, ומכ"ש אם לא נכנס המוכיח בגדר זה
כלל שדברי תוכחה שלו הוא משפה ולחוץ ולא מקירות לבו בודאי שטוב לו שתיקותו
מדיבורו . . . Cf. *T.* 66a.

64 *T.* 163b.

65 *P. Y.* 57c.

66 *T.* 101d. Jerusalem Talmud, Berakhot IV, f. 7d.

NOTES TO APPENDIX

1 Horodetzky, *op. cit.*, Vol. 1, p. 130.

2 *T.* 84d.

3 *P. Y.* 91c.

4 *K. P.* 1a.

5 *P. Y.* 89b: דרוש לשבת הגדול שנת תק כ"ז ;92a: דרוש לשבת הגדול שנת ;
דרוש לשבת תשובה שנת תק כ"א :95c; דרוש לשבת תשובה שנת תק"ה :93c; תק כ"ה
K. P. ;דרוש לשבת תשובה שנת תק כ"ז :101c ;(no date) :98d; דרוש לשבת הגדול
דרוש לשבת פרשת מצורע שנת :24c; דרוש לשבת פרשת מצורע שנת תק כ"א :22d
תק כ"א לפ"ק.

6 שמעתי ממורי ש'ן (שיחיה נצח). *T.* 35d, 41b, 182c.

7 See Dubnow, *op. cit.*, p. 69, note 1.

8 Actually the earliest material in R. Yaakov Yosef's works which is
dated, is found in his responsa. One שאלה is addressed to מהור'ר יוסף
הכהן אב"ד דק"ק ראשקוב, *P. Y.* 88a. Since he was rabbi in Rashkov
c. 1748–1752 (see chapter 2, note 4), it must have been written during that
period, probably toward the beginning of it, since he writes that he possesses
few books, having had to leave them in Sharograd. See *P. Y.* 88a.

9 *T.* 15d, 195a; *P. Y.* 24d; *Z. P.* 16d. See also *T.* 154c. Once in quoting
from the Besht he says הראה לו רבו, *T.* 195a. The expression, השיבו למורי, *T.*
38c, is obscure, especially since it is in the plural.

10 *T.* 32a, 69c, 96a, 170b, 178b.

11 *P. Y.* 71b, 22d.

12 *T.* 107b.

13 *T.* 82c, *K. P.* 43c.

14 *T.* 194c.

15 *T.* 40d.

16 *P. Y.* 24d.

[17] *Z. P.* 7b.

[18] *T.* 13a.

[19] *T.* 12c.

[20] *T.* 130c.

[21] Dr. Joshua Bloch believed that the Meziboz edition was only a legendary invention of the hasidim, which allowed them to blame Rabbi Ezekiel Landau of Prague for burning all extant copies. See Bloch, *op. cit.*, pp. 245–257. Dubnow, though he questions the source of A. Tauber (דפוס קאריץ, *Kirjath Sepher*, Vol. 1, 1924, p. 305) who reports the burning by Rabbi Landau, seems to believe that there was, in fact, a Meziboz edition, which Ben Yakov in his אוצר הספרים refers to. See Dubnow, *op. cit.*, p. 138, note 2.

[22] Found on the preface page of the Koretz edition (1780), but omitted in later editions.

[23] *T.* 9c.

[24] *T.* 27d.

[25] *T.* 127a.   [26] *T.* 4a.

[27] *P. Y.* 2c.

[28] *P. Y.* 11a, d, 16c, 17d, 18a, 19b, d, etc.

[29] *P. Y.* 78a–82c.

[30] *P. Y.* 82c–89b. On 102d a שאלה is printed out of place. שאלה זו מקומה בדף פ'א ומחמת איזה מניעה שהיה בבית הדפוס נדפסה התשובה קודם השאלה.

[31] *P. Y.* 89b–102d.

[32] *P. Y.* 106, 7.

[33] Preface to *T.*: ... ועד ידו נטוי' עשות ספרים הרבה אשר בכתובים על סוגיות הו'ת וש'ח אבע'א נמרא ואבע'א סברא. ודין קמצא הכהן אפס קצהו להטעים מיעוט הדבש לזכות הרבים ביראת ה' טהורה. השם יאריך ימיו ושנותיו ויזכרהו להוציא מחשבתו לפועל כל שישנו בזכירה ...

[34] *T.* 46b.

[35] *T.* 37c.

[36] *T.* 135a.

[37] *T.* 104c: ובזה כתבתי בספרי פ' הש'ס .... Horodetzky, *op. cit.*, p. 130, misreads this to mean that his book was פירוש הש'ס. The words פ' הש'ס refer not to ספרי, but to the following words, thus: ... פירש הש'ס י'ח קללות קילל ישעיה.

[38] Furthermore, we find references to a קונטרס אחרון, *T.* 27b: כמו שכתבתי בקו' [בקונטרס] האחרון: שכרתי בקונ' [בקונטרס] אחרון.

[39] *T.* 94d, 111c, 117a, 148d, 169d.

[40] *T.* 49c.

[41] *T.* 164d: שמעתי מפי החסיד המפורסם מוהר'ן. Though the place-name קאסויר is not mentioned here and the abbreviation מוהר'ן, at times, also applies to ר' נחמן האירידנקע, I assume it is ר' נחמן קאסויר who is meant here, since the noun חסיד is never used with מוהר'ן האירידנקע while it is frequently used with מוהר'ן קאסויר.

⁴² A fourth הספד may be in *T.* 87c: תצטער ותבכה ותספד אחר שתדע...
שהוא הנשמה וחיות גוף כללות העולם הוא שנסתלק. ולכך. ואחיכם כל בית ישראל יבכו את
השרפה אשר שרף ה' " שנשארו כגוף בלא נשמה וכיתמי בלא אבא ובידה בלא מנהיג וראוי
לצעוק על הספינה שאבדה קברניטה, ואז מכפר, והבן. But no name is given here.

⁴³ *T.* 100a: הניבור הוא ראש הדור צדיק יסוד עולם היודע בקטרי המלחמה לעמוד...
נגד הצורר אותנו תמיד וכלי זיינו הם תלמידיו הלומדים טכסיסי מלחמה וישמשו אותו או
שאר צדיקים שבדור הנטפלים עמו שע"י קישור ואיסור תפלתם יחד לזרוק חצים ובליסטראות
אל חויא כנודע משא'כ השונא בתחבולת ונב כלי זיינו שאחד המיוחד שבעדר
הצדיקים חטפו מהעולם הוא מוהר'ר ליב פינסטר זלה'ה
שהיה מנן בעד כמה אלפים מישראל ושאר צדיקים
ונאונים. This statement would seem to indicate that he considered ר'
ליב פיסטנר as the greatest of all the zaddikim.

⁴⁴ *T.* 86a: המנוח הצדיק ר'ל פיסטנר.

⁴⁵ *T.* 24c.

⁴⁶ Fifty-seven times. He is usually quoted as הרב המגיד, but sometimes
simply as מוהר'ם which may refer to him or to a person with a name having
the same abbreviation mentioned in *P. Y.* p. 26b: בשם החסיד מוהר'ם מבראד.
One is tempted to emend מבראד to מבאר, but the appellative חסיד is never
once given to the Maggid Menaḥem of Bar.

⁴⁷ Who is הרב הגדול המנוח מוהר'י? Two tentative alternatives may be presented. Firstly, since in the eulogy מוהר'י is called הרב הגדול, we would be led
to believe that, as important as מוהר'ם was (he is the most frequently quoted
person in R. Yaakov Yosef's works apart from the Besht), מוהר'י was *more*
important. In addition, the date of the eulogy is תק'כ and, to the best of our
knowledge (see Dubnow, *op. cit.*, p. 69, note 1), the Besht himself died in that
year. Furthermore the name ישראל would fit the abbreviation, thus מוהר'י
[ישראל בעל שם טוב]. Arguing against this supposition is the fact that he is
not referred to as מורי, which would surely have been the case in a eulogy
for the Besht. Furthermore, it is doubtful that he would present a eulogy
for the Besht in connection with anyone else, no matter how highly he
considered him.

The only other alternative, on the basis of the names found in Yaakov
Yosef's works, is הרב מו' יצחק פיסטנר, *P. Y.* 35a. Apart from the fact that his
name likewise commences with I, it should be noted that he is called הרב.

⁴⁸ *Z. P.* 30a.

⁴⁹ See above, p. 44; chapter 10, note I.

⁵⁰ According to Horodetzky, *op. cit.*, p. 131, R. Yaakov Yosef insisted upon
being buried next to the Mokhiaḥ over which two graves a single wall was later
erected. The Mokhiah's book קול אריה, קאריץ, תקנ'ח, bears resemblance,
in his criticism of the rabbis, to R. Yaakov Yosef's works.

⁵¹ He is quoted three times: *T.* 153b, 189a; *P. Y.* 14c.

⁵² הרבני הוותיק מוהר'ן האריזנקע, *T.* 21d, 28c, 147c, 195c; *K. P.* 40c (the simple
abbreviation מוהר'ן may refer either to נחמן קאסויר or נחמן האריזנקע, but if it

is preceded by הרבני, thus: הרבני מוהר'ן, it refers to נחמן האורידנקע; while if it is preceded by החסיד or המנוח, it refers to נחמן קאסויר).

[53] ה ח ס י ד דוב בער טורצינר, K. P. 12b; המנוח ה ח ס י ד מוהר'ר חיים לאניזר, P. Y. 93a. (A. Heschel, op. cit., p. 222 has identified him as the Maggid of Mezritch). ניסי ה ח ס י ד המפורסם, P. Y. 26b; ה ח ס י ד מוהר'ם מבראד, Z. P., הרב ה ח ס י ד מוהר'ר אברהם מניר, P. Y. 99d; מוהר'נ(?) זלה'ה, המנוח החסיד מוהר'ר אפרים זלה'ה (דק'ק בראד), Z. P. 16b; T. 48b, 126b; הרב הגדול מו' משה מקוטוב, T. 91a; הגאון ה ח ס י ד מוהר'י הולש, T. 85; המנוח הוותיק מוהר'ר נח זלל'ה (מראשקוב), Z. P. 4d, 44c; T. 33b.

[54] T. 91c.

[55] T. 147a; see also P. Y. 67d.